AMERICAN FURNITURE 2013

Edited by Luke Beckerdite

Published by the CHIPSTONE FOUNDATION

Distributed by University Press of New England

Hanover and London

Cover: Detail, tall-case clock with movement by Augustin Neisser, Philadelphia area, Pennsylvania, ca. 1745. Walnut and mixed-wood inlay with tulip poplar and pine. H. 93½", W. 22½", D. 12½". (Courtesy, Historical Society of Berks County, Reading, Pa.; photo, Gavin Ashworth.)

Design: Wynne Patterson, Pittsfield, VT
Copyediting: Fronia Simpson, Bennington, VT
Typesetting: Mary Gladue, Windsor, CT
Printing: Meridian Printing, East Greenwich, RI

Published by the Chipstone Foundation
Distributed by University Press of New England
1 Court Street
Lebanon, New Hampshire 03766
upne.com

© 2013 by the Chipstone Foundation
All rights reserved
Printed in the United States of America 5 4 3 2 1
ISSN 1069–4188
ISBN 978-0-9827722-3-2

Contents

Figure 1 John Townsend, high chest of drawers, Newport, Rhode Island, 1756. Mahogany with white pine and ash. H. 88½", W. 40¼", D. 21⅛". (Private collection; photo, Gavin Ashworth.) This high chest descended in the Arnold family of Warwick, Rhode Island. It retains its original finial, cast brass hardware, and finish.

American Furniture

Editorial Statement

American Furniture is an interdisciplinary journal dedicated to advancing knowledge of furniture made or used in the Americas from the seventeenth century to the present. Authors are encouraged to submit articles on any aspect of furniture history, essays on conservation and historic technology, reproductions or transcripts of documents, annotated photographs of new furniture discoveries, and book and exhibition reviews. References for compiling an annual bibliography also are welcome.

Manuscripts must be typed, double-spaced, illustrated with black-and-white prints, transparencies, or high resolution digital images, and prepared in accordance with the *Chicago Manual of Style*. The Chipstone Foundation will offer significant honoraria for manuscripts accepted for publication and reimburse authors for all photography approved in writing by the editor.

Luke Beckerdite

Erik Gronning and Amy Coes

The Early Work of John Townsend in the Christopher Townsend Shop Tradition

▼ J O H N   T O W N S E N D (1733–1809), born in Newport, Rhode Island, on February 17, 1733, was the first son of Christopher Townsend (1701–1787) and his wife, Patience Easton (1703–1789), and is accepted by many as one of America's greatest cabinetmakers. John Townsend's work has been studied at length by many scholars. Among the most comprehensive publications was Morrison H. Heckscher's *John Townsend: Newport Cabinetmaker* (2005). The exhibition that accompanied that book assembled for the first time nearly all of the known works by Townsend. Therefore, it was with great surprise that in March 2011 an unknown signed and dated John Townsend high chest was discovered (fig. 1). Researching the high chest initiated a string of discoveries not only about John Townsend but also about his apprenticeship with his father.[1]

Christopher Townsend, the son of Solomon and Catherine Townsend, was born in Oyster Bay, Long Island, and arrived in Newport with his family in 1707. Between 1715 and 1722 Christopher trained as a joiner and cabinetmaker with an unknown Newport master. In December 1723 he married and settled on Easton's Point, where his wife's family had significant landholdings and ties in the furniture, shipbuilding, and house building trades. In 1725 Christopher purchased lot 51 in Newport for his house and shop, which still stand today at 74 Bridge Street.[2]

Christopher began his career during the 1720s working as a house carpenter or housewright. He described himself as a "joiner" or "shop joiner" and likely built his own house and shop (the latter measuring 12 by 20 feet), which was located down the street from the house of his older brother, Job Townsend (1699–1765). In 1729 he became a freeman and received commissions for a number of public and private buildings in Newport, including the Colony House (1739–1749) and perhaps Trinity Church (1725–1735), as well as the Seventh Day Baptist Meeting House (1725–1730). He may have established his cabinet shop by 1732, when he purchased hardware, nails, and other materials. Two years later, a local merchant sold him a large quantity of hardware for case furniture, including desks.

Christopher's shop supplied furniture to several important local merchants, including Abraham Redwood and Isaac Stelle. The workshop was spacious enough for five or six workbenches, which were manned by his sons, John and Jonathan (1745–1773), whom Christopher trained, as well as other apprentices and journeymen. Christopher's working career spanned nearly sixty years, during which time he amassed an estate larger than those of anyone else in his extended family, owing in part to his wife's assets.[3]

John Townsend's life paralleled his father's in many ways over his nearly fifty-year career. John probably began his apprenticeship in 1747 and completed his term during the mid-1750s. He described himself as a "joiner" in a contract with the house carpenters Henry Peckham and Wing Spooner in 1754, but at that time he may still have been working in Christopher's shop.[4]

Figure 2 High chest of drawers attributed to John Townsend, Newport, Rhode Island, ca. 1770. Mahogany with yellow poplar. H. 84½", W. 41", D. 21". (Private collection.) This high chest descended in the Dyer family of Providence, Rhode Island.

The high chest illustrated in figure 1 is the earliest example of that form documented to John Townsend. It does not have his archetypal front legs with flat incised carving; sharp, angular, anisodactyl claw feet; rear legs with pad feet; or conventional concave shell (fig. 2). Rather, this chest has four delicate unadorned legs, each supported with open-talon claw-and-ball feet, and an obverse convex shell, oriented with the lobes extending down. If not for its prominent signature, this object might never have been ascribed to John Townsend. Dated 1756, the chest may have been the first major commission he received. The original owners, Lieutenant Colonel Oliver Arnold (1725–1789) and his wife Mary (1725–1762), were married in that year, and their choice of John Townsend to make the chest attests to the latter's elevated status within Newport's cabinetmaking community at the young age of twenty-three.[5]

The importance that Townsend placed on the Arnold chest is evident from the profuse graphite inscriptions he placed on it. "Made By John Townsend / Newport 1756" (fig. 3) is written on the inside of the top drawer of the lower case, "John Townsend" is penciled on the upper-case drawer divider, and the letter "M"—matching that in the word "Made" and used as a finishing mark—is written on different components at least five times (fig. 4). Large calligraphic finishing marks are characteristic of Townsend's work and consistently appear on other examples of his furniture. On the Arnold chest, he used the letters "A," "B," "C," "D," "E," and "F" to differentiate the drawers of the upper case. The drawers of the lower case are also

Figure 3 Detail of the graphite signature on the high chest illustrated in fig. 1. (Courtesy, Sotheby's.)

Figure 4 Detail of an "M" finishing mark on the backboard of the high chest illustrated in fig. 1. (Courtesy, Sotheby's.)

inscribed: "A" on the back of the upper drawer, "B" on the back of the center drawer below, and "A" and "B" on the backs and sides of the flanking drawers. In addition, letters occur on several drawer dividers and drawer sides (figs. 5, 6).[6]

Townsend wrote the name "Polly" and "£14 Wigg" on the bottoms of two drawers of the upper case (figs. 7, 8). The first inscription is likely a ref-

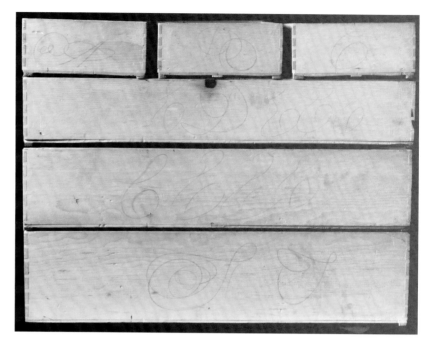

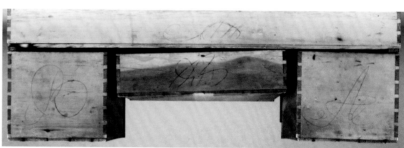

Figure 8 Detail of the inscription "£14 Wigg" on the bottom of a drawer in the upper case of the high chest illustrated in fig. 1. (Courtesy, Sotheby's.)

erence to Mrs. Arnold, since "Polly" was a common nickname for Mary in the eighteenth century. The second inscription corresponds to the price of a wig in Newport in the 1750s, when it was common practice to spell the word with two *g*'s. Writing of a somewhat personal nature is also present on the chest but is otherwise unknown in John Townsend's work. The upper left drawer of the upper case is inscribed "W Richardson / J Robinson / E Wanton / J Townsend / To Ride out next Wednesday" (fig. 9). This writing refers to William Richardson, Joseph Robinson, Edward Wanton, and John Townsend and probably to the day the chest was to be delivered. All four men were from elite Quaker families, who lived near one

Figure 9 Detail of the inscription "W Richardson/J Robinson/E Wanton/J Townsend/to Ride out next Wednesday" on the upper left drawer of the upper case of the high chest illustrated in fig. 1. (Courtesy, Sotheby's.)

Figure 10 Detail of the inscription "Woman Is By / Nature False & Inconstan(t) / W[ ]fill / W Richardson" and letter "A" on the upper left drawer of the upper case of the high chest illustrated in fig. 1. (Courtesy, Sotheby's.)

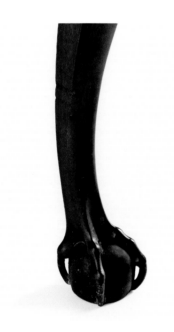

Figure 11 Detail of the leg and foot of the high chest illustrated in fig. 1. (Photo, Gavin Ashworth.)

another on Easton's Point in Newport and were variously connected through business and marriages.[7]

William Richardson (1736–1769) was the son of Thomas Richardson (1680–1761), a Newport merchant, general treasurer of Rhode Island (1748–1761), and presiding clerk of the New England Yearly Meeting of Friends (1729–1760), and his wife, Mary Wanton (1700–1777), who married in 1729. Mary Wanton's brother Gideon (1693–1767) served as governor in 1745 and 1747. William Richardson and Joseph Robinson were partners in Thomas Robinson & Co., one of the leading mercantile businesses in Newport. Richardson was Thomas Robinson's (1731–1817) brother-in-law and was undoubtedly related to Joseph. On November 5, 1761, all three men represented their firm in an agreement to manufacture spermaceti candles with Obadiah Brown & Co., Richard Cranch & Co., Naph Hart & Co., Isaac Stelle & Co., Aaron Lopez & Co, Collins & Rivera, and Edward Langdon & Son. Captain Edward Wanton (1734–1773) was the son of Governor Gideon Wanton (1693–1767) and Mary Cadman (d. 1780) and a cousin of William Richardson. Born on April 12, 1734, Edward was described as a merchant in several Newport court cases. His brother Gideon Jr. (b. 1724) married John Townsend's sister Mary (1735–1783).[8]

The upper left drawer of the Arnold chest bears the inscription "Woman Is By / Nature False & Inconstan(t) / W[ ]fill / W. Richardson" (fig. 10), a playful commentary on marriage that reinforces the theory that the chest was made around the time of Oliver and Mary Arnold's wedding. The first part of the inscription was inspired by a quote in *The Orphan; or, the Unhappy Marriage*, a play written by Thomas Otway (1652–1685) in England in 1680. A story of unrequited love, the play was one of the most influential domestic tragedies of the seventeenth century, and it remained popular in English and American theaters well into the nineteenth century. The larger quote that inspired Townsend's quip was excerpted from the play and published widely. It appeared in an essay on marriage written by Joseph Addison (1672–1719) for the *Spectator* in 1711. Reissued in eight volumes in 1747, the *Spectator* was available for circulation at the Redwood Library, which was founded in Newport in that year. The Townsends, Wantons, Robinsons, and Richardsons were among the library's first members.[9]

The Arnold high chest is the earliest dated Rhode Island example with an ogee head. Although the pediment has fully developed features that became standard in Newport work from 1760 to 1780—an enclosed ogee pediment with two moderately sized oculi and two applied tympanum panels—it was made just when the flat-top form that had been popular for the previous fifty years was passing out of fashion for all but the least expensive chests. The absence of quarter columns on the upper case and carving on the knees and presence of four pierced claw-and-ball feet and a downward oriented convex shell provide further evidence that the Arnold chest represents a transitional phase in Newport high chest design.

The Arnold chest is also unusual in having four claw-and-ball feet (most later Newport examples have turned pad feet at the rear) and is the earliest dated example with pierced talons (fig. 11). Although not verified through microscopy, the balls have a dark finish that may have been intended to simulate ebony and contrast with the lighter, more transparent finish of the anisodactyl claws. The claws have rounded knuckles and are thinner and less angular than those on later feet from Townsend's shop. Characteristic of all the claw-and-ball feet on his furniture, the hallux or rear talon has no knuckle. This sets his work apart from feet on furniture documented and attributed to John Goddard, which have a well-defined, rounded knuckle on the rear talon.[10]

Figure 12   Detail of the shell on the high chest illustrated in fig. 1. (Photo, Gavin Ashworth.) The shell is applied and the lobes are carved through into the skirt below. The joint is visible near the bottom of the shell.

Figure 13   Detail showing the lamination line of the shell and skirt of the high chest illustrated in fig. 1. (Photo, Gavin Ashworth.)

Of all the features of the Arnold chest, the shell is perhaps the most distinctive (fig. 12). Unlike most of the shells on later Newport high chests and dressing tables, which are somewhat semicircular in shape and oriented with the lobes facing up, the shell on the Arnold chest is fan-shaped and oriented in the opposite direction. The carver of the Arnold chest began by transferring the design of the shell to a ½-inch-thick mahogany board, cutting the rough outline with a bow saw, and partially carving the outermost convex lobes. After gluing the board to the skirt, he completed the carving with gouges (used right side up to cut the flutes and upside down to model the convex surfaces), a parting tool (used to establish the fillets between the convex and concave lobes), and abrasive (used to remove tool marks from the convex lobes). The glue line is visible where the carver cut through the laminate into the skirt below (fig. 13). Only two other pieces are known with this type of shell: a pier table with ball-and-claw feet and a high chest (figs. 14, 16).

This unique shell design may have influenced cabinetmakers working in and around nearby Stonington, Connecticut. Several objects from this region, including a high chest of drawers with a history of descent in the Smith and Hyde families and a dressing table, have skirts with integral "drops" having the same basic outline as this early Newport shell (figs. 1, 12, 15). Decorative arts scholars Minor Myers Jr. and Edgar Mayhew attributed the Smith high chest to a member of that family and suggested as a candidate Jonathan Smith, who was working in Stonington during the second half of the eighteenth century.[11]

Figure 14   Pier table, Newport, Rhode Island, 1750–1765. Mahogany with red cedar. H. 30", W. 50", D. 25". (Courtesy, Redwood Library and Athenaeum, Newport, Rhode Island; photo, Gavin Ashworth.) The feet are similar to those on furniture documented and attributed to John Goddard. This table has been extensively reworked. The drawers are later additions, and the original top was probably marble.

Although Rhode Island designs were undoubtedly transmitted to other coastal New England towns, the most diagnostic construction techniques employed by John Townsend and his Newport contemporaries were rarely imitated. As exemplified by the work on the Arnold chest, Townsend's drawer dovetails are fine and evenly spaced, and the top of each drawer side is finished with a shallow torus molding. Each of the three short drawers of the upper case is secured with a wooden spring lock (often referred to as a "Quaker" lock) rather than a conventional metal lock. Otherwise, Townsend would have had to place the escutcheon plate too high on the

Figure 15   Dressing table, Stonington area, Connecticut, ca. 1765. Maple. H. 27½", W. 31¾", D. 20". (Private collection; photo, Sotheby's.)

drawer face and disturb the chest's proportions. The mahogany he chose was very dense and highly figured, ranging from a striped pattern on the drawer fronts to a curled pattern for the cornice moldings and shell laminate. Most of the secondary wood in the chest is clear white pine, including the vertical glue blocks used to secure the legs to the inner corners of the lower case frame, which reinforce the area where the partitions between the lower drawers join the skirt and stop the drawers. As is the case with other furniture documented and attributed to John Townsend, the Arnold chest has a small amount of mahogany secondary wood. The glue blocks securing the front legs to the skirt are made of that wood and chamfered to remain hidden from view. Collectively, these construction and design characteristics are hallmarks of Townsend's work and crucial in identifying other early pieces.

The high chest illustrated in figure 16 was probably made circa 1755. Notations on a piece of parchment glued to a drawer side state that the chest was originally owned by Governor Gideon Wanton and bought at auction following his death by Perry Weaver, John Goddard's son-in-law. The chest descended in the Freeborn branch of the Weaver family until its acquisition by the current owners. Although significantly larger than the Arnold high chest, the Wanton example is similar in having plain knees, claw-and-ball

Figure 16 High chest of drawers attributed to Christopher Townsend and John Townsend, Newport, Rhode Island, ca. 1755. Mahogany with tulip poplar. H. 92¼", W. 44¼", D. 22¾". (Private collection; photo, Gavin Ashworth.) The horizontal moldings at the base of the finial plinth are missing, but the chest retains its original hardware.

Figure 17 Detail of the leg and foot of the high chest illustrated in fig. 16. (Photo, Gavin Ashworth.)

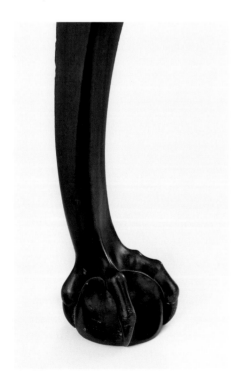

Figure 18   Detail of the shell on the high chest illustrated in fig. 16. (Photo, Gavin Ashworth.)

Figure 19   Detail showing the pediment back-board of the high chest illustrated in fig. 1. (Photo, Gavin Ashworth.) The upper portion of central plinth is lost.

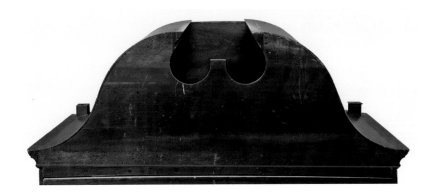

Figure 20   Detail showing the pediment back-board of the high chest illustrated in fig. 16. (Photo, Gavin Ashworth.)

feet at the front and back, and a downward-oriented convex shell. It also has the same drawer lettering system and related "M" finishing marks on the backboard.[12]

The carving on the Wanton chest differs from that on the Arnold example. The feet have compressed balls, larger toes with subtly modeled knuckles, and talons that are not pierced (fig. 17). Although conventional in design, the feet of the Wanton chest are superior in execution to those on much Newport furniture. The shell on the Wanton chest is less complex than that on the Arnold example (fig. 18), but it is glued up in the same manner. On both shells, the carver cut through the laminate into the skirt below.

The Arnold and Wanton high chests share several construction features: the backboards of the heads are cut to mirror the oculi and plinths of the tympana (figs. 19, 20); the cyma-shaped cornice moldings are attached with interior screws; mahogany glue blocks are used to secure the front legs to

Figure 21   Detail of the glue blocks securing the left front leg of the high chest illustrated in fig. 1. (Photo, Gavin Ashworth.)

Figure 22   Detail of the glue blocks securing the left front leg of the high chest illustrated in fig. 16. (Photo, Gavin Ashworth.)

Figure 23   Detail of the glue block attached to the skirt and a vertical drawer divider on the high chest illustrated in fig. 1. (Photo, Gavin Ashworth.)

Figure 24   Detail of the glue block attached to the skirt and a vertical drawer divider on the high chest illustrated in fig. 16. (Photo, Gavin Ashworth.)

the skirt (figs. 21, 22); and the glue blocks reinforcing the joint between the vertical dividers of the lower drawers terminate in chamfered points (figs. 23, 24). Variations in the construction of these pieces are largely a factor of design. The pediment of the Wanton high chest has a mahogany board behind the oculi and moldings around them (fig. 16). The board is dadoed and wedged into the cornice returns and front-to-rear framing boards below (fig. 25). The plinth of the tympanum originally had a base molding, but the latter is missing. Ogee heads that are fully enclosed at the front are relatively common on Newport case pieces, but the unusual attachment of the board behind the oculi of the Wanton chest suggests that it was an early attempt to achieve that design.[13]

The design and construction of these chests suggest that they were made in the same shop. This relationship becomes even more apparent when the marks on the objects are compared under infrared light. The Wanton high

Figure 25   Detail of the board behind the oculi of the pediment of the high chest illustrated in fig. 16. (Photo, Gavin Ashworth.)

Figure 26   Detail of an "M" finishing mark on the high chest illustrated in fig. 16. (Photo, Erik Gronning.) John Townsend may have inscribed this finishing mark.

Figure 27   Detail of an "M" finishing mark on the high chest illustrated in fig. 16. (Photo, Erik Gronning.) Christopher Townsend may have inscribed this finishing mark.

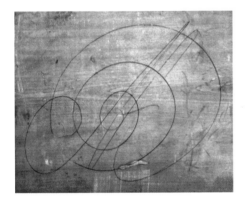

Figure 28   Detail of the "B" inscribed on the high chest illustrated in fig. 16. (Photo, Erik Gronning.) The belly of the "B" is not nearly as exaggerated as that shown in fig. 29.

Figure 29   Detail of the "B" inscribed on the high chest illustrated in fig. 1. (Courtesy, Sotheby's.)

chest has letter designations, but it is inscribed with an "M" finishing mark seven times. The "M" marks are by two different hands; one begins with a distinctive triple loop (fig. 26) and is nearly identical to the "M" marks on the Arnold high chest (fig. 4), while the other lacks the loops and has a concentric spiral (fig. 27). The letter "B" on the Wanton chest also differs from that on the Arnold example (figs. 28, 29). Inscriptions on a desk-and-bookcase signed by Christopher Townsend and made for the Reverend Nathaniel Appleton (1693–1784) and his wife, Margaret (Gibbs) (1699–

Figure 30 Christopher Townsend, desk-and-bookcase, Newport, Rhode Island, ca. 1750. Mahogany throughout. Dimensions not recorded. (Private collection; Image © Metropolitan Museum of Art.) The brackets are original, but the ball feet below are conjectural replacements. As is the case with the Arnold and Wanton high chests (figs. 19, 20), the upper backboard of the Appleton bookcase is shaped to mirror the tympanum.

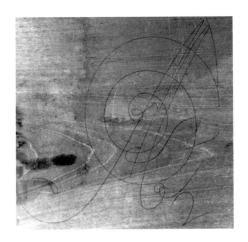

1771), of Cambridge, Massachusetts, offer an explanation for the similarities and differences observed in the marks on the Wanton and Appleton high chests (fig. 30). The "M" finishing marks on the backboards of the desk-and-bookcase and the Wanton high chest are nearly identical (figs. 27, 31). Moreover, the calligraphic "B" on the Wanton high chest is identical to the "B" in the inscription "Made By Christopher Townsend" (figs. 28, 32). Therefore, one may surmise that Christopher Townsend and his son John collaborated in the production of the Wanton high chest.

The Appleton desk-and-bookcase has "plum-pudding" mahogany primary wood and solid silver hardware made by Newport silversmith Samuel Casey (1723–ca. 1773). It retains its original urn-and-flame finials, which are simi-

Figure 31 Detail of an "M" finishing mark on the desk-and-bookcase illustrated in fig. 30. (Courtesy, Sotheby's).

Figure 32 Detail of the inscription "Made By Christopher Townsend" on the desk-and-bookcase illustrated in fig. 30. (Photo, Charlotte Hale, Sherman Fairchild Paintings Conservation Center, Metropolitan Museum of Art, Image © Metropolitan Museum of Art.)

lar to the one John Townsend made for the Arnold high chest (figs. 33, 34). Imported British case furniture or architectural design books may have influenced Christopher's or his client's choice of an arched pediment, since only one other Newport case piece with that type of head is known. The desk-and-bookcase is also unusual in having fallboard supports faced with

Figure 33 Detail of the cornice molding and left finial of the desk-and-bookcase illustrated in fig. 30. (Photo, Gavin Ashworth.)

Figure 34 Detail of the finial on the high chest illustrated in fig. 1. (Courtesy, Sotheby's.) The softer, more elliptical shape of the flame is unique in John Townsend's work. The lowermost section of the finial is restored and would originally have been shorter, like the finial shown in fig. 33.

Figure 35 Detail of the silver mount on the left fallboard support of the desk-and-bookcase illustrated in fig. 30. (Courtesy, Sotheby's.) The eyes are made from a cylinder of agate.

silver birds with inlaid agate eyes (fig. 35). Christopher Townsend appears to have favored this motif, since he used birds with a similar profile on the staircase frieze in his house on Bridge Street in Newport. Another distinctive feature of the Appleton desk-and-bookcase may have been lost. The writing height of the fallboard is relatively low, which suggests that the feet are not full height. Inside each bracket are two mahogany glue blocks that abut to form a square hole (fig. 36). If the Appleton desk-and-bookcase followed the design of elevated English baroque examples, a compressed ball foot with a square tenon may have fit into the holes (fig. 37).[14]

A recently discovered slant-front desk with a history of descent in the Simon Pease family of Newport shares details with the Appleton desk-and-

Figure 36 Detail showing the foot blocking on the desk-and-bookcase illustrated in fig. 30. (Photo, Leslie Keno.) The glue blocks are neatly finished to conform to the shape of the brackets.

Figure 37 Desk-and-bookcase, England, 1700–1720. Oak with pine. H. 81⅛", W. 43⅞", D. 23½". (Metropolitan Museum of Art, Gift of James De Lancey Verplanck and John Bayard Rogers Verplanck, 1939 [39.184a,b]. Image © Metropolitan Museum of Art.)

Figure 38 Christopher Townsend, desk, Newport, Rhode Island, ca. 1750. Mahogany with
mahogany, cedrela, and tulip poplar. H. 37¼",
W. 35⅝", D. 20¼". (Private collection; photo,
Gavin Ashworth.) The lower portions of the feet
are missing, but the desk has its original brass,
hardware, and finish.

bookcase; the brasses are aligned vertically, the interior design and foot construction are similar, and the shells on the small drawers are virtually identical (figs. 38–40). The bottom board of the desk is signed "Made by C T," and the backsides of the exterior drawers are inscribed with a chalk finishing mark (figs. 41, 42). The three large drawers are also marked sequentially in graphite, "B," "C," and "D" (fig. 43).[15]

A related slant-front desk with brass lopers identical in shape and size to those on the Appleton desk-and-bookcase has graphite letters inscribed

Figure 39 Detail showing the foot blocking of the desk illustrated in fig. 38. (Photo, Gavin Ashworth.)

Figure 40 Detail of a shell on an interior drawer of the desk illustrated in fig. 38. (Photo, Gavin Ashworth.)

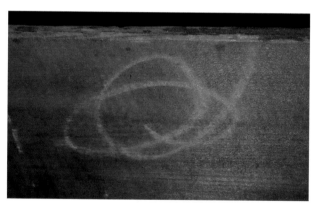

Figure 41 Detail of the inscription "Made by C T" on the bottom of desk illustrated in fig. 38. (Photo, Erik Gronning.)

Figure 42 Detail of a chalk finishing mark on the back of an exterior drawer of the desk illustrated in fig. 38. (Photo, Erik Gronning.)

 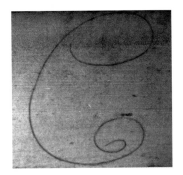 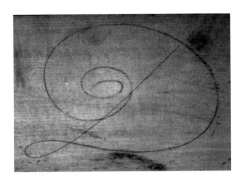

Figure 43 Details showing the letters on the backs of the exterior drawers of the desk illustrated in fig. 38. (Photo, Erik Gronning.)

Figure 44 Desk attributed to Christopher Townsend, Newport, Rhode Island, ca. 1750. Mahogany with tulip poplar, chestnut, cedrela, and white pine. H. 42", W. 36½", D. 22". (Private collection; photo, Sotheby's.) The feet are replaced.

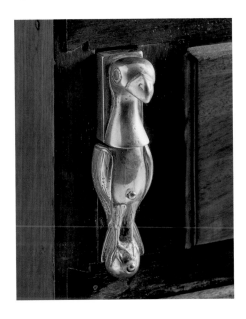

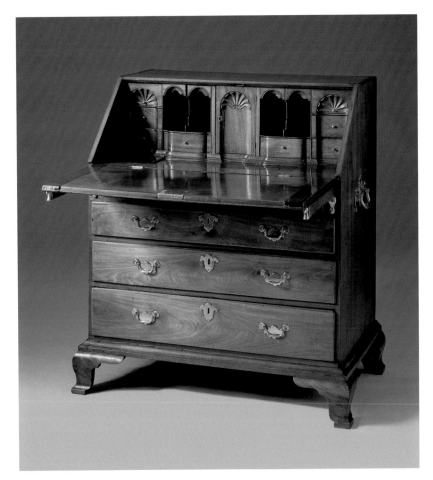

Figure 45 Detail of the brass mount on the left fallboard support of the desk illustrated in fig. 44. (Courtesy, Sotheby's.) The eyes are made from a cylinder of agate.

on the back of the exterior drawers in Christopher Townsend's hand (figs. 44–46). The other notable differences include a more detailed prospect door shell and intricate sliding wooden locks securing the uppermost exterior drawer. The current feet are replacements and may possibly have originally been of the two-part form found on the desks in figures 30 and 38. On one interior drawer is a graphite mark (fig. 46). A similar mark was found on a drawer of the Wanton high chest.[16]

Another slant-front desk possibly made for the export market has details suggesting that it originated in Christopher Townsend's shop (fig. 47). Made of cedar, this object has an "M" finishing mark similar to those on other pieces documented and attributed to him as well as drawer

Figure 46 Details of the inscription on the back of an exterior drawer of the desk illustrated in fig. 44. (Photo, Erik Gronning.) The upper image shows the orientation of the board when the inscription was made prior to assembly. The lower image is as it appears with the grain oriented horizonally.

Figure 47 Desk attributed to Christopher Townsend, Newport, Rhode Island, ca. 1750. Cedar. H. 41¼", W. 35⅞", D. 19¾". (Courtesy, Caxambas Foundation; photo, Gavin Ashworth.)

backs with Christopher's script lettering system. Moreover, the precisely rendered dovetails, rounded edges of the drawer sides, and chamfered top edges of the drawer backs are consistent with his work. Christopher Townsend is documented as having made several cedar desks for export over the course of his career, including "2 Cedar Desks, and Casing" in 1748. John Banister paid him £83. 12. 6. for those pieces, which were shipped on the sloop *Little Polly* bound for Jamaica. In 1764 Captain Peleg Bunker purchased a red cedar desk from Townsend and agreed to make payment after returning from the West Indies.[17]

The high chest of drawers illustrated in figure 48 represents another collaborative effort between Christopher and John Townsend; it is inscribed in graphite on the lower-case drawer blade "John T" and "Christopher Townsend" (figs. 48, 49). The chest has a history of descent in the Smith family of Philadelphia, but an original brass lock escutcheon engraved in period script "Thos. Robinson" suggests that the original owners were Thomas (1731–1817) and Sarah (Richardson) Robinson, who married in Newport in 1752. The shaped pediment backboard, glue blocks, molding profiles, upper drawer Quaker locks, cabriole legs, and feet are very similar to those on the Arnold high chest (figs. 11, 50). The graphite lettering of the drawers and "M" finishing marks on the back of the upper and lower cases of those objects are also identical. Were it not for the concave shell (fig. 51) and inscription, this high chest would almost certainly be ascribed to John Townsend alone. The chest is unique in having bonnet

Figure 48 Christopher Townsend and John Townsend, high chest of drawers, Newport, Rhode Island, ca. 1755. Mahogany with yellow poplar, chestnut, white pine, and mahogany. H. 87¹³⁄₁₆", W. 40½", D. 22¾". (Courtesy, Philadelphia Museum of Art; photo, Gavin Ashworth.) The chest retains its original hardware.

Figure 49 Detail showing the "John T" and "Christopher Townsend" inscriptions on the lower-case drawer blade of the high chest illustrated in fig. 48.

Figure 50   Detail of a leg and foot of the high chest illustrated in fig. 48. (Photo, Gavin Ashworth.)

Figure 51   Detail of the shell on the high chest illustrated in fig. 48. (Photo, Gavin Ashworth.)

Figure 52   Detail of a piece of molding used in the construction of the pediment of the high chest illustrated in fig. 48. (Photo, Gavin Ashworth.)

Figure 53   John Townsend, dining table, Newport, Rhode Island, 1756. Mahogany with soft maple, red oak, and hickory. H. 28¾", W (open). 62¼", W (closed). 17½", D. 58¼". (Metropolitan Museum of Art, Gift of Stuart Holzer and Marc Holzer, in memory of their parents, Ann and Philip Holzer, 2012. Image © Metropolitan Museum of Art.)

Figure 54   Detail of the incsription " John Townsend 1756/3," on the dining table illustrated in fig. 53. (Image © Metropolitan Museum of Art.)

dust boards made of mahogany. These boards may represent the use of left-over wood, rather than a material option, since a section of scrap molding was used as a brace on the interior of the pediment (fig. 52).[18]

Made the same year as the Arnold high chest is a dining table inscribed "John Townsend 1756/3," " John Towns[en]d" and "John" (figs. 53, 54). The table's tall cabriole legs terminate in claw-and-ball feet that are identical to those on the Arnold chest (figs. 11, 55). As he did on that high chest, Townsend inscribed the table with the owner's name—"For Israel / A" (fig. 56). A similar undated table may be an antecedent for the signed example (fig. 57). Likely made in the shop of Christopher Townsend, it has his characteristic feet, which are similar to John's but distinguished by having thicker toes and much shorter talons.[19]

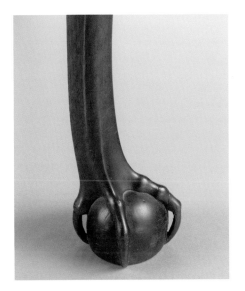

Figure 55   Detail of a leg and foot of the dining table illustrated in fig. 53. (Image © Metropolitan Museum of Art.) The central talon on the foot is replaced.

Figure 56   Detail of the inscription "For Israel / A" on the dining table illustrated in fig. 53. (Image © Metropolitan Museum of Art.)

Rectangular tea tables with angular cabriole legs, slipper feet, ovolo rail moldings, and tray tops rabbeted on the underside to fit inside the frame are generic Newport forms that were likely made by members of both the Townsend and Goddard families. The example illustrated in figure 58 is unusual in being signed in chalk on the underside of the top: "C Townsend joynd the piece" (fig. 59). Given the similarities in their construction of case furniture, it is not surprising that John Townsend's version of this slipper-foot form is virtually identical to Christopher's.[20]

John Townsend also offered claw-and-ball feet as an option on this standardized tea table form. With a history of descent in the Sweet or Abbott family of Rhode Island, the example illustrated in figure 60 has feet that are identical to those on the Arnold chest. Other than having the underside of the top notched in the corners, its construction is the same as that of other Newport tea tables including the one signed by his father (fig. 59).[21]

Figure 57 Dining table attributed to Christopher Townsend, Newport, Rhode Island, ca. 1755. Mahogany. H. 30½", W (open). 69", D. 62". (*Antiques* 110, no. 98 [September 1970]: 292.)

Figure 58 Christopher Townsend, tea table, Newport, Rhode Island, ca. 1750. Mahogany. H. 25¾", W. 21⅜". (Private collection; photo, Sotheby's.)

Figure 59 Detail of the inscription "C Townsend joynd the piece" on the tea table illustrated in fig. 58. (Courtesy, Sotheby's.)

Figure 60 Tea table attributed to John Townsend, Newport, Rhode Island, ca. 1760. Mahogany. H. 26¼", W. 19⁵⁄₁₆", D. 19⅜". (Courtesy, Museum of Art, Rhode Island School of Design, Providence; photo, Erik Gould.)

Christopher Townsend's earliest known work is a flat-top high chest of drawers that is signed and dated in graphite on the bottom board of the upper case, "Christopher Townsend made 1748" (figs. 61, 62). According to a paper label on the chest, the original owner was Newport ship captain William Van Deursen, who, during the Revolution, lived in Middletown, Connecticut, where he commanded the privateer brig *Middletown*. With its dovetailed lower case, legs secured with glue blocks inside the frame, and cyma-shaped skirt, the Van Deursen chest shows that Newport case design

Figure 61 Christopher Townsend, high chest of drawers, Newport, Rhode Island, 1748. Walnut with white pine. H. 70", W. 38½", D. 20½". (© 2013. Collection of Gerald and Kathleen Peters; photo, Gavin Ashworth.)

Figure 62 Detail of the inscription "Christopher Townsend made 1748" on the high chest illustrated in fig. 61. (Photo, Charlotte Hale, Sherman Fairchild Paintings Conservation Center. Image © Metropolitan Museum of Art.)

and construction became standardized very early, which gave the city's cabinetmakers an advantage in the coastal furniture trade.[22]

A very similar high chest can be attributed to Christopher Townsend based on its graphite inscriptions (fig. 63). The original owner was George Hussey (d. 1782) of Nantucket, Massachusetts. At his death the chest passed to Clothier Pierce Sr., a merchant in Newport, and next through the Potter family of Dartmouth, Massachusetts. Though not signed, the high chest has Christopher Townsend's large calligraphic finishing mark "M" in graphite on the interior bottom of the lowest long drawer of the upper case, as well as his signature lettering system (fig. 64). Its drawer arrangement differs

Figure 63 High chest of drawers attributed to Christopher Townsend, Newport, Rhode Island, ca. 1750. Mahogany with white pine and yellow poplar. H. 72", W. 39", D. 21". (Private collection; photo, Israel Sack, Inc., Archive, Yale University Art Gallery.) This high chest was originally made for George Hussey (d. 1782) of Nantucket, Massachusetts.

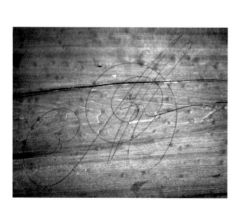

Figure 64 Detail of the "M" finishing mark on the high chest illustrated in fig. 63. (Photo, Erik Gronning.)

slightly from the signed example but is the same as that of the Arnold and Robinson high chests. As with the Wanton high chest, the sides of the lower case are rabbeted to receive the squares of the legs (figs. 1, 48).[23]

A high chest of drawers with china shelves backed by an elaborately scalloped board is the most architecturally elaborate example of the New-

Figure 65 High chest of drawers attributed to Christopher Townsend, Newport, Rhode Island, ca. 1755. Mahogany with white pine and yellow poplar. H. 83⅝", W. 40½", D. 22¼". (Chipstone Foundation; photo, Gavin Ashworth.) The chest retains its original cast brass hardware and finish. Made in three sections and secured with glue blocks, the china shelves are inscribed twice with a chalk "A." As is the case with other flat-top high chests documented and attributed to Christopher Townsend, the rear legs are glued into a shallow rabbet in the backboard.

Figure 66 Detail of a claw-and-ball foot of the high chest illustrated in fig. 65. (Photo, Gavin Ashworth.)

Figure 67 Bureau table with legs attributed to John Townsend, Newport, Rhode Island, ca. 1760. Mahogany with chestnut and tulip poplar. H. 27", W. 40¼", D. 22". (Courtesy, Schuyler Mansion State Historic Site, New York State Office of Parks, Recreation and Historic Preservation.) The case has fine dovetails and a deep shell carving consistent with furniture from John Townsend's shop, but owing to alterations, only the legs and feet can be attributed to him. This object may have started out as a pier table or side table.

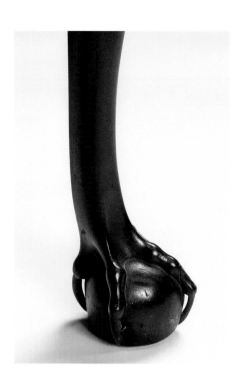
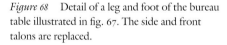

Figure 68 Detail of a leg and foot of the bureau table illustrated in fig. 67. The side and front talons are replaced.

port flat-top form (fig. 65). Originally owned by Rhode Island Governor Samuel Ward (1725–1776), the chest can be attributed to Christopher Townsend's shop based on structural and stylistic affinities with the Van Deursen and Hussey high chests. The distinctive claw-and-ball feet, with thicker elongated phalanxes and flattened balls, relate closely to those of the Wanton high chest (figs. 17, 66). The balls also appear to be ebonized like those of the Arnold and Ward high chest (figs. 11, 66) and of a heavily altered table that descended in the Schuyler and Van Rensselaer families of New York (figs. 67, 68). The original owner of the table may have been Philip Schuyler, who married Catherine Van Rensselaer in 1755.[24]

In the Townsend shop tradition, claw-and-ball feet with pierced talons occur on furniture documented and attributed to both Christopher and John. In some instances, their work is relatively easy to separate. The feet on a tea table that reputedly descended in the Weeden family of Jamestown, Rhode Island, are related to those on the Wanton chest in that the second phalanges of the side toes are more elongated than that of the center toe (figs. 69, 70, 17). This design and carving feature is more closely associated

Figure 69   Tea table attributed to Christopher Townsend, Newport, Rhode Island, ca. 1760. Mahogany with chestnut. H. 26", W. 33½", D. 20½". (Courtesy, Museum of Fine Arts, Houston, Bayou Bend Collection, gift of Miss Ima Hogg.) The table has a chestnut cross-brace dovetailed at the midpoint of the long rails and a top secured with glue blocks. The knee returns are replaced.

Figure 70   Detail of a leg and foot of the tea table illustrated in fig. 69.

with Christopher than with John. In contrast, the feet on a marble-top tea table from the Rodman family of Rhode Island could be ascribed to either maker (figs. 71, 72).[25]

A dressing table with a history in the Chase family of Rhode Island has legs and feet that are closely related to those of the Rodman table (figs. 73, 74). The elongated second phalanges on the side toes and the shorter

pierced talons of the feet follow the design associated with Christopher Townsend, and the graphite letters on the backs of the drawers and spiral finishing marks also appear to be in his hand. The balls also appear to be ebonized like those on the Arnold and Ward high chests and altered Van Rensselaer table (figs. 11, 66, 68, 74). As is typical of early high chests and dressing tables associated with Christopher and John Townsend, the front legs of the Chase table are secured with contoured mahogany glue blocks, and the rear legs with rectangular white pine glue blocks, the latter notched to act as drawer stops. The glue blocks on the inside of the skirt are shaped in the same manner as those of the Arnold and Wanton high chests (figs. 21–24). Other early features can be observed in the design and execution of the carved shell, most notably the way it is contained within an arch and its open center (fig. 75). The Robinson high chest has a related shell, but the center is not cut out (fig. 51).[26]

Several early Newport case pieces have shells with a hollowed lobe extending up between opposing scroll volutes, a motif some Newport fur-

Figure 73   Dressing table attributed to Christopher or John Townsend, Newport, Rhode Island, ca. 1755. Mahogany with white pine, yellow poplar, chestnut, and mahogany. H. 31", W. 35¾", D. 22". (Courtesy, Museum of Fine Arts, Houston, Bayou Bend Collection, gift of Miss Ima Hogg.)

Figure 74   Detail of a leg and foot of the dressing table illustrated in fig. 73.

Figure 75   Detail of the shell of the dressing table illustrated in fig. 73.

niture scholars have interpreted as a stylized fleur-de-lis. A high chest of drawers with this detail is inscribed on the top long drawer of the upper case, "No. 28 / Made By / John Townsend / Newport / 1759" (figs. 76, 77). The piece has "signature" attributes of John's shop, including his florid lettering system on the backs of the drawers. Like other objects documented

Figure 76 John Townsend, high chest of drawers, Newport, Rhode Island, 1759. Mahogany with chestnut, eastern white pine, and cottonwood. H. 88¾", W. 39⅜", D. 22⅛". (Courtesy, Yale University Art Gallery, New Haven, Connecticut, bequest of Doris M. Brixey.) Christopher Townsend may also have used the fleur-de-lis broken motif seen on the shell of this chest. A mahogany high chest base with that feature has ball-and-claw feet remarkably similar to those made by Christopher (CRN Auctions, *Americana and English Antiques, American and European Works of Art, Chinese, and Jewelry*, Cambridge, Massachusetts, September 9, 2012, lot 107).

Figure 77 Detail of the inscription "No. 28 / Made By / John Townsend / Newport / 1759" on the high chest illustrated in fig. 76.

Figure 78 Detail of a leg and foot of the high chest illustrated in fig. 76.

and attributed to him, it is well made and highly finished. The inner edge of the skirt shell is chamfered, the drawer sides have a torus molding at the top, glue blocks are contoured where required, and wooden spring locks secure the small upper drawers. Although made only three years after the Arnold chest, the Brixey example is designed quite differently. On the latter, tympanum panels are smaller, the oculi are larger, two equal-size drawers are in the upper row, the knees are carved, the rear legs end in pad feet, and the feet are pierced above the ball (figs. 78, 79). Indeed, the Brixey chest is the earliest documented example from Townsend's shop with those features.[27]

The most atypical object associated with John Townsend earliest period is a document cabinet with three shells, each with his characteristic fleur-de-

Figure 79 Detail of a foot of the high chest illustrated in fig. 76. A space can be seen above the ball.

Figure 80 John Townsend, document cabinet, Newport, Rhode Island, ca. 1755. Mahogany. H. 27½", W. 25¾", D. 12⅞". (Private collection; photo, Christie's.) The cabinet has Townsend's drawer lettering system. The backs of the drawers are inscribed in graphite "A," "B," "C," "D," from top to bottom on the right, and "E," "F," "G," and "H," from top to bottom on the left. Townsend used book-matched pieces of wood for drawers A and E, consecutive pieces cut from the same log for drawers B and D, and contiguous pieces from the same flitch for drawers G and H.

Figure 81 Detail of the inscription "John Townsend / Newport" on the document cabinet illustrated in fig. 80. (Photo, Gavin Ashworth.)

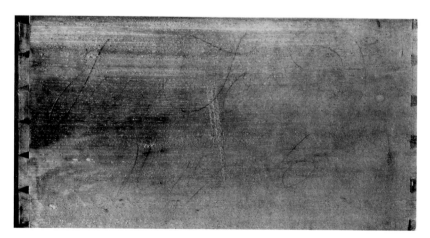

Figure 82 Detail of the shell on the door of the cabinet illustrated in fig. 80. (Photo, Christie's.)

lis (fig. 80). Inscribed in graphite "John Townsend/Newport" on the right side of the lower left drawer, the cabinet is one of the earliest block-and-shell case pieces made by him (fig. 81). The shelves and dividers in the interior have scalloped edges similar to those in the Appleton desk-and-bookcase, and the door shell, confined within an arch, continues a design likely introduced by Christopher Townsend (figs. 30, 82). The shells are taller than those on John Townsend's later block-and-shell pieces. One of the most

Figure 83   Chest of drawers attributed to John Townsend, Newport, Rhode Island, ca. 1756. Mahogany with eastern white pine and yellow poplar. H. 38⅛", W. 38½", D. 20⅛". (Courtesy, Diplomatic Reception Rooms, U.S. Department of State, Washington, D.C.) The chest retains its original hardware, but the bottom 3½ inches of the feet are replaced. The top drawer is secured with a spring lock that is reached by opening the drawer below.

Figure 84   Detail showing the two-piece construction of the shell on the chest of drawers illustrated in fig. 83. (Photo, Erik Gronning.)

unusual aspects of the cabinet's design is its compressed ball feet. Both their use and the possible incorporation of ball feet on the Appleton desk-and-bookcase and desk illustrated in figure 30 attest to the continued influence of baroque design on John Townsend's early work.[28]

A chest of drawers with a history in the Milnor family of Woodstock, Connecticut, can be attributed to John Townsend based on its carved shells and graphite inscriptions (fig. 83). Aside from being larger, the shells are almost identical to those on the document cabinet. On both objects, the applied convex shells were made in two pieces, a lobed section and a blocking section below (fig. 84). The back of each drawer is inscribed with graphite letters in John Townsend's distinctive hand, and the top drawer has his characteristic "M" finishing mark. As is the case with several other examples of his work, the chest also bears the owner's name, "Moses," written in graphite (fig. 85).[29]

Figure 85   Detail of the inscription "Moses" on the chest of drawers illustrated in fig. 83. (Photo, Erik Gronning.)

Figure 86   Slant-front desk attributed to John Townsend, Newport, Rhode Island, ca. 1755. Mahogany. H. 42", W. 37", D. 19½". (Private collection; photo, Sotheby's.) The desk retains its original hardware, but the feet are replacements.

The desk illustrated in figure 86 is the only slant-front example having a shell with the stylized fleur-de-lis motif. It retains a partially legible graphite signature, "J [ ] Newport," on the bottom board and has the name "James Harden"—likely an owner or journeyman—inscribed in Townsend's hand (figs. 87, 88). Its interior is similar to the Appleton desk-and-bookcase, but its more elaborate pigeonhole dividers are finished with scalloped sides similar to those found on the interior dividers of the document cabinet.[30]

Figure 87   Detail of the partial inscription "J [ ] Newport" on the desk illustrated in fig. 86. (Photo, Erik Gronning.)

Figure 88 Detail of the inscription "James Harden" on the desk illustrated in fig. 86. (Photo, Erik Gronning.)

A high chest that descended in the Potter family of Kingston, Rhode Island, and a card table that came down in the family of Stephen Hopkins are from John Townsend's early period, but their knee and foot carving differs from that on other examples examined in this study (figs. 89, 90). The toes of their front feet have an extra knuckle, the piercing above the ball

Figure 89 High chest of drawers attributed to John Townsend, Newport, Rhode Island, ca. 1757. Mahogany with mahogany and white pine. H. 87", W. 40¾", D. 22". (Photo, 2012 Museum of Fine Arts, Boston.) The construction of this high chest is consistent with John Townsend's early work, but the backboard of the pediment has a semicircular cutout rather than shaping that matches the tympanum. All of the drawer fronts were veneered at a later date.

Figure 90 Card table attributed to John Townsend, Newport, Rhode Island, ca. 1760. Mahogany with maple and white pine. H. 27½", W. 35½", D. 18½". (Courtesy, Chipstone Foundation.) This table descended in the family of Stephen Hopkins (1707–1785), who was a governor of Rhode Island and a signer of the Declaration of Independence.

Figure 91 Detail of the knee carving on the high chest illustrated in fig. 89. (Photo, 2012 Museum of Fine Arts, Boston.)

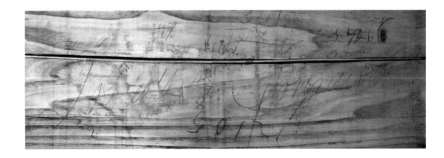

Figure 93   Detail showing the graphite signature
on the bureau table illustrated in fig. 92. (Photo,
Erik Gronning.)

is larger, and the tendons are significantly more defined (fig. 91). John
Townsend used his standard lettering system on the drawers and drawer
dividers of the chest, and his characteristic "M" finishing mark occurs in
five places.[31]

Evidence suggests that John Townsend's brother Jonathan also trained
in Christopher's shop, but the only documented piece by the younger man
is a bureau table with a history of descent in the Pell family of Newport and

Figure 94 John Townsend, card table, Newport, Rhode Island, 1762. Mahogany with chestnut, maple, and white pine. H. 27¼", W. 35", D. 16½". (Courtesy, 63rd Street Equities; Image © Metropolitan Museum of Art.)

Figure 95 Detail showing the graphite signature on the card table illustrated in fig. 94. (Image © Metropolitan Museum of Art.)

New York (fig. 92). The piece had his florid signature and other writing in graphite on the underside of the top drawer (fig. 93). As this bureau suggests, it is very likely that some of the furniture historically attributed to John Townsend was made by Jonathan instead.[32]

Made when he was thirty years old and signed in graphite "John Townsend / Newport / 1762," the card table illustrated in figure 94 is the latest piece of furniture with a graphite signature by Townsend (fig. 95). It marks a turning point in his career, from the baroque objects with delicate claw-and-ball feet that characterize his earlier output to the more aggressive legs and feet with taller balls and longer talons that typify his later work (fig. 96). The distinct knee carving is in his mature style, with tendrils on the knee brackets that nearly reach the knee and the lower section fanning out across the width of the leg.[33]

As one would expect, John Townsend's earliest furniture reflects his training in Christopher's shop. What is more surprising is the level of elite patronage John received at such an early age. Christopher had established

Figure 96 Detail of the knee carving on the card table illustrated in fig. 94. (Image © Metropolitan Museum of Art.)

strong ties with wealthy Newport residents long before John received his first order, and those relationships certainly benefited John as he ventured out on his own. John did, however, begin to develop his own style as his confidence grew and he gained exposure to new foreign design sources.[34]

ACKNOWLEDGMENTS   For their assistance with this article, the authors wish to thank David Bayne, Luke Beckerdite, Charles Burns, Dennis Carr, Sarah Anne Carter, Tara Cederholm, Maria Saffiotti Dale, Mr. and Mrs. Prescott Dunbar, Remi Dyll, Virginia Hart, Morrison Heckscher, Heidi Hill, Andrew Holter, Patricia Kane, Peter Kenny, Leigh Keno, Leslie Keno, Mrs. Angela Kilroy, Alexandra Kirtley, Caren Kraska, Mrs. Phyllis Kurfirst, Deanne Levison, Ann Smart Martin, Whitney Pape, Todd Prickett, Jonathan Prown, Robert Trent, Lynn Turner, Nick Vincent, Susan Walker, Gerald Ward, Ann Woolsey, and the institutions and collectors who allowed us to study and photograph their objects.

1. Charles O. Cornelius, "John Townsend, an Eighteenth Century Cabinet-Maker," *Metropolitan Museum Studies* 1, no. 1 (November 1928): 72–80; Mabel Munson Swan, "The Goddard and Townsend Joiners," *Antiques* 49, no. 4 (April 1946): 228–31; Mabel Munson Swan, "The Goddard and Townsend Joiners," *Antiques* 49, no. 4 (May 1946): 292–95; Joseph Downs, "The Furniture of Goddard and Townsend," *Antiques* 52, no. 6 (December 1947): 427–31; Ralph Carpenter, *The Arts and Crafts of Newport, Rhode Island, 1640–1820* (Newport, R.I.: Preservation Society of Newport County, 1954); Houghton Bulkeley, "John Townsend and Connecticut," *Connecticut Historical Society Bulletin* 25, no. 3 (July 1960): 80–83; Wendell Garrett, "The Goddard and Townsend Joiners: Random Biographical Notes," *Antiques* 94, no. 3 (September 1968): 391–93; Wendell Garrett, "The Family of Goddard and Townsend Joiners: More Random Biographical Notes," *Walpole Society Note Book* (Portland, Maine: Anthoensen Press, 1973), 32–42; Liza Moses and Michael Moses, "Authenticating John Townsend's Later Tables," *Antiques* 119, no. 5 (May 1981): 1152–63; Wendell Garrett, "The Goddard and Townsend Joiners of Newport: Random Biographical and Bibliographical Notes," *Antiques* 121, no. 5 (May 1982): 1153–55; Morrison Heckscher, "John Townsend's Block-and-Shell Furniture," *Antiques* 121, no. 5 (May 1982): 1144–52; Liza Moses and Michael Moses, "Authenticating John Townsend's and John Goddard's Queen Anne and Chippendale Tables," *Antiques* 121, no. 5 (May 1982): 1130–43; Michael Moses, *Master Craftsmen of Newport: The Townsends and Goddards* (Tenafly, N.J.: MMI Americana Press, 1984); and Morrison Heckscher, *John Townsend: Newport Cabinetmaker* (New York: Metropolitan Museum of Art, 2005). On p. 76 of *John Townsend: Newport Cabinetmaker*, Heckscher notes that Townsend was twenty-four years old when he made the dining table with his signature and the date 1756. For an illustration of that object, see his fig. 50 and cat. 1, pp. 76–79.

2. For additional information on Christopher Townsend, see Luke Beckerdite, "The Early Furniture of Christopher and Job Townsend," in *American Furniture*, edited by Luke Beckerdite (Hanover, N.H.: University Press of New England for the Chipstone Foundation, 2000), pp. 1–30. Heckscher, *John Townsend: Newport Cabinetmaker*, pp. 48–57. Moses, *Master Craftsmen of Newport*, pp. 65–70, 247–50. Margaretta Lovell, "'Such Furniture as Will Be Most Profitable': The Business of Cabinetmaking in Eighteenth-Century Newport," *Winterthur Portfolio* 26, no. 1 (Spring 1991): 52–56; Margaretta M. Lovell, *Art in a Season of Revolution: Painters, Artisans, and Patrons in Early America* (Philadelphia: University of Pennsylvania Press, 2004), pp. 255–56.

3. Abraham Redwood purchased a desk-and-bookcase from Christopher Townsend. On February 4, 1738, Christopher wrote Redwood regarding the delivery of the desk-and-bookcase: "According to thy Request . . . I indevoured to finish a Desk and Book Case Agreeable to thy directions to send thee by Brother Pope but could not quite finish . . . and understanding it was not for thee but a friend of thine, I concluded it would be Equal to thee, If I send it by another opertunity. And having an opertunity to send it by Brother Solomon, I . . . ordered him to Deliver it to thee or thy order, thou paying him one Moyodore freight, the Desk and

Bookcase amounts to Sixty Pounds this currency; includeing the two Ruf cases which is equal to fourteen heavy Pistole at £4.5.8 or fourty-four ounces and a half of Silver . . . I may let thee know that I sold such a Desk and Book Case without any Ruf cases, for £58 in hand this winter. Brother Job, also sold one to our Collector for £59. I mention this, that thou may know that I have not imposed on thee." Christopher Townsend to Abraham Redwood, February 4, 1738, MS 93-96, Newport Historical Society, reprinted Beckerdite, "The Early Furniture of Christopher and Job Townsend," p. 10. Christopher Townsend sold Isaac Stelle another desk-and-bookcase for £65 in 1742 and appears to have also sold other furniture to Samuel Ward, who was governor of Rhode Island during the 1760s and a client of Job's. For additional information, see Beckerdite, "The Early Furniture of Christopher and Job Townsend," p. 10. At his death in December 1787, Christopher was very wealthy. His estate inventory included extensive real estate on Easton's Point and considerable silver, financial instruments, furniture, and other fine possessions. In his will dated 1773, in which he described himself as a "Shop-joiner," he left his son John real estate holdings, including his house and adjoining shop and lots 81, 82, and 84 on Easton's Point, as well as all of his joiner tools, mahogany, other shop joinery stock, all his desk furniture, and one-third part of all of his new desks and other joiners' ware for sale. He also left John two of his largest silver porringers and one feather bed. To his son and namesake Christopher, a clockmaker and engraver, he left a significant amount of silver and furnishings including his "Clock and Clock Case, and Silver Watch, silver Tankard, Two silver Porringers . . . One large Mahogany Oval Table, one small Mahogany oval Table . . . one large Mahogany desk, which his brother Jonathan made, the Mahogany Desk," which stood in his Great Room, his "large looking Glass," two roundabout great chairs, six leather-bottomed chairs, and five large maps in frames. He left his daughter, Mary (d. 1782), real estate on Easton's Point and his feather bed, looking glass, six maple-framed chairs, two silver porringers, and one silver cream pot. Since she predeceased her father, these items were redistributed to her children in a 1786 codicil to his will. Christopher Townsend's will dated 1773, codicil dated 1786, and inventory dated 1792, in Heckscher, *John Townsend: Newport Cabinetmaker*, pp. 199–202.

4. Heckscher, *John Townsend: Newport Cabinetmaker*, p. 52; and Moses, *Master Craftsmen of Newport*, p. 66.

5. The high chest remained in the family of the original owners for 255 years. Its provenance identifies Lieutenant Colonel Oliver and Mary Arnold of East Greenwich, Kent, Rhode Island, as the first owners. Oliver Arnold was born to William Arnold (1681–1759) and Deliverance (Whipple) (1679–1765) of Warwick, who married circa 1705. He is listed as a freeman in Warwick in 1755 and married Mary the following year. After Mary's death, he married Almy Greene (1727–1789) in Warwick on March 11, 1762, and served as lieutenant with the rank of lieutenant colonel under the command of Captain Benjamin Arnold of the Pawtuxet Rangers or Second Independent Company for the county of Kent, a militia chartered by the Colony of Rhode Island and Providence Plantations on October 29, 1774. Oliver Arnold appears in the 1774 Rhode Island census as living in Warwick. He is also listed in the 1777 military census for Rhode Island and the 1782 tax list for the township of East Greenwich. See Bruce C. Macgunnigle, *Rhode Island Freemen, 1747–1755: A Census of Registered Voters* (Baltimore, Md.: Genealogical Publishing Co., 1982), p. 12. Oliver Arnold's name appears on the petition presented to the General Assembly to establish the Pawtuxet Rangers, dated October 29, 1774. The census was taken on June 1, 1774. See John R. Bartlett, *Census of the Inhabitants of the Colony of Rhode Island & Providence Plantations for 1774* (Warwick, R.I.: Providence, Knowles, Anthony & Co., 1858), p. 59. Given that Townsend was born on February 17, 1733, he was twenty-three years old in 1756, not twenty-four.

After Oliver Arnold died in East Greenwich on December 6, 1789, and his second wife Almy's subsequent death, this chest descended to their daughter Sarah "Sally" Arnold (1770–1826), who married Orthneil Gorton Wightman (1763–1806) of Warwick on November 4, 1790. At Sally's death on December 1, 1826, this chest was among the part of her estate bequeathed to her daughter Almy Maria Wightman (1793–1879), who married Stukley Wickes (1788–1873), a tailor and town clerk of East Greenwich, on February 24, 1817. Their daughter Sarah Arnold Wickes (June 1, 1824–January 1911) of Warwick was the next to own the chest. She never married and died without issue, leaving her possessions to her nieces, Almy "Allie" Wickes (1858–1914) and Mary "Minnie" LeMoine Wickes (1860–1916), daughters of her brother Oliver Arnold Wickes (1820–1905) and his wife, Harriet Elizabeth Mawney (1820–1875). Allie and Minnie, who never married, lived at the Stone House, the family homestead built by their father in 1855 on Major Potter Road in East Greenwich (now Warwick), and the high chest stood in the southeast bedroom upstairs. At the death of Oliver Wickes in 1905, the ownership of the Stone House passed to his son, Edward Stukley Wickes (May 20, 1866–July 22, 1944), a farmer, although Allie and Minnie continued to live there until their deaths in 1914 and 1916, respectively. See Warwick Will Book 8, pp. 261, 313, City of Warwick. Sally Arnold Wightman's inventory dated January 8, 1827, records property valued at $214.55. Half of this was bequeathed to her daughters, Almy Wickes and (Ann) Catherine Wightman (1806–1885). The other half was sold at auction and the proceeds divided among six of her heirs. Sarah Arnold Wickes will, September 25, 1910, recorded February 23, 1911, Warwick Will Book 23, p. 285. Almy Wickes wrote her will on October 22, 1908, and it was recorded on September 11, 1914. In it she left her entire estate to her sister Mary. Warwick Will Book 24, p. 272. Mary Wickes died without a will but left an inventory of an estate valued at $21,788.53. Her estate included notes secured on mortgage on real estate and deposits in trust companies and banks. See Warwick Will Book 24, p. 565.

When Edward Stukley Wickes died in 1944, he left the Stone House to his nephew Edward Irving Wickes (1910–1972), noting in his will, "if the highboy now in my house should be there at my decease the same is the property of my niece Harriet and was given to her several years ago." He is referring to his niece Harriet Almy Wickes (1908–1996), daughter of William Sands Wickes (1863–1944) and sister of Edward I. Wickes, who had inherited the chest from her Aunt Minnie. She never married and resided at the Stone House with her brother and his family. This chest remained in the southeast bedroom of the house until 1976, when she gave it to her niece. See Edward S. Wickes will, Warwick Probate Records Book 39, p. 58. The high chest was sold at Sotheby's, *Important Americana: Furniture, Folk Art, Silver, Porcelain, Prints and Carpets*, New York, January 21, 2012, lot 186.

6. Lovell, "'Such Furniture as Will Be Most Profitable,'" pp. 27–62. The large calligraphic letter "M" was used several times as a finishing mark: once on the back of the upper case, once on the back of the lower case, once on the bottom of the middle long drawer of the upper case, and once in the bottom of the central short drawer of the lower case. For additional discussion of the "M" finishing mark, see Moses, *Master Craftsmen of Newport*, p. 88, figs. 3.9 and 3.10. The "A" appears on the top left upper-case short drawer, the "B" on the top center drawer, and the "C" on the top right short drawer, and "D," "E," and "F" on the long drawers. Townsend inscribed several "E"s and "F"s on their respective drawers while also adding several "E"s to the drawer designated with a "D."

7. Martha H. Willoughby notes Job Townsend Jr. buying a wig for £12.10 on December 22, 1752. Martha Willoughby, "The Accounts of Job Townsend, Jr.," in *American Furniture*, edited by Luke Beckerdite (Hanover, N.H.: University Press of New England for the Chipstone Foundation, 1999), p. 126.

8. *Rhode Island Friends Record—Births and Deaths. Commerce of Rhode Island, 1726–1800*, 2 vols. (Boston: Massachusetts Historical Society, 1914), vol. 1, *1726–1774*, pp. 88–92. *Commerce of Rhode Island, 1726–1800*. Janet Fletcher Fiske, *Gleanings from Newport Court Files, 1659–1783* (Boxford, Mass.: J. F. Fiske, 1998), pp. 770, 1116, 1129, 1166, 1167. Thomas Robinson's grandfather Rowland (1664–1716) was a settler of the Narragansett area and landowner in the Pettaquamscutt and Point Judith areas, and his father, William (1693–1751), served as deputy governor of Rhode Island from 1745 to 1748. Thomas married Sarah Richardson in 1752. John Russell Bartlett, *History of Wanton Family of Newport, RI* (Providence, R.I.: Sidneys Rider, 1878), p. 54.

9. The play was first produced at the Dorset Garden Theatre in London. English essayist Joseph Addison wrote about *The Orphan* in the October 17, 1711 edition of the *Spectator*. The Redwood Library in Newport owns a copy of the 1747 publication as well as a four-volume reprint issued in 1854.

10. The anisodactyl foot is the most common arrangement of digits in birds, with three toes pointed forward and one back.

11. The dressing table was sold at Sotheby's, *Fine American Furniture, Folk Art, Folk Paintings, and Silver*, New York, June 26, 1986, lot 174. It was formerly owned by Israel Sack, Inc. and illustrated in *American Antiques from Israel Sack Collection* (Washington, D.C.: Highland House Publishers, 1988), vol. 1, p. 65, no. 204. Minor Myers Jr. and Edgar Mayhew, *New London County Furniture, 1640–1840* (New London, Conn.: Lyman Allyn Museum, 1974), p. 27, no. 22-3. See also two high chests sold at Christie's, *The Collection of Marguerite and Arthur Riordan, Stonington, Connecticut*, New York, January 18, 2008, lots 581, 585.

12. The label is inscribed, "This Case of Drawers was formerly owned by Gov Gideon Wanton whose house stood on Coddington Street and after his Death it was sold at auction

and bought by my Grand Father Perry Weaver and after his Death it came to my Mother Sarah Freeborn and after her Death it came to me. Perry W Freeborn." Joseph K. Ott, *The John Brown House Loan Exhibition of Rhode Island Furniture* (Providence, R.I.: Rhode Island Historical Society, 1965), p. 94, no. 61. See also Moses, *Master Craftsmen of Newport*, pp. 182–83, figs. 3.101, 3.101a, 3.101b. Richard Pratt, *The Second Treasury of Early American Homes* (New York: Hawthorn Books, 1954), p. 46. It is included in the Rhode Island Furniture Archive at the Yale University Art Gallery as object number RIF816.

13. Note that each corner of the lower-case sides has a shallow vertical trench, measuring approximately 3/32 inch, matching the width of the leg tenon or square. This construction characteristic, while not found on the Arnold high chest, is found on the John Townsend high chest at Yale University (1984.32.26). While providing a slightly better surface area to secure the leg to the case, it was possibly done to avoid further shaping of the leg tenon.

14. The desk descended in the family of the Reverend Nathaniel Appleton and was inherited at his death by his son Nathaniel Appleton Jr. (1731–1789). After Nathaniel Jr.'s death in 1789, his wife, Rachel, may have sent it to their eldest surviving son, John Appleton (1758–1829), who was living in France as the American consul to Calais. His son John-James Appleton (1792–1864) inherited the piece. From him, it descended through three more generations of the Appleton family until a descendant sold it at Sotheby's, New York, *Important Americana*, January 16–17, 1999, lot 704. See also Leigh Keno and Leslie Keno, *Hidden Treasures* (New York: Warner Books, 2000), pp. 255–83, who note that there may be additional Christopher Townsend signatures on the piece. For the staircase in the Christopher Townsend house, see Moses, *Master Craftsmen of Newport*, p. 71, fig. 2.1a. This desk is also discussed in detail in Beckerdite, "The Early Furniture of Christopher and Job Townsend," pp. 18–22, figs. 33, 34, 37–39. It is included in the Rhode Island Furniture Archive at the Yale University Art Gallery as object number RIF242. The most avant-garde feet of the period were those produced by an as-yet-unidentified shop in Boston, Massachusetts. Alan Miller, "Roman Gusto in New England: An Eighteenth-Century Boston Furniture Designer and His Shop," in *American Furniture*, edited by Luke Beckerdite (Hanover, N.H.: University Press of New England for the Chipstone Foundation, 1993), pp. 160–200. Marijn Manuels presented the lecture "Newport Furniture: A Conservator's Perspective" at the John Townsend Newport Cabinetmaker Symposium, Friday, May 20, 2005, where he discussed the possibility that the flame on the finials and the shells on the bookcase doors were covered with silver leaf. He also postulated that the ball feet, if originally present, may have been treated similarly.

15. In the desk interior, the valance drawers are marked "C" and "D." The concave side drawers are marked "A," "C," and "E," top to bottom on the proper right side, and "B," "D," and "F" on the proper left side. The lowest drawer behind the prospect door is inscribed "C," whereas the markings on the drawers above are illegible. The desk was sold at Joseph Kabe Estate Auction, Milford, Connecticut, on April 10, 2010.

16. The exterior drawers are marked "A," "C," and "D." The interior drawers when marked are done with chalk and are numbered. The desk was included in the exhibition "The Arts and Crafts of Newport Rhode Island, 1640–1820" and illustrated with later feet in the accompanying catalogue, Carpenter, *The Arts and Crafts of Newport, Rhode Island, 1640–1820*, no. 46. The desk was subsequently purchased by Harry Arons, who reportedly replaced the feet with ones salvaged from an eighteenth-century piece of Goddard-Townsend furniture. The desk was sold at Sotheby's, *Important American Furniture from the Collection of the Late Thomas Mellon and Betty Evans*, New York, June 19, 1998, lot 2144. It is included in the Rhode Island Furniture Archive at the Yale University Art Gallery as object number RIF459.

17. A label in the third interior drawer reads, "Sold by John C. R. Tompkins Antiques, Millbrook, N.Y." The desk has replaced brasses. Heckscher, *John Townsend: Newport Cabinetmaker*, p. 48.

18. The backs of the long drawers of the upper case feature the calligraphic letters "D," "E," and "F" in graphite. Two drawer dividers are numbered "I" and "II" in chalk, while one short drawer of the lower case in inscribed "B" in graphite, and the middle drawer, "C." It is included in the Rhode Island Furniture Archive at the Yale University Art Gallery as object number RIF817.

19. Christopher dovetailed three cross braces to the upper edge of the rectangular frame and dovetailed and nailed two cross braces to the bottom edge. Two legs swing on a knuckle-joint mechanism to support the oval top when open and cover a portion of the skirt when closed. The ends of the skirt are finished with applied convex moldings that continue the curve of the knees. Fine dovetailing and small dowels are evident throughout the piece. The hinged maple

rails are worm-infested, as is seen on other pieces of Townsend's work that used maple as a secondary wood. Heckscher, *John Townsend: Newport Cabinetmaker*, pp. 76–79, cat. 1. It is well preserved, retaining fifteen of its sixteen original open talons and an early finish. It is included in the Rhode Island Furniture Archive at the Yale University Art Gallery as object number RIF20. The Christopher Townsend table is illustrated in two John Walton advertisements: *Antiques* 98, no. 3 (September 1970): 292, and *Antiques* 110, no. 3 (September 1976): 380. It is cited twice in the Rhode Island Furniture Archive at the Yale University Art Gallery as object numbers RIF302 and RIF4238. It is also cited as no. 755 in the Decorative Art Photographic Collection (DAPC), Winterthur Museum. Another nearly identical drop-leaf dining table is in the collection of the Art Institute of Chicago. Its claw-and-ball feet, however, are more typical of John Townsend, and it has a cross-brace construction and skirt molding that are very closely related to his signed and dated table at the Metropolitan Museum of Art. It is illustrated in Moses and Moses, "Authenticating John Townsend's and John Goddard's Queen Anne and Chippendale Tables," p. 1134, figs. 11, 11a. It is included in the Rhode Island Furniture Archive at the Yale University Art Gallery as object number RIF914 and in DAPC as no. 666. A drop-leaf dining table with square leaves in a private collection shares many similar details with this group of tables but can be attributed to Christopher Townsend on the basis of its distinctive claw feet. The frame is supported on cabriole legs that terminate in claw feet with more compressed balls, thicker digits, longer second digits, and pierced talons. This latter table is illustrated in Moses, *Master Craftsmen of Newport*, p. 150, fig. 3.72, as the property of Peter Eliot.

20. The table was sold at Sotheby's, *Important Americana*, New York, January 20–22, 2006, lot 554, as the property of Mr. and Mrs. Thornton B. Wierum. Thornton Wierum inherited it from his paternal grandmother, Mary Briggs Thornton Wierum, and the table may have descended to her through the Briggs, Howard, and Church branches of her family.

21. Christopher P. Monkhouse and Thomas S. Michie, *American Furniture in Pendleton House* (Providence, R.I.: Museum of Art, Rhode Island School of Design, 1986), pp. 133–34, no. 71.

22. This chest is illustrated in a foreword by Alice Winchester in *Antiques* 79, no. 5 (May 1961): 450–51, as the property of Mr. and Mrs. William C. Harding of Norwichtown, Connecticut. It is illustrated in Ott, *The John Brown House Loan Exhibition of Rhode Island Furniture*, pp. 86–87, fig. 57, and included in the Rhode Island Furniture Archive at the Yale University Art Gallery as object number RIF205.

23. The high chest is included in the Rhode Island Furniture Archive at the Yale University Art Gallery as object number RIF1558. The interior backs of the top short drawers are marked in chalk "A," "B," "C," and "D," "E," and "F" on the interior backs of the long drawers of the upper case. The same long drawers are inscribed in graphite "B," "C," and "D." The top long drawer of the lower case displays a chalk letter "A" on the interior back, while the three short drawers below are lettered with a chalk "A," "B," and "C." It is illustrated along with a portion of George Hussey's estate inventory in Israel Sack, Inc., *American Antiques from Israel Sack Collection* (Alexandria, Va.: Highland House Publishers, 1988), vol. 2, p. 556, no. 1300.

24. The top short drawers are lettered in Christopher's signature manner with a chalk "A," "B," and "C," while the top drawer of the lower case is marked in chalk with an "A." The chest is included in the Rhode Island Furniture Archive at the Yale University Art Gallery as object number RIF1215. It is illustrated in Oswaldo Rodriguez Roque, "Living with Antiques: Chipstone near Milwaukee," *Antiques* 133, no. 5 (May 1988): 1154, pl. 16; and Beckerdite, "The Early Furniture of Christopher and Job Townsend," pp. 11, 16, 17, figs. 20, 30, 31. Beckerdite associates this high chest with Christopher Townsend on pp. 16–17 of his article. Anna K. Cunningham, *Schuyler Mansion: A Critical Catalogue of the Furnishings & Decorations* (Albany, N.Y.: Division of Archives and History, New York State Education Dept., 1955), pp. 52–53, no. 24.

25. David Warren, *Bayou Bend* (Houston, Tex.: Museum of Fine Arts, 1975), p. 56, no. 105. David Warren et al., *American Decorative Arts and Paintings in the Bayou Bend Collection, Museum of Fine Arts, Houston* (Houston, Tex.: Museum of Fine Arts, 1998), pp. 63–65, no. F111. Neither Christopher nor John is known to have made the rectangular tea table form with more elaborate turreted corners. Two other simple rectangular tea tables are known, but their feet are carved in a manner associated with John Goddard. Keno and Keno, *Hidden Treasures*, pp. 108–9. Parke-Bernet Galleries, *The Notable American Collection of Mr. and Mrs. Norvin H. Green*, New York, December 1–2, 1950, lot 492. Ott, *The John Brown House Loan Exhibition*, pp. 32–33, no. 30. H. O. McNierney, Stalker & Boos, Inc., *The Charles H. Gershenson Collection*, public auction, October 23–24, 1972, lot 128.

26. Warren, *Bayou Bend*, p. 60, no. 115. Warren et al., *American Decorative Arts and Paintings in the Bayou Bend Collection*, pp. 76–77, no. F126. Moses, *Master Craftsmen of Newport*, p. 187, fig. 3.105, described this object as associated with John Townsend. The backboard bears the inscription "Bought of Miss Charlotte Foster to whom her sister left her Mother's furniture." The top is supported by three cross braces secured to the back with blind dovetails and to the front rails with mortise-and-tenon joinery. The holes on the braces indicate that the original top was attached with nails. The drawers have poplar sides and bottoms, which is consistent. The dovetails are similar to those used for his other work, although drawer A has smaller dovetails, apparently made by another craftsman. It is included in the Rhode Island Furniture Archive at the Yale University Art Gallery as object number RIF827.

27. This piece is illustrated and discussed in Moses, *Master Craftsmen of Newport*, pp. 177–79, figs. 3.99, 3.99a–d; Gerald W. R. Ward, *American Case Furniture in the Mabel Brady Garvan and Other Collections at Yale University* (New Haven, Conn.: Yale University Art Gallery, 1988), pp. 265–68, no. 140; Heckscher, *John Townsend: Newport Cabinetmaker*, cat. 8, pp. 90–92. It is included in the Rhode Island Furniture Archive at the Yale University Art Gallery as object number RIF3606.

28. Christie's, *Important American Furniture and Folk Art*, New York, January 20, 2012, lot 113. It is included in the Rhode Island Furniture Archive at the Yale University Art Gallery as object number RIF21.

29. The backs of the drawers display letters in florid script, with the top drawer lettered "A" in chalk, the second drawer from the top lettered "B C D E" in graphite, the third with a "C" in graphite, and the bottom drawer with "A B C D E F" in graphite. The bottom board glue blocks are significantly chamfered on their outer edge, as are found on other Townsend pieces. As with the Arnold high chest, the backsides of the drawer fronts are toothed with a toothing plane. Of note: the front base molding is pieced in the concavity, probably to avoid using a thicker piece of wood. The top is secured with nails driven through the white pine subtop, and the top drawer can be opened only by releasing the wooden spring lock attached to the drawer's bottom. The bottom 3½ inches of the feet are replaced. Clement E. Conger and Alexandra Rollins, *Treasures of State: Fine and Decorative Art in the Diplomatic Reception Rooms of the U.S. Department of State* (New York: H. N. Abrams, 1991), pp. 125–26, no. 45. It is included in the Rhode Island Furniture Archive at the Yale University Art Gallery as object number RIF664.

30. Sotheby's, *Fine Americana*, New York, June 17, 1998, lot 1191.

31. This high chest is included in the Rhode Island Furniture Archive at the Yale University Art Gallery as object number RIF811. The "M" finishing mark appears five times in graphite: on the exterior bottom of the long drawers of the upper and lower case and on the bottom board between the cases. This table is included in the Rhode Island Furniture Archive at the Yale University Art Gallery as object number RIF311 and published in Oswaldo Rodriguez Roque, *American Furniture at Chipstone* (Madison: University of Wisconsin Press, 1984), pp. 322–23, no. 151. A high chest of drawers with the same overall form and carving as the Brixey high chest and a history in the Lyman Hazard family of Peace Dale, Rhode Island, is signed by Benjamin Baker (ca. 1735–1822) of Newport and appears clearly influenced by John Townsend's work. It has the distinctive broken scroll with a stylized fleur-de-lis centered in the shell of the skirt as well as the same pierced brass hardware as the Milnor family chest of drawers at the State Department and the slant-front desk with John Townsend's partial signature. Dennis Carr notes that Benjamin Baker had a professional relationship with John Townsend and that the two cabinetmakers lived on Easton's Point near one another for eighteen years. Baker's extant account book records charges to Townsend from May to June 1782 for making twenty-two mahogany chair frames, repairing a mahogany chair, working on coffins, and making a counter and a shelf for the shop. Although the high chest he signed has many parallels with the work of John Townsend, its construction is not consistent with Townsend practice and its carving is not as precise as Townsend's work. Dennis Andrew Carr, "The Account Book of Benjamin Baker," in *American Furniture*, edited by Luke Beckerdite (Hanover, N.H.: University of New England Press for the Chipstone Foundation, 2004), pp. 46–89, fig. 1. It sold at Parke-Bernet Galleries, *Important 18th Century American Furniture and Decorations*, New York, May 22, 1971, lot 199, as attributed to John Goddard. It is included in the Rhode Island Furniture Archive at the Yale University Art Gallery as object number RIF1210.

32. The bureau table was sold at Christie's, *Important American Silver, Furniture, Folk Art, Prints, English Pottery and Chinese Export Art*, New York, January 24, 25, and 28, 2013, lot 157

and appears to be dated 1767. Four block-and-shell bureaus with the same hardware are illustrated in Heckscher, *John Townsend: Newport Cabinetmaker*, pp. 128–31, cats. 24–27.

33. This table is included in the Rhode Island Furniture Archive at the Yale University Art Gallery as object number RIF19. It is constructed with fine dovetailing, central upper and lower medial cross braces, and a knuckle-joint swing mechanism with legs overlapping a portion of the skirt when closed. This table is illustrated in Heckscher, *John Townsend: Newport Cabinetmaker*, pp. 80–83, cat. 2. Heckscher notes in the entry that a possible mate with a history in the Slade family of Fall River, Massachusetts, is pictured in an old photograph in the curatorial files of the Metropolitan Museum of Art. The Slade family piece is virtually identical, with wood cut from the same boards. Moses and Moses, "Authenticating John Townsend's and John Goddard's Queen Anne and Chippendale Tables," pp. 1131, 1133, figs. 2, 2a.

34. One furniture form not investigated in this study is the tall-case clock. While traditionally many of the cases housing works by James Wady have been attributed to Job Townsend, superficial examination and comparison of the carved shells on the waist doors suggests that some of these cases were actually made by Christopher Townsend. More research is necessary to support this hypothesis.

Figure 1 Ceremonial armchair, Britain, ca. 1750.
Mahogany with beech. H. 49" (with modern
arched board added to the crest), W. 21½",
D. 24½" (seat). (Courtesy, Colonial Williamsburg Foundation, photo, Hans Lorenz.) The
footstool is a reproduction.

Leroy Graves

New Insights on the Virginia Royal Governor's Chair

▼ THE CEREMONIAL armchair made for the royal governor's use in the Capitol Building at Williamsburg, Virginia, is one of the most iconic seating forms with an American history, but its place of manufacture, original appearance, and specific function have been the subject of decades of debate (fig. 1). Furniture historians have traditionally attributed the chair to England or Williamsburg; speculated about whether the crest was originally straight, arched, or fitted with a royal coat of arms; and suggested that the chair could have been used in the General Court or the Council Chamber. Although little new scholarship pertaining to the governor's chair has emerged over the last fifteen years, the recent discovery of two related backstools owned by a descendant of an eastern Virginia family prompted new research (see fig. 10). This essay will show how the structural and upholstery evidence of these three chairs sheds light on their origin, ceremonial context, changes in design, and how those objects were perceived.[1]

History and Historiography

The history of the armchair is essential to understanding how it looks today. Although presumably made for the second Capitol Building in Williamsburg and taken to Richmond when the seat of government moved there in 1780, the earliest reference to the chair is in the June 16, 1866, issue of *Frank Leslie's Illustrated Newspaper* (fig. 2). Leslie reported that the chair was "made in England, and sent over, with the stoves, as presents for the House of Burgesses." His stylized illustration shows the chair with crossstretchers; an upholstered seat, back, and arms (which he described as "lined in red"); a book rest attached to the lion-head terminal of the left arm; and an arched crest and stiles faced with wooden strips. Tradition maintains that the chair was subsequently stored in the attic of the State Capitol Building, then given to William McKie Dillard (1856–1902), who was doorkeeper of the House of Delegates. Richmond antiques dealer Hugh Proctor Gresham purchased the chair from Dillard's son and sold it to a local dealer named J. F. Biggs by 1928, when John D. Rockefeller's agent the Reverend W. A. R. Goodwin acquired the chair for the Colonial Williamsburg Foundation.[2]

The earliest accession records indicate that the chair was sent to the New York City firm W. H. Sloane for restoration to be supervised by R.T.H. Halsey. That work included removal of the arched crest and nineteenth-century upholstery, repair of damaged or missing areas of the rear feet, and installation of new upholstery (figs. 3, 4). When the chair was displayed at the

Figure 2 Engraved image of the armchair illustrated in fig. 1 published in *Frank Leslie's Illustrated Newspaper*, June 16, 1866.

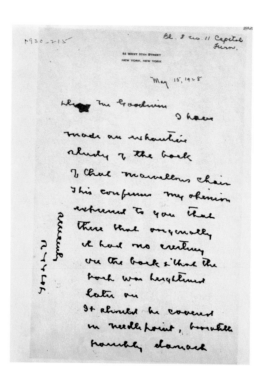

Figure 3   Letter from W. H. Soane to W.A.R. Goodwin, May 15, 1928.

Figure 4   Drawing of the armchair illustrated in fig. 1 marked "RECEIVED / FEB 11 1929 / PERRY, SHAW & HEPBURN."

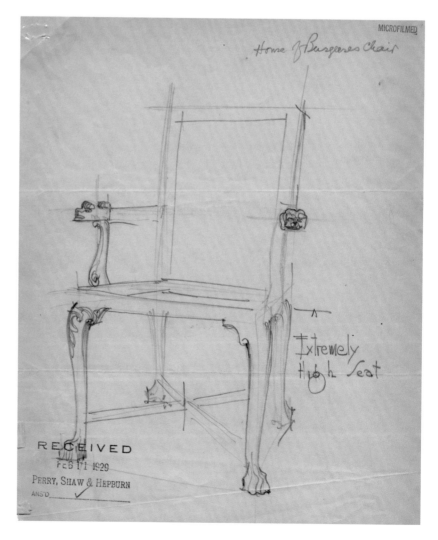

Figure 5 Photograph of a hall vignette in the
"Girl Scouts Loan Exhibition," New York, 1929.
The armchair is visible in the left rear corner.

"Girl Scouts Loan Exhibition" in 1929, it had a square back, cross-stretchers, and damask upholstery (fig. 5). Aside from removal of the nineteenth-century stretchers and replacement of the missing knee blocks, little was done to change the design of the governor's chair until 1977, when a board was added to the crest to elevate the back and create an arched profile. From that point until now, scholars have assumed that the chair originally had a "rounded crest," which "had been cut off, leaving a short square back." In changing the profile, Colonial Williamsburg curators and conservators looked to contemporaneous British and southern ceremonial chairs, most of which have tall backs. They also noted that the seat height mandated the use of a footstool, as was the case with the thrones of George II and III and the chair depicted in John Singleton Copley's portrait of Henry Laurens, who served as governor of South Carolina from 1775 to 1776 (fig. 6).[3]

The most significant scholarship on the governor's chair is presented in Wallace Gusler's *Furniture of Williamsburg and Eastern Virginia, 1710–1790* and Ronald L. Hurst and Jonathan Prown's *Southern Furniture, 1680–1830: The Colonial Williamsburg Collection*. Gusler theorized that the chair was made for "the Governor's [use] . . . in the General Court," that it was likely displayed beneath an elaborate canopy, and that "a set of similar chairs of

Figure 6 John Singleton Copley, *Henry Laurens*, 1782. Oil on canvas. 54¼" x 40⅝". (Courtesy, National Portrait Gallery, Smithsonian Institution, Washington, D.C., gift of Andrew Mellon, 1942.)

regular height may have accompanied it." He also pointed out relationships between the governor's chair and a master's chair made for Williamsburg Masonic Lodge Six, specifically the use of lion-head arm terminals, arm supports with leaf carving on their outer faces and geometric designs on the inner face, and knees with asymmetrical scroll and acanthus. Based on those shared details, Gusler attributed the construction of the governor's chair to the Anthony Hay shop and the carving to James Wilson, a London-trained artisan who advertised in Williamsburg in 1755. Hurst and Prown's interpretation differed in two respects. They felt that the chair was probably made for the governor's Council Chamber, and that its place of manufacture could have been either Britain or Williamsburg.[4]

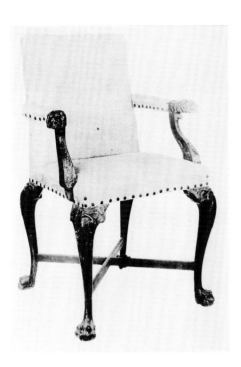

Photographs in the accession file for the governor's chair document five different upholstery treatments. The earliest upholstery, likely done under the supervision of New York decorator Ernest LoNano before 1929, featured a damask show cloth and brass nails with central bosses and milled edges spaced approximately two inches apart (fig. 7). By 1963 the damask had been replaced with leather, and small brass nails were applied, end to end, around the lower edge of the arms and seat, rear edges of the crest and rear stiles, and lower edge of the rear seat rail (fig. 8). In 1977 Williamsburg conservators removed the leather, added an arched board to the crest, and applied new leather upholstery and nails. The tight upholstery lines from that treatment reflected new understanding about period upholstery practices (fig. 9). Additional information gleaned from the study of British ceremonial seating led the foundation's curators and conservators to replace the leather with red silk velvet and apply fringe on the lower edge of the arms and seat and rear edges of the back stiles in 1985. That treatment remained in place until 2012, when the upholstery was removed to facilitate comparison of the frame with the frames of the recently discovered backstools.[5]

Figure 7   Photograph of the armchair illustrated in fig. 1, taken ca. 1930.

Figure 8   Photograph of the armchair illustrated in fig. 1, taken in 1963.

Figure 9   Photograph of the armchair illustrated in fig. 1, taken in 1977. The arched crest and new leather upholstery were added in preparation for the chair's exhibition in "Furniture of Williamsburg and Eastern Virginia: The Product of Mind and Hand," Virginia Museum, Richmond, 1978. Wallace Gusler curated that show.

The Backstools

In the summer of 2012, Fredericksburg antiques dealer Bill Beck sold the Colonial Williamsburg Foundation two backstools with ornament executed by the carver of the governor's chair (fig. 10). The backstools were described as a "Pr. Mahogany side chairs [with], paw feet, acanthus carved knees, [and] upholstered backs" in the October 6, 2011, estate sale of William N. Wilbur. His deceased wife, Mary Tyler McCormick Wilbur (1915–1981), had descended from several eastern Virginia families. Microanalysis verified the use of several secondary woods, including red pine, which provided strong evidence that the backstools and governor's chair were made in Britain.[6]

All three chairs have sculptural paw feet and knees decorated with asymmetrical shell and acanthus carving, a formula common in British furniture

Figure 10   Backstool, Britain, ca. 1750. Mahogany with oak, cherry, beech, and ash. H. 40", W. 25", D. 22" (seat). (Courtesy, Colonial Williamsburg Foundation, Friends of Colonial Williamsburg Collections Fund and the TIF Foundation in Memory of Michelle A. Iverson; photo, Craig McDougal.) The other backstool has red pine in its construction.

of the mid-eighteenth century (figs. 11, 12). This knee design also occurs in Boston and New York furniture, but the carving on those objects is not as professionally rendered as that on the backstools and governor's chair. On the latter objects, the leaf and shell motifs are subtly modeled and shaded

Figure 11 Details showing the knee carving on the armchair illustrated in fig. 1 (left) and one of the backstools represented by the example illustrated in fig. 10 (right).

Figure 12 Details showing the paw feet on the armchair illustrated in fig. 1 (left) and one of the backstools represented by the example illustrated in fig. 10 (right).

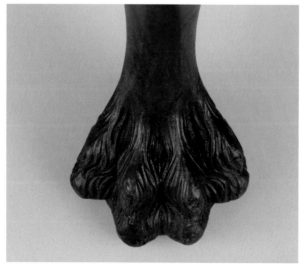

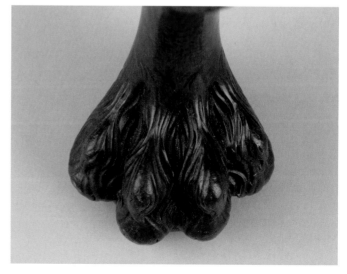

Figure 13 Details showing the side knee blocks of the left front legs of the armchair illustrated in fig. 1 (left) and one of the backstools represented by the example illustrated in fig. 10 (right). On the armchair knee block, the carver snapped off the volute and had to modify his design.

with carefully regulated flutes made with a very small gouge. Other than minor differences in scale and one design adjustment that reflected a mistake on the part of the carver (fig. 13), the foot and knee carving on the backstools and armchair is nearly identical.[7]

Structural details suggest that the shop responsible for the backstools made them from stock-in-trade side chairs with over-the-rail upholstery, probably to fulfill a large order that also included the governor's chair. Evidence of conversion is the rounded back edge of the rear posts (fig. 14), replaced seat rails (fig. 15), and unusual attachment of the back, which was simply glued and screwed to the sawn-off rear posts of the repurposed side chairs (fig. 16). The screw threads are die-cut rather than filed, indicating a mid-eighteenth-century date (fig. 17). On most backstools, the stiles of the back frame extend below the lower rail and are set in notches in the side rails. The addition of an upholstered back, which would have been about 1½ inches thicker than a splat, necessitated the use of longer side rails. Because this changed the geometry of the seat, the front rail had to be replaced as well. The maker simply sawed through the original beech front and side

Figure 14 Detail showing a rounded rear post on one of the backstools, represented by the example illustrated in fig. 10.

Figure 15   Detail showing replaced front and side rails on the seat frame of one of the backstools, represented by the example illustrated in fig. 10.

Figure 16   Detail showing the back attachment of one of the backstools, represented by the example illustrated in fig. 10.

Figure 17   Detail of a screw used in the back attachment of one of the backstools, represented by the example illustrated in fig. 10.

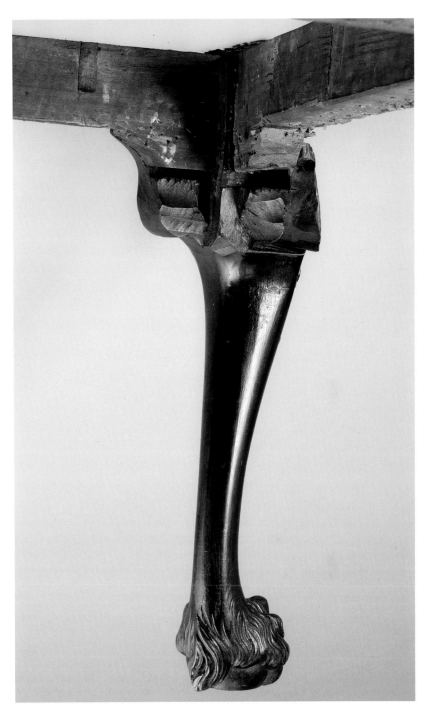

Figure 18 Detail showing altered knee blocks on one of the backstools, represented by the example illustrated in fig. 10.

Figure 19 Details showing remnants of the original red wool (top) and silk (bottom) surviving on one of the backstools, represented by the example illustrated in fig. 10.

rails, leaving their glued-in tenons in place (see fig. 15). Because the traditional joint location had been compromised, he cut new mortises that were more centered on the leg stock and lower than the originals. This new tenon location required the use of front and side rails that descended lower at their juncture with the legs and required alteration of the knee blocks (fig. 18). The blocks, which were originally attached to the stiles of the front legs, were sawn and chopped out to fit over and under the new rails.

The upholstery evidence on the backstools supports the theory that they are period conversions made to accompany the governor's chair. Fragments

Figure 20   Detail showing the brass nail pattern
on one of the backstools, represented by the
example illustrated in fig. 10.

of the original dark red silk show cloth are trapped under nails on the front
(fig. 19), and fragments of matching red wool are under nails on the back.
Period brass nail shanks, which occur at approximately two-inch intervals
on both the back and seat frame, indicate that the backstools were upholstered at the same time (fig. 20).

The Governor's Chair
Subsequent examination of the frame of the governor's chair revealed tiny
fragments of red silk and matching red wool in the same contexts as those
on the backstools, along with brass nail shanks at two-inch intervals
(figs. 21–23). The shanks on the front and side rails of the seat and arms are
approximately one inch above the lower edge, denoting the use of one-inch

Figure 21 Armchair illustrated in fig. 1 with upholstery removed.

Figure 22 Detail showing a remnant of the original red silk show cloth on the armchair illustrated in fig. 1.

Figure 23 Detail showing the brass nail pattern on the armchair illustrated in fig. 1.

fringe. Presumably, the footstool received a similar treatment. As is the case with their nearly identical carving, the upholstery evidence on the governor's chair and backstools supports the theory that they were purchased as a suite. If the suite were made for use in the Council Chamber, a dozen backstools would have been required to seat each member.

With its more elaborate upholstery, the governor's chair reflected that person's position as the Crown's representative in Virginia. As previous scholars have suggested, the chair may have been displayed under a canopy and raised on a platform similar to those shown in the engraving *A View of the House of Peers. The King Sitting on the Throne, the Commons Attending Him at the End of the Session, 1755* (fig. 24). Like the armchairs on either side of George II's throne, the backstools would likely have sat at floor level.[8]

Figure 24 A View of the House of Peers. The King Sitting on the Throne, the Commons Attending Him at the End of the Session, 1755, engraved by B. Cole, London, 1755. (Courtesy, Colonial Williamsburg Foundation.)

Scholars have also speculated about the display of a royal coat of arms with the governor's chair, and whether that armorial was attached to or suspended above the crest. Precedent for an attached armorial can be found in contemporaneous ceremonial seating from Britain as well as an armchair made for the royal governor of South Carolina (fig. 25). The coat of arms

Figure 25 Ceremonial armchair with carving attributed to the shop of Henry Hardcastle (d. 1756), Charleston, South Carolina, 1755–1756. Mahogany with sweet gum. H. 53⅜", W. 37⅜" (arms). (Collection of the McKissick Museum, University of South Carolina; photo, Museum of Early Southern Decorative Arts.)

Figure 26 Detail of the mortises and screw holes in the crest of the armchair illustrated in fig. 25.

on the South Carolina chair is missing, but mortises and screw holes in the back of its crest demonstrate that the chair had an armorial attached with a wrought-iron armature (fig. 26). X-radiography and visual examination of the wood surfaces and nail shanks on the Virginia governor's chair indicate that the crest was reduced in height and rabbeted on the back but uncov-

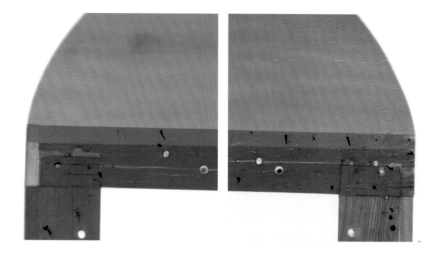

Figure 27   X-radiographs of the crest rail of the armchair illustrated in fig. 1.

Figure 28   Detail showing the original placement of a mahogany strip added to the armchair illustrated in fig. 1 during the nineteenth century.

Figure 29   Detail showing the partial mortise in the top of the mahogany strip and alignment with a patched partial mortise in the crest rail of the armchair illustrated in fig. 1. The marks left by the lead and outer cutter of the center bit are visible at the bottom of the mortise on the strip and below the patch on the crest.

Figure 30 Detail showing a center bit similar to the example used to bore the mortises in the mahogany strip and crest rail of the armchair illustrated in fig. 1.

ered no evidence for an attached coat of arms (fig. 27). Although these alterations make it impossible to exclude an attached or integral coat of arms as part of the original design, it is far more likely that the chair originally had a square back and a coat of arms suspended above. The crest rail shows no sign of catastrophic damage, which would likely have been present if an integral coat of arms broke off, or evidence for the attachment of an armorial.[9]

When the governor's chair was upholstered in 1977, two strips of mahogany were removed from the frame and placed in storage, where they remained until 2013. Nail evidence indicates that the long strip was attached to the left rear stile (fig. 28) and the shorter strip to the right rear stile. The discovery of a partial mortise drilled in the top of the long strip led to a closer study of the crest, which had been patched at both ends (fig. 29). The mortise was cut with a center bit, which had a short lead and outside cutter (fig. 30). Removal of one of the patches on the crest revealed another partial mortise that matched the one on the mahogany strip (fig. 31). These mortises and the one-half-inch rabbet on the back edge of the crest (fig. 32)

Figure 31 Detail showing the partial mortises on the mahogany strip and crest of the armchair illustrated in fig. 1 with a patch removed.

Figure 32 Detail showing the rabbeted upper rear edge of the crest of the armchair illustrated in fig. 1.

were probably related to the attachment of an arched extension, installed before Frank Leslie illustrated the chair in 1866 (see fig. 2). The individual responsible for that work probably cut off the top edge of the crest, presumably to remove a surface compromised by holes from upholstery nails. If the stock used to make the crest was of the same dimensions as the stiles of the back frame, which is the case with the backstools, only one half inch is missing from the top. That would have been enough space to attach the original upholstery. The back of the governor's chair did not have webbing like the backstools. To support the foundation, the upholsterer nailed a single piece of linen to the front face of the back frame of the governor's chair. In contrast, the seat frame of that chair has nail sites from period webbing.[10]

Between the 1930s and 1960s, original materials used to cover upholstered seating furniture made or used in the American colonies was often removed and, more often than not, discarded. Important evidence was lost in the process. Although the governor's chair, too, was reupholstered by the Colonial Williamsburg Foundation, the process was well documented, and each element that was removed from the frame was preserved, making it

Figure 33 Armchair, backstool and reproduction stool illustrated in this article, with red silk, wool upholstery, and fringe. (Photo, Craig McDougal.)

possible to meticulously examine the piece in order to return it to what we believe was its original appearance (fig. 33).[11]

No study of this type can be undertaken in isolation. Although the physical evidence on the frame of the governor's chair was the most important consideration in determining its likely original appearance, paintings and prints depicting British ceremonial chairs provided a wealth of information about the upholstery and use of contemporaneous examples. Another important source consulted during this study was Colonial Williamsburg's extensive collection of seating furniture with original upholstery, which documents many methods used by early craftsmen to create the various contours and profiles. Decades spent intensely studying those objects provided the basis for our understanding of period techniques and reinforced the conclusions drawn from the evidence surviving on the frame of the governor's chair. The results of the foundation's commitment to the study and preservation of upholstered furniture will be published next year in a lavishly illustrated book, *Reading the Evidence: The Craft and Preservation of Early Seating Upholstery* by Leroy Graves.

1. Accession file no. 1930-215, Colonial Williamsburg Foundation (hereafter CWF), Williamsburg, Va. Wallace B. Gusler, *Furniture of Williamsburg and Eastern Virginia: The Product of Mind and Hand* (Richmond: Virginia Museum, 1978), pp. 11, 12, fig. 4; Wallace B. Gusler, *Furniture of Williamsburg and Eastern Virginia, 1710–1790* (Richmond: Virginia Museum, 1979), pp. 70–72, fig. 46; Morrison H. Heckscher and Leslie Greene Bowman, *American Rococo, 1750–1775: Elegance in Ornament* (New York: Harry N. Abrams for the Metropolitan Museum of Art and the Los Angeles County Museum of Art, 1992), p. 167, fig. 39; Ronald L. Hurst and Jonathan Prown, *Southern Furniture, 1680–1830: The Colonial Williamsburg Collection* (New York: Harry N. Abrams for the Colonial Williamsburg Foundation, 1997), pp. 185–89, no. 52.

2. The Capitol Building was completed ca. 1754. Accession file no. 1930-215, CWF. An October 25, 1989, memo from John O. Sands states that "Ms. Vera Goodman . . . inquired some months ago about the Governor's chair in the CW collections. She thought that it looked like a chair that her father had described playing in as a child of three or four, then the property of his great uncle. . . . She suggests that the chair was given to William McKie (Mack) Dillard (1856–1902), who was the doorkeeper of the House of Delegates. It appears that the chair had been relegated to storage, and was given to Dillard, probably upon retirement. On his death, it passed to his brother Thomas Massenburg Dillard (1848–1929), of 211 South High Street, Blackstone, Virginia. That house still stands, and it was there that her father played on the chair. Apparently, upon the death of T. M. Dillard, it went into the hands of an antiques dealer." This account of the ownership of the chair after William McKie Dillard differs from others, which maintain that the piece passed directly to his son.

3. Accession file no. 1930-215, CWF. Colonial Williamsburg furniture conservator Albert Skutans added an arched board to the crest between 1977 and 1978, when the chair was being readied for exhibition in "Furniture of Williamsburg and Eastern Virginia: The Product of Mind and Hand." Hurst and Prown, *Southern Furniture*, p. 187. Gusler cited the throne of George III in *Furniture of Williamsburg and Eastern Virginia*, p. 70; and Hurst and Prown illustrated and discussed *A View of the House of Peers. The King Sitting on the Throne, the Commons Attending Him at the End of the Session, 1755*, an engraving by B. Cole of London (p. 187). Hurst and Prown also illustrate a chair made for use by the royal governor of South Carolina. That object has a tall back and a crest rail with mortises and screw holes in the back, presumably from the attachment of a carved coat of arms.

4. Gusler, *Furniture of Williamsburg and Eastern Virginia*, pp. 70–74, 103–9. Hurst and Prown, *Southern Furniture*, pp. 185–89, no. 52.

5. The leather upholstery applied in 1977 or 1978 was subsequently tufted.

6. See accession file no. 2012-25, CWF, for a copy of the microanalysis (Alden Wood I.D., October 27, 2011), a copy of the sale advertisement, and a genealogical report.

7. For Boston chairs with this carving formula, see Luke Beckerdite, "Carving Practices in Eighteenth-Century Boston," in *New England Furniture: Essays in Memory of Benno M. Forman* (Boston: Society for the Preservation of New England Antiquities, 1987), pp. 123–36. Most of the New York pieces with this knee design are card tables, most dating between 1760 and 1780. See accession file no. 2012-25, CWF.

8. Gusler, *Furniture of Williamsburg and Eastern Virginia*, pp. 70–72; Hurst and Prown, *Southern Furniture*, pp. 185–87.

9. For more on the South Carolina chair, see Bradford L. Rauschenberg, "The Royal Governor's Chair: Evidence of the Furnishing of South Carolina's State House," *Journal of Early Southern Decorative Arts* 6, no. 2 (November 1980): 1–32. Rauschenberg attributed the chair to the cabinet firm of Elfe and Hutchinson based on a March 14, 1758, entry in the journal of the Commons House of Assembly, which recorded their bill for "Furniture for the Council Chamber amo £728.2.6"; and Act 874 of the 1758 Statutes at Large of South Carolina, which noted that the firm's "Extraordinary" charge was for chairs and tables for the Council Chamber (pp. 8–9). Luke Beckerdite later attributed the carving on the South Carolina governor's chair to the shop of Henry Hardcastle, a British-trained carver who immigrated to New York by 1751 and moved to Charleston, South Carolina, between July 1755 and the artisan's death in October 1756 (Luke Beckerdite, "Origins of the Rococo Style in New York Furniture and Interior Architecture," *American Furniture*, edited by Luke Beckerdite [Hanover, N.H.: University Press of New England for the Chipstone Foundation, 1993], pp. 32–37). According to Beckerdite, the entries cited by Rauschenburg do "not mention the Governor's chair and probably referred to chairs and tables for the members of the Upper House of Assembly." He further notes that Elfe and Hutchinson's charges reflect the exchange rate for Charleston and English currency, which was 7:1 in 1758 as compared with 1.7:1 in New York and 1.6:1 in Pennsylvania. Beckerdite suggests that the South Carolina governor's chair was ordered in 1756, citing "the treasurer's advance to pay tradesmen's bills for furniture on July 6 of that year, Hardcastle's working dates in Charleston, and an order for a mace for the governor, robes for the speaker, and a gown for the clerk in March 1756."

10. The author thanks Colonial Williamsburg furniture conservator Albert Skutans for information pertaining to the seating frame in 1977.

11. Wallace Gusler and Albert Skutans were responsible for preserving all of the components added to the frame.

F. Carey Howlett and
Kathy Z. Gillis

Scientific Imaging
Techniques and
New Insights on the
WH Cabinetmaker:
A Southern Mystery
Continues

▼ A N   I N S C R I P T I O N on the surface of a piece of furniture can be an outstanding aid to research, sometimes providing definitive identification of a maker, owner, retailer, or user. An inscription can also be an interesting but rather mundane vestige from the age of handcraftsmanship—a remnant of a cabinetmaker's work in the form of an alignment mark, orientation mark, cost notation, or list of materials. Whatever their original purpose, inscriptions are often faint, worn, incomplete, obscured, or poorly written. Interpreting such inscriptions on furniture can be difficult at best and speculative at worst, sometimes resulting in misinformation and faulty attributions.

By maximizing the possibilities for obtaining new and useful information from inscriptions, scientific imaging is a powerful tool for extending the eyes of the conservator, curator, and scholar. Forensic scientists and conservators have used specialized imaging techniques for years, but only since the advent of digital photography have some of them become cost-effective and accessible to anyone interested in learning them. The techniques discussed here are beneficial, whether providing a solid foundation of physical evidence to document the maker of a particular object or simply adding details to our knowledge of its history of manufacture, ownership, and use.

This article demonstrates a range of imaging techniques and their applicability by looking at several examples of furniture associated with northeastern North Carolina's enigmatic WH cabinetmaker, so called because a number of objects have finely executed calligraphic monograms bearing the initials "WH." This group of more than thirty objects has been of considerable interest to scholars for years, because of curiosity about the identity or meaning of "WH" and because of their idiosyncratic structure and ornament. Many objects in the WH group have histories of descent in families from Halifax, Northampton, Bertie, and Hertford counties, and all have details associated with the Roanoke River basin school of cabinetmaking—a designation used by furniture scholar John Bivins in *The Furniture of Eastern North Carolina*. In an attempt to explain the presence of Germanic features on objects made in a region populated largely by people of English descent, he speculated that the maker may have been a Hessian soldier who deserted Cornwallis's army during the American Revolution and settled near Halifax, North Carolina. Certain ornamental details used by that maker are unique in American case furniture: the unusual relief-carved and ebonized compass-work designs often found on pediments of the WH group are signature features and may indicate a northern European source.

The highly detailed putty-inlaid monograms, meanwhile, are more akin to the work of a metal engraver than a cabinetmaker. Despite these singular features, no documentary or physical evidence survives to associate the group with a particular maker.[1]

A recent book written by Thomas R. J. Newbern and James R. Melchor brought scholars and collectors the news that the mystery of the WH cabinetmaker had been solved. Their monograph reported the discovery of numerous inscriptions identifying house carpenter William Seay as the maker of the group. His work in the building trade is documented by two indentures. In 1774 Seay took Charles Rhodes as an apprentice "carpenter" and Joel Bird as "carpenter and joiner." Similarly, Seay's purchase of lumber, tools, and hardware at the 1802 estate auction of Bertie County cabinetmaker Thomas Sharrock suggests that the former may have made furniture. But, since many regional house carpenters and joiners did the same, Newbern and Melchor's contention that Seay was the maker of the WH group is linked almost entirely to the inscriptions the authors cite.[2]

Several factors made furniture in the WH group ideal for a case study on imaging techniques. Foremost was Newbern and Melchor's assertion that William Seay's name appears on several case pieces as well as on architectural elements. Although a single inscription is rarely sufficient to identify an individual as the maker, the appearance of the same name on multiple objects in a group can, in the right context, warrant attribution. The authors' book also contains intriguing references to illegible script, which suggests that specialized photographic techniques might enhance legibility. Because the authors presented their evidence in a nontraditional manner—usually an untouched image of markings or features accompanied by a duplicate "enhanced" image altered with pencil, ink, or chalk—imaging provides an unbiased basis for evaluation and interpretation of their findings.

A desk in the collection of the Virginia Museum of Fine Arts provided special impetus for this study (fig. 1). According to Newbern and Melchor, the desk has six inscriptions associated with Seay and is "one of the most fully documented pieces of Southern furniture, a true Rosetta stone for this group." Based on their findings, the authors developed a history for the desk that extended well beyond its known provenance. In contrast, an investigation undertaken by the museum revealed no inscriptions on the desk, which raised questions regarding other marks associated with the WH group.[3]

This study demonstrates several effective techniques for enhancing the legibility of inscriptions on furniture, but informed interpretation relies on several factors. Experience in paleography, the study of historic handwriting, is very helpful, as knowledge of period letter forms, historic abbreviations, spelling, and other conventions can simplify interpretation. A good understanding of traditional writing implements, as well as a logical sense of those most likely to have been used by a cabinetmaker or an owner, is also helpful. Indeed, it is clear that owners were more likely to inscribe names in ink, whereas makers' names are generally in pencil, red crayon, and occasionally chalk—all materials typically found in a cabinetmaker's or joiner's toolbox. Access to archival documents in the form of deeds, tax lists, inven-

Figure 1 Desk attributed to the WH cabinet-maker, northeast, North Carolina, 1780–1790. Walnut with walnut and yellow pine. H. 47¾", W. 46", D. 22⅝". (Courtesy, Virginia Museum of Fine Arts; photo, Katharine Wetzel.) This desk was found in Halifax, North Carolina.

tories, indentures, and other records is beneficial when testing the plausibility of a discovered name, particularly if signatures are located for comparison with those found on furniture. The context and location of any suspected inscription are also of paramount importance. Experience and logic indicate that makers' names most frequently occur on surfaces of upper drawers or on backboards, where they are easily observed in a cursory examination. Owners' names generally occur in the same locations, though they are even more likely to be found on desk interiors and are unlikely to be associated with inscriptions made before assembly. Makers' names also occasionally appear in locations indicating pre-assembly writing, while logic dictates that owners' names were generally inscribed after construction.

When searching for inscriptions, a healthy skepticism is important. One should never assume from the outset that writing will be found, and, if present, that it was intended for posterity. Most surviving examples of American furniture are not inscribed with names, and when they are, the name is rarely that of the maker.

The techniques used in this study were based on the nature of the materials undergoing examination. This study used Reflectance Transformation Imaging (RTI), a recently developed technique ideal for looking at low-relief objects, to examine a few incised surfaces; cross-polarization to examine faint chalk inscriptions and one inscription below a yellowed coating; and infrared reflectography to examine graphite (pencil) inscriptions.

Figure 2 Secretary press attributed to the WH cabinetmaker, northeast, North Carolina, 1785–1795. Walnut with walnut, yellow pine, and oak. H. 110¼", W. 48¼", D. 22." (Courtesy, Historic Hope Foundation; photo, Gavin Ashworth.)

Ultraviolet fluorescence examination, a common technique for characterizing coatings, is largely ineffective when examining inscriptions, especially graphite and calcium carbonate, but UV reflectance photography proved useful in searching for inscriptions in iron gall ink. All of the techniques and equipment used to obtain the photographs in this study are presented in the appendix to this article.

Secretary Press, Hope Plantation, Windsor, North Carolina

The secretary press illustrated in figure 2 has many features characteristic of WH case pieces dating from the early to mid-1790s: an enclosed scrolled pediment; a tympanum decorated with ebonized low-relief leaf carving flanking a roundel with putty inlay; a pierced anthemion-like central finial (largely replaced); and drawer bottoms flush-mounted with the sides. The monogram is unique to the group and might ultimately prove useful in identifying the original owner (fig. 3). Earlier researchers have interpreted the initials to be "CRT" or "CRJ," but comparison with letters in George Fisher's *The Instructor*, an American writing manual published in 1786, suggests that the conjoined letters are "PRT." Indeed, the striking similarity of the letters on the roundel and those in Fisher's "Flourishing Alphabet" raises the strong possibility that the maker of the roundel owned, or had access to, a copy of *The Instructor* (fig. 4).[4]

Figure 3   Detail of the monogram from the secretary press illustrated in fig. 2. (Photo, F. Carey Howlett).

Figure 4   "Flourishing Alphabet," from George Fisher, *The Instructor, or American Young Man's Best Companion. . . .* (Worcester, Mass.: Isaiah Thomas, 1786), pl. 3. (Courtesy, Massachusetts Historical Society.)

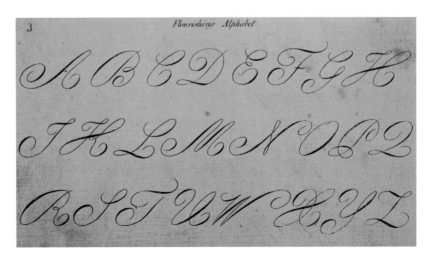

INCISED INSCRIPTION: "WILLIAM SEAY"—MAKER OR OWNER?

Technique: Reflectance Transformation Imaging

Newbern and Melchor discovered the inscription "William Seay" on the secretary press in 2009, but they failed to detect a partial second name, "Elizabeth Cou[illeg.]." The entire inscription, though approximately 4⅞ inches long with capital letters ½ inch high, is barely visible near the upper edge of the inner face of a side of the third large drawer (fig. 5). The second name is less legible: the inscription is partially crossed out with scratches made by what appears to be the same tool used to make the lettering; the scratches are centered on the first word of the second name. Standard photography using raking light proved somewhat effective at enhancement, clearly indicating this word to be "Elizabeth," but the final word remains indecipherable (fig. 6).

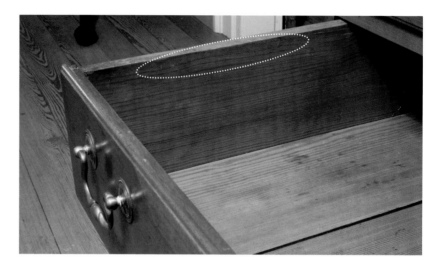

Figure 5 Detail of the secretary press illustrated in fig. 2, showing the location of the inscribed names. (Courtesy, Historic Hope Foundation; photo, F. Carey Howlett.)

Figure 6 Raking-light image of the inscription on the secretary press illustrated in fig. 2 (Courtesy, Historic Hope Foundation; photo, Gavin Ashworth.)

Since the inscription is incised, we decided to examine it more thoroughly using Reflectance Transformation Imaging (RTI), a technique recently developed for enhancing the visibility of nearly illegible low-relief surfaces such as corroded ancient coins or worn heiroglyphic tablets. The technique involves taking a series of photographs of the object using a fixed camera position but changing the position and angle of a single light source for each image at regular intervals and at the same distance from the object. The images are compiled into a single file using specially designed software. The file is then opened in the RTI viewer, which has a circular trackpad that permits viewing of the photographed object as if it were being illuminated in real time and from any angle using a variety of rendering modes, thereby permitting a detailed examination of the three-dimensional form of an object.[5]

This form of examination has several advantages over standard photography. Once the images are captured and compiled, an examiner can take as much time as needed working at the computer to rearrange the lighting virtually in infinite variations. Markings can be fully analyzed, providing insight into the tools that made them. By manipulating the lighting, one can minimize unrelated features that can be mistaken for part of the inscription or those that interfere with its legibility, such as the scratches across the name "Elizabeth." Words that are unclear because of odd spellings or misshapen letters, such as the last word of the second name, can be thoroughly examined letter by letter at higher magnification to search for faint line extensions or loops that may be visible only under specific lighting conditions.

RTI examination led to a number of insights about the inscription. The names were apparently written using a metal stylus. The lines range from nearly imperceptible depressions to deeper visible scratches cutting through wood fibers, and the writer wrote much as he or she would have written with a quill pen, using greater pressure on the downstrokes than on the upward-moving arcs. Each "i" in "William" is emphatically dotted with a circular puncture, additional evidence pointing to a metal stylus. A faint "M" followed by a smaller mark suggesting a superscript "r" is visible before the name "William." The name "Seay" was inscribed twice—perhaps the first version was too faint (fig. 7). A single letter appears between "Seay" and "Elizabeth"—either a "y" from the first attempt at "Seay" or a typical shorthand notation for "et" (and). A slight amount of color darkens the recessed lines, but there is no ink or graphite present: either someone rubbed a small amount of dark pigment into the recesses of the inscription at some point to make the letters more visible, or dirt became embedded in the inscription over time.

Figure 7 A portion of the inscription illustrated in fig. 6 showing the name "William Seay" viewed using Reflectance Transformation Imaging (RTI) rendered in static mode. (Courtesy, Historic Hope Foundation; photo, Travis Fullerton.)

Figure 8 A portion of the inscription illustrated in fig. 6 showing the name "Elizabeth Cou[illeg.]" viewed using Reflectance Transformation Imaging (RTI) rendered in unsharp mask mode. (Courtesy, Historic Hope Foundation; photo, Travis Fullerton.)

The final word of the second name remains unclear, demonstrating that there are limitations to any examination technique (fig. 8). The word is undoubtedly the work of the same hand using the same tool and written at the same time as the other words, but the writer was constrained by two factors. First, the names were intentionally inscribed on a wide, soft earlywood band in the yellow pine, and the first three words all fit reasonably well within a fairly wide horizontal section of the band. The earlywood begins to narrow and slope downward at the beginning of the fourth word, and the resistance of the hard latewood interfered with the flow of the writing, sloping the name and constricting the letters. Second, it is likely that the tight confines of the drawer inhibited the writer, since the writing arm was pressed against the drawer back while the final word was inscribed.

Interpreting the inscription "Elizabeth Cou[illeg.]" is problematic. There is convincing evidence that William Seay married Elizabeth Rutland Tyler (widow of John Tyler) by 1790, when he appeared in the federal census as a resident of Hertford County. However, that fails to explain why "Elizabeth" was crossed out or to clarify the remaining inscription, "Cou[illeg.]." It is tempting to interpret the last letters as the beginning of "Courtney" or "Coventry," but those surnames are not documented in the Roanoke River basin during the late eighteenth or early nineteenth centuries. One might also speculate that "Elizabeth Co[illeg.]" refers to Elizabeth City County (a former county of Virginia, now the city of Hampton) approximately one hundred miles northeast of the region associated with WH furniture, or to the town of Elizabeth City, North Carolina, approximately the same distance directly east. However, there is no evidence linking William Seay to either of those places, and again, the number and arrangement of the letters making up the final part of the inscription do not clearly spell the words "City" or "County."[6]

The location of the inscription indicates it was made after the drawer was fabricated and assembled: it would be impossible to inscribe names right-side up anywhere else on the inner surface of a drawer side, and the upper loop of the "S" in the name "Seay" extends onto the rounded-over upper edge of the drawer side. The writer was probably right-handed, as the writing, which is on the inner face of a proper right drawer, begins about eight inches from the front corner of the drawer, an impossible location for a left-handed writer to begin.

The incising on the drawer can be compared with three ink signatures by Seay, two dating from 1774 and a third from 1800. All four inscriptions have an even rightward slope, and while there is general consistency with the forms of nearly all the letters, the "W" is perhaps the most telling. Each "W" starts with a simple arc flourish that begins near the highest point of the letter, curves down no lower than the letter's midpoint, then rises up to the top of the first leg. Downstroke legs are slightly S-curved, with at least one

Figure 9 Signature of William Seay on an indenture document for Joel Bird, May 11, 1774. (Courtesy, North Carolina State Archives.)

in each signature and in the incised name showing a distinct loop at the bottom leading into an upstroke. The final upstroke in the ink signatures as well as the incised name are simple, slightly outward-curving lines ending abruptly just above the midpoint (fig. 9).

Although Seay inscribed the secretary press, that does not mean he was the maker. The near imperceptibility of the inscription under normal lighting conditions, its strange and unobtrusive location high on the upper inner face of the third large drawer, the uncommon manner in which it is incised in the wood, the fact that it was written after assembly, and the presence of a second name—possibly that of William Seay's wife or an earlier Elizabeth of his acquaintance—strongly suggest that "William Seay Elizabeth Cou[illeg.]"denotes ownership or use rather than authorship. The only circumstance that would lend support for Seay's being the maker of the WH group would be the discovery of similar inscriptions on other related examples. As will be shown, the inscription on this secretary press is unique in its execution, and that object is the only known piece bearing the name "William Seay."

CHALK INSCRIPTION:
A JOURNEYMAN'S NAME OR A SIMPLE REMINDER?
Technique: Cross-polarization
Newbern and Melchor note that the secretary press has another inscription on the inner face of the proper right side of the bottom drawer (fig. 10). This inscription is in white chalk, a material historically used by cabinetmakers as an aid in assembling parts during construction. Calcium carbonate inscriptions are notoriously difficult to read. By its nature, the material is ephemeral: a light surface dust easily smudged, brushed, or wiped away. Such inscriptions are often frustrating even when they can be read. More

Figure 10 Chalk inscription on the inner face of the proper right side of the bottom drawer of the secretary press illustrated in fig. 2. (Courtesy, Historic Hope Foundation; photo, Travis Fullerton.)

often than not, an inscription initially interpreted as a name or signature, usually because of prominent but typical eighteenth- or nineteenth-century flourishes to the letters, will ultimately reveal itself as something less significant, such as "Bottom," "Top," or "Right."

Newbern and Melchor interpreted the inscription to read, "Made by Britain" and postulated that Britain was a journeyman who lived near Seay's property in Roxobel, Bertie County. The inscription actually reads, "Left side/inside," a practical reference to the orientation of the drawer side for proper assembly. The words "side" and "inside" are reasonably legible in a conventional photograph, but to bring out the faint lettering of the word "Left," we used cross-polarization photography followed by contrast enhancements using Adobe Photoshop (fig. 11).

Cross-polarization is a technique generally used for photographing highly reflective surfaces such as silver and glass, but it can enhance the visibility of a chalk inscription on bare wood by eliminating glare from the wood surface. Such reflectivity is barely noticeable in most situations, but it can interfere with the visibility of fine details such as very faint chalk inscriptions. In cross-polarization photography, a polarizing filter is placed over the light source and a polarizing ring is placed over the camera lens. When the ring is rotated to the correct position, the light waves reaching the camera sensors are all oriented in the same plane. Light scatter is eliminated, so the surface is visible with no interfering glare.

The word "Left" was visible initially as a series of very faint diagonal lines. Cross-polarized light enabled the camera to read more of the surface, and Photoshop enhancement followed by magnified inspection of the "L" provided clear visual evidence of its previously unseen upper and lower loops. While the "e" has been wiped away and the "ft" remains fragmentary, the phrase "Left side / inside" is a convincing interpretation of the handwriting, especially in light of its location on the drawer and the fact that chalk lettering typically served a utilitarian function for a cabinetmaker or joiner.

Secretary Press, Chrysler Museum of Art, Norfolk, Virginia
The only example of ink lettering found in this study is present on a secretary press illustrated in figure 12. The two-part press is very similar in form and ornament to the preceding example (fig. 2), with the chief difference occurring in the lower carcass: rather than containing full drawers, it is fitted with walnut doors enclosing four painted yellow pine linen slides. The scrolled pediment retains its original ebonized decoration on the cornice

Figure 12 Secretary press attributed to the WH cabinetmaker, northeast, North Carolina, 1785–1795. Walnut with yellow pine and walnut. H. 107½", W. 44¾", D. 22½". (Courtesy, Chrysler Museum of Art; photo, Gavin Ashworth.) This press descended in the Smithwick family of Hartford County, North Carolina.

bead as well as on the low-relief leaf carving surrounding a well-executed "WH" monogram. An unusual slatted slide is fit into the lower case above the desk interior. The upper rails of the glazed doors are shaped, and the original feet survive nearly intact.

INK INSCRIPTION: A LONE "W" OR MORE?
Techniques: Cross-polarization, Reflected Ultraviolet Light
The letter "W" is located on the yellow pine top of the lower case, approximately 6 inches from its front edge and thus hidden from view when the piece is assembled and in use. It is a bold, calligraphic letter, standing approximately 1 inch high, with a pronounced contrast between thin and thick strokes. The width and form of the strokes suggest application of ink with a small brush rather than a quill pen. Somewhat lower and a few inches to the right is a considerably smaller, less-definite ink stroke that appears to be the upper portion of a letter. A somewhat opaque yellowed varnish residue obscures any remainder of this letter, and no additional lettering is visible in normal light (fig. 13).

Figure 13 Inscription on the top of the lower case of the secretary press illustrated in fig. 12. (Photo, Gavin Ashworth.)

Newbern and Melchor maintain that this inscription reads "W Seay" and that it is written in the same hand as the incised inscription on the secretary press illustrated in figure 2, but there is no evidence to support either assertion. There is too little of the second letter to indicate that it is an "S," and there is no visible evidence of the letters "eay" following it. The form and execution of the "W" are very different from those in William Seay's signatures and the incised name visible in figure 7. On the secretary press illustrated in figure 12, the "W" is somewhat vertical and awkwardly formed with only slight curves to all strokes, except for a long, initial, thin-lined arc, a flourish that constitutes more than half the overall length of the letter. This flourish swoops down to the imaginary line at the base of the letter, an unusual feature for an eighteenth-century "W," which makes the letter easily confused with an "M." The thick downstroke legs are connected to the thin upstroke lines with abrupt, acute angles and no continuous loops, and there is no curve to the final upstroke. It is very unlikely that the same hand produced the incised names on the other secretary press (figs. 2–8).

Attempts to improve the visibility of the second letter and to search for additional lettering proved fruitless. As the "W" and the additional stroke were most likely produced using iron gall ink, reflected ultraviolet photography was considered the best option for enhancing any faint lettering, as iron gall ink tends to absorb UV radiation, making it stand out against a wood background in a reflected UV photograph. Here the technique did not reveal any new information. Either there is no additional lettering, or it is too obscured by varnish to become visible in a reflected UV photograph (UV radiation does not penetrate deeply). A second photograph was taken using cross-polarization in an attempt to cancel out any unwanted light scatter and "see through" the yellowed varnish. Once again, no additional lettering became visible (fig. 14).

Figure 14 Inscription illustrated in fig. 13 viewed using cross-polarization to search for additional evidence of ink. (Photo, F. Carey Howlett.)

In sum, there is insufficient evidence to assume the writer of the letter "W" and maker of the secretary press are one and the same or to demonstrate that the "W" is a partial signature of William Seay. It is also unlikely there is additional writing beneath the yellowed varnish. The varnish is sufficiently thin to reveal the contrast between the early- and latewood, so any lettering produced by iron gall ink, a material of marked contrast to the yellow pine, should also be visible.

Desk, Virginia Museum of Fine Arts, Richmond, Virginia

The desk illustrated in figures 1 and 15 is one of the most exceptional examples from the WH group. It is notable for the pronounced blocking of the façade and desk interior, which, in addition to its shaped, square quarter-columns, gives it a Continental baroque appearance rare in furniture from the American South. Indeed, numerous structural elements, including the abundant use of closely spaced nails attaching the drawer beading, the square form of the beading, the heavy blocking of the feet, and the thickness of the drawer sides suggest that the maker trained in a German cabinetmaking/joinery tradition. Although the desk does not exhibit the ornament that most graphically defines the work of the WH cabinetmaker—a relief-carved ebonized floral motif or a calligraphic monogram—several other objects in the group bear these ornamental details as well as

Figure 15 Desk illustrated in fig. 1 with fallboard open. (Courtesy, Virginia Museum of Fine Arts.) Furniture scholar John Bivins published this image in a section on the WH cabinetmaker in *The Furniture of Eastern North Carolina.*

the unique combination of Continental structural elements described above. Since the desk contains the earliest stylistic and structural features associated with the WH group and reflects the purest European influence, it may be the earliest object associated with the WH cabinetmaker.

The desk has two paper labels on components of the interior, both with the ink inscription "Ursula M. Daniel, Halifax, NC." Before it was sold to the Virginia Museum of Fine Arts in 1949, the desk appears to have descended in the Daniel or Garry families of Halifax; letters from the Daniel family at the Virginia Museum of Fine Arts attest to that tradition. The desk received heavy use as a work surface during part of its existence: there are numerous abrasions and scratches, and the writing surface of the desk lid and the secondary wood of one of the interior drawers are defaced with imprints of an unidentified stamping tool.[7]

Newbern and Melchor reported the discovery of six previously undocumented inscriptions on the desk: two separate signatures of the name "W Hill" on an exterior face of a large drawer and on one of the lid supports, two adjacent signatures showing the name "W Seay" on the interior face of a large drawer, the initials "TBH" on the bottom edge of the bottom large drawer, and the cipher "MW" on the other lid support. The authors postulate a history of the desk that predates its Daniel family ownership: the desk was made by William Seay on commission from Whitmell Hill as a gift for his son Thomas Blount Hill. The cipher "MW" showed that Micajah Wilkes, a supposed journeyman working for William Seay, contributed to the construction of the desk.[8]

On learning of these findings by Newbern and Melchor, a team of conservators, a curator, and the staff photographer at the Virginia Museum of Fine Arts examined all the sites described above, with the intent of securing publishable photographs of any newly discovered inscriptions for the authors. We conducted examinations using normal lighting, raking light, ultraviolet fluorescence, and infrared reflectography, but the examination proved fruitless. In a recent follow-up examination, Reflectance Transformation Imaging was used in addition to the earlier techniques, and additional time was taken to ensure that all sites were thoroughly evaluated. Once again, no names or initials came to light. Although a range of imaging techniques was used in examination of these sites (except for RTI, which was used only in the examination of the incised cipher), the photographs shown here were selected as the best means to illustrate the features incorrectly identified as inscriptions by Newbern and Melchor.

REPORTED SIGNATURES (2): "W SEAY" IN CHALK, BOTTOM DRAWER, INNER FACE OF PROPER RIGHT SIDE
Technique: Raking Light, Cross-polarization
According to Newbern and Melchor, the name "W Seay" is written in chalk twice on the inner face of the large bottom drawer, one inscription appearing just above and one directly below the residue of an apparent mud dauber's nest. Chalk, as a fine powder on the surface of an object, tends to show well in raking light, and, as mentioned earlier, cross-polarization can eliminate any reflective interference. While chalk may appear more pronounced when viewed with the light coming from a particular angle, photos taken from any angle should reveal some evidence of it. Photographs of the site demonstrate clearly that no chalk is present. In the first image the raking light source was placed well to the right of the drawer side and nearly parallel with the wood grain, clearly reflecting the wavy-grained walnut of

Figure 16 Raking side-lit cross polarized image of the inner face of the bottom drawer of the desk illustrated in fig. 1. No chalk is present, although the sloping wavy figure of the walnut resembles handwriting. (Courtesy, Virginia Museum of Fine Arts; photo, Travis Fullerton.)

Figure 17 Wavy figure is not visible in a raking top-lit cross polarized image of the same view as fig. 16. The surface reveals jackplane marks but no presence of chalk. (Courtesy, Virginia Museum of Fine Arts; photo, Travis Fullerton.)

the drawer side, with the waviness sloping to the right in a manner suggestive of handwriting (fig. 16). In the second image the light comes from above and is essentially perpendicular to the grain (fig. 17). From this angle the wood is evenly reflective: the wavy grain is imperceptible, and nothing is visible on the surface except jackplane marks and the mud dauber residue. The tendency for cabinet woods such as walnut to display so much variance in reflectivity is a desirable characteristic known as *chatoyance*, or the cat's-eye effect. Here the effect led to the misinterpretation of the wood grain as a chalk inscription reading "W Seay."

Figure 18 Standard photograph (left) of the wavy figure on one of the lid supports of the desk illustrated in fig. 1. No ink is visible. (Photo, Travis Fullerton.) A second image using reflected ultraviolet photography (right) demonstrates that no ink is present.

REPORTED SIGNATURE: "W HILL" IN INK, PROPER RIGHT LID SUPPORT, OUTER FACE

Technique: Normal Lighting, Reflected Ultraviolet Light

Newbern and Melchor also refer to a very small ink inscription reading "W Hill" on the outer face of one of the lid supports. No examination technique used by the team at the Virginia Museum of Fine Arts revealed any evidence of ink. Here, reflected ultraviolet light photography was particularly useful, as it revealed no evidence of historic iron gall, logwood, or carbon ink. As the photographs shown here illustrate, the authors appear to have misinterpreted sloping wavy-grained walnut to be an inscription (fig. 18).

REPORTED SIGNATURE: "W HILL" IN INK, BOTTOM DRAWER, OUTER FACE OF PROPER RIGHT SIDE

Technique: Normal Lighting, Reflected Ultraviolet Light

Newbern and Melchor published an enhanced image showing the name "W Hill" in large letters running perpendicular to the length of the bottom drawer side. Examination revealed no evidence of ink on the surface and

Figure 19 Standard photography (left) of the outer surface of the side of the bottom drawer of the desk illustrated in fig. 1 reveals a series of angled scratches and a reflected ultraviolet image (right) shows no evidence of an ink inscription. (Photo, Travis Fullerton.)

proved conclusively that the "inscription" is a cluster of abrasions on the wood surface, once again sloping in a manner suggestive of handwriting (fig. 19).

REPORTED INITIALS:
"TBH" IN CHALK, BOTTOM DRAWER, BOTTOM EDGE
Technique: Normal Lighting
Newbern and Melchor reported finding the initials "TBH" in chalk on the bottom edge of the bottom drawer. This location is problematic for an inscription of any kind: one would not typically expect to find writing, particularly the name of an owner, in such a concealed location that is so vulnerable to wear. The markings interpreted as chalk initials are visible as light-colored bands as much as ¼ inch wide. Similar bands occur on the edges of all side and bottom edges of the large drawer faces. They are clearly patterns of blanching made by solvent drips associated with a twentieth-century finish removal. Most are straight drips, but in the case of the drips interpreted as "TBH," the bottom drawer was apparently turned ninety degrees in mid-drip, thereby crossing the "T" and connecting the legs of the "B" and "H" (fig. 20).

Figure 20   Standard photograph of the bottom edge of the bottom drawer of the desk illustrated in fig. 1 reveals blanched surface drips associated with refinishing rather than the initials "TBH." A second image (bottom) shows similar drips on another drawer. (Photos, Travis Fullerton and F. Carey Howlett.)

REPORTED CIPHER: INCISED "MW," PROPER LEFT LID SUP-
PORT, OUTER FACE

Technique: Reflectance Transformation Imaging

Newbern and Melchor illustrate markings identified as an incised cipher of the letters "MW" on the outer face of one of the lid supports and relate those letters to a much clearer "MW" cipher found on the rear rail of a Roanoke River basin bottle case in the collection of the Colonial Williamsburg Foundation. The markings are very faint and barely visible in normal light, partly because the lid support shows numerous fine abrasions on all surfaces, evidence of very hard use. As the markings are definitely scratched into the surface, Reflectance Transformation Imaging was selected as the best option for enhancing their visibility. Two photographs are provided to show fully the features the authors referred to as a cipher. The first shows the lid support illuminated by raking light from the right just above the center point. Rendered in "image unsharp masking" mode and viewed with high-gain, specular light, the photo reveals an uneven six-legged zigzag beginning on the upper side face of the applied bead on the vertically grained end of the lid support and extending several inches before ending along the top edge of the support (fig. 21). When raking light is shifted to the upper left and the image is rendered in diffuse gain mode, an unrelated, shallow, V-shaped depression appears to overlay a portion of the zigzag, roughly suggesting the appearance of a cipher (fig. 22). RTI demonstrates the random nature of this juxtaposition: no initials are inscribed on the lid support.[9]

Figure 21 A photo captured using Reflectance Transformation Imaging (RTI) in image unsharp mask mode showing an uneven six-legged zigzag scratched into a lid support of the desk illustrated in fig. 1, clearly not handwriting. (Photo, Travis Fullerton.)

Figure 22 With light position changed in the RTI viewer and RTI photography rendered in diffuse gain mode, an unrelated V-shaped depression is visible crossing the zigzag scratch, suggesting an overlapping cipher. (Photo, Travis Fullerton.)

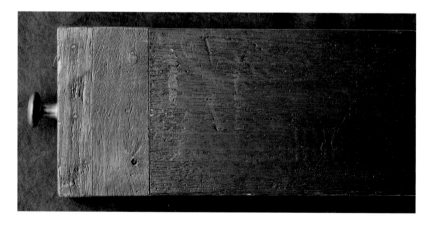

The result of this investigation is that the desk in the collection of the Virginia Museum of Fine Arts does not support an attribution to William Seay or anyone else: the history postulated by Newbern and Melchor has no basis in fact. In a search for the identity of the maker of the WH group of furniture, the desk proved more of a blank slate than a Rosetta stone, and the desk's provenance remains unchanged.

Figure 23 Hope Plantation House, Windsor, North Carolina, completed ca. 1803. (Courtesy, Historic Hope Foundation.) Hope was the home of home of David Stone, a former governor of North Carolina.

Figure 24 Standard photograph of a stair riser at Hope Plantation, showing an inverted "W" at right and several other pencil markings. (Courtesy, Historic Hope Foundation; photo, F. Carey Howlett.)

Figure 25 An infrared photograph of the stair riser illustrated in fig. 24 shows the differing intensities and orientations of the pencil-inscribed letters on the stair riser, clear evidence they were written at different times; no names are present. (Courtesy, Historic Hope Foundation; photo, F. Carey Howlett.)

Staircase Riser, Hope Plantation, Windsor, North Carolina

Newbern and Melchor identified William Seay as both the WH cabinetmaker and the primary builder of a number of large houses in the Roanoke River basin. Among the most prominent is David Stone's residence at Hope Plantation, completed circa 1803 (fig. 23). The attribution of the house to Seay is based on the authors' discovery of the inscription "W Seey" on the reverse of a riser in a service staircase at the house, visible inside a small closet entered from the staircase landing. The authors also attribute the writing to one of Seay's apprentices.[10]

Visual inspection of the stair riser reveals an inverted "W" and a few additional letters in pencil. The style of the handwriting is correct for the period of the house, and, as stated by the authors, the inscriptions predate assembly (fig. 24). Infrared reflectography was chosen as the best technique for additional examination: it is ideal for looking at pencil inscriptions because of the strong absorption of infrared light by graphite, making it stand out more clearly than it does in normal light. In the infrared photograph, the inverted "W" is visible at right with an illegible scribble below it, both in bold pencil. A large "D" in finer pencil is at left, and a smaller "g" or "J" in the same hand lies between the "W and the scribble. The "W" and "D" are not only oriented differently, they are unrelated and by different hands. The "D" and a few nondescript smudges within its bounds do not spell "Seey" (fig. 25).

The primary builder of the Hope Plantation house remains unknown. Local tradition associates the house with Jeremiah Bunch and his brothers, a family of free black house builders living close to Hope Plantation at the time. There is also reason to believe the Sharrock family of Roxobel, North Carolina, contributed to the interior woodwork, but there is no known document associating William Seay with the construction of David Stone's house at Hope Plantation. Indeed, Newbern and Melchor's attribution of at least three other houses to William Seay is inaccurate: Seay died in Hertford County in 1803, several years before the building of Woodbourne (1808) in Roxobel, the Pugh-Griffin House (1812) in Woodville, and the Sally-Billy House (1810) in Halifax County.[11]

Figure 26 Sideboard associated with the WH group of furniture, northeast, North Carolina, 1810–1820. Walnut with yellow pine, H. 39½", W. 69½", D. 23¾". (Courtesy, Historic Hope Foundation; photo, Gavin Ashworth.)

Sideboard, Hope Plantation, Windsor, North Carolina

The sideboard illustrated in figure 26 is, perhaps, the latest example attributed by previous scholars to the WH group. This attribution is largely based on the perceived relationships between the blocking on that object and that on the preceding desk (fig. 1). The blocking is an early stylistic feature that, combined with an otherwise standard neoclassical form, makes the sideboard unconventional in American furniture. Many of the characteristic WH-group structural features are absent: drawer bottoms are set in dadoes rather than flush-nailed to the bottoms of drawer sides; no pins secure stile and rail joints; and the conventionally applied veneer is not found on any other WH pieces. In addition, the profile of the blocking on the desk is more refined, with fillets canted rather than parallel to the façade as on the sideboard, and the execution very different. These departures have led to the supposition that the sideboard was made by a journeyman in the WH shop who had trained elsewhere or in a second shop influenced by the WH group.

Newbern and Melchor discovered a large inscription on the inner surface of the yellow pine backboard of the sideboard and interpreted part of the writing as the name "Wilmot Peeas" or "Wilmot Seeas," which they felt might signify a relative of William Seay or one of his unrelated journeymen. They also identified a partially obscured second name as "John Weedo[n]" and noted that the remainder of the inscription was a list of dimensioned boards supplied by one of the two names.[12]

The inscriptions were written in pencil, so here again infrared reflectography served as the best technique for improving legibility (figs. 27, 28). If noth-

Figure 27   Standard photograph of the inner surface of the back of the sideboard illustrated in fig. 26 showing a large, lengthy, but nearly illegible pencil inscription. (Photo, Gavin Ashworth.)

Figure 28   In a reflected infrared image of the inscription illustrated in fig. 27, the handwriting is completely legible. (Photo, F. Carey Howlett.)

ing else, the resulting IR photograph proved that John Weedo[n] was the tradesman who likely provided the lumber. The inscription reads as follows:

6 Walnut Pieces 1 inch Thick
4 Pine ditt ¾ Thick 4½ Wide
1 4½ Wide @ ½ Thick
John Weedo—

Misinterpreting "Walnut Pieces" as "Wilmot Peeas" in normal light is understandable: an old graphite inscription does not stand out on an oxidized wood surface. Illegibility obscured not only the lettering but also the entire context of the inscription, and it is obvious that the presence of two oversize words beginning in sweeping capital letters was highly suggestive of a proper name. The use of infrared reflectography makes the words and context of this graphite inscription very clear.

Curiously, the sideboard is the sole example from the WH group examined thus far that bears a pencil inscription. The name "John Weedo[n]" (or a similar variation) does not appear in any known documents from the Roanoke River basin. The sideboard has no provenance, and it may date considerably later than previously thought: the torus moldings of the top and base edges, if original, indicate a classical revival influence. While it would be imprudent to remove the sideboard from inclusion in the WH group at this time, these observations and the fact that its construction differs in many ways from other WH pieces raise questions. Additional research should be conducted to explore other possible origins for this unusual sideboard.

Tympanum Board, Private Collection, Atlanta, Georgia
The final item examined in the study is a tympanum board from a case piece in the WH group (fig. 29)—one of four documented examples (three on intact pieces) featuring a federal eagle clutching Masonic emblems. The elaborate eagle is ebonized, incised, and inlaid with putty. It holds the scales of justice in its beak, a Masonic square, compass, and sunburst in its right

Figure 29 Tympanum board attributed to the WH cabinetmaker, northeast, North Carolina, 1792–1796. Walnut, ebonized ornament and putty inlay. H. 18", W. 44". (Private collection; photo, Craig McDougal.)

talons, and a level in its left. Above the eagle is a banner of fifteen stars, probably representing the states of the Union at the time the pediment was constructed, dating it between 1792 and 1796. On either side are the relief-carved, ebonized tendrils and leaves typical of the WH group, here laid out in a more delicate pattern than usual and outlined in white. The bead and ogee moldings of the scrolls are also ebonized, as are the ground and central star motif of each pinwheel roundel.

REPORTED INSCRIPTION: "HASKETT" IN CHALK, REVERSE OF TYMPANUM BOARD
Technique: Cross-polarization Followed by Black-and-White Conversion and Digital Filtration in Adobe Photoshop
A large chalk inscription is present on the back of the typanum in probable late eighteenth-century script, approximately 16 inches long and 3 inches high (fig. 30). The walnut was apparently sealed with varnish or a pigmented wash before the inscription was made, and portions of the writing are worn, smudged, and difficult to read against the dirty and yellowed coating.

Figure 30 Cross-polarization photo of the large chalk inscription on the back of the tympanum board illustrated in fig. 29. (Photo, F. Carey Howlett.)

Newbern and Melchor interpreted the first marks of the inscription as the sketch of an eagle and the surname that follows as "Haskett," reading the final double letters, although made with open loops, as crossed to form a double "T." They associate the inscription with Jesse Haskett, a Perquimans County man they suggest was living in Roxobel in the mid-1790s working as a journeyman for William Seay. Haskett, they argue, likely ornamented the pediment.

To evaluate this interpretation, this study employed cross-polarization followed by black-and-white conversion and additional processing in Adobe Photoshop. This enhanced legibility to some extent, though some parts of the inscription remain unclear. Additional imaging with UV fluorescence revealed no additional information.

The first mark of the inscription is very faint (fig. 31). It does not appear to be the sketch of an eagle, as no chalk lines representing a head, beak, or body are present. The mark consists of two mirror-image arcs, similar to those in the letter "H," but differences with the more clearly legible "H" in the surname introduces uncertainty to this interpretation. The arcs overlap near their midpoints in the first mark, whereas they remain apart in the surname "Haskell," joined only by the crossbar. Moreover, the "H" in the surname has additional flourishes. Compared with other examples of period script, the first initial could also be interpreted as an "X."

Imaging indicates the surname is probably "Haskell," as no chalk is present to indicate that the final double "l" was crossed to form a double "t" (fig. 32). More writing is present: at least four smaller letters slope upward

Figure 31   Processed cross-polarization photo of the first letter of the inscription illustrated in fig. 30. (Photo, F. Carey Howlett.)

Figure 32   Processed cross-polarization photo of the name "Haskell" and additional lettering illustrated in fig. 30. (Photo, F. Carey Howlett.)

from the upper right corner of the "H" in "Haskell," suggesting a first name also beginning in "H," such as "Harry" or "Harvy."

Does the name "H [or X] Haskell" identify a maker, either the decorator of the tympanum or the maker of the entire pediment? The size of the lettering, its location, and the chalk used to inscribe it all suggest this is possible, but it remains far from certain. Three known WH pediments have eagles below fifteen stars, indicating a relatively short time period for their construction. It is possible that these objects, and others like them, were fabricated nearly simultaneously: the inscribed name, possibly that of the individual who commissioned the piece, may have been a useful means to distinguish otherwise similar objects.

The benefits of imaging in the examination and analysis of markings on furniture are clear. Imaging techniques enhance legibility, improve the accuracy of interpretations, and help prevent unfounded speculation. This study was limited to six objects in the WH group, but inscriptions reputedly found on three of those pieces—the Hope Plantation secretary press, the Chrysler Museum of Art secretary press, and the Virginia Museum of Fine Arts block-front desk—were the foundation for Newbern and Melchor's attribution. Imaging showed that two of these objects do not bear

Seay's name and that his only signature on a piece of furniture almost certainly denotes ownership or use rather than authorship. As was the case when John Bivins published *The Furniture of Eastern North Carolina*, there is insufficient documentary and physical evidence to attribute the WH group to any maker. The richness, diversity, and unique character of the group remain intriguing. The mystery continues.

1. John Bivins Jr., *The Furniture of Coastal North Carolina, 1700–1820* (Chapel Hill: University of North Carolina Press for the Museum of Early Southern Decorative Arts, 1988), pp. 291–322.

2. Thomas R. J. Newbern and James R. Melchor, *WH Cabinetmaker: A Southern Mystery Solved* (Benton, Ky.: Legacy Ink Publishing, 2009). North Carolina Archives, Raleigh, CR.010.101.7, folder 1774–75. Thomas Sharrock Estate Papers, Bertie County Record of Estates, State Archives of North Carolina, CR.010.508.90. Newbern and Melchor also propose that William Seay descended from a family of woodworkers, citing a June 4, 1768, court record documenting an agreement by James Seay (possibly an uncle of William Seay) to apprentice his orphaned nephew Abraham Seay, then two years old, as a "house carpenter" (Bertie County Court Minutes, 1763–1771). They failed to note the subsequent formal indenture document signed by James Seay and dated June 26, 1768, in which he agreed to teach Abraham Seay "the art and calling of a cordwainer" (State Archives of North Carolina: Apprentice Records CR.010.101.7, folder 1768).

3. Newbern and Melchor, *WH Cabinetmaker*, p. 59. The staff of the Virginia Museum of Fine Arts informed Newbern and Melchor of their findings before *WH Cabinetmaker: A Southern Mystery Solved* went to press. Susan J. Rawles, Assistant Curator for American Decorative Arts, email message to James Melchor, May 11, 2009: "I am sorry to be the bearer of bad news, but our staff of conservators and photographers have all spent a great deal of time examining and re-examining the WH block-front desk in an effort to identify period signatures and markings — unfortunately, to no avail. While they have examined your photos against the evidence of the object and can, in a few instances, acknowledge variations in the surface areas akin to markings, they cannot confirm that those markings are signatures — as opposed to variations in the wood born of salt or humidity or scratches, etc. Consequently, we are unable to provide you with the images you requested. I sincerely hope that . . . other physical evidence and historical documentation on the cabinetmaker and patron . . . will more than compensate for this turn of events." Individuals who examined the desk include consulting conservator F. Carey Howlett; staff conservators Kathy Gillis, Carol Sawyer, and Bruce Suffield; chief conservator Stephen Bonadies; assistant curator Susan Rawles; and photographer Katherine Wetzel.

4. George Fisher, *The Instructor, or American Young Man's Best Companion Containing Spelling, Reading, Writing and Arithmetic* (Worcester, Mass.: Isaiah Thomas, 1786).

5. Reflectance Transformation Imaging is a product of Cultural Heritage Imaging, a nonprofit corporation. Software for capturing and viewing RTI images is available at no cost at http://culturalheritageimaging.org/Technologies/RTI/.

6. John E. Tyler, "A History of the Tyler Family of Bertie and Hertford Counties, North Carolina," manuscript, p. 18, archives, Historic Hope Foundation. The manuscript discusses the marriage of Elizabeth Rutland Tyler, widow of John Tyler, to a "Mr. Seay." This is probably William Seay, as it explains his 1800 guardianship of Peggy Andrews, the orphaned daughter of Stephen Andrews and Celia Tyler. Celia was the daughter of Elizabeth Rutland Tyler, making Peggy Andrews the orphaned step-granddaughter of William Seay (Stephen Andrews estate papers, State Archives of North Carolina, CR010.508.1). The 1800 federal census for Hertford County, North Carolina, lists William Seay as heading a household of four white people, one male over forty-five (Seay), one female over forty-five (probably Elizabeth Rutland Tyler), one female sixteen to twenty-five (probably Celia Tyler Andrews, widow of Stephen Andrews), and one female under ten (probably Peggy Andrews).

7. Frank L. Horton. "The Work of an Anonymous Carolina Cabinetmaker," *Antiques* 101, no. 1 (January 1972): 169–76. See also Virginia Museum of Fine Arts objects file for the desk, acc. no. 1949.11.17.

8. Newbern and Melchor, *WH Cabinetmaker*, pp. 58–63.

9. Ibid., p. 243; Ronald L. Hurst and Jonathan Prown, *Southern Furniture, 1680–1830: The Colonial Williamsburg Collection* (New York: Harry Abrams for the Colonial Williamsburg Foundation, 1997), pp. 534–36.

10. Newbern and Melchor, *WH Cabinetmaker*, pp. 173–81.

11. Conversation with David Serxner, Historic Hope Foundation. See the entry for Jeremiah Bunch in North Carolina Architects and Builders: A Biographical Dictionary, http://ncarchitects. lib.ncsu.edu/. Bivins, *The Furniture of Coastal North Carolina*, p. 64. Thomas Sharrock and son Steven witnessed a will at Hope Plantation while the house was under construction. Seay is listed as "William Seay dcd" in a June 13, 1803, document transferring his guardianship of Peggy Andrews to John Andrews (Stephen Andrews estate papers, State Archives of North Carolina, CR010.508.1). Newbern and Melchor, *WH Cabinetmaker*, pp. 104–13, 120–26, 230–36. The authors reported finding the inscription "Seay Sharrock" on the drawer bottom of a built-in cupboard at the Pugh-Griffin House, supposed evidence of a collaboration by William Seay and the Sharrock family of cabinetmakers. The drawer bottom was not included in this study because the house was built after Seay's death.

12. Newbern and Melchor, *WH Cabinetmaker*, pp. 229–31.

Appendix

Imaging Techniques and Equipment

Following is a brief discussion of the equipment used during the course of this project. For more detailed information, the authors recommend Jeffrey Warda, ed., *The AIC Guide to Digital Photography and Conservation Documentation* (Washington, D.C.: American Institute for Conservation of Historic and Artistic Works, 2011). This book presents a range of technical information in a concise, understandable format and includes a number of imaging techniques not used in the foregoing study. There are also numerous informative websites for photographers interested in cost-effective approaches to multispectral imaging, such as Ben Lincoln's www.beneaththewaves.net/Photography.

Reflectance Transformation Imaging (RTI)

RTI is a computer-based means to compile two-dimensional images into a format that enables a three-dimensional study of an object's surface. The technique is usually conducted using standard photography and a single, movable light source. The Virginia Museum of Fine Arts (VMFA) employed a Canon 5D Mark 2 and a handheld flash to examine the incised names on the Hope Plantation secretary press (figs. 7, 8) and the zigzag scratches on the lid support of the VMFA desk (figs. 21, 22). While RTI can be performed using a consumer-model digital camera, the VMFA's full-frame sensor Canon ensures optimal quality, resolving extreme detail and providing sharp images with very little distortion.

Cross-polarization

This visible-light technique can be used with any digital camera to control specular and diffuse reflections. Minimizing or eliminating these reflections enhances contrast and saturation, distinguishing various features on a surface. A linear polarizing film is placed in front of the light source and a circular polarizing filter on the camera lens; the polarizer on the camera is rotated perpendicular to that of the film for maximum extinction of glare. Cross-polarization photos of the VMFA desk(figs. 16, 17) and the Hope Plantation secretary press (fig. 11) were made using a studio flash filtered using a Rosco #7300 neutralizing linear polarizing film and a B+W Circular Pol-E filter on a 50megapixel 4-shot Hasselblad H4D50-MSRTI (www.bhphotovideo.com). Cross-polarization photos of the Chrysler Museum secretary press (fig. 14) and the WH eagle tympanum (figs. 31, 32) were made using a Nikon D70 and the same polarizing filters as above.

Cameras and Filters for Reflected Infrared and Reflected Ultraviolet Photography
Digital camera sensors are sensitive to the full spectrum of light, visible and invisible. This makes them ideal for multispectral imaging but presents problems in the production of standard visible-light images because of the interference of the invisible portion of the spectrum, particularly the infrared. Manufacturers have gradually increased the internal filtration of the invisible portions of the spectrum, such that no current consumer digital cameras are useful as purchased for multispectral imaging. In addition, both infrared and ultraviolet light present a focusing problem when working with standard lenses. While special lenses permit the focusing of infrared and ultraviolet light in the same plane as visible light, they tend to be very expensive to produce. Consequently, most multispectral photographic systems are costly and serve a very limited professional forensic market.

Fortunately, there are numerous options available for those interested in conducting infrared and ultraviolet photography, employing either used equipment or new cameras converted for use in IR and UV photography. The cameras and light sources used during the course of this project follow.

(1) Sony "Nightshot" feature: For basic infrared images, older Sony digital cameras with a "Nightshot" feature (discontinued after the A100 series) are a simple solution requiring no added filters. With "Nightshot" engaged, the camera's internal infrared-blocking filter is removed from the light path. The feature was designed as a point-and-shoot means to take images in near darkness, not specifically as an IR technique, so the resulting image is a hybrid of available visible and infrared light. Though there is no flexibility to the technique (aperture and shutter speed are fixed), photos taken carefully in "Nightshot" mode can often reveal as much information as a pure reflected infrared photograph. The IR photograph of the Hope Plantation stair riser (fig. 25)was taken using a Sony Cybershot F717 in "Nightshot" mode and standard tungsten photo lamps.

(2) Fuji Finepix S3 UVIR: Fuji manufactures multispectral cameras that take infrared and ultraviolet photographs when used with the appropriate filters. The infrared photograph of the Hope Plantation sideboard inscription was taken using a Fuji FinePix S3 UVIR, a camera discontinued before 2010 and now supplanted by the company's IS Pro UV-IR digital SLR. The FinePix S3 has a full-frame sensor with 12.3 megapixels. The spectrum is roughly 350 to 1000 nanometers (nm) (from the UV-A to near infrared). It has a Nikon lens mount and requires the use of filters for the desired imaging technique. The camera allows considerable flexibility in settings to achieve optimal exposures. The Hope sideboard inscription (fig. 28) was revealed using standard tungsten photo lamps and an infrared filter from Edmund Optics with a cutoff below 830 nm (www.edmundoptics.com /optics/optical-filters/bandpass-filters). To take the photo, the camera was

first manually focused with no filter present. The filter was then added and focus adjusted over several trial exposures to achieve a single good image.

(3) Nikon D70: The Nikon D70, discontinued only a few years ago, can take good photographs in both infrared and ultraviolet portions of the spectrum without modification, as Nikon's internal blocking filter remained relatively weak until fairly recent generations of its consumer digital SLRs. Like the Fuji Finepix camera, filters are necessary for both infrared and reflected ultraviolet photography. Because the internal filters block some of the desired wavelengths, the camera requires longer exposures and/or wider aperture settings than the Fuji Finepix camera. Unpublished reflected ultraviolet photographs of the "W" on the Chrysler Museum's secretary press were taken using a Nikon D70 with a B+W 403 ultraviolet bandpass filter (blocking all visible light) (http://diglloyd.com/articles/Filters/spectral-B+W-403.html) stacked with a LDP LLC X-Nite CC1 filter (www.maxmax.com/axnitefilters.htm) to block out infrared light, ensuring only reflected UV-A light reached the camera's sensors. The camera was initially focused without filters using the auto-focus feature. While auto-focus was still locked, the filters were placed on the lens, then the lens was set for manual focus. As with the Fuji Finepix, focus was manually adjusted over several trial exposures to achieve a single good image. Reflected infrared photos taken with the Nikon D70 during this project (not shown here) used both a Hoya R72 (cut-off at 720 nm) and a B+W 093 (cut-off at 830 nm). Light sources for both infrared and reflected UV photography are described below.

(4) Converted digital SLR cameras: For optimal results using a recently made digital SLR camera, one can convert an off-the-shelf camera into a UV/IR camera either by using a purchased conversion kit to replace the internal UV/IR filters or by sending the camera to one of several businesses that perform the conversions for a fee (see www.lifepixel.com or www.maxmax.com/IRCameraConversions.htm). If a new camera is converted, it is important to know that the conversion will void a manufacturer's warranty. The Virginia Museum of Fine Arts uses a converted Canon 5D Mark 2, a 21-megapixel camera that has been modified to see and record both infrared and UV wavelengths of light. The reflected infrared range is ~715–1200 nm; reflected UV, 350 nm–400 nm. This camera was used to search for reported ink markings on the VMFA desk using reflected ultraviolet light photography (figs. 18 right and 19 right), employing filters equivalent to those described above in section 3.

Lighting for Reflected Infrared Photography
Cameras that have weak infrared filtration or have had internal filters removed are very sensitive to infrared and near-infrared light. Both sunlight and the tungsten light traditionally used for photography contain sufficient light in the near-infrared wavelengths to ensure adequate exposure. Indeed, hot spots (areas of overexposure to near-infrared wavelengths) are a bigger problem than underexposure, whether the light source is the sun or tungsten filaments. Standard tungsten photo lamps were used for all visible light, cross-polarized light, and reflected infrared photographs.

Lighting for Reflected Ultraviolet Photography

Unlike UV-fluorescence photography, which produces best results when the light source is restricted to ultraviolet wavelengths (usually UV-A, approximately 350–400 nm), reflected ultraviolet photography can be performed using daylight or any other visible light source that includes the ultraviolet portion of the spectrum. Lighting must be relatively intense, as the filters (described above in Nikon D70) are visually opaque, and exposures can often take several seconds. Tungsten lighting cannot be used as it contains virtually no ultraviolet component. High-pressure mercury vapor lamps and xenon lamps are suitable but can be very expensive. The reflected ultraviolet images in figures 18 and 19 were taken using a Broncolor Unilite strobe flash with a Broncolor UV attachment (www.bron.ch/broncolor/products/lamps/showproduct/unilite=1600). As a less-expensive alternative, surfaces can be lit using daylight or, if indoors, two fluorescent fixtures, each containing an 18-inch 15-watt UV-A fluorescent tube (Sylvania F15 T8 G13 BL368 - Quantum 368 nm, available at www.barbizonspecialtylighting.com). These specialty tubes provide much more UV-A light than commonly available BLB (black light blue) fluorescent tubes. While all fluorescent tubes are considerably less intense than mercury vapor lamps, they work well for close illumination of inscriptions, which generally cover a small surface area.

Enhancing Images in Adobe Photoshop

All of the techniques described above benefit from processing in Adobe Photoshop (www.adobe.com/Photoshop), an essential tool for enhancing images in order to extract as much visual information as possible. Its capabilities are greatest when images are captured and processed in RAW format, although images can be considerably improved even after conversion to high-resolution TIFF files.

It is generally useful to convert images to black and white. Among other things, this addresses the distracting appearance of reflected infrared and reflected ultraviolet photographs, which come from the camera with a reddish or a purplish cast, respectively. Rather than converting an image directly to grayscale, which discards all color information, it is often best to use the black-and-white conversion tool, which preserves color information on separate channels, permitting one to adjust the relative intensities of particular colors even after the image is converted. When processing a cross-polarized image of chalk on wood, for instance, reducing the intensity of the red and yellow channels, which generally make up the color of the wood background, invariably improves contrast between the chalk and the wood.

Next, "levels" are adjusted to improve the overall exposure and the relative intensity of lights and dark shades, a step that once again enhances contrast. Finally, adjustments are made using the "brightness and contrast" sliders, adding a final measure of contrast to distinguish the elements of an inscription from its background.

Figure 1 Newel post attributed to Thomas Day, Littleton Tazewell Hunt House, Milton Township, Caswell County, North Carolina, ca. 1855. (Photo, Tim Buchman.) This is one of twenty-five distinctive S-shaped newels attributed to Day.

Patricia Dane Rogers
and Laurel Crone Sneed

The Missing
Chapter in the Life
of Thomas Day

▼ L A T E I N T H E S P R I N G of 1835, a rising young African American furniture maker from Milton, North Carolina, named Thomas Day (1801–ca. 1861) traveled to Philadelphia (fig. 1). Under normal circumstances, it would have been logical for a professional artisan to visit this bustling commercial hub in search of new business contacts and the latest fashions in furniture making, but circumstances were not normal. After Nat Turner's bloody insurrection in August 1831, white-on-black violence targeting free blacks and antislavery activity had increased and spread. It was dangerous for any free person of color, let alone a southerner, to be in the so-called City of Brotherly Love, where white mobs had attacked and demolished African American businesses and gathering places in that very year as well as in 1832 and 1834.

Day was in Philadelphia for a different purpose: to attend the Fifth Annual Convention for the Improvement of the Free People of Colour in the United States. This event attracted the nation's most prominent free African American antislavery leaders, a group described as "men of enterprise and influence" who were on hand to forward an ambitious and wide-ranging platform. In the course of five days, the attendees formally called for improved African American access to schools and jobs and a boycott of sugar produced by slave labor. They railed against the growing number of proposed plans for African colonization by former slaves and free blacks and pledged temperance, thrift, and moral reform. The delegates also vowed to blanket Congress with a pamphlet campaign to outlaw slavery in the District of Columbia "and its territories." Most emphatically, the group proclaimed its belief in universal liberty and racial equality: "We claim to be American citizens and we will not waste our time by holding converse with those who deny us this privilege unless they first prove that a man is not a citizen of that country in which he was born and reared."[1]

For a southern person to attend this event was startling enough. For a free person of color who ran a successful business in a small southern market center, going to Philadelphia was a radical act. Had Day's white neighbors and patrons in the slave-powered tobacco region of Caswell County known of his presence at this historic black abolitionist meeting, he and his family would have been in grave danger. In North Carolina, anyone merely in possession of a pamphlet containing so much as a whiff of abolitionist propaganda risked being accused of sedition, a crime punishable by imprisonment, whipping, and even death. Indeed, in the years leading up to the Civil War, fomenting racial unrest was a felony in that state, and the meeting Day attended could not have posed a more seditious threat to the public order at his home some four hundred miles to the south.[2]

Day's participation in the convention is all the more remarkable because just five years earlier, North Carolina's attorney general, Romulus M. Saunders, had informed members of the state legislature that they could trust Thomas Day, who was petitioning for residency status for his African American wife. "In the event of any disturbance amongst the Blacks," Saunders stated, "I should rely with confidence upon a disclosure from him as he is the owner of slaves himself as well as real estate." Saunders, a Milton resident, could not have envisioned his accommodating neighbor in a crowd promoting racial uplift and abolition. But Day's presence there provides evidence of another side to him—a life that he kept hidden from his clients and neighbors. A growing body of evidence reveals that Thomas Day moved within abolitionist circles to a degree that Saunders and his southern white associates never would have imagined. In their eyes not only was he a good local businessman, but he was also a fellow slave owner. Enslaved African Americans worked not only in his furniture shop but also the tobacco fields and timberland that he owned outside Milton. Viewed through a modern lens, Thomas Day seems something of an enigma, a man in the middle whose life, work, and personal convictions regarding the most pressing cultural issue of the day moved back and forth. At the height of his career, he wrote to his daughter admonishing her to be pleased with her lot in Milton. Yet, he sent her and his two sons to Wesleyan Academy (now Wilbraham & Monson Academy), an abolitionist-led boarding school in faraway Wilbraham, Massachusetts.[3]

Since 2009, when the present authors first published this new information about Day's attendance at the convention in Philadelphia, a number of influential publications and exhibitions about him have come out. All overlook evidence that corroborates Day's Philadelphia visit and his close personal relationships with known abolitionists who had direct ties to the antislavery movement. The pivotal discovery relating to Day's abolitionist connections was finding his name on the list of attendees at the event in Philadelphia and the supporting proof of where he sought lodging. A newspaper advertisement called "A Card" firmly links him to these black conventioneers, and it first appeared in the July 11, 1835, issue of William Lloyd Garrison's abolitionist paper, *The Liberator*. More recently, the discovery of the diary of the Reverend John Francis Cook—a leading black abolitionist and delegate to the 1835 convention—provides further proof of Day's long-standing ties to African American activists in the North. On May 12, 1850, Cook recorded a visit from Thomas Day of Milton, North Carolina, who was accompanied by two of his children. For historian Ira Berlin, the diary corroborating Day's ties to Reverend Cook is highly significant. "We had a hint that Day was different because of his connection with the abolitionist school and his trip to the Philadelphia convention confirmed this." But Cook's words, he says, "completely change our understanding of Thomas Day" and offer further insight into the complex world of antebellum race relations, especially "relations between southern free people of color and those in the North." Unearthed during the past seven years while conducting research for a Thomas Day documentary film-in-progress, *The Thin Edge of Freedom: Thomas Day and the Free Black Experience, 1800–1860*, these bits and pieces of information—the "Card," Cook's diary, and Day's personal correspondence—add up to a new understanding of the cabinetmaker and his world.[4]

For many decades, Thomas Day has been a celebrated historical figure. Thanks to early scholarly work by Carter G. Woodson and John Hope Franklin, this furniture maker's legacy is well known within African American history circles. He is equally well known in the parts of north-central North Carolina and south-central Virginia where his furniture and architectural work were concentrated. Local interest also can be traced back to popular articles written in the 1920s and 1940s. Using the fading memories of Milton's "old timers," Caroline Pell Gunter reported that Day was educated in Boston and Washington. Although that was factually wrong, Gunter's story greatly expanded recognition of this talented artisan and held a grain of truth. An essay that Day's great-grandson William A. Robinson wrote for Woodson's pioneering journal, *The Negro History Bulletin*, in 1950 shed further light on Day's history, including the names of his children, the Massachusetts town where their school was located, and his own words—expressed in two previously unknown letters to his daughter. On a visit to Milton, the irony of seeing the town's "old rotting mansions and formal gardens gone to pot" was not lost on Robinson. When an attempt to purchase a signature sideboard from a descendant of his great-grandfather's wealthiest client was rebuffed, he reported the white man's telling response, "We got to hold onto the past."[5]

In the 1970s Day was the focus of several important exhibitions and academic research projects. Ira Berlin cited Day's work in his seminal book on free people of color, *Slaves without Masters: The Free Negro in the Antebellum South*. In 1975 the North Carolina Museum of History acquired eighteen pieces of furniture that Thomas Day was commissioned to make for Governor David Reid. This purchase, generously funded by members of the North Carolina chapter of the national black sorority and service organization Delta Sigma Theta, led to the first major exhibit of his work, "Thomas Day, Cabinetmaker." Historian Rodney A. Barfield chronicled what was known about Day's life in the exhibition catalogue in which an endnote contained a surprise: the cabinetmaker's daughter, Mary Ann, had been educated in the North before she went to school in Wilbraham. Ironically, interest in Day accelerated after 1989, when a fire nearly destroyed his home and workshop. (The ensuing restoration spearheaded by a group of dedicated Milton citizens who organized themselves as the Thomas Day House/Union Tavern Restoration, Inc. garnered national publicity.) An award-winning children's book published in 1994 was followed by intensive biographical research into Day's life and family supervised by historian John Hope Franklin. During the course of that research, Laurel Sneed and Christine Westfall of the Thomas Day Education Project identified the cabinetmaker's birthplace and the rest of his family, including his parents, John and

Mourning Stewart Day, his brother, John Day Jr. (a well-known Baptist missionary to Liberia), and his maternal grandfather, Thomas Stewart, a "doctor" from Dinwiddie County, Virginia.[6]

The Day renaissance reached critical mass in 1996 with a second show at the North Carolina Museum of History and a traveling exhibit with eleven pieces attributed to him. When a major North Carolina manufacturer unveiled twenty-four Thomas Day reproductions at the High Point international furniture market, the *Washington Post* took notice and came up with news of its own: the discovery of the cabinetmaker's Bible in a Baltimore suburb and the revelation that his daughter-in-law was from the nation's capital. Annie Washington, later Annie Day, was the first principal of the Stevens School, the premier grammar school for "colored" children in the District of Columbia. The school was named for Thaddeus Stevens, a radical abolitionist congressman from Pennsylvania and champion of the Thirteenth Amendment that ended slavery. Additional explorations of Day's life and work included critical insights from two candidates for master's degrees. Janie Leigh Carter transcribed and annotated letters written from Liberia by Day's older brother John, and Michael A. Paquette, a master cabinetmaker, provided an insider's perspective on the organization of Day's shop and business practices. In 1998 the Winterthur Museum held a scholarly symposium on race and ethnicity in American material culture, where decorative arts and material culture scholar Jonathan Prown explored Day's legacy as a craftsman. In light of recent interpretations, he specifically cautioned against Afro-centric interpretations of Day's work without firmer scholarly and aesthetic evidence. Prown also suggested that some objects that were being attributed to Day, who typically did not label or sign his pieces, might have been made by other artisans, although perhaps some were initially trained in the maker's shop.[7]

Today, Thomas Day is in the national spotlight more than ever. Much of the new attention centers on an ambitious exhibition held at the North Carolina Museum of History, "Behind the Veneer: Thomas Day, Master Cabinetmaker," and the handsome catalogue raisonné that accompanied it, *Thomas Day: Master Craftsman and Free Man of Color*. The authors, Patricia Phillips Marshall and Jo Ramsay Leimenstoll, raised the subject of his "potential" abolitionist connections but ultimately cast doubt on the issue. A subsequent installation at the Renwick Gallery of the Smithsonian American Art Museum provided a more elegantly distilled presentation of Day's work, focusing on his furniture as art. That exhibition similarly missed the opportunity to discuss the recent discoveries about Day's multifaceted history and specifically to point out his close personal ties to leading abolitionists in the District of Columbia.[8]

The purpose of this essay is not to focus on Thomas Day's furniture making legacy but, rather, to add to his historiography the ever growing body of evidence related to his abolitionist ties, which in turn suggest a new way of thinking about Day as both a man and a maker. Added to what is already known, this work strives to illuminate the part of his life that he intentionally kept under wraps for his own protection and that of his family.

In the process, it both expands and complicates our understanding of the man and effectively serves as a vital chapter that to date has been excluded from his extraordinary story.

Present-day visitors to the hamlet of Milton, North Carolina—population 166—cannot avoid either hearing about Thomas Day or encountering one of the many local sites associated with him. A common starting point for tours is the red brick Presbyterian Church on Broad Street, where he was not only a member but also made the handsome walnut pews that are still in use today (figs. 2, 3). Church records document his family's membership from 1841 to 1864. Nearby, the template Day used to make the distinctive S-shaped arms of the pews was discovered during the restoration of the

Figure 4   Union Tavern, Milton, North Carolina, ca. 1818. (Photo, Tim Buchman.) Formerly
known as the Yellow Tavern, Thomas Day's
home and workshop is on the town's main street.
The tavern was a major stagecoach stop
on the route to Petersburg, Virginia.

Union Tavern (fig. 4), his former home and workshop. But this is where
facts about Day and the pews end and two conflicting oral traditions or
interpretations begin.

According to one tale passed down in Milton, Day agreed to make the
pews on condition that he would be allowed to sit in the main sanctuary so
his slaves could look down from the balcony and see him and his family
among the white parishioners. In the other version—told mainly by his
descendants—he made the pews with the stipulation that his slaves would
be allowed to join him and his family downstairs in the sanctuary. For cultural historian Juanita Holland, these tales reflect two dominant and very
different contemporary views. In the first case, Thomas Day is a man who
desires to segregate himself from his slaves and to "distance himself from
being black," and in the second, Day was "insinuating himself and those he
cared about into the [white-dominated] system as much as he could."[9]

Thomas Day's story is full of such contradictions; however, this essay
will show that many of them can be explained by the fact that Day led a
double life: one among white neighbors and customers who wished to
maintain the status quo of race-based slavery, and another life among ardent
black and white abolitionists. Day had to behave very differently in those
polarized worlds.

Even a cursory glimpse into the world of Thomas Day opens up an
understudied and underappreciated aspect of American history: the experi-

ence of so-called free African Americans in the generations between the American Revolution and the Civil War. "Free blacks" or "free people of color" constituted a caste that was neither white nor free, though technically they were not enslaved. Their ambiguous status kept them on the alert at all times. In the South in particular, they were considered a threat to the white slave-holding society and were increasingly subjected to restrictive laws designed to keep them under control. Franklin described their experience in North Carolina before the Civil War:

> Free blacks in North Carolina, as Thomas Day came into manhood, could not move freely from one community to the other. If you wanted to go from Milton or Yanceyville to Raleigh, you needed permission to do that. And it was dangerous for you to do that, because . . . if you turned up where nobody knew you, it would be assumed that you were a runaway slave, and you had no defense against an accusation that you were a runaway. Now he could be seized, and he could be jailed, and the jailer could advertise that he had taken up a runaway slave. . . . Now if that free black, let's say it was Thomas Day, said, "I am not a slave, I am free," they'd say, "Yeah, how're you going to prove it?" "I can prove it in court." They'd say, "You have no standing in court. You cannot take an oath. You cannot swear on the Bible because you are not a person." You see?[10]

Southern states, including North Carolina, enacted repressive laws after widely publicized slave insurrections in Virginia in 1800 and South Carolina in 1822. They clamped down even harder after 1829, when David Walker, a free black North Carolina–born abolitionist in Boston, published a bold call for slaves to rise up and fight for their rights. Walker's appeal unapologetically justified violence if whites would not acknowledge that slavery was a sin, repent, and embrace African Americans as their brothers in Christian fellowship. In North Carolina, the cluster of restrictive statutes included the "seditious publications" act, which banned any printed material that might "excite insurrection, conspiracy or resistance in slaves or free negroes and persons of colour within the State." From 1830 on, it was illegal for free people of color to teach a slave to read or write, to marry a slave, to preach in public, to "peddle" goods outside the county in which they lived without a license, or to leave the state for more than ninety days and then seek to reenter. It was also next to impossible to free a slave. Anyone contemplating such an action had to publish intent six weeks in advance, petition the state's Superior Court, and pay the astronomical sum of "one thousand dollars for each slave named." The penalty for "concealing," "harboring" or "helping a slave escape from the state" was "death without benefit of clergy."[11]

It was in such a legally and socially circumscribed milieu that Day lived and worked for more than three decades, making furniture and architectural components for prominent local planters, merchants, and leading citizens, including former North Carolina governors David Lowry Swain and David Settle Reid. In 1847, when he was president of the University of North Carolina, Swain hired Day for a major project. In 1855 and 1858 Day filled large furniture orders for Reid after the latter had become a U.S. senator. In an era when most free African Americans in the South were illiterate, untrained in a marketable skill, and denigrated as a group, Thomas Day stood out as an educated, accomplished artisan, businessman, and family man whose talent, personal integrity, work ethic, and seeming acceptance of prevailing regional values won him the respect of the white community. Making exceptions for individual free blacks who were upright citizens—contributors to their communities who supported the status quo of white domination or gave the appearance of doing so—was part of the white mind-set in the old South. According to historian Melvin Patrick Ely,

> There are always white hardliners who go out of their way to disparage free blacks, declaring that people of African descent can't possibly succeed as free people. And at the same time you find free blacks and whites doing business together, sometimes marrying, founding churches together, even hitching up wagons and moving west together. So what's going on is considerable fluidity and inconsistency against the backdrop of a pretty thoroughly repressive system.

Figure 5 Newel post attributed to Thomas Day, Woodside, Milton, North Carolina, ca. 1838. (Courtesy, Historic Woodside House; photo, Tim Buchman.) Woodside was built by planter and foundry owner Caleb Hazard Richmond. The house is noted for having interior architectural details fabricated by Thomas Day and for being the site where Confederate general Dodson Ramseur married Richmond's daughter Mary.

Figure 6 Detail of a newel post attributed to Thomas Day, William Long House, Blanch Community near Milton, North Carolina, ca. 1856. (Photo, Tim Buchman.) This design may have been inspired by Day's initials.

Day was certainly treated as an exception, not only because he owned slaves but also because his trade served the needs of the local planter class. In addition to making household furniture, Day's shop produced cribs, caskets, and architectural components. Although he kept up with the latest designs, Day's repertoire was innovative and, occasionally, idiosyncratic. His newel posts are unique in being tightly spiraled or formed in a shape resembling his initials (figs. 5, 6). Similarly, some of his otherwise conservatively designed sideboards have exuberant and decidedly oversize ornamental scrolls (fig. 7).[12]

It is likely that Day found inspiration in popular British and American design books, but high-style furniture imported into the piedmont region of North Carolina may also have influenced his work. As Marshall notes, Day "developed his aesthetic vision over time. The majority of his documented furniture dates from 1840 to 1860, roughly the last twenty years of

Figure 7 Detail of a scrolled mirror support on a sideboard attributed to Thomas Day, Milton, North Carolina, 1840–1855. Mahogany and mahogany veneer with yellow pine, tulip poplar, and walnut. (Collection of the North Carolina Museum of History, donation Museum of History Associates and Mr. Thomas S. Erwin; courtesy, Renwick Gallery of the Smithsonian American Art Museum; photo, Amy Vaughters.) The sideboard was made for Caleb H. Richmond.

Figure 8 Lounge attributed to Thomas Day, Milton, North Carolina, 1845–1855. Walnut with yellow pine. H. 27⅜", W. 88⅝", D. 23⁷⁄₁₆". (Collection of the North Carolina Museum of History, purchase with state funds; courtesy, Renwick Gallery of the Smithsonian American Art Museum; photo, Tim Buchman.) Day made twelve documented settees that he referred to as "lounges." This example descended in the Bass-Engle family.

Figure 9 Sofa attributed to Karsten Petersen, Salem, North Carolina, 1830–1850. Cherry with tulip poplar. H. 25", W. 72", D. 23½". (Courtesy, Old Salem Museum & Gardens.)

his life. The earliest of these present his interpretations of somewhat staid European American designs, while the later pieces are full of motion." Day's work was also shaped by interactions with other regional craftsmen, including the Siewers brothers from Salem in 1838. According to some furniture historians, the "lounges" Day began to produce a few years later resemble contemporaneous Moravian examples in their incorporation of German classical, or Biedermeier, designs (figs. 8, 9). Although Day was receptive to new designs and endeavored to offer his clients the latest furniture fashions, his work remained highly individualistic (fig. 10). For art historian Richard Powell, Day's work reflects an improvisational impulse analogous to jazz.[13]

The recent exhibition and the publication *Thomas Day: Master Craftsman and Free Man of Color* offer a much-needed overview of his material legacy as a maker of furniture and architectural detail, but a fuller understanding of his life and work hinges on incorporating the newly found evidence about his abolitionist connections. This essay does not posit that the

Figure 10 Detail of the left term support of a chimneypiece documented to Thomas Day, William Long House, Blanch Community near Milton, North Carolina, ca. 1856. (Photo, Tim Buchman.)

maker's progressive social and political sentiments shaped his work, but it does aim to present that side of the story for future scholars to take into account. This new understanding begins with the discovery of the newspaper advertisement in which Day and others praised the amenities of the black boardinghouse they patronized in Philadelphia during the Fifth Convention for the Improvement of the Free People of Colour.

Serena Gardiner, an active member of that city's large free black community, owned the boardinghouse and provided rooms and meals for twenty-one men, including Thomas Day, for the duration of the convention. These boarders, in turn, signed the "Card" at the end of their stay, recommending her establishment as well as citing their reason for being in the city (fig. 11):

> We, the undersigned, having availed ourselves during the session of the colored Convention held in Philadelphia, June 1835 of Mrs. Serena Gardiner's select boarding house, No. 13, Elizabeth-street, are happy to say, that with its pleasant situation, the cleanliness of its apartments, the good order therein preserved, and its good table, we were highly pleased; and *to persons of color* visiting this city, who are prepared to appreciate the above advantages, we freely recommend her house, as possessing superior inducements to their patronage and support.

A CARD.

WE, the undersigned, having availed ourselves during the session of the colored Convention, held in Philadelphia, June, 1835, of Mrs. Serena Gardiner's select boarding house, No. 13, Elizabeth-street, are happy to say, that with its pleasant situation, the cleanliness of its apartments, the good order therein preserved, and its good table, we were highly pleased; and to persons of color visiting this city, who are prepared to appreciate the above advantages, we freely recommend her house, as possessing superior inducements to their patronage and support.

Wm. P. Powell, New Bedford.
Dr. James H. Fleet, District of Columbia.
Augustus Price, Washington, D. C.
John F. Cook,   do.
Henry Ogden, Newark, N. J.
John D. Closson,   do.
Alfred Niger, Providence, R. I.
Francis C. Lippins, Easton, Pa.
Justin Reynolds, North Carolina.
Charles C. Remond, Salem, Mass.
Nathen Gilbert, Providence, R. I.
Samuel Hardenburg, New York.
Wm. Hamilton,   do.
Wm. H. Noland, Washington, D. C.
John Peck, Carlisle, Pa.
Joseph J Roberts, Liberia, W. A.
Wm. N. Cobston, Petersburg, Va.
Wm. Whipper, Columbia, Pa.
Henry Scott, Worcetster, Mass.
Wm. Nickins, late of New Orleans.
Thomas Day, North Carolina.

Figure 11 "A Card," *Liberator*, August 8, 1835, p. 127. (Facsimile.)

Figure 12   *Liberator*, January 1, 1831. (Courtesy, Massachusetts Historical Society, Boston, Massachusetts.) The front page of the first edition features William Lloyd Garrison's famous "Open Letter to the Public," in which he stated, "I am in earnest—I will not equivocate—I will not excuse—I will not retreat a single inch and I WILL BE HEARD."

Figure 13   Photograph of William Lloyd Garrison. 3¼" x 3". (Courtesy, Prints of American Abolitionists Collection, Massachusetts Historical Society, Boston, Massachusetts.) An uncompromising moralist, Garrison was editor and publisher of the *Liberator* for more than thirty years and a founder of the American Anti-Slavery Society.

Eager for additional business, Gardiner published the "Card" in the *Liberator* (figs. 12, 13). It included the names and home states of all the men. Three were from the South, including Day, who appears last on the list as "Thomas Day, North Carolina." In her exuberance to advertise her business, Gardiner was not thinking that it would be dangerous for these southern men at home to be identified and linked to abolitionists in a national antislavery publication.[14]

Since Day was a common name and other Thomas Days resided in North Carolina, it is fitting that the identity of this person be questioned. Census records show that six men named Thomas Day lived in the state around this time. However, four were white and must be excluded since, with the exception of a handful of well-known white abolitionists named as "honorary delegates," the convention was black and so was the boardinghouse. No white

North Carolinians would have patronized an establishment for "genteel" and/or "respectable persons of color," as Gardiner and her husband, Peter, characterized it in multiple *Liberator* ads. Of the two black Thomas Days, the Caswell County cabinetmaker is the only one who fits the professional profile of Gardiner's elite and educated guests. The only other free black named Thomas Day was an illiterate, impoverished tenant farmer from Person County. His descendant Aaron Day, a noted genealogist, said that his ancestor did not have the means to travel far beyond Person County.[15]

The risk taken by Day in attending the convention cannot be overstated, and he would not have traveled north to meet with high-profile black activists in Philadelphia unless he was seriously interested in their beliefs and policies. The city, with its frequent white-on-black mob violence and escalating attacks on organized antislavery activity, was simply not a safe place for anyone of African descent in the late spring of 1835, and Day was the young parent of at least two children dependent on the well-being of their father.

Evidence of Day's presence in Philadelphia and his identification as a black abolitionist was hiding in plain sight for more than thirty years in *The Black Abolitionist Papers, 1830–1865: A Guide to the Microfilm Edition*. Issued before the release of the five-volume print series, *The Black Abolitionist Papers*, the *Guide* is an index to the massive collection of microfilmed documents and narratives gathered to identify the most significant black abolitionists in the Americas and the British Isles. The scholarly foreword explains how the activist figures were selected, and the *Guide* lists Thomas Day and all the guests at Mrs. Gardiner's boardinghouse. The "Card," the document that placed them there, has been part of the public record since 1981, when the *Guide* was published, but until 2009 no researcher had ever identified Thomas Day, the black abolitionist in Philadelphia, as the cabinetmaker from Milton.[16]

The discovery of the "Card" casts new light on Day's secret life and suggests the need to consider more closely his ancestry and formative years. Until the publication of Sneed and Westfall's 1995 research report, little was known about Day before his arrival in Milton. Census records indicated that he was born in Virginia but did not specify exactly where he was from or how he ended up in North Carolina. A passing mention of John Day Sr. in the Chancery Court records of Dinwiddie County brought the identities of Thomas's parents and grandfather to light. Citing "John Day and Mourning, his wife, formerly Mourning Stewart, one of the heirs . . . of Thomas Stewart the elder," the document contains details pertaining to the estate of a free black man, "Dr. Thomas A. Stewart," and listed the spouses of his many heirs. It was significant because an eighty-four-year-old woman named "Morning S. Day," presumably Thomas Day's mother, was listed in his Milton household in the 1850 census. She and Mourning Stewart Day turned out to be one and the same.[17]

Mourning's father, Thomas Stewart, like his grandson and namesake Thomas Day, was a prominent member of his community as well as a slaveholder. While not common, free black ownership of slaves was a fact of life not only in the South but also in the North. According to Franklin, "at no time during the antebellum period were free negroes in North Carolina without slaves." In Stewart's 1804 will, the first of two, he left a female slave to his grandson, "John Day, the son of Mourning," which made it clear that Mourning and John Day had a son named John as early as that year. In his study of hundreds of free black families born in Virginia, North Carolina, and South Carolina, genealogist Paul Heinegg listed a John Day, born in 1797, who had immigrated to Liberia and become a well-known missionary and statesman. Because that John Day was identified as a "cabinetmaker," Heinegg hypothesized that he was Thomas's brother. Heinegg had no proof of a fraternal relationship between the two Days but cited, as a source, a eulogy for John prepared at the time of his death. It appeared in the *African Repository*, the mouthpiece of the American Colonization Society, the organization that spearheaded the colonization of Liberia. The eulogy revealed that "Rev. John Day" had begun his work abroad with the "Northern Baptist Board of Missions" but had "subsequently become connected with the Southern Baptist Convention." From 1847 to 1859 he had served as superintendent for the Southern Baptist Foreign Missions Board and had overseen its missionary work in Sierra Leone, Central Africa, and Liberia "up to the hour of his death." Heinegg was correct in speculating that John was Thomas's brother.[18]

John Day was one of the most prolific correspondents of all nineteenth-century Baptist missionaries. He sent more than one hundred letters to the Reverend James B. Taylor, the corresponding secretary of the church's Foreign Mission Board. One John Day letter, written in 1847, confirmed what the court records from Dinwiddie County had implied: "My mother was the daughter of a coloured man of Dinwiddie County, Virginia, whose name was Thomas Stewart, a medical doctor, but when or how he obtained his education in that profession, I know not."[19]

Thomas Stewart, Thomas and John Day's grandfather, was born circa 1727 and was the son of a black man who remains unidentified and a white indentured servant, most likely a woman named Elizabeth Stuard, from whom, by law, he inherited his free legal status. Before the American Revolution, most southern free blacks were the mixed-race progeny of black enslaved or indentured men and white female indentured servants. Invariably identified in his adult years as "Dr. Stewart" in the tax rolls of Dinwiddie and Mecklenburg counties, Virginia, he owned substantial property and was by all accounts a well-known and respected local practitioner. Thomas Day's mother, Mourning Stewart Day, was the second daughter of at least fourteen children born to Dr. Stewart. She was the first child born after the death of his first wife and was apparently named in commemoration of the mourning period. In his autobiographical 1847 letter, John Day also identified his father as a cabinetmaker named John Day (Sr.). A letter written by the missionary's widow in 1860 confirmed that John and Thomas Day were brothers.[20]

Thomas Day was born into this respected and well-educated family in rural Dinwiddie County, about twenty-five miles southwest of Petersburg.

When he was six years old, his father, John Day Sr., moved the family to neighboring Sussex County, where John Jr., age ten, was boarding with a white acquaintance and being educated by white Baptist tutors. Thomas was apparently sent to the same school as his brother, and their father trained both sons in his trade. The Days moved in 1807, the same year Congress outlawed importation of slaves from Africa, but conditions for free black families in Virginia were precarious at best. Several factors, in addition to the opportunity to educate the sons, could have influenced the family's decision to move to Sussex, including prospects for work and an opportunity to buy property. Sussex had, in addition to Baptists, sizable Quaker and Methodist populations, and the Days were aware that members of those denominations could be important allies. Between 1784 and 1806, more than seventy-five Quaker and Methodist slaveholders in Sussex County manumitted 378 slaves. During the late eighteenth century, Quakers had become increasingly opposed to slavery (fig. 14), including those in Virginia, which had more free and enslaved people of African descent than any other state. One study shows that as early as 1767, Virginia

Figure 14 Jeremiah Paul, *Manumission of Dinah Nevill*, Philadelphia, Pennsylvania, ca. 1795. Oil on canvas. 50" x 39". (Private collection; photo, Gavin Ashworth.) This emotionally charged picture depicts Quaker tailor Thomas Harrison purchasing the freedom of "mulatto" slave Dinah Nevill from Benjamin Bannerman, Virginia planter. In 1773 Bannerman bought Nevill and her three children from Nathaniel Lowry of New Jersey and arranged for the family to be transported to Philadelphia. On their arrival in the city, Nevill made a public plea claiming that she and her children were free people. A group of Quakers filed suit to void Bannerman's claims, but the court ruled in the latter's favor. This decision and similar cases involving African Americans led to the formation of the Society for the Relief of Negroes Unlawfully Kept in Bondage, which would eventually become the Pennsylvania Abolition Society. Thomas Harrison (1741–1815), who was a founding member of that society, continued the effort to free Nevill and her children, and on May 18, 1779, he manumitted them with money provided by Quaker brewer Samuel Moore.

Quakers were "training enslaved people to be laborers in a free market. Monthly meetings loaned money to African American tradesmen and established apprenticeships for their children."[21]

Sussex lies northeast of Greensville County, where the family also had strong ties. Free black Days and Stewarts had lived in Greensville since before the American Revolution, and John Day Jr. was born there, at Hick's Ford (later Hicksford and now Emporia) in 1797. In an autobiographical letter, he claimed that his mixed-race father was the illegitimate son of a white woman and her black coach driver and was born in South Carolina and reared in North Carolina. Greensville County records strongly support, however, the view that John Day Sr. had Virginia roots, like his sons' maternal grandparents, the Stewarts. Heinegg's research points to another free black Greensville County man named John Day as the father of John Day Sr. This John Day paid taxes in the county from 1782 until his death in 1802. More to the point, he owned properties adjacent to known acquaintances of the free black Days, members of the Robinson and Jeffreys families.[22]

John and Thomas Day came of age during tumultuous times that included white retaliation for slave uprisings in which free blacks were often implicated for no reason other than they were already free. By the second decade of the nineteenth century, gradual improvements in roads and transportation had increased the flow of manufactured products, as large urban shops sold domestic goods and furniture through wider networks. This, in turn, affected many local artisans who could not compete with cheaper, and often more fashionable, factory-made products, including furniture. John Day Sr. was one of the artisans who had a hard time staying ahead financially, in part because he developed a drinking problem. John Jr. later recalled his own youthful efforts to keep his head above water after his father became "intemperate":

> In 1817 my father went over to North Carolina and left me in Dinwiddie to pay a debt he owed to Mr. John Bolling. I carried on a little cabinetmaking business in a village in that part of the county . . . paid my father's debt, and was likely to do well in the world's estimation, but associating myself with—young white men, who were fond of playing cards, contracted that habit. Mr. John L. Scott, a merchant and friend of mine came . . . to see me and I told him that if I continued in that place . . . I should ruin myself. He procured a shop for me about 7 miles off of Mrs. Ann Pryor's. I commenced well . . . but a drunken journeyman set fire to my shop and consumed all I had. The neighbors spoke of reinstating me, but I would not accept any thing but a coat and hat of my friend J. L. Scott. I went on my feet to Warren County, North Carolina and got in possession of my father's tools, borrowed money off a gentleman, and commenced work there.

It is not clear where Thomas and his mother were while John Jr. was working off the debt. Possibly Thomas worked for his father in North Carolina or spent some of the time helping his older brother meet family obligations while honing his own cabinetmaking skills.[23]

Research initiated in 1996 explored three centuries of Day family history and led to the discovery of Thomas Day's Bible, which was in the possession of his great-great-great-grandson Thomas Day V (fig. 15). Like many

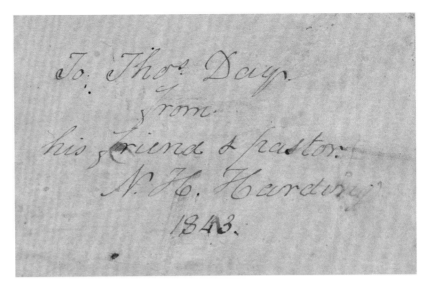

Figure 15 Inscription in Thomas Day's Bible written by his pastor, Nehemiah Henry Harding. (Collection of Dr. and Mrs. Thomas Baker Day; photo, courtesy, North Carolina Museum of History.)

Figure 16 The Reverend Nehemiah Henry Harding. (Courtesy, Presbyterian Heritage Center, Montreat, North Carolina.)

family Bibles, Thomas's is full of names and dates, including that of Annie Washington Day, that establish Thomas Day's connections to people in the North, including leading abolitionists. One of the most important names was that of N. H. Harding, who inscribed the Bible in 1843 and identified himself as Day's "friend and pastor."[24]

As noted by historian Peter H. Wood, "if Thomas Day offers one window into the complex world of antebellum race relations, his minister provides another." The Reverend Nehemiah Henry Harding, the minister of the Milton Presbyterian Church and a graduate of Princeton Theological Seminary, was from New England (fig. 16). The scion of a family of seafaring merchants, he experienced a shipboard conversion during a storm and changed careers. He arrived in Milton in 1835, the same year that Thomas Day attended the black convention in Philadelphia. "Slavery was the most controversial issue of the day," says Wood, "and everyone had strong opinions. Advocates could be found for armed revolt, peaceful petitioning, immediate freedom, gradual emancipation, African colonization or continued enslavement. As controversy swirled, individuals shifted their stance on the matter." This is particularly clear in the case of Harding, who "wrestled with this thorny issue." In the 1830s, on visits home to Brunswick, Maine, the abolitionist hotbed where Harriet Beecher Stowe would later write *Uncle Tom's Cabin*, Harding's position on slavery continued to evolve. On one visit, after a decade of living in a slave state, he said he was "pro slavery" when a Congregational minister asked where he stood. But, after returning to the South, he wrote back to the minister and said that he had experienced a change of heart. "After mature deliberation," Harding insisted, "I am now a strong-antislavery man . . . the sworn enemy of slavery in all its forms and with all its evils." During a subsequent visit north, he shifted course again and made what northern activists considered to be "'gratuitous and invidious remarks about the increasing militancy of abolitionists.' Asked to read an announcement addressing 'the duty of Christians . . . toward the colored people' he refused and preached a sermon warning Brunswick's citizens to beware of excessive zeal regarding their 'duty to the colored people.'"

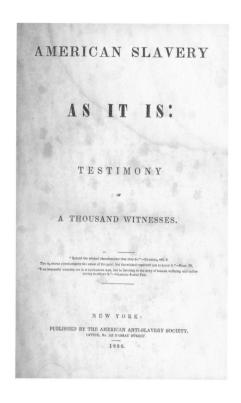

AMERICAN SLAVERY

AS IT IS:

TESTIMONY

OF

A THOUSAND WITNESSES.

"Behold the wicked abominations that they do."—Ezekiel, viii. 9.
The righteous considereth the cause of the poor; but the wicked regardeth not to know it."—Prov. 29.
"True humanity consists not in a squeamish ear, but in listening to the story of human suffering and endeavoring to relieve it."—Charles James Fox.

NEW YORK:
PUBLISHED BY THE AMERICAN ANTI-SLAVERY SOCIETY,
OFFICE, No. 143 NASSAU STREET.
1839.

Figure 17 Frontispiece, Theodore Dwight Weld, *American Slavery As It Is: Testimony of a Thousand Witnesses*, 1839. (Courtesy, Wilson Library, University of North Carolina, Chapel Hill, North Carolina.) This publication is a documentary account of slavery in all its brutality through first-hand testimonials and recollections of former slaves as well as white witnesses. It was distributed widely and is considered one of the most influential antislavery tracts. The Reverend Nehemiah Henry Harding, pastor of the Milton Presbyterian Church and friend of Thomas Day, is represented in the book with a quotation in which he condemns the immorality of slavery as an institution.

Harding likely assumed the changing story was playing out only in his inner circle, but his vacillations became public when a local antislavery advocate printed his letter in the *Liberator* in 1838 and parts of the letter were extracted and republished by Theodore Dwight Weld in the influential American Anti-Slavery Society publication, *American Slavery As It Is: Testimony of a Thousand Witnesses* (fig. 17):

> I am greatly surprised that I should in any form have been the apologist of a system so full of deadly poison to all holiness and benevolence as slavery—the concocted essence of fraud, selfishness and cold-hearted tyranny and the fruitful parent of unnumbered evils to the oppressor and the oppressed, the one thousandth part of which has never been brought to the light.

According to Wood, the influence of the book in which Harding's harsh condemnation of the institution of slavery appeared was second only to *Uncle Tom's Cabin*. "Perhaps Harding's views changed again during the last decade of his life through interaction with his most prominent black parishioner. . . . After all, he and Thomas Day were learning from experience that racial enslavement in the United States might outlast them both and that they needed to be guarded in their stated public opinions if they were to endure and prosper in North Carolina."[25]

Racial enslavement was indeed deeply rooted in the upper South and also in Thomas Day's own family, going back to his maternal grandfather and slave owner Thomas Stewart. Recent research into Day's formative years has uncovered an 1820 map of Dinwiddie County that pinpoints his birthplace: Thomas Stewart's homestead (fig. 18). The search also yielded the first contemporaneous confirmation of Stewart's medical practice, which appeared in the November 13, 1778, edition of the *Virginia Gazette*:

> I Nathaniel Hobbs of Dinwiddie County do hereby certify, that in the month of May last my negro boy Tom received a kick from a stallion in the forehead, which deprived him of his senses from Sunday until Tuesday evening in which time he lost a quantity of blood, and many ounces of matter, supposed to be part of his brain, but by the assistance of Dr. Thomas Stewart, of Dinwiddie, and his specifick balsam, he is now perfectly well and as sound and sensible as ever.

Beyond dispensing patent medicines, Stewart was a successful farmer and entrepreneur. He also was a free person of color who achieved a surprising level of success and who passed on his ideals and love of learning to his offspring and grandchildren. Details culled from the chancery proceedings and property records revealed that, in addition to large tracts of land, he owned a mill and a popular tavern located in his "mansion house." He ran these diverse operations with the help of his family and numerous enslaved workers.[26]

In 1810, the year he died, Stewart owned more than nine hundred acres in Dinwiddie County and, at the peak of his ownership, may have had as many as thirty-two slaves. His upward mobility undoubtedly was largely achieved through some combination of talent, resolve, and good fortune. However, the ownership of enslaved men, women, and children was

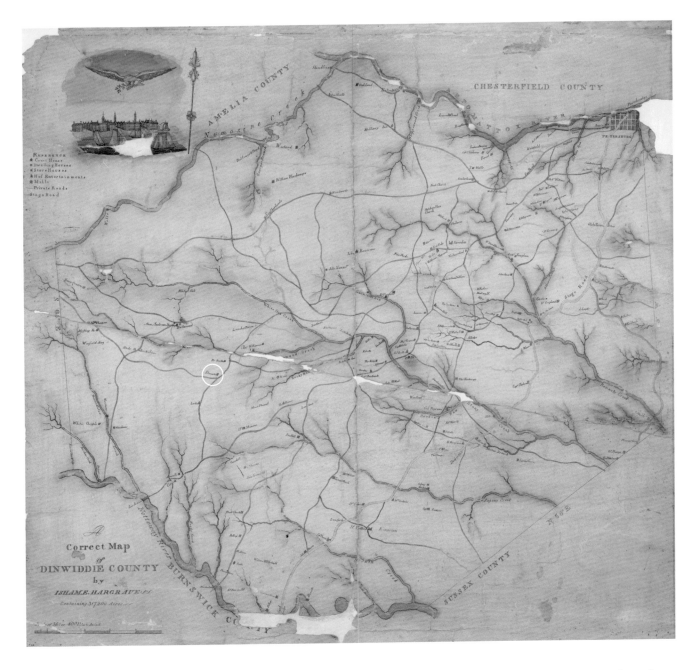

Figure 18   Isham E. Hargrave, "Correct Map of Dinwiddie County, Virginia containing 317,200 acres," ca. 1820. (Courtesy, Library of Virginia, Richmond, Virginia.) This map shows the "mansion house" of Thomas Day's maternal grandfather, Dr. Thomas Stewart, on present-day Old White Oak Road. Hargrave was the county's deputy surveyor.

another central factor in his climb, and this raised obvious questions about the mixed-race doctor's relationship with his slaves. Evidence suggests that Stewart's connection to his enslaved workers was not as exploitative as one might expect, given his driving ambition. In his 1804 will, he listed twenty-seven slaves by name and requested that sixteen of them be freed on his death. He also asked that some unnamed boys "whom I have emancipated" each be sent to school and then trained in a "good trade." The will was contested by "divers witnesses," likely family members to whom the slaves were more valuable as property that could be sold, and, based on their testimony, the court refused to admit the will to the record. After Stewart's death, twenty slaves he named in his will sued his heirs for their freedom but, ultimately, were unsuccessful in court.[27]

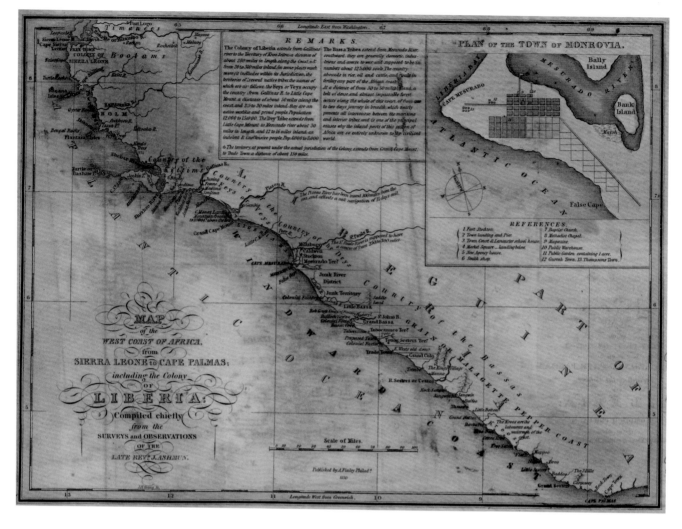

Figure 19 Jehudi Ashmun, "Map of the West Coast of Africa from Sierra Leone to Cape Palmas, including the Colony of Liberia," printed by A. Finley, Philadelphia, Pennsylvania, 1830. (Courtesy, Geography and Map Division, Library of Congress, Washington, D.C.) Thomas Day's brother John Day Jr. sailed for Liberia the same year this map was printed. John lived in Monrovia, which is depicted on this map, before embarking on his career as a missionary.

By 1820 both John and Thomas Day were in North Carolina living with their parents in a place identified in early census records as the Nutbush Voting District. This rural area lies in modern Bullocksville in what is now Vance County but was then part of Warren County. During this period, as in earlier generations, many free blacks crossed the Virginia border, heading south to escape escalating racist laws in the Old Dominion and to find cheaper, more fertile land in North Carolina. Soil depletion, the result of decades of tobacco cultivation, was another factor that compelled movement out of Southside Virginia. In John Day Sr.'s case, finding work was the likely motive. Many fine houses were built in the Nutbush region, and the inventory of tools from his 1832 estate papers suggests he was a house joiner as well as a furniture maker.[28]

In 1821 the Day brothers left Nutbush. Thomas, then twenty years old, went to Hillsborough, North Carolina's former capital. He opened a furniture-making shop, which he described in an advertisement as a "Stand," where he produced walnut and mahogany furniture. John Jr. moved to Milton, forty miles north of Hillsborough, to begin formal training to become a Baptist preacher. After completing his studies, however, white Baptist examiners accused him of misinterpreting church doctrine and refused to admit him to their ranks. It was a particularly disillusioning setback, and John strongly believed that he had been disapproved on spurious grounds. With a wife and young family to support, he needed to find a different way to uphold his beliefs and find his way in the world. One prospect was to leave America.

Many disheartened free blacks were drawn to the idea of migrating to Africa after the formation of the American Colonization Society in 1816. This did not reflect disloyalty to America but, rather, a loss of hope that Americans of African descent would ever be treated equally in the United States. "We love this country and its liberties," wrote a free black man in Illinois, "if we could share an equal right in them." White politicians who feared slave unrest, especially in the South, endorsed the idea of resettlement. In the dozen years after the American Colonization Society acquired control of Liberia in West Africa, more than 250 colonization societies sprang up across the South (fig. 19). Quakers and other religious sects initially supported colonization as a humane alternative to racial oppression in the United States. Eventually, however, many early supporters rejected the colonization movement as a racist scheme to rid the country of African Americans. Yet, along with nearly four thousand other free people of color from Virginia, John Day pulled up stakes and took his family to Africa in 1830, and over the course of the next half century, nearly fifteen thousand free black Americans did the same. The manifest of the ship on which Day traveled listed his occupation as cabinetmaker. In the years that followed, he emerged as a major religious and political leader, a proponent of Liberian colonization, and a critic of the institution of slavery.[29]

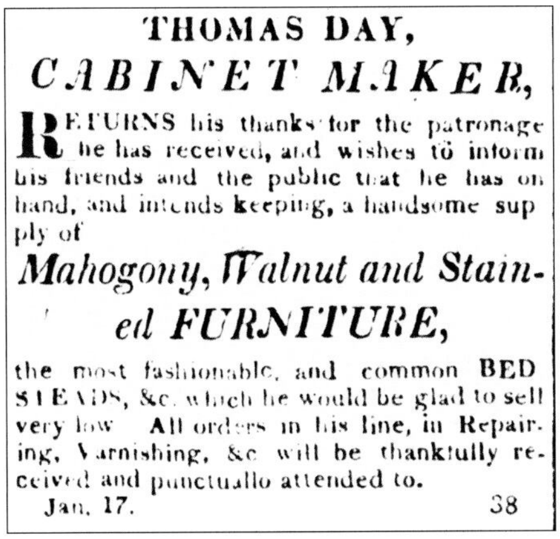

THOMAS DAY,

CABINET MAKER,

RETURNS his thanks for the patronage he has received, and wishes to inform his friends and the public that he has on hand, and intends keeping, a handsome supply of

Mahogony, Walnut and Stained FURNITURE,

the most fashionable, and common BED STEADS, &c. which he would be glad to sell very low. All orders in his line, in Repairing, Varnishing, &c. will be thankfully received and punctuallo attended to.

Jan. 17. 38

Figure 20 Advertisement for Thomas Day's shop, *Milton Gazette & Roanoke Advertiser*, March 1, 1827. (Courtesy, North Carolina Office of Archives and History, Raleigh, North Carolina.)

Historian Jill Baskin Schade recently discovered evidence that John Day initially worked as a cabinetmaker in Monrovia and that some of his furniture was exported to the American market. A March 1835 advertisement in the *African Repository* listed "African curiosities," including furniture made of Liberian wood by John Day, "a first rate cabinet-maker." Another advertisement placed in May 1836 reported that orders had been received from Baltimore and that two worktables had been shipped. Day's work as a missionary appears to have begun just two months later.[30]

Thomas Day had moved to Milton in the mid-1820s, and he remained in North Carolina. Perhaps recalling the ways that his grandfather had successfully navigated a slave-based society, he invested in the American free enterprise system despite its glaring inequalities. Day must have realized that in order to thrive in the South as a free person of color, he had to position himself as a part of mainstream society. He bought property in Milton and in 1827 opened a furniture-making shop. In an early advertisement in the *Milton Gazette & Roanoke Advertiser*, Day thanked his patrons for their furniture orders and assured them of punctual service (fig. 20). By this time, it appears that he was already a well-known and respected figure, one who gained unusual support from North Carolina's white political class.[31]

In 1826 the North Carolina state legislature enacted a law barring free blacks from entering the state. The law stipulated a $500.00 penalty, and anyone unable to pay could "be held in servitude" for up to ten years. After marrying Aquilla Wilson, a free black woman from nearby Halifax County, Virginia, on January 6, 1830, Day solicited help from his white neighbors, sixty-one of whom signed a petition requesting an exemption for his wife. The most prominent signature was that of Attorney General Saunders on the accompanying affidavit. This remarkable imprimatur from the state's highest legal authority not only expedited Day's legal request but also legitimized him in the eyes of the most powerful members of the state's gentry.[32]

The petition offers a telling example of the complicated and, at times, seemingly counterintuitive ways in which Day needed to operate in order to ensure his own financial success and local acceptance of his family. In the North, free African Americans and former slaves, like Frederick Douglass, who escaped enslavement in Maryland in 1838, could risk taking strong public stands against slavery. Day's situation, below the Mason-Dixon Line, however, was far more precarious and required subtle forms of resistance. According to Ira Berlin:

> He [Day] accepts the law but requests exceptional treatment. This makes him different from someone like Douglass who challenges the legal system and demands the abolition of slavery and the discriminatory racist laws that support it. . . . We see a "personal" approach—enlisting one's customers and neighbors rather than . . . directly challenging the . . . system.[33]

As with many other successful African American business people, Day developed strategies that allowed him to live and work within the prevailing system and thrive as a member of the local community. By all outward accounts, he appeared to be someone who played by the rules of the day and did not stray too far afield from accepted social practice. But as was the case with many other free people of color, Day seems to have led a far more complicated life, one that was characterized by covert actions and beliefs that ran counter to his public persona.

Political scientist James C. Scott provides useful terms to describe the ways that subordinate groups, including free and enslaved African Americans during the antebellum period, resisted domination and found ways to survive and live within extremely constrained, inhumane circumstances. Scott's theory spells out the universal practice of marginalized people who pretend to support their suppressors and their institutions rather than suffer the dire consequences they would incur with overt challenges. They protect themselves by wearing a "mask" of accommodation. In North Carolina, a frontal attack on racist laws by a black man would have provoked certain retaliation. Scott calls the professed acceptance of the status quo a "public transcript," and what subordinated people actually say and do behind their suppressors' backs, a "hidden transcript." From his perspective, Day and other free blacks in the South were forced to create a "public transcript," as both political strategy and survival tactic. Day's apparent acceptance of state law and his personal petition for his wife's exemption from it did not overtly threaten the racist status quo. Instead, the petition demonstrated that he was willing to work within the established system. Basing their actions on the side of Thomas Day they thought they knew, the leading citizens of

Milton had publicly attested to their belief that he seemed cautious and accommodating on racial matters, unwilling to organize with others openly to fight long-standing discrimination. Scott takes note of the "immense political terrain that lies between quiescence and revolt." It is this political "middle ground" between complete acquiescence and outright defiance that Day and many other free blacks in the South cultivated for their survival.[34]

Had Day lived long enough or written more, scholars today might have clearer insight into his true feelings about slavery as well as his strategies for navigating society in Milton. Despite lack of access to whatever thoughts he privately entertained, some understanding can be gleaned from a variety of historical sources. The furniture maker's sole specific pronouncement on the subject is ambiguous. When his daughter Mary Ann blamed her older brother Devereux's "depraved" behavior on being raised in a "shop of the meanest of God's avocation," Day rose to his own defense, praising the "respectable" character of the shop and the honesty of its "hands," many of whom were not slaves at that time. Mary Ann went on to claim that "being born in the Oppressive South has had a miserable influence on our family." Again, Day assumed the mantle of a loving father who seemingly was content with the world that he had created for his family: "It pleased the Lord to create Adam and Eve in Eden & it also pleased the Lord to permit you to [be] born in Milton & the best thing you do will be to improve the privileges before you and make yourself acquainted with useful learning and embrace all possible opportunities for spiritual and temporal knowledge."[35]

Day's measured response indicates that he understood his marginalized position and the necessity of being well regarded by white elites. However, some of his comments are open to different interpretations. In a letter to Mary Ann, Day wrote, "Ever regard your Caracter more than your life." Although this can be read as an admonition to maintain respectability at all costs, he may have been advising his daughter, in somewhat veiled manner, to remain true to her own values no matter what situation arises. Maintaining an unassailable reputation was the best protection for Day and his family. Ownership of slaves gave him something in common with his white neighbors and reaffirmed their belief that he was an exception to the prevailing assumption of white superiority and black inferiority. Yet, just as Day's writings are more complicated than they first appear, so too was his ownership of slaves. The respect accorded to Day by fellow African Americans and white activists in the abolitionist cause suggests motives other than profit and self-protection.[36]

Slavery was pervasive in the South, and free African Americans of means—almost all, like Day, of mixed racial heritage and appearance—were often active participants. Southern whites were three times more likely to own slaves than southern free blacks, a group that constituted a relatively small percentage of the total population, but in 1830 in North Carolina alone, nearly two hundred free blacks owned slaves. According to historian Juliet E. K. Walker, a leading scholar of the African American business tradition, "Facing competition from slave-owning white craftsmen, free black craftsmen needed slave ownership to have any chance of success. In a slave owning society, was there an alternative to unpaid labor?" Slave ownership also guaranteed a dependable source of labor that, in Day's case, could be supplemented with hired help when a particular job paid enough to justify it.[37]

One of the challenges to understanding ownership of slaves by free blacks is interpreting and weighing the evidence. Most information pertaining to slaves in free black households comes from census records, which are notoriously prone to error. Census takers did not require the person being interviewed to provide documentation regarding the number of family members and/or slaves in a household or their ages. And because slave ownership was one of the best ways for free blacks to demonstrate compliance with the prevailing social system, it was in their best interest to report and even inflate the numbers of slaves they owned. Increasingly, historians are giving credence to this "self-protection" motive. Of course, owners had to pay

Figure 21 "Whatnot," or étagére, attributed to Thomas Day, Milton, North Carolina, 1853–1860. Mahogany and mahogany veneer with yellow pine, tulip poplar, and walnut. H. 69¾", W. 40", D. 16". (Private collection; courtesy, Renwick Gallery of the Smithsonian American Art Museum; photo, Tim Buchman.) Day made this étagére for Milton merchant John Wilson.

property tax on slaves claimed to be in their possession, but for a free African American living in the racist South, that "insurance" may have been well worth the price.

Thomas Day took a hands-on approach to his business, acting as workshop manager, craftsman, and salesman. As the owner of his shop, he employed whites and free blacks as well as slaves throughout his career (figs. 21, 22). When he recruited five white Moravian artisans, including the Siewers brothers from Salem at the end of the 1830s, Day owned three slaves and employed "some fifteen hands, both white and colored." Records show that he owned slaves for at least three decades, increasing his holdings from two in 1830 to fourteen at the apex of his career in 1850. The "Slave Schedule" for the U.S. census that year indicates that six of the fourteen were males between the ages of fifteen and thirty and four were children under ten, the

Figure 22 Thomas Day, lady's open pillar bureau, Milton, North Carolina, 1855. Mahogany and mahogany veneer with yellow pine and tulip poplar. H. 85", W. 42⅛", D. 20⅞". (Collection of the North Carolina Museum of History, purchase funds provided by Delta Sigma Theta Sorority, Inc.; courtesy, Renwick Gallery of the Smithsonian American Art Museum; photo, Tim Buchman.) Day made this bureau for former North Carolina governor David S. Reid, who lived in Rockingham County.

Figure 23 Thomas Sully, *Joseph Jenkins Roberts* (1808–1876), Philadelphia, Pennsylvania, 1844. Oil on canvas. 33⅞" x 29⅜". (Historical Society of Pennsylvania Collection; courtesy, Philadelphia History Museum at the Atwater Kent, Philadelphia, Pennsylvania.) Roberts, a Petersburg, Virginia, merchant, was the first president of Liberia and one of the twenty-one men who lodged in Mrs. Gardiner's Philadelphia boardinghouse during the black abolitionist convention of 1835.

youngest being seven years old. According to this same census, five of the seven cabinetmakers in the shop were white, the only free blacks being Day and his seventeen-year-old son Devereux, both designated mulatto or mixed race. By 1860 he was one of only eight free black slaveholders remaining in North Carolina, with two slaves listed in residence and one as fugitive. Many free blacks left the state in the decades before the Civil War as a result of increasingly constricting social and economic conditions.[38]

Day bravely countered the rising racial restrictions by traveling beyond the scrutiny of white Milton, in part to explore what the abolitionist movement had to offer, including educational and professional opportunities. The 1835 convention, which took place at Philadelphia's second largest black church, had been heavily promoted in the abolitionist press, and the city was packed with attendees who "despite their wealth and degree of refinement . . . could not be sure of getting a room in one of Philadelphia's hotels." Eleven of Serena Gardiner's guests were official delegates, and three had been delegates to previous conventions, as had her husband. In addition to Day, the gentlemen she listed included Charles Lenox Remond, a fiery orator from Salem, Massachusetts, and a regular on the international antislavery lecture circuit; Joseph Jenkins Roberts of Monrovia, the future

Figure 24 William Whipper, attributed to William Matthew Prior, Philadelphia, Pennsylvania, 1835. Oil on canvas. 24¾" x 20⅛". (Courtesy, Fenimore Art Museum, Cooperstown, New York, gift of Steven C. Clark; photo, Richard Walker.) Whipper was a wealthy Pennsylvania lumber and coal merchant and a founder of the American Moral Reform Society. He delivered the keynote address at the 1835 convention in Philadelphia and signed the "Card," which places him in the city and the boardinghouse with Thomas Day and John Francis Cook. When a white mob tried to destroy Cook's school in Washington two months after the convention, he fled to Whipper's hometown, Columbia, Pennsylvania.

Figure 25 The Reverend John Francis Cook, shown in a copy of a newspaper photograph presented to the Moorland-Spingarn Research Center of Howard University in Washington, D.C. by Cook's descendants. (Courtesy, Moorland-Spingarn Research Center, Howard University, Washington, D.C.)

first and seventh president of Liberia and close friend of the Reverend John Day; William Hamilton of New York, the keynote speaker at the previous convention; Samuel Hardenburgh, also from New York, grand marshal in the parade that marked the end of slavery in New York State; and William Whipper, a Pennsylvania coal and lumber merchant, one of the wealthiest free black men in America (figs. 23, 24). Whipper operated a major Underground Railroad station in Columbia, Pennsylvania, for more than twenty years, often concealing fugitive slaves in his company's shipping cars. After slavery ended and he was safe to discuss his role, he described his home, a safe harbor at the end of a bridge across the Susquehanna, as a main "point of entry" for fugitives fleeing Maryland and Virginia.[39]

Others who signed the "Card" included three Washington, D.C., delegates: Dr. James H. Fleet, John Francis Cook, and Augustus Price. An accomplished music teacher, Fleet was "conceded to be the foremost colored man in culture, in intellectual force and general influence in the District at that time." Cook was a former slave who devoted his life to educating black children and in 1841 founded the esteemed Washington institution now known as the Fifteenth Street Presbyterian Church (fig. 25).

Emancipated two and a half years before the Philadelphia convocation, he served as its secretary and was an organizer of the American Moral Reform Society. (Its formation was a centerpiece of the 1835 convention, and the organization actually superseded the convention originally planned for the following year.)[40]

Cook, born in 1810, came from a family of activists. His aunt Alethia Browning Tanner purchased her own freedom and that of at least eighteen friends and relatives, including Cook, his mother, and his siblings. She was an astute real estate investor and a leader of Washington's early free black community. She also purchased slaves with the express purpose of setting them free. Cook's uncle George Bell cofounded the city's first school for colored children in 1807. Cook's son George later became the first superintendent of the District's "colored schools," and his son John served as the city's tax collector and represented the city at three Republican National Conventions during Reconstruction. At the time of the convention, Augustus Price, a co-author of Whipper's keynote speech—the American Moral Reform Society's manifesto—was an aide to Andrew Jackson, the sitting president of the United States. Described as "the president's trusted servant," "private secretary," and "White House doorkeeper," Price was "present at private White House meetings and cabinet discussions" and also "apparently helped the president draft important documents."[41]

Cook and Price were deeply involved in local abolitionist efforts. Cook had organized a secret debating club, where he led passionate antislavery discussions and distributed "seditious" publications such as the *Liberator* to young blacks. Following the June convention, he "breathed the gospel of freedom and reform as never before . . . and told them that white Americans and their laws sorely abused them as people of color." That August Washington experienced its first major episode of white mob violence against African Americans. Hundreds of armed white men attacked black people, and both Price and Cook were targeted. After his school was nearly destroyed, Cook fled the city on horseback and headed for Columbia, Pennsylvania, where his friend William Whipper resided. For distributing incendiary papers "from the North," Price was chased by an angry mob that threatened to "enter and search the White House" for him. Price was admitted b ut the mob was stopped at the door.[42]

While attending the 1835 convention, Day must have been struck by the cultural contrasts between Milton and Philadelphia. The northern city had a large free black population and was the birthplace of the first abolition society established in the western world. By 1838 the city was home to sixteen black churches, twenty-three day schools, four literary societies, three debating societies, three libraries, four temperance societies, and eighty relief or beneficial organizations. It would be difficult to imagine Day not visiting one or more of these organizations, socializing with activists developing the convention platform at Mrs. Gardiner's boardinghouse, or seeking out local power brokers who once called North Carolina home.[43]

A short list of transplanted North Carolinians living in Philadelphia at this time included former slave Frederick Augustus Hinton, a prosperous

Figure 26 Edward Williams Clay, "Philadelphia Fashions, 1837," printed and published by H. R. Robinson, New York City, ca. 1837. Lithograph. 18½" x 12¾". (Courtesy, The Library Company of Philadelphia.) This image is one of a series of racist cartoons that satirized the dress and manners of Philadelphia's most affluent African Americans. The male figure is believed to be the well-known barber and social activist Frederick Augustus Hinton and the female, his second wife, Eliza Willson. African American stereotypes such as this were pervasive in mid-nineteenth-century America and reveal that racism was accepted in the North despite the fact that free blacks had more freedoms and greater opportunities there than in the South.

barber from Raleigh; Hinton's father-in-law, oyster seller Richard Howell; and Junius C. Morel, a militant writer and educator (fig. 26). All had close ties to the black convention movement since 1830, when forty free black leaders gathered in the city to form the American Society of Free Persons of Colour. (Morel and Richard Allen, founder of the African Methodist Episcopal Church, wrote and signed the manifesto that called for the first official convention in 1831 and promoted immigrating to Canada rather than Liberia.) Historian Julie Winch noted that Hinton, the Howells, and the Gardiners were all related by marriage. Hinton, a "tireless crusader for abolition" who promoted the radical journal *The Rights of All*, was also an agent for the *Liberator*. He was involved in multiple activist causes including the Pennsylvania Anti-Slavery Society and the Philadelphia Library Company of Colored Persons. He pressed for the restoration of free black suffrage after Pennsylvania took it away in 1838, and he was active in the American Moral Reform Society. Junius Morel, the son of a white slave owner, wrote for and raised funds for abolitionist newspapers and fought African colonization, likening Liberia to "Golgotha" and "a kind of Botany Bay for the United States." After the passage of the Fugitive Slave Law, he grew even more radical and encouraged African Americans to "defend themselves with force if force was used against them." Morel's closest friend was the first

Figure 27 Engraving depicting Charles Bennett Ray, from Carter G. Woodson, *The Negro in Our History* (Washington, D.C.: Associated Publishers, 1922), p. 146. Ray was a businessman, preacher, and operative with the Underground Railroad. He also served as an agent and later as publisher and editor of the influential black abolitionist newspaper the *Colored American*, which encouraged the moral, social, and political improvement of African Americans and endorsed a peaceful end to slavery. A native of Falmouth, Massachusetts, he was the first black graduate of Wesleyan Academy in Wilbraham, the same abolitionist-led school where Thomas Day later sent his three children.

black graduate of Wesleyan Academy in Wilbraham, Massachusetts, the Reverend Charles Bennett Ray, publisher and editor of the *Colored American*, an early New York–based black weekly (fig. 27). Ray was a founding member of the New York City Vigilance Committee.[44]

The convention of 1835 and subsequent antislavery meetings were widely covered in the abolitionist press and closely followed by educated African Americans. Free black elites were a small but extremely well-connected group. If they did not know one another personally, they certainly knew about each other. According to historian Winch, sail maker James Forten, one of Philadelphia's wealthiest and most influential black abolitionists, "received a constant stream of guests and callers . . . dozens of visitors from all over the United States and Britain, referred . . . by his network of acquaintances." Such northern networks overlapped whenever possible with others in the South, where many slaves were clearly cognizant of free blacks and whites who might offer assistance with their flight or resettlement. When Harriet Jacobs fled from Edenton, North Carolina, to Philadelphia in 1842, a member of that city's Vigilance Committee spotted her and took her to a safe house. "She had come to Philadelphia with the names of black folks from Chowan County who had settled in the city and with the knowledge repeatedly condemned by the *Edenton Gazette*, that the poor slave had many friends in the North." Evidently, so did Thomas Day.[45]

While Day was in Philadelphia, white North Carolinians convened a state constitutional convention in Raleigh, where voting rights took center stage. In the end, the right to vote was extended to white men who did not own property and taken away from free black men, including property holders like Thomas Day. The vote was close—sixty-six "yeas" and sixty-one "nays"—with Caswell County's two representatives voting for disenfranchisement and Day's future benefactor, then Governor Swain, voting to retain free black suffrage. On July 4, the *Liberator* published a letter that had appeared earlier in the *Fayetteville Observer*, noting that the state's two wealthiest free black slave owners, Louis Sheridan and John Carruthers Stanly, had been in a unique and powerful position to protest the loss of their right to vote. The letter stated, "free Negroes such as . . . Sheridan . . . and . . . Stanly . . . should have plead trumpet-tongued in behalf of the more respectable portion of this degraded class." But there is no evidence that either of them—or Thomas Day—uttered a word of protest. Taking an overt political stand would have been useless and self-destructive.[46]

As affluent, mixed-race North Carolina businessmen and slave owners, Sheridan and Stanly shared many similarities with Day, especially survival strategies used to deflect criticism and circumvent the shoals of racism in the state. Of the three, Stanly was the wealthiest and owned more slaves than any other free black man in the South. Born into slavery in New Bern in 1774, he was of Day's parents' generation, the son of a white merchant with extensive shipping interests and an enslaved African. Privately tutored and highly literate, Stanly was a barber. Like Day, he was extremely concerned about his public image. Emancipated at the age of twenty-one, unsatisfied that his "free papers" constituted sufficient certification of his legal status, he successfully petitioned the General Assembly in 1798 to "confirm, establish, and Secure [your] petitioner his Freedom with the rights and privileges attendant thereon." As Day would later do with his petition on behalf of Aquilla, Stanly used this request both as a means to reinforce the legitimacy of his freedom and as a tool to publicize himself.[47]

A member of the Presbyterian Church in New Bern, he sat in the sanctuary with the white congregation—as did Day in Milton—instead of in the upstairs gallery reserved for other persons of color. Stanly also had numerous business dealings with leading whites, the most important of whom was his half brother, a congressman and banker. Even though his prominent kinsman was a known highflyer and speculator, Stanly cosigned a bank note for him. Saddled with debt when the loan came due, Stanly was forced to mortgage many of his properties, which was the beginning of a downward financial spiral from which he never recovered. At the height of his success, he owned four plantations—a total of 2,600 acres—exclusive of his city holdings and more than 150 slaves. Stanly has often been considered a banner example of exploitative free black slave ownership whose views meshed inextricably with those of white New Bern. At the time of his death circa 1846, "few of his white neighbors considered him much different from themselves in the feeling that the South's 'peculiar institution' was the capstone of a unique and advanced civilization." According to one neighbor, "J. C. Stanly was a man of dignified presence, and lived in fashionable style, his sons and daughters being well educated and always making a good appearance as bright mulattoes. No citizen of Newbern would hesitate to walk the streets with him. He was uniformly courteous and unobtrusive."[48]

Had Stanly's white associates looked beyond appearances, they might have detected ways that he and his family were different from them. While Stanly has been described as a "hard task-master . . . who fed and clothed [his slaves] indifferently," he was also directly involved in obtaining the freedom of nearly thirty slaves. Franklin described him as the "most influential free Negro in the manumission movement."[49]

Louis Sheridan, who was born circa 1788, was another notable free African American businessman and slave owner who was later chastised for failing to stand up to the loss of free black suffrage. Born in Elizabethtown, he was also the offspring of a white man and an enslaved woman. After gaining his freedom, he prospered as the owner of a dry goods store, became a major real estate investor, and purchased numerous properties in town and in surrounding Bladen County. Like Day and Stanly, Sheridan built a large network of social and business relationships with whites in high places and appeared to accept the norms of white supremacy by owning slaves. His immediate circle included former governor John Owen, an Elizabethtown native who had openly opposed the loss of suffrage for free blacks. There were, however, cracks in Sheridan's mask of accommodation, and in time they deepened. In 1828 his name appears as an authorized agent for the nation's first black newspaper, *Freedom's Journal*. Though he later denied it, he also appears to have served as agent for that paper's radical successor, *The Rights of All*, disassociating himself from the publication after the *Cape Fear*

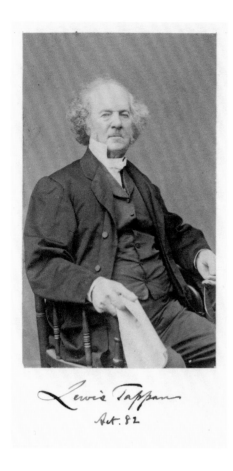

Figure 28　Photograph of Lewis Tappan. 9" x 6" (Courtesy, Massachusetts Historical Society, Boston, Massachusetts, Prints of American Abolitionists Collection.) Tappan, a prominent New York City merchant, and his brother Arthur were among the founders of the American Anti-Slavery Society and their credit-reporting firm was the precursor of Dun & Bradstreet. The diary of the Reverend John Francis Cook of Washington, D.C., reveals that Lewis Tappan was among the many prominent northern abolitionists who corresponded with and visited the minister.

Recorder denounced him for supporting it. In a letter to the editor, he disclaimed "all connection" with northern political elements and exploited his impeccable reputation to ingratiate and distance himself:

> I will appeal to my general conduct in society and to all who know me of every class in the community and challenge one and all to produce any evidence of a solitary instance in which I have by word or deed hinted at or countenanced such mischievous effects as are attributed to the "Rights of All" and to other papers or pamphlets published in the Northern States.[50]

The letter appeased Sheridan's critics, but his words and actions over the next few years suggest that he shared sentiments articulated in northern antislavery publications, including *The Rights for All*. In the end, he freed his slaves and sailed for Liberia. In August 1838, eight months after his departure, the *Colored American* quoted from a letter he had written to New York City businessman and abolitionist Lewis Tappan (fig. 28), citing his growing desperation at the overt racism he was experiencing:

> Our cast being that in which the smallest degree of interest is conceived, nothing possible to be done is left unattempted to degrade and bring us down below the standing of their very slaves and the consequence is that under the now existing state of things, we the free people of color are denuded of all privileges marking the attributes of a man.

Originally Sheridan considered Liberian colonization the greatest "humbug ever palmed off on the American people," but after being disenfranchised, he thought it only a matter of time before blacks would be banished from the United States. On December 30, 1837, he emigrated with his immediate family and more than fifty of his former slaves. The expatriation proved disastrous. He lost family members to disease, and by the time of his own death in 1844, he had become persona non grata in Liberia because of his public condemnation of government corruption there.[51]

Like Day, Stanly and Sheridan exemplify the complexities and seeming contradictions of free black identity in a time and place where whites held all the cards. For all their grand visions and bold initiatives, the success of these two men was ultimately measured in the terms of property they amassed, especially human chattel. Yet, even after he emancipated sixteen slaves in order to go to Liberia, Sheridan felt that he was still not "freed from the tyranny of the white man even on African soil." For generations, many mainstream historians stressed that most free people of color who possessed slaves did so to conform to white planter values and to participate in the profits of the "peculiar institution" often in imitation of their own white forebears. Growing evidence, however, suggests that some free blacks "owned" slaves in order to protect and or free them. Stanly and Sheridan's motives for slave-holding appear to be equally mixed: exploitative, in that forced labor clearly gave them the economic advantage they sought; self-protective, in that slave ownership elevated them in the esteem of their white neighbors; and benevolent, especially when it came to purchasing relatives and close acquaintances. Nowhere is this divide more evident than in Stanly's case. By all accounts, he thought nothing of breaking up families of slaves who worked his fields, but he felt quite differently about the enslaved relatives he diligently fought to manumit. His 1802 petition to free two of his sons whom he had purchased from white owners illustrates the remarkably stark difference in his feelings toward the latter. "It is inconsistent with nature," he wrote to the members of the North Carolina General Assembly, "for the parent to wish his child in a state of vassalage, either to another or himself."[52]

With the newer understanding of Day's ties to abolitionist events, schools, and ideational leaders, questions emerge about exactly how he might have interacted with or supported his own slaves. Aside from extolling their good character to Mary Ann, all that is known from the written record is that he and his wife hosted a church session meeting at their home when their "servant," Cory, joined the Presbyterian congregation, and that Day trusted two slaves, Samuel and David, to handle money. Oral history in the Milton area continues to circulate stories of Day's hiding fugitive slaves in his basement and smuggling them out in furniture and caskets. Some descendants of Thomas Day and of other free black families in North Carolina also mention hearing that Thomas Day was protecting and assisting slaves. Existing documents, including one of Day's letters to his daughter, suggest that this hypothesis merits further investigation.[53]

Historian Peter Wood presented a possible scenario for the true nature of Day's cabinetmaking operation. When asked, "How might a southern-born free black also be an abolitionist?" Wood responded, "We don't know for sure but we suspect" that Day's shop "could have been a far South station of the Underground Railroad." Day "could have treated his slaves hard or he could have been playing within the system and protecting them. He goes with the law but doesn't resist it in overt ways." Considering the circumstances, "it makes sense that he is not taking a Nat Turner role. Instead, he could have told his slaves 'I am the boss. I'm going to help you learn a trade. You can't get out of here immediately on your own, but here you'll get better treatment than you'd get at the tobacco plantation down the road.' . . . So someone could work for Day and later perhaps move on to the North and have a skill and be out from under slavery." Certainly Day's shop was capable of offering considerable artisanal training to white and African American workers alike.[54]

By 1850 the shop in Milton produced one-sixth of all furniture made in the state, a stunningly high proportion given that location. A pillar of the community, Day owned three properties in town, a 270-acre farm in the county, and shares in the local bank. After winning a contract from the University of North Carolina to furnish and fabricate architectural details for two debating society libraries and halls, he purchased the Union Tavern, the most significant piece of real estate in Caswell County. A fine example of federal architecture, the tavern had been a popular public hostel and stagecoach stop since its completion in 1818. Day's ownership of property was not unusual since free blacks were not legally excluded from doing so. However, his purchase of Milton's most prominent building and conversion of that structure into his home and business were at odds with the prevailing social norms of North Carolina. The 1842 narrative of Lunsford Lane, who had purchased his own freedom with funds earned while still an enslaved entrepreneur in Raleigh, describes a more common mode of comportment:

> I had endeavored . . . not to become obnoxious to the white inhabitants knowing as I did, their power and their hostility to the colored people. . . . First I had made no display of the little property or money I possessed but in every way I wore as much as possible the aspect of poverty. Second, I had never appeared to be even so intelligent as I really was. This all colored at the south, free and slaves, find is necessary for their own comfort and safety to observe.[55]

Day (who was a good bit wealthier, and whiter, than Lane) did not feel compelled to hide his success, intelligence, or confidence in his abilities. When advised that he had been selected to make shelves for the debating society libraries in Chapel Hill, he wrote President Swain and asked him to "measure the length of your Books and the Depth of the shelves accurately." In a similar vein, Day occasionally disagreed with white patrons over matters of taste. He countered a proposal to furnish the university's debating halls with chairs by proposing high-backed benches, which he considered more practical: "anything you please . . . rather than chairs tumbling about the rising floors." He subsequently stated that the "common" red damask selected for upholstering the benches would look "too cheap" and persuaded the debating societies' representatives to approve an expensive corded "figured damask," which would be "more durable & a great deal handsomer." Although it is now clear that Day withheld some of his criticisms, the mere fact that he was willing to vigorously disagree with his white patrons is significant. As historian Loren Schweninger notes, "even the most prosperous mulattoes were constantly reminded that the slightest miscalculation, the most innocent breaching of social etiquette, an ill chosen word, could result in a violent confrontation."[56]

There are several reasons that perhaps explain why Thomas Day was able to sidestep the normal behavioral expectations of people of color. Affluent whites in the Carolina piedmont were anxious to acquire his work, and some of his property acquisitions may have been seen as beneficial to the Milton community. The fact that the Union Tavern came on the market in 1848 suggests that it needed to be repurposed to be productive. The consistently rising level of production of Day's shop and the elevated social standing of his clientele indicate that his business skills and political acumen were exceptional. His light skin color—he was described in censuses as a "mulatto"—also likely contributed to the level of acceptance he had among whites. Milton locals reportedly described him as a "straight-haired West Indian" married to a "Portuguese" woman, intimating that neither he nor his wife was dark-skinned. Day's level of education also gave him a demonstrable advantage in his interactions with the citizens of Milton, the majority of whom were less educated than Day.[57]

By the 1840s meaningful educational opportunities for free people of color in North Carolina were virtually nonexistent. A proposal "prohibiting a free Negro from teaching his own children or causing them to be educated" was introduced at the 1834–1835 session of the General Assembl—just five months before Day's trip to the Philadelphia convention. The measure failed to pass, but the handwriting was on the wall. In 1844 the state excluded all people of color from its "common" or public schools. Although there was no statute against teaching free blacks privately, "public opinion refused to countenance any such procedure." In 1850 only 217 free blacks in North Carolina "were receiving some form of education." According to one study, private schools for blacks in the upper South were "inferior," which led some parents of means to send their children to "John Francis Cook's Union Seminary School in the District of Columbia where the curriculum included reading, composition, recitation, sculpture, physiology and health."[58]

Day sent his children to Wesleyan Academy (fig. 29), which was more than six hundred miles from Milton. The head of the Massachusetts school was the Reverend Miner Raymond, a noted Methodist cleric whom a contemporary described as a "flaming abolitionist." Day could have learned about the school from any number of sources, including contacts within the

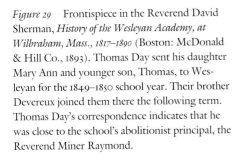

Figure 29 Frontispiece in the Reverend David Sherman, *History of the Wesleyan Academy, at Wilbraham, Mass., 1817–1890* (Boston: McDonald & Hill Co., 1893). Thomas Day sent his daughter Mary Ann and younger son, Thomas, to Wesleyan for the 1849–1850 school year. Their brother Devereux joined them there the following term. Thomas Day's correspondence indicates that he was close to the school's abolitionist principal, the Reverend Miner Raymond.

convention movement, but a likely source was John Cook, who corresponded with Day and had abolitionist connections all over the country. Day could also have heard about Wesleyan from his minister, whose sister, Sophia Harding Snow, lived in Boston, which was home to many Wesleyan students. The school offered a broad and advanced curriculum that was heavy on mathematics, science, and languages. The academy's "Teacher's Department" could also have been an enticement, especially for Mary Ann, who, in fact, became a teacher. According to its 1849–1850 catalogue, the school launched a new course to future educators to teach reading, writing, arithmetic, and spelling the semester that Mary Ann arrived. It is also possible that Day learned about Wesleyan while attending an abolitionist convention. Berlin has asserted that Day's participation in such gatherings, "together with his connection with the abolitionist school in Massachusetts, reveals another side of him." This "secret life" included "ties with important elements of the activist black community engaged in self-help, racial uplift and anti-slavery projects."[59]

Five years after the Philadelphia convention, a man identified as "Thomas Day Jr." appears on the attendance roster of a similar, but larger, gathering in New York City: the Seventh Annual Meeting of the American Anti-Slavery Society, which convened at the Fourth Free (Presbyterian) Church just off Chatham Square (fig. 30). This individual is listed with the New York City delegation. No Thomas Day Jr. is noted in the city directory for that year or in the 1840 census, and no other American Thomas Day can be identified who was associated with the antislavery movement. Thomas Day of Milton had business contacts and friends in New York City, so his inclusion in the New York delegation is plausible. By 1840 he had worked with an old-guard hardware firm, W. N. Seymour & Co., for at least five years as well as with a commission agent named James Hunter. As for the suffix "Jr.," a disclaimer on the roster admits to errors "in the orthography of names and towns" due to the "hurry and confusion of such a large assembly," so it is possible that the "Jr." was a transcription mistake for "Sr.," that "NC" was misread as "NY," or that the name "Thomas Day" is partly or wholly in error. Another possibility is that he was put into a northern delegation to disguise his southern roots, or simply because no southern delegations were listed. Given the Milton cabinetmaker's social standing and political sentiments, as well as his previous attendance at the Philadelphia convention, it is likely that he was the man listed on the New York roster.[60]

If Thomas Day of Milton attended the Seventh Annual Meeting of the American Anti-Slavery Society, he could have met the delegation from

Figure 30 Fanny Palmer, "Chatham Square. New York," for N. Currier. Lithographer, New York City, ca. 1847. Aquatint on paper. Plate, 8" x 12½". (Courtesy, Museum of the City of New York, New York.) W. N. Seymour & Co., the hardware emporium where Thomas Day conducted business for many years, is the white building with the flag in the background.

Wilbraham, Massachusetts, which included several prominent men associated with Wesleyan. By that date, the racially integrated American Anti-Slavery Society had 250,000 members and hundreds of auxiliaries, and, as was the case with previous conventions, it disseminated names of schools that welcomed black students. Many other delegates at the New York convention were also familiar with egalitarian institutions like Wesleyan. The Reverend Jehiel Beman of Boston, the recently appointed director of the Massachusetts Abolition Society's Agency in Behalf of the Free People of Color, was the point man for aiding "people of color in . . . obtaining the advantages of education for their children." Charles B. Ray of New York was an alumnus of Wesleyan, Abel Bliss was a founder of the academy, and Frederick Merrick would later become the president of Wesleyan College. John W. Dadman was a member of the academy's Examining Committee for New England students, and William Rice, who had once distributed antislavery notices on campus, was valedictorian of the class of 1840. Wesleyan Academy advertised widely in mainstream newspapers in New York and throughout New England, in abolitionist broadsheets including the *Liberator* and the *Colored American*, and in the Methodist Episcopal weekly, *Zion's Herald*, whose Boston publisher, Jacob Sleeper, was a prominent Wesleyan trustee. Ray's broadsheet, the *Colored American*, reported that "thousands" had attended.[61]

The Day children were still babies when Thomas went to Philadelphia in 1835, but his presence at that convention suggests that he was very concerned about their future. Racial uplift through education was at the top of that convention's agenda, and the Committee on High Schools had identified a handful of northern institutions known to accept black youth "on an equal footing with whites." The list included the Oneida Institute in Whitesville, New York; Mount Pleasant Academy in Amherst, Massachusetts; McGrawville College in McGrawville, New York (later New York Central College); and Canaan (later Kimball Academy), in Meriden, New Hampshire. By the time Day's children were ready to attend high school, the list had expanded to include such coeducational options as Wesleyan, H. H. Kellogg's Domestic Seminary and Clinton Grammar School, in Clinton, New York (which Devereux possibly attended before he went to Wesleyan); Oberlin, in Ohio, originally the Oberlin Collegiate Institute, which opened its doors to whites, blacks, males, and females in 1833; and Comer's Commercial College, established in Boston in 1840. Highly regarded all-black schools included the Philadelphia Institute for Colored Youth, chartered in 1827, and Avery College in Pittsburgh, founded in 1849 to train young men as ministers and teachers. With John Cook as a personal guide, Day would have had contacts at several of these schools.[62]

According to Wesleyan's catalogues, Mary Ann and Thomas were there from 1849 through 1852. Devereux, whose name does not appear in the catalogue of 1849–1850, did not join them until their second year. A postscript on an undated letter from the elder Thomas to Mary Ann at Wesleyan shows how close a friend he was to the ardent abolition leaders of Wesleyan: "Give my love to Mr. R and Mr. M and tell them within five days, I will send them the money due the Seminary." Since Day had mentioned both men by their full names in the body of the letter, it is clear that "Mr. R" refers to Miner Raymond, principal of the academy, and "Mr. M" to John Merrick, the treasurer of the school's board.[63]

Founded by Methodists in 1817, Wesleyan had been a bastion of abolitionist sentiment since the early 1830s. "Trustees, teachers and students" had been swept away by "the new impulse." A contemporaneous history of the school notes that the student leader in the movement was William Rice, and that the chapel was an active Underground Railroad station. During the time period when the Day children were at Wesleyan, the entire community was even more radical, a fact that would not have eluded Thomas and Aquilla Day. The arrival of their children in Massachusetts coincided with the vitriolic debates consuming Congress and culminating in the passage of the Fugitive Slave Act on September 18, 1850. The floor of the Capitol had become a battleground, where one Mississippi senator threatened to lynch an abolitionist senator from New Hampshire should he "go ten miles into the interior of the . . . good state" of Mississippi. The law and the related Compromise of 1850, which extended slavery to the western territories, gave slave hunters authority in all states and required the cooperation of local officials. Federal marshals and even bystanders who refused to participate in apprehending fugitives were subject to a $1,000 fine. Free blacks without proper documentation were also targeted, kidnapped, and sold into slavery, particularly when the price for cotton in the South was high and labor was in greater demand. Considering the noxious political climate, Thomas Day was incredibly brave to escort his children from Milton to Wilbraham and back. A poster dated April 24, 1851, warned "all" people of color in Boston, eighty miles east of Wilbraham, about policemen acting as slave catchers (fig. 31).[64]

The Milton community apparently turned a blind eye when Day broke North Carolina law and traveled beyond Caswell County without the requisite license and when his children stayed out of state longer than the ninety-day limit, but in communities where free blacks had high standing, officials often looked the other way. Moreover, there were so many statutes on the books ostensibly "controlling" free black activity that there was no way that the myriad laws could be consistently enforced with the limited number of officials available. Yet any law could be enforced at any time, which created a sense of threat and even terror. An 1838 Virginia law prohibiting "a Free Negro who left the state to study" from ever returning underscores the risk that parents took by sending their children away to school. Just across the border in North Carolina, Thomas and Aquilla understood that secrecy was their best protection.[65]

With the Fugitive Slave Law in effect, it is unlikely that Day would have ventured beyond familiar territory without a testimonial letter from a known authority. When Louis Sheridan traveled from Bladen County to New York City in 1834, he carried a letter of introduction from John Owen, a former North Carolina governor. Ten years later, Boston minister Jehiel C. Beman had to present a letter signed by the governor of Massachusetts to gain passage on a train from Baltimore to Washington, but he was still

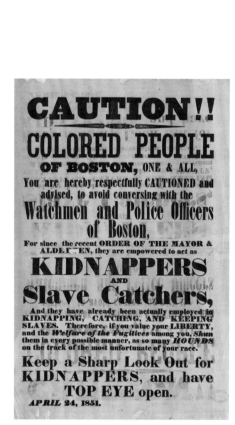

Figure 31   Caution!! Colored People of Boston. Boston, Massachusetts, April 24, 1851. Ink on paper. 16" x 10½". (Courtesy, Trustees of the Boston Public Library/Rare Books Collection.)

required to sit in "the Jimmy," the sooty Jim Crow car. Day also would have needed letters of introduction to open accounts in cities where he conducted business, including Petersburg, Virginia, Baltimore, and New York. Given his standing in North Carolina, he could have obtained references from any number of prominent clients and neighbors.[66]

Day was undoubtedly attuned to the growing hostility toward all people of color in the South. Evidence of the latter is seen in two particularly odious bills that were introduced, albeit unsuccessfully, in the North Carolina legislature in late 1850. One called for shipping all 345 free black residents of Duplin County to Liberia. Those who preferred to remain would be "sold and become slaves." The other bill would have compelled "all the free Negroes of North Carolina to emigrate to the Abolition and Free Soil States," the assumption being that resident abolitionists in those states would feel less kindly toward their new neighbors when confronted by such a large dose of "black medicine." The poisonous words of South Carolina senator John C. Calhoun were also widely reported:

> It is a great and dangerous error to suppose that all people are equally entitled to liberty. . . . It is a reward reserved for the intelligent, the patriotic, the virtuous and deserving—and not a boon to be bestowed on a people too ignorant, degraded and vicious, to be capable either of appreciating or enjoying it.[67]

Day's white neighbors and clients typically addressed him as "Mr. Day" instead of "Tom," and some sat side by side with his family in the church next to his shop, but few, if any, of those people would have considered him a social equal. In November 1851 Day cautioned Mary Ann to "expect cool Comfort as far as human intercourse is concerned" when she returns from school, citing the "frail . . . affection of Friends." He understood that the realities of life in Milton were at odds with his daughter's experiences at Wesleyan. In the same letter, he expressed contempt for the daughters of some white neighbors "who learn a little of one thing" and "a little of another . . . [and] return to their country homes knowing nothing but . . . scoff at persons they think inferior to themselves." In an especially pointed dig at the local gentry, he added that the behavior of "such children they raise here are Just a such as could be Expected from such parents." Day could never have said this publicly, yet in an undated letter to Mary Ann, then a student at Wesleyan, his sense of isolation is palpable:

> No doubt my great concern at this time & will be is to get some suitable place for you and your Brothers—all of us—to settle down—I want you to be in some place where your turn of feelings & manners can be well met with associates—& I fully Expect to affect my purpose if I live long enough.

Poignantly, Day added, "There is nothing here but to make a little money & that but little to induce us to stay here." Despite his wishes for his children, it appears that he was resigned to his fate in Milton, perhaps believing that by this late date he already had stayed too long. He appears to have expressed similar sentiments to his brother in Liberia. In a letter published by the Colonization Society, John Day wrote, "My brother in America has asked me 'how it is that colored men in America are so insignificant and here

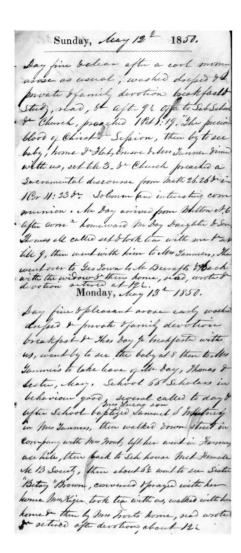

Sunday, *May 12ᵗ* 1850.

[handwritten diary entry]

Monday, *May 13ᵗ* 1850.

[handwritten diary entry]

Figure 32 Detail of the Reverend John Francis Cook's diary entries describing a visit from Thomas Day and two of his children on May 12 and May 13, 1850, box 3, Cook Family Papers, 1827–1869. (Courtesy, Moorland-Spingarn Research Center, Howard University, Washington, D.C.)

so great?'" Despite his own individual success, the abolitionist inclinations in Thomas Day allowed him to think more broadly about the perverse implications of slavery and racial inequity in America. Still, he and his peers continued to be constrained in their ability to openly state their beliefs.[68]

Accounts of former Underground Railroad operatives reveal that most were extremely careful to be discreet and destroy their records after the Fugitive Slave Law went into effect. Thomas Day's old friend John Cook, having been victimized by racially motivated mob violence, knew better than to reveal his true thoughts even in his diary. At first glance, Cook's diary appears to be a sober account of mundane daily activities, interspersed with vague references to correspondence "rc'd." or letters written "in response." He did not record that his good friends J. B. Vashon of Pittsburgh, Dr. J. J. Gould Bias of Philadelphia, and the Reverend Leonard Grimes of Boston were major Underground Railroad operatives, that Joshua Leavitt of New York was the editor of the *Emancipator*, or that Lewis Tappan, who visited his Sunday school on March 3, 1850, was a founding member of the American Anti-Slavery Society and enlisted thousands of members to bombard Congress with abolitionist pamphlets.[69]

Cook's entry on the occasion of the Days' visit to Washington suggests that he knew them well: "Mr. Day arrived from Milton, N.C. Mr. Day, Daughter [whom Cook later identifies as "Mary"] & son, Thomas all called, set & took tea with me until 9, then went with him to Mrs. Tanner" (fig. 32). The next morning, Cook "breakfasted" with Thomas Jr. and took him to see his infant son, who was being cared for by a friend. In the year and three months that he kept his diary, no one but Thomas Day stayed overnight with Cook's beloved aunt and benefactor Alethia Tanner, and Thomas Jr. is the only nonfamily member Cook took to see "the baby." Seven years later, Thomas Jr. married Mary Virginia Washington, the eldest daughter of Cook's close friend and neighbor Mary Washington. Thomas and his first wife, who went by the name Virginia, had three children before her death in North Carolina in 1867. Four years later, Thomas Jr. returned to Washington to marry her younger sister, Annie.[70]

William Robinson later confirmed Cook's close ties to the Days. In 1927 he wrote Carter Woodson, known today as the Father of Black History, to "find George M. Cook to see if he knew of a Thomas Day [Jr.] of Milton, N. C. who married a Miss Annie Washington, first principal of Stephen's [*sic*] school" (fig. 33). Robinson would have learned of Cook's direct involvement with his family from his mother, Annie Day Shepard (fig. 34), the younger daughter of Thomas Day Jr. and Virginia. After Virginia's death, young Annie and her sister Minnie were sent to the District of Columbia to live with their aunt, Annie Washington, and to attend her school. This raises the question of how George M. Cook, born in 1860, came to know about Thomas Day's children. George, who was John F. Cook's nephew, was Annie Washington's student at Stevens when she married Thomas Day Jr. As one of the few surviving members of the Cook family who would have known them both personally, he might also have known if Annie and Mary Ann were educated together and whether Cook's school, where Annie

Washington was once a student, was the one that Mary Ann attended in the North before she and her brothers went to Wesleyan. Since the records of Cook's Union Seminary are no longer extant and only one diary maintained by John Cook is known to survive, we may never know for certain; however, one has to wonder how Thomas Jr. came to join this abolitionist minister and teacher's inner circle. If Thomas Day Jr. was educated in Washington as well, that could explain why the Milton "old timers" told Caroline Pell Gunter in the 1920s that Thomas Sr. attended schools in those cities; they simply confused father and son. Thomas Jr.'s subsequent marriages to Cook's neighbors, the Washington sisters, explain the close association of his generation with the free black community of Washington, further buttressing this theory.[71]

In 1840 Thomas Day's net worth was $40,000. Although the following decade was his most productive period (figs. 35, 36), buying and selling on credit and investing in expensive shop machinery left him in arrears by the mid-1850s. Day's health also deteriorated, and in 1856 he sold off most of his farm. A year later, a national financial panic wiped out one of every three businesses and effectively ended his storied success. As Jonathan Prown has argued, rising racial tensions in the South also likely contributed to Day's financial and physical demise. In the summer of 1858, the North Carolina credit agent for R. G. Dun & Co. of New York City took note of the state of the Milton furniture business in his ledger: "[Mr. Day is] [b]roke all to pieces—prop'y under a deed of trust. When he gets through his present debts, he won't have much of anything left." A few months earlier, Day had declared insolvency, and a year after that most of his personal property was sold at public auction. Although six of his slaves, including David, were eligible for sale, their names do not appear on the deed recording the event. A notation in his Bible states that he died on "October 20, 1859 at the age of 59," but he appears in the 1860 census. His actual date of death remains an unresolved mystery because while there is an alleged gravesite on his former farm near Milton, it has not been authenticated and no obituary has yet been found.[72]

Figure 35   Thomas Day, bedstead, Milton, North Carolina, 1853. Mahogany veneer with yellow pine and tulip poplar. H. 87½", L. 82", W. 65½". (Collection of the North Carolina Museum of History, purchase with state funds; courtesy, Renwick Gallery of the Smithsonian American Art Museum; photo, Tim Buchman.) Day made this bedstead for Azariah Graves II of Oak Grove plantation in present-day Stony Creek Township, Caswell County, North Carolina.

Figure 36   Passage rack, or hall tree, attributed to Thomas Day, Milton, North Carolina, ca. 1857. Tulip poplar; mahogany graining. H. 86", W. 35", D. 23½". (Courtesy, Town of Hillsborough, North Carolina, gift of Dr. and Mrs. H. W. Moore as part of town renovation of the Ruffin Roulhac House as Hillsborough's Town Hall; courtesy, Renwick Gallery of the Smithsonian American Art Museum; photo, Amy Vaughters.) The rack was made for C. H. Moseley of Caswell County, North Carolina.

An article in the April 15, 1865, issue of the *Christian Recorder*, the newspaper of the African Methodist Episcopal Church, noted that Thomas Day Jr. was in Wilmington, North Carolina (fig. 37). That date would have resonated in his memory as the day Abraham Lincoln died, scarcely a week after Lee's surrender at Appomattox. The same article reported that a "Miss Day" [Mary Ann] had been teaching in Wilmington's "underground" schools. A skilled cabinetmaker in his own right, Thomas borrowed money from some of his father's white business creditors to save the Union Tavern and likely occupied his father's old home and workshop until January 1864, when he finally paid off the debt. His mother transferred her membership from the Milton church to the First Presbyterian Church of Wilmington the following October. This suggests that the family was already living in the latter town. The *Christian Recorder* described the politics of the vibrant free black community that embraced the Days as kindred spirits:

The people [in Wilmington] are generally refined and well informed . . . Union to the bone, liberal and modest. Almost or I may say all of the colored people have been engaged in the business of hiding Yankee prisoners. Almost every house in the city occupied by colored people has done this favor for our prisoners.[73]

As the Confederacy was disintegrating, Thomas Day's long-hidden political sympathies were emerging, albeit in the values and examples passed down to his children. Mary Ann was working to improve the lives of African Americans in Wilmington even before Union forces occupied the city on February 22, 1865. She had helped establish an "underground" school for African American children at a time when teaching them was still forbidden. The March 11, 1865, issue of the *Christian Recorder* reported that she, three other teachers, and nearly seven hundred recently emancipated children assembled in the basement of the city's largest Methodist Church on Front Street to meet Union leaders as well as representatives from the Freedmen's Bureau and the American Missionary Association. The American Missionary Association was one of several benevolent societies that funded schools throughout the South. A later edition of the same newspaper reported that Mary Ann's future husband, the Reverend James A. Chresfield, was also in town, running a school in the very church to which Aquilla Day transferred her membership.[74]

Wilmington's leading black citizens, including Thomas, were characterized as individuals "who have friends and relatives in the North." They were also a close-knit, politically active group. Two "underground" teachers who assisted Mary Ann in her work were daughters of Wilmington's wealthiest free black resident, James D. Sampson. (The newspaper had identified them as the "Misses Day [singular] and Sampsons.") Sampson (d. 1861) was a cabinetmaker and builder who owned numerous slaves and educated his children in the North. Initially, they were tutored at home alongside his slaves, a transgression for which he barely escaped being tarred and feathered. One Sampson son, John Patterson Sampson, founded an antislavery

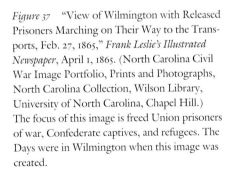

Figure 37 "View of Wilmington with Released Prisoners Marching on Their Way to the Transports, Feb. 27, 1865," *Frank Leslie's Illustrated Newspaper*, April 1, 1865. (North Carolina Civil War Image Portfolio, Prints and Photographs, North Carolina Collection, Wilson Library, University of North Carolina, Chapel Hill.) The focus of this image is freed Union prisoners of war, Confederate captives, and refugees. The Days were in Wilmington when this image was created.

newspaper in Cincinnati, the *Colored Citizen*, later known as the *National Negro War*. It was circulated to thousands of black soldiers during the Civil War, and, because of this, John Patterson Sampson achieved national fame as a journalist and abolitionist.[75]

A subsequent letter from Mary Ann to the American Missionary Association described the children she was teaching. She reported that they were so poor they could not afford books, and she elected to pay for the texts by having the cost "deducted" from her salary. Her involvement in establishing one of the first schools in Wilmington for formerly enslaved children further suggests that Thomas and Aquilla Day selected Wesleyan because they wanted their children to be empowered by that training ground for abolitionists. Numerous graduates of the school, white as well as black, became leaders and activists. Many served as ministers and educators; some graduates and their offspring even took part in founding schools and colleges. Alumnus Charles B. Ray was a founder of the New York Society for the Promotion of Education among Colored Children.[76]

After their marriage in 1867, Mary Ann and her husband, James Chresfield, moved to Lexington, North Carolina, where he established a church and school. Mary Ann died three years later, but letters in the National Archives to officials at the Freedmen's Bureau survive as a testament to her deep involvement with James's fledgling operation. The education of African Americans was of paramount concern for other members of Thomas and Aquilla's family, including their daughter-in-law Annie Washington Day, granddaughter Annie Day Shepard, and great-grandson William Robinson, the son of Annie Day Shepard by her first husband, Dr. D. A. Robinson. William served as director of North Carolina's African American secondary school system, and many family members across generations played significant roles in the education of African Americans.[77]

Unanswered questions remain about Thomas Day, the Milton furniture maker and patriarch of this impressive family. He was not an overt abolitionist like David Walker, who moved from Wilmington to Boston in the early 1820s and who publicly demanded immediate change. Nor did he become a violent insurrectionist, like Nat Turner, who, like Day, was born in Southside Virginia. But in Day's own distinctive way, he contributed to the cause of African American equality, if only through the shining example of his own individual success. New historical evidence reveals that he had irrefutable ties to some of the most powerful abolitionists in the country, and that these ties came with enormous risk to his safety and that of his family.

Because Day's activities beyond Milton were so well hidden, it is still impossible to document the full extent of his participation in the abolition movement. In the years to come, more documents likely will emerge and help create a more complete and more complex portrait. Day was remarkably daring to go to Philadelphia for the abolitionist convention in 1835 (and probably the meeting of the American Anti-Slavery Society in New York in 1840). In those acts alone, the depth of his commitment to equality can hardly be questioned. Equally revealing is his choice of Wesleyan Academy for his children's education and the Day family's ties to that school's ardent abolitionist leaders and to John F. Cook, a major abolitionist figure in Washington, D.C. Such avowed abolitionists would not have been on close personal terms with a slave owner had he not assured them, by actions as well as words, that he was sympathetic to their cause. It is also difficult to imagine that Cook's protégées Virginia and then Annie Washington would have married Thomas Jr. without firsthand knowledge of their father-in-law's egalitarian social convictions. It now seems clear that by sending his children to Wesleyan, Day was preparing them to be agents of change. His daughter's devotion to secretly teaching in Wilmington's "underground schools" and the involvement of Day descendants in the education of African Americans testify to his legacy.

1. "Attention! Colored Americans," *Emancipator* (New York), May 26, 1835. *The Black Abolitionist Papers: The United States, 1830–46*, edited by C. Peter Ripley, Roy E. Finkenbine, Michael F. Hembree, and Donald Yacovone, 5 vols. (Chapel Hill: University of North Carolina Press, 1991), 3: 146–51. The quotation appears in the convention's keynote address announcing the formation of the American Moral Reform Society and was authored by delegates William Whipper, Alfred Niger, and Augustus Price.

2. *Acts Passed by the General Assembly of the State of North Carolina at the Session of 1830–31* (Raleigh, N.C.: Lawrence & LeMay, 1831), chap. 5, secs. 1–3, pp. 10–11.

3. Journal of the House of Commons of North Carolina, 1830–1831, p. 238, Office of Archives and History (hereafter OAH), Raleigh, N.C. Saunders and sixty-one white citizens of Milton used this occasion to allow Day's wife, Aquilla Wilson Day, a Virginian, a special dispensation from an "act to prevent free persons of colour from migrating into the State" (*Acts Passed by the General Assembly of North Carolina at Its Session Commencing on the 25th of December, 1826* [Raleigh, N.C.: Lawrence & Lemay, Printers to the State, 1827], chap. 21, sec. 1, p. 67.

4. Laurel Crone Sneed and Patricia Dane Rogers, *The Hidden History of Thomas Day* (Research Triangle Park, N.C.: Apprend Foundation, 2009). This essay was supported by a grant from the North Carolina Humanities Council. "A Card," *The Liberator*, July 11 and August 8, 1835. The "Card" was discovered on the Accessible Archives database (accessible.com) at the Library of Congress in 2006 in the course of researching a documentary film about Thomas Day. Cook Family Papers, 1827–1868, Moorland-Spingarn Research Center, Howard University, Washington, D.C. Work on the documentary film, *The Thin Edge of Freedom: Thomas Day and the Free Black Experience, 1800–1860*, is still in progress. The creative director and executive producer is Laurel Sneed, director of the Apprend Foundation and director of the Thomas Day Education Project/Crafting Freedom workshops. The film was awarded an NEH Media-Maker's grant for 2009–2010 for the development of a script. The scriptwriter is Stephen Stept, an award-winning documentary producer and writer.

5. Carter G. Woodson wrote about Day's business success in *The Mis-Education of the Negro* (Washington, D.C.: Associated Publishers, 1933), pp. 169–70. John Hope Franklin's doctoral thesis was published as *The Free Negro in North Carolina, 1790–1860* (Chapel Hill: University of North Carolina Press, 1943). Articles by Caroline Pell Gunter, "Tom Day—Craftsman," *Antiquarian*, September 1928, *News & Observer*, June 30, 1929, and Paul Ader, "Tom Day," *State* 8, no. 5 (February 15, 1941), relied primarily on local oral histories. In "Tom Day—Craftsman," p. 60, Gunter said Day was born between 1785 and 1787 on his parents' farm near Milton and that his mother had mortgaged the farm to send him to school in Boston and Washington, where he studied for three years. William A. Robinson et al., "Thomas Day and His Family," *Negro History Bulletin* 8 (March 1950): 122–26, 140. In a letter to Woodson dated September 16, 1927, Robinson enclosed transcribed copies of letters from Thomas Day to Mary Ann, one dated November 27, 1851, the other undated, stated that he had the originals, and offered to send "photographic copies" to Woodson for $2 per letter. Woodson's files at the Library of Congress contain Robinson's typed transcriptions but not images of the originals. Today, these transcriptions and two one-page fragments from each of the letters are in the archives of the late Mary Satterfield, a Milton community historian. For more on the Robinson-Woodson correspondence, see Carter Godwin Woodson Papers, 1916–1927, part 1, box 1.6, reel 3-4, Library of Congress, Washington, D.C. The authors thank Lewis Wyman, Reference Librarian, Manuscript Division, for this citation.

6. Ira Berlin, *Slaves without Masters: The Free Negro in the Antebellum South* (Oxford: Oxford University Press, 1974), pp. 239–40. *Records of the Moravians in North Carolina*, edited by Minnie J. Smith (Raleigh, N.C.: State Department of Archives and History, 1964), 9 (1838–1847): 49; on June 28, 1847, Thomas Day requested that his sixteen-year-old daughter educated in the "North" be allowed to study music with a Salem Academy teacher. The children's book is Mary E. Lyons, *Master of Mahogany: Tom Day, Free Black Cabinetmaker* (New York: Charles Scribner's & Sons, 1994). Laurel Sneed and Christine Westfall, *Uncovering the Hidden History of Thomas Day: Findings and Methodology* (1995; updated, Durham, N.C.: Thomas Day Education Project, 1996).

7. Patricia Phillip Marshall, "With All Necessary Care and Attention: The Artistry of Thomas Day," North Carolina Museum of History, Raleigh, September 3, 1996–March 2, 1997. African American collector Derrick Beard was the driving force behind the exhibition "Sankofa: A Celebration of African American Arts & Crafts, 1790–1930," which traveled to venues including the Maryland Historical Society in Baltimore and the DuSable Museum of African American History in Chicago. Craftique, Inc. launched "The Thomas Day Collection" in 1996, but the firm is no longer in business. According to Marian Thomas, former director of the Thomas Day House/Union Tavern Restoration project, Craftique, Inc. made a "generous" donation toward the restoration and contributed royalties for each piece sold. Patricia Dane Rogers, "Carved in History, Thomas Day: A Success in an Unlikely Time and Place," *Washington Post*, February 13, 1997. Janie Leigh Carter, "John Day: A Founder of the Republic of Liberia and the Southern Baptist Liberian Missionary Movement in the Nineteenth Century (master's thesis, Wake Forest University, 1998). Michael A. Paquette,"Thomas Day: An Inquiry into Business and Labor Practices in an Antebellum Cabinetshop," *Journal of the North Carolina Association of Historians* 6–7 (Fall 1998–99): 6–22. Jonathan Prown, "The Furniture of Thomas Day: A Reevaluation," *Winterthur Portfolio* 33, no. 4 (Winter 1998): 215–29.

8. The exhibit opened in June 2010 and closed in January 2013. Patricia Phillips Marshall and Jo Ramsay Leimenstoll, *Thomas Day: Master Craftsman and Free Man of Color* (Chapel Hill: University of North Carolina Press for the North Carolina Museum of History, 2010). Based on the exhibition organized by the North Carolina Museum of History, the Renwick Gallery's "Thomas Day: Master Cabinetmaker and Free Man of Color" ran from April 12 to July 28, 2013.

9. Patricia Phillips Marshall, "The Legendary Thomas Day: Debunking the Popular Mythology of an African American Craftsman," in Rodney D. Barfield and Patricia M. Marshall, *Thomas Day, African American Furniture Maker* (Raleigh: North Carolina Office of Archives and History, 2005), p. 50. There are variations among the stories of Day's descendants, but most portray him as benevolent toward his slaves. Marshall notes that evolving myths regarding Day account for the seeming incongruities in his life, such as the fact that he was black yet attended a predominantly white church and owned slaves. There is no documentary evidence in church records that Day agreed to make the pews on condition that he and/or his slaves receive special seating. Juanita Holland, filmed interview by Laurel C. Sneed, 1998, Thomas Day Education Project archives (hereafter TDEP), Durham, N.C.

10. John Hope Franklin, filmed interview by Laurel C. Sneed for *Thomas Day, American*, October 1995, TDEP.

11. David Walker's antislavery pamphlet, *Walker's Appeal in Four Articles; Together with a Preamble, to the Coloured Citizens of the World but in Particular and Very Expressly, to Those in the United States of America, Written in Boston, State of Massachusetts, September 28, 1829, David Walker. Third and Last Edition with Additional Notes, Corrections, &c.* (Boston: David Walker, 1803), p. 73, stated: "America is more our country than it is the whites—we have enriched it with our *blood and tears*." *Acts Passed by the General Assembly of the State of North Carolina at the Session of 1830–1831* (Raleigh, N.C.: Lawrence & Lemay, 1831), chap. 4, secs. 1–3, pp. 9–10 ("An act to more effectively prevent intermarriages between free negroes or free persons of colour and white persons and slaves"); chap. 6, secs. 1–2, p. 11 ("An act to prevent all persons from teaching slaves to read or write, the use of numbers excepted"); chap. 7, sec. 1, p. 11 ("An act to prohibit free persons of colour from peddling . . . granted annually by the county court . . . when 7 or more justices are present"); chap. 9, sec. 1, pp. 12–13 ("An act to regulate the emancipation of slaves in this State"); chap. 8, p. 12 ("An act providing . . . punishment for harboring or maintaining runaway slaves").

12. Melvin Patrick Ely, interview for the film *The Thin Edge of Freedom: Thomas Day*. Marshall and Leimenstoll, *Thomas Day: Master Craftsman*, p. 132. The authors attribute as many as eighty architectural projects to Day.

13. Marshall and Leimenstoll, *Thomas Day: Master Craftsman*, p. 76. August Fogle Letters, 1820–1897, Moravian Archives, Winston-Salem, N.C., as quoted in Paquette, "Thomas Day: An Inquiry," p. 7. Johanna M. Brown, Curator of Moravian Decorative Arts, Old Salem Museums & Gardens, email message to Patricia Rogers, June 6, 2013. According to Brown, four cabinetmakers from Germany (including one who was originally Danish) came to Salem and brought with them "a Teutonic interpretation of neoclassical design which later seemed to include Biedermeier influences." She also notes, Karsten Petersen, the former Dane, trained Jacob Siewers and that there appears to have been "an exchange of design and style ideas" between Siewers, his brother, John, and Thomas Day. Decorative arts historian Sumpter Priddy III and Jerome Bias, a North Carolina cabinetmaker and Day scholar, have also observed Salem influences in Day's work, but Bias notes that the construction of Day's lounges does differs from the Salem versions. Richard Powell's observation was recorded in October 1995 in a video interview for the Thomas Day Education Project archives.

14. Aiming to attract a "genteel" black clientele, Serena Gardiner and her husband, African Methodist Episcopal minister Peter Gardiner, a delegate to all of the previous conventions, took out twenty-three additional *Liberator* ads for the Elizabeth Street boardinghouse and its predecessor at 19 Powell Street.

15. The Fifth Census of the United States, 1830, Population Schedule of Surry, Currituck, Person and Caswell County, North Carolina; Sixth Census of the United States, 1840, Population Schedule of Carteret, Surry, Person and Caswell County, North Carolina, National Archives, Washington, D.C. These documents list five men named Thomas Day, but the convention took place five years later, eliminating anyone who moved into the state after 1830, so the Thomas Days in the 1840 census, who could have moved into the state at any time after 1830, must also be counted. The 1830 census lists three white men named Thomas Day and two free men of color with the same name. Of the three whites, two are from Surry County and the third, from Currituck County. A fourth white Thomas Day from Carteret County is enumerated in the 1840 census. The two black Thomas Days remain the same: one from Caswell County and one from neighboring Person County. Genealogist Aaron Day, who has studied his Person County relatives, described the Thomas Day living in that county as poor and illiterate, a tenant farmer and bushwhacker who cleared land for crops and roads. He signed two deeds of debt with an "X," indicating illiteracy (Person County Deed Book G, January 6, 1824, pp. 100–101; Deed Book L, August 1, 1835, p. 374, North Carolina Office of Archives and History, State Archives, Raleigh, N.C.).

16. *Black Abolitionist Papers, 1830–1865: A Guide to the Microfilm Edition*, edited by George E. Carter, C. Peter Ripley, and Jeffrey Rossbach (Sanford, N.C.: Microfilming Corporation of America, 1981), pp. 1–4. The *Guide* lists the 14,000 documents and almost 300 individuals on which the five *Black Abolitionist Papers* books published by the University of North Carolina Press between 1985 and 1992 were based.

17. Dinwiddie County Chancery Order Book 1, 1832–1852, microfilm reel 18, Library of Virginia (hereafter LVA), Richmond, Va. The document, dated April 2, 1834, refers to an earlier court order. Seventh Census of the United States, 1850: Caswell County, North Carolina, Population Schedule, National Archives, Washington, D.C. Day's household, listed under "Free Inhabitants," included two mulatto females—"Morning S. Day, 84" and "Aquila Day, 49." The only other family members listed were Thomas Day, aged 49, and his son, Devereux, who is identified as a 17-year-old cabinetmaker.

18. Franklin, *The Free Negro*, p. 59. Thomas A. Stewart left two wills, one dated September 22, 1804, and the other May 18, 1808. In the first, he left his grandson a slave named Rhoda. In the second he gave "unto my grand son John Day, a girl named Rhody." Several transcribers wrote the name of this slave as "Thody," but the correct name is clear on the first original (Dinwiddie County, Virginia Wills, 1801–1869, microfilm reel 57, LVA). Conversation between Paul Heinegg and Laurel C. Sneed at a symposium sponsored by the Thomas Day Education Project titled "Navigating the Labyrinth of Race," Yanceyville, N.C., November 11, 2000. "Eulogy of Rev. Edward W. Blyden, on the Rev. John Day, Monrovia, 1859," *African Repository* 37, no. 5 (1861): 154–58.

19. John Day to James B. Taylor, October 16, 1847, John Day Missionary Correspondence to the Southern Baptist Foreign Mission Board, Southern Baptist Historical Library and Archives, Nashville, Tenn.

20. *The Vestry Book and Register of Bristol Parish, Virginia, 1720–1789*, transcribed and published by Churchill Gibson Chamberlayne (Richmond, Va.: privately printed, 1898), pp. 24, 58. These transcribed parish papers detail baptisms, deaths, and births, including those of sev-

eral mulatto children of "Eliz. Stuard." A 1731 vestry order notes that two "Melettos," Tom and Will, were bound to Captain Peter Wynn who owned property near Thomas Stewart's future Dinwiddie County landholdings. (Wynn's stepmother, the widow of his father Joshue Wynn[e], may have been the "Mrs. Fran. Wynn" who owned the house where "Eliz. Stuard" gave birth to another "mulatto" son in 1725.) Berlin, *Slaves without Masters*, p. 6. There is no record of Stewart's attendance at either of America's earliest medical schools: the Medical Department of the College of Philadelphia, established in 1765 (predecessor of the University of Pennsylvania Medical School), or the Faculty of Physic of King's College in New York, established in 1776 (now, Columbia University Medical School). He could have received training from any number of sources, including an apothecary, a root medicine practitioner, or a physician. Paul Heinegg, *Free African Americans of North Carolina, Virginia, and South Carolina from the Colonial Period to about 1820*, 5th ed., 2 vols. (Baltimore, Md.: Clearfield, 2005), 2: 1091–92. Heinegg lists fourteen children in order of birth date, with Mourning (born ca. 1766) as Stewart's fourth child and second daughter. Court testimony by Stewart's granddaughter Hannah, however, indicates that Mourning was the fifth-born child. Hannah stated that Stewart had married twice and that his first wife had one daughter and three sons (Hannah Stewart v. Elizabeth Chavis, not dated, Mecklenburg County Chancery Causes, 1872-007, LVA). If Stewart was officially married twice, Mourning's mother may have been a common-law wife. Stewart married his second wife of record, Winifred Atkins, on February 5, 1795 (Catherine Lindsay Knorr, *Marriage Bonds and Minister's Returns of Sussex County, Virginia, 1754–1810* [Pine Bluff, Ark.: Purdue Co., 1952], p. 77). Will of Thomas A. Stewart, September 22, 1804. Stewart left his daughter Mourning and her heirs twenty-five pounds. John Day to James B. Taylor, October 16, 1847; John Day to James B. Taylor, December 22, 1847; Catharine Day to James B. Taylor, May 23, 1860, John Day Missionary Correspondence. Catharine wrote, "I have not received since the death of my husband, a line from his brother, Mr. Thomas Day, who, when I last heard was residing in Milton, N.C. I do not know whether he is alive or dead; whether he has removed or still lives in Milton."

21. John Day to James B. Taylor, October 16, 1847, John Day Missionary Correspondence. John noted that his father had owned a "pretty little plantation" in Sussex County, Virginia. By 1810 John Day Sr. had acquired about sixty acres near present-day Jarratt (Gary M. Williams, *Sussex County, Virginia: A Heritage Recalled by the Land* [Petersburg, Va.: Dietz Press, 2012], p. 90 n. 119). To this day, the property is known as Johnny Day Field. According to a direct descendant of Thomas Eppes, Thomas Day lived nearby and was likely responsible for the interior woodwork in Eppes's house, including the massive chimneypiece (Katherine Eppes Jarratt to Patricia Dane Rogers, November 19, 2011). Williams, *Sussex County*, pp. 77, 90 n. 114 (Williams cites p. 84 in G. Michael Wildasin, "The Methodist and Quaker Challenge to Slavery in Jeffersonian Virginia" [Ph.D. diss., College of William and Mary, Williamsburg, Va., 1972]). The original list of "Manumitters in Sussex County, Virginia, 1782–1806," is in the Sussex County Courthouse, Sussex, Va. Donna McDaniel and Vanessa Julye, *Fit for Freedom, not for Friendship: Quakers, African Americans, and the Myth of Racial Justice* (Philadelphia: Quaker Press, 2009), p. 112.

22. Sneed and Westfall, *Uncovering the Hidden History of Thomas Day*, pp. 5–7, 20–23. Although John Day Jr. is usually a reliable correspondent, and many statements from his autobiographical letter can be proven, his account of his father's birth and childhood has yet to be verified. For tax and land records pertaining to the elder John Day of Greensville County, see Heinegg, *Free African Americans*, 1: 399 n. 88. When Thomas Day married in 1830, Uriah Jeffreys of Greensville County, Virginia, was his bondsman.

23. John Day to James B. Taylor, October 16, 1847, John Day Missionary Correspondence. John Bolling was likely John Peyton Bolling (1788–1861), scion of a Petersburg family with large landholdings. In 1817, the year that John Day Sr. left his son to pay his debt, Bolling owned 1,160½ acres of farmland in the same Dinwiddie neighborhood where the elder Day rented property before moving to Warren County, North Carolina. *Land Records Dinwiddie County, Virginia, 1752–1820*, compiled and indexed by Thomas P. Hughes and Jewel B. Standefer (Memphis, Tenn: Thomas P. Hughes, 1973), p. 47.

24. Dr. and Mrs. Thomas Baker Day of Columbia, Maryland, own the Bible, which was first reported in the *Washington Post*, February 13, 1997.

25. Quotations and comments are excerpted and paraphrased from the sidebar about Harding in Peter H. Wood, "Who Was Nehemiah Henry Harding: A Minister Wrestles with His Conscience," in the first edition of Sneed and Rogers, *The Hidden History of Thomas Day*, pp. 11–12. Wood's article was based on "A Recreant Minister," *Liberator*, June 29, 1838.

26. Map of Dinwiddie County, Virginia, surveyed by Isham E. Hardgrave, 1820, Dinwiddie County Courthouse, Dinwiddie, Va. Stewart's property was about five miles west of present-day McKenney, Virginia. According to the U.S. Federal Census of 1850, Thomas Day was born in 1801. He was likely born on his grandfather's property since Dinwiddie County tax lists show his father lived there with sons of Dr. Stewart from 1800 to 1802 (Dinwiddie County Property Taxes, 1782–1799, reel 113.7, Seimes Microform Center, Daughters of the American Revolution Library, Washington, D.C.). Kay Moss, *Southern Folk Medicine, 1750–1820* (Columbia: University of South Carolina Press, 1999), p. 46. "Specifick balsam" is likely a popular patent medicine known as "the Balsam of Life." Developed by London merchant Robert Turlington in 1744, it was used for external and respiratory complaints. Hobbs's signed notice appeared on page 3, column 1, of this popular newspaper, published by Dixon and Hunter. The original is in the John D. Rockefeller, Jr. Library, Colonial Williamsburg, Williamsburg, Va., http://research.history.org/DigitalLibrary/VirginiaGazette/VGImagePopup.cfm?ID=6314&Res=HI.

27. *Land Records Dinwiddie County*, p. 6. Stewart was taxed on 903 acres in Dinwiddie County in 1809. For the slave figure, see Heirs of Thomas Stewart v. Heirs of Thomas Stewart, Chancery Cases, 1876-083, folder 3, Chancery Causes, Manuscripts and Archives, LVA. Will of Thomas A. Stewart, September 22, 1804, Dinwiddie County Wills, 1801–1869, microfilm reel 57, LVA, Richmond, Va. Peachy R. Grattan, *Reports of Cases Decided in the Supreme Court of Appeals and in the General Court of Virginia from April 1, 1848 to April 1, 1849*, vol. 5, no. 46 (Richmond, Va.: John Colin, 1849), pp. 61–62. A summary of an appeal in the case of Worsham v. Hardaway's Administrators in 1840 cites the crux of the case of Stewart's slaves versus Stewart's heirs in Chancery Court in Richmond and its dismissal in 1827.

28. For a list of tools and furniture listed in the John Day Sr. estate papers, see Marshall and Leimenstoll, *Thomas Day: Master Craftsman*, pp. 195–97. Jerome Bias notes, "the tools suggest that he [John Day Sr.] was building houses. I am basing this on the presence of augers. They would have been used to build timber frame houses" (Bias, email message to Laurel Sneed, November 11, 2009). The presence of paint and an oilstone in the inventory also suggests that John Day could have been painting interior woodwork. In an interview with Patricia Rogers on June 8, 2013, Gregory Tyler, the researcher who discovered the John Day estate papers in the North Carolina Archives in Raleigh, said county records show that John Day made at least three caskets in 1830. David B. Gammon, *Abstracts of Wills, Warren County, North Carolina, 1779–1844* (Raleigh, N.C.: David B. Gammon, 1995), p. 117. On July 27, 1841, John Wadkins left his grand-daughter Eliza "a chest of drawers and a bed made by John Day." Gammon's transcription is from Warren County, North Carolina Wills, Book 38, p. 510.

29. Abraham Camp, as quoted in *The Mind of the Negro as Reflected in Letters Written during the Crisis, 1800–1860*, edited by Carter G. Woodson (New York: Russell & Russell, 1969), pp. 2–3. Signed by Francis Scott Key and three others, the 1820 petition to Congress to form the "American Society for Colonizing the Free People of Color in the United States" begins with the statement that if the "rapid increase of free people of color" continues at the same rate, "it will appear how large a proportion of our population will, in the course of even a few years consist of persons of that description . . . this description of persons are not, and cannot be either useful or happy among us . . . . No nation has it so much in its power to furnish proper settlers . . . no nation has so deep an interest in thus disposing of them." McDaniel and Julye, *Fit for Freedom, not for Friendship*, pp. 56–59. The manifest describing the "Ship Carolinian's Company, arrived at Monrovia December 4, 1830," lists John Day as a cabinetmaker who could read and write. It can be accessed online in the Samuel J. May Anti-Slavery Collection of the Cornell University Library. See *Tables Showing the Number of Emigrants and Recaptured Africans Sent to the Colony of Liberia by the Government of the United States: Also, the Number of Emigrants Free Born, Number That Purchased Their Freedom, Number Emancipated andc: Together with a Census of the Colony, and a Report of Its Commerce, andc, September 1845* (Washington, D.C.: Government Printing Office, 1845).

30. Jill Baskin Schade, email message to Janie Leigh Carter and Patricia Rogers, July 24, 2013. Schade is a doctoral candidate at the University of Virginia, whose dissertation explores the visual and material culture of African Americans in Liberia from 1821 to 1865. She notes that a material analysis of Thomas Day's work might indicate whether he used African woods. She also raises the question of whether early work that appears to be by Thomas Day is actually by his brother. In addition to the *African Repository*, the initial notice about John Day's interest in exporting furniture was published in the *Spectator* (New York) on May 4, 1835. The September 15, 1836, edition of that paper reported that "John Day, a cabinetmaker," had moved to the

Caldwell settlement on July 30, 1836, to take charge of a boys' school supported by the "American Baptist Foreign Mission," the earliest report of his work as a missionary in Liberia.

31. "Thomas Day, Cabinet Maker," *Milton Gazette & Roanoke Advertiser*, March 1, 1827.

32. *Acts Passed by the General Assembly of North Carolina at Its Session Commencing on the 25th of December, 1826* (Raleigh, N.C.: Lawrence & Lemay, 1827), chap. 21, p. 67: "An act to prevent free persons of colour from migrating into this State for the good government of such persons resident in the State, and for other purposes." *Journals of the Senate and of the House of Commons and General Assembly of the State of North Carolina at the Session of 1830–31* (Raleigh, N.C.: Lawrence & Lemay, 1831), pp. 237–38. The bill permitting Aquilla Day to reside in North Carolina passed 74 to 40. The petition, with Saunders's imprimatur, was ordered published in the official record the same day, Christmas Eve, 1830. The bill appears in *Acts Passed by the General Assembly of the State of North Carolina at the Session of 1830–31* (Raleigh, N.C.: Lawrence & Lemay, 1831), chap. 81, sec. 1–2, p. 79: "An act to authorize Aquilla Day, otherwise called Aquilla Wilson, to reside in the State." Research by Dr. G. C. Waldrep III of Bucknell University has identified Aquilla as the daughter of Martin Wilson and Priscilla Matthews, both descended from long lines of free people of color in Halifax County. The Wilsons lived near Halifax Court House, and the Matthews were in the county as early as 1760. Born in 1805 or 1806, Aquilla was the sixth of twelve children. In 1837 the entire family migrated to Jennings County, Indiana. A letter from Day to his daughter indicates that either Priscilla or Aquilla's sister Frances (who married a cousin named William Wilson and lived in Pike County, Ohio) visited the Days in Milton as late as 1851. G. C. Waldrep, telephone interview with Patricia Rogers, October 10, 2006. Journal of the House of Commons of North Carolina, 1830–1831, 238, OAH.

33. Ira Berlin to Laurel Sneed, March 2007, TDEP.

34. James C. Scott, *Domination and the Arts of Resistance: Hidden Transcripts* (New Haven, Conn.: Yale University Press, 1990), pp. 4, 13–14, 87–90, 164–65, 199.

35. Thomas Day to Mary Ann Day, not dated, collection of Mary Satterfield (1911–2003), Milton, N.C.

36. Thomas Day to Mary Ann Day, November 27, 1851, collection of Mary Satterfield (1911–2003), Milton, N.C.

37. David L. Lightner and Alexander M. Ragan, "Were African American Slaveholders Benevolent or Exploitative? A Quantitative Approach," *Journal of Southern History* 71, no. 3 (August 2005): 552, 555. The authors conclude that in 1830, a white person was only three times as likely as a free person of color to own a slave. Free blacks totaled 2.01 percent of North Carolina's total population in 1830 and 3.01 percent in 1840. Franklin, *The Free Negro in North Carolina*, pp. 18, 236–37. Juliet E. K. Walker, *The History of Black Business in America: Capitalism, Race, Entrepreneurship* (New York: Twayne Publishers, 1998), p. 38.

38. Paquette, "Thomas Day: An Inquiry," pp. 13–14. Paquette details the relationship between Day and the Siewers brothers and quotes the journal entry from Augustus Fogle describing Day's workforce. See Augustus Fogle, Travel Accounts for the Years 1832–1895, Augustus T. Fogle Letters, 1820–1897, Moravian Archives, Winston-Salem, North Carolina. Seventh Census of the United States, 1850, Caswell County, North Carolina, Slave Schedule, National Archives, Washington, D.C. The enumeration of Day's slaves was taken on two different dates. The list also included a sixty-six-year-old man, a woman, fifty-five, and two females in their early twenties. People identified as mulatto in the census were sometimes described as "bright" or "yellow," meaning that they were not dark-skinned. Day's daughter Mary Ann is classified as mulatto in the 1850 census when she was at school in Wilbraham. Her brother Thomas has no racial designation. Franklin, *The Free Negro in North Carolina*, p. 237.

39. Daniel R. Biddle and Murray Dubin, *Tasting Freedom: Octavius Catto and the Battle for Equality in Civil War America* (Philadelphia: Temple University Press, 2010), p. 78, notes that Brick Wesley African Methodist Episcopal Church on Lombard Street had a seating capacity of eight hundred. *The Elite of Our People: Joseph Willson's Sketches of Black Upper Class Life in Antebellum Philadelphia*, edited by Julie Winch (University Park: Pennsylvania State University Press, 2000), p. 130 n. 37. Peter H. Wood, "What We Know of the 20 People Who Were with Thomas Day in Philadelphia," notes shared with the Thomas Day Education Project, June 13, 2007. William Whipper is profiled in *The Black Abolitionist Papers: The United States, 1830–46*, 3: 129–30. The reference to Whipper's clandestine Underground Railroad activities is from William Still, *The Underground Rail Road* (Philadelphia: Porter & Coates, 1872), pp. 735–36.

40. M. B. Goodwin, "History of Schools of the Colored Population," in *The American*

Negro: His History and Literature (New York: Arno Press and *New York Times*, 1969), p. 213. This "History" is a reprint of "Section C of the *Special Report of the Commissioner of Education on the Improvement of Public Schools in the District of Columbia, 1871.*" The report was originally issued by Henry Barnard, the first U.S. Commissioner of Education. It provided a detailed account of the development of the District's African American schools and substantial biographical information about Reverend John Francis Cook, James H. Fleet, and Thomas Day's daughters-in-law, Virginia and Annie Washington (pp. 196, 200–203, 205, 207–11, 213–14, 216–17). Dorothy S. Provine, *District of Columbia Free Negro Registers, 1821–1861*, 2 vols. (Berwyn Heights, Md.: Heritage Books 1996), 2: 229. Cook was manumitted on December 10, 1832, and his emancipation was recorded three days later under Registration No. 1069: "Lethee (Lethe) Tanner, in consideration of five dollars, manumits her 'servant man' named John Francis Cook, who is about twenty-two years old."

41. Provine, *District of Columbia Free Negro Registers*, 1: 154. Tanner's activities are detailed in a lengthy note accompanying Registration No. 705, the July 9, 1829, manumission paper for John Cook's brother Alfred. The list of people Tanner emancipated is derived from this note and from cross-checking the manumission records of people listed in the index under Tanner and Cook. Augustus Price's full name and his close relationship to Andrew Jackson are reported in *The Black Abolitionist Papers: The United States, 1830–46*, 3: 153. This relationship was also noted by James Parton, a nineteenth-century Jackson biographer who interviewed Jackson's official private secretary, Nicholas Trist (James Parton, *Life of Andrew Jackson*, 3 vols. [New York: Mason Brothers, 1861], 3: 606–7). According to historian Peter Wood, Gardiner's guests were "a veritable who's who of the black elite. . . . Almost all of them seem to have achieved remarkable economic success. All have confronted the issues of social and civic leadership (integration vs. separation, Africa vs. America, open abolitionism vs. accommodationist gradualism, acceptance vs. confrontation) that are uppermost in the country in that turbulent year" (Peter Wood to Laurel Sneed, June 13, 2007, TDEP).

42. Jefferson Morley, *Snow-Storm in August: Washington City, Francis Scott Key, and the Forgotten Race Riot of 1835* (New York: Nan A. Talese/Doubleday 2012), pp. 89, 104, 105, 154, 214. Robert Vincent Remini, *Andrew Jackson: The Course of American Democracy, 1833–1845*, 3 vols. (Baltimore, Md.: Johns Hopkins University Press, 1998), 3: 269. Faced with demands to fire Augustus, Jackson responded, "My servants are" responsible to "me alone" and are "entitled to protection at my hands" (Parton, *Life of Andrew Jackson*, 3: 606–7).

43. *The Present State and Condition of the Free People of Color of the City of Philadelphia and Adjoining Districts as Exhibited by the Report of a Committee of the Pennsylvania Society for Promoting the Abolition of Slavery, &c.* (Philadelphia: the Society, 1838), pp. 1, 26–28. The population figure of 13,591 free black individuals appears on page 5.

44. Information about Peter and Serena Gardiner is on pp. 130 n. 35 and 147 n. 60; on Frederick Augustus Hinton, pp. 58–60, 150–51 n. 72; on Junius Morel, pp. 135–37 nn. 49–50 and p. 150 n. 71. All, Winch ed., *The Elite of Our People*. Charles Bennett Ray is mentioned several times in the story and we felt this bolstered the claim that Wesleyan was a training ground for abolitionists. No academic we consulted had ever seen anything like this spelled out in writing. It sets us up for raising a question about Day's use of the same terms. M. N. Work, "Life of Charles B. Ray," *Journal of Negro History* 4, no. 4 (October 1919): 369–70. Correspondence between Ray and Washington attorney Jacob Bigelow offers rare documentation of coded language Underground Railroad operatives used, this time in a plan to transport "a little parcel" to Canada: a ten-year-old slave girl disguised as a boy. According to Ray, railroad terminology was used to "more effectively secure concealment" of fugitive slaves; "box" and "package" also referred to human cargo; "depot" and "station," to a safe destination. Bigelow asks Ray to inform him of the "arrival of the package without breakage or injury" and to return the disguise, its "wrapper . . . for I have another similar parcel to send."

45. Erica Armstrong Dunbar, *A Fragile Freedom* (New Haven, Conn.: Yale University Press, 2008), p. 135. Julie Winch, *A Gentleman of Color: James Forten* (New York: Oxford University Press, 1997), p. 260. Hinton was a member of Forten's inner circle as well as William Lloyd Garrison's. Jean Fagan Yellin, *Harriet Jacobs: A Life* (New York: Basic Civitas Books, 2004), p. 65.

46. *Journal of the Convention, Called by the Freemen of North-Carolina to Amend the Constitution of the State, which Assembled in the City of Raleigh on the 4th of June 1835, and Continued in Session until the 11th Day of July Thereafter* (Philadelphia: J. Gales & Son, 1835), pp. 22–23. Article 1, section 3 of the amended constitution states that "No free Negro, free mulatto or free persons of

mixed blood descended from negro ancestors to the fourth generation inclusive, though the ancestor of each generation may have been a white person, shall vote for members of the Senate or House of Commons." "Negro Voters," *Liberator*, July 4, 1835.

47. Loren Schweninger, "John Carruthers Stanly and the Anomaly of Black Slaveholding," *North Carolina Historical Review* 67, no. 2 (April 1990): 165, 178. Schweninger concludes that Stanly owned more than twice as many slaves as the individual widely alleged to be the second largest free black slave owner in the South.

48. Ibid., pp. 177, 192. Schweninger notes that in 1830 Stanly owned all but a few of the 163 slaves listed as living on his various properties. Stephen Franks Miller, *Recollections of Newbern Fifty Years Ago: With an Appendix Including Letters from Judges Gaston, Donnell, Manly and Gov. Swain* (Raleigh, N.C.: S. D. Poole, 1874), p. 21. The recollections of this ninety-year old attorney, newspaper editor, and former New Bern resident are available through the Eastern North Carolina University Digital Library, http://digital.lib.ecu.edu/13575 (accessed December 5, 2013).

49. Schweninger, "John Carruthers Stanly and the Anomaly of Black Slaveholding," p. 178. The author identifies John D. Whitford as the resident who described Stanly as a "harsh taskmaster." Colonel John Dalton Whitford, a local historian, was elected mayor of New Bern at twenty-one, president of the Atlantic & North Carolina Railroad at twenty-nine, and a delegate to the state convention that voted for secession in 1861. See Bill Hand, *A Walking Guide to North Carolina's Historic New Bern* (Charleston, S.C.: History Press, 2007), p. 67. Franklin, *The Free Negro in North Carolina*, p. 31.

50. "Negro Voters," *Liberator*, July 4, 1835. *Cape Fear Recorder*, September 10, 1830.

51. "Important Intelligence from Liberia," *Colored American*, December 8, 1848. Sheridan's lengthy letter from Liberia to abolitionist Lewis Tappan, Tappan's response, and this revelation that Sheridan had originally told him that he regarded colonization efforts as a "humbug" consumed the entire front page and part of the second of this edition of the newspaper. "From the Pennsylvania Freeman: Louis Sheridan," *Colored American*, August 4, 1838. The newspaper reprinted an undated article and anonymous letter that had appeared in the *Pennsylvania Freeman*, a publication edited by John Greenleaf Whittier. The *Colored American* did not reveal the identity of the letter's author until four months later.

52. The source for Stanly's Petition PAR 11280205 to free two mulatto boys is available online at http://library.uncg.edu/slavery/details.aspx?pid=735.

53. According to an online transcription of the "session minutes" of the Milton Presbyterian Church by librarian Martha Spencer, a Caswell County native, Cory became a member on April 6, 1845. http://www.roots.web.ancestry.com/~nccaswel/misc/milton-ses.htm (accessed December 5, 2013). Marshall and Leimenstoll, *Thomas Day: Master Craftsman*, p. 29. A member of the audience at the panel discussion "Thomas Day: Man, Maker and Mogul," at the Renwick Gallery of the Smithsonian American Art Museum on May 10, 2013, asked if Day was involved with the Underground Railroad. Panelists did not address the question, but attendee Marian Thomas, the former director of the Thomas Day House/Union Tavern Restoration, Inc., stated that the rumor of Day's involvement originated with a Milton resident who lived in the tavern before it burned and whose forebears knew Day personally.

54. The podcast of Peter H. Wood's interview can be accessed at http://ashp.cuny.edu/?podcast=free-blacks-in-the-south-life-of-thomas-day.

55. Lunsford Lane, *The Narrative of Lunsford Lane, Formerly of Raleigh, N.C., Embracing an Account of His Early Life, the Redemption by Purchase of Himself and Family from Slavery. And His Banishment from the Place of His Birth for the Crime of Wearing a Colored Skin, Published by Himself* (Boston: J. G. Torrey, 1842), p. 31.

56. Thomas Day to David L. Swain, November 17, 1847, University of North Carolina Papers (#40005), University Archives, Wilson Library (hereafter WL), Chapel Hill. Thomas Day to Benjamin S. Guion, November 17, 1847, Papers of the Philanthropic and Dialectic Societies, WL. Thomas Day to Peter E. Hines, November 1, 1848, Papers of the Philanthropic and Dialectic Societies, WL. Loren Schweninger, *Black Property Owners in the South, 1790–1915* (Champaign: University of Illinois Press, 1990), 136.

57. James L. Roark, Samuel Candler Dobbs Professor of American History at Emory University, comments about "the many lives and interests," "Thomas Day: Man, Maker and Mogul," Renwick Gallery, May 10, 2013. William A. Robinson, quoting Caroline Pell Gunter and Paul Ader in "Thomas Day and His Family," pp. 123–24. Gunter described Day's wife as "Portuguese" in the *News & Observer*, June 30, 1929. Ader said Day was West Indian in the *Greensboro Daily News*, February 9, 1941. Recent assumptions about Day's appearance have

been based on a frequently published image of a fair-skinned man long believed to be John Day Jr. and therefore assumed to resemble his brother to some degree, but the picture has now been determined to have been misidentified. In a telephone interview with Patricia Rogers on June 6, 2013, Ann Shumard, Curator of Photographs at the Smithsonian's National Portrait Gallery and curator of "A Durable Memento: Portraits by Augustus Washington," a 1999 exhibition that included daguerreotypes of prominent black Americans living in Liberia. Shumard said that there is "no way that could be a portrait of John Day," because John Day died in 1859 and the costume of the man in the photograph is considerably later. The image identified as John Day's portrait first appeared in Nan F. Weeks and Blanche Sydnor White, *Liberia for Christ: Presenting the Story of Virginia Baptists in the Colonization, Development, and Christian Conquest of the Republic of Liberia* (Richmond, Va.: Women's Missionary Union by Virginia, 1959), p. 11.

58. *Laws of the State of North Carolina Passed by the General Assembly at the Session of 1844–1845* (Raleigh, N.C.: Thomas J. Lemay, 1845), chap. 36, sec. 14, pp. 152–53. An amendment to previous acts, the law excluded blacks by stating that "any branch of English education may be taught in said schools; and all white persons over the age of four years old shall be permitted the school of their district, as scholars, and receive instruction therein." Franklin, *The Free Negro in North Carolina*, p. 164. Schweninger, *Black Property Owners in the South, 1790–1915*, p. 138.

59. David Sherman, *History of the Wesleyan Academy at Wilbraham, Mass., 1817–1890* (Boston: McDonald & Gill Company, 1893), p. 286. *Twenty-fifth Annual Catalogue of the Wesleyan Academy, Wilbraham, Mass., 1849–1850* (Springfield, Mass.: George W. Wilson Printer, 1850), p. 21. Ira Berlin to Laurel C. Sneed, March 2007, TDEP.

60. "American Anti-Slavery Society. Roll of Members and Delegates, Present at the Late Annual Meeting of the Anti-Slavery Society," *Liberator*, May 29, 1840. Caswell County Deed Book 2, March 11, 1858, pp. 508–9, Office of the Register of Deeds, Caswell County Courthouse, Yanceyville, N.C. One of Day's creditors was "Seymore & Company of New York," likely the prominent hardware retailer W. N. Seymour & Co. on Chatham Square. E. Didier depicted the exterior of the building and its name in his painting *Auction at Chatham Square* (Museum of the City of New York). The museum also owns "Chatham Square. New York," an N. Currier lithograph that shows the Seymour hardware emporium in the background. In an undated letter to Mary Ann, Day notes that receipt of a "box of goods" that "Mr. James Hunter of New York" shipped to her at school has not been acknowledged. Day insists that she go to the Wilbraham "depot" with Wesleyan's principal, Miner Raymond, to ascertain the whereabouts of the "box." Given the town's reputation as an Underground Railroad stronghold with a bevy of safe houses, Day's now known ties to abolitionists associated with the Underground Railroad and long-standing rumors of his own involvement, one may infer that the references to the "box of goods" and "depot" are code for fugitive slaves and a safe haven.

61. Sherman, *History of the Wesleyan Academy*, p. 280. "Agency in Behalf of the Free People of Color," *Colored American*, December 7, 1839. The announcement of Beman's employment included a request for "information of all schools and seminaries of higher grades, where persons of color may enjoy the same advantages accorded to the whites." *Colored American*, May 23, 1840.

62. *Minutes of the Fifth Annual Convention for the Improvement of the Free People of Colour in the United States: Held by Adjournments, in the Wesley Church, Philadelphia, from the First to the Fifth of June, Inclusive, 1835* (Philadelphia: William P. Gibbons, 1835), p. 17. Yellin, *Harriet Jacobs*, p. 298 n. 97. Louisa Jacobs, daughter of Harriet Jacobs, an escaped slave from Edenton, North Carolina, attended Kellogg's integrated school in 1848. In his undated letter to Mary Ann, Day wrote, "Devereux was worse when he came home from Clinton by a great deal than when he left home" (Collection of Milton community historian, Mary Satterfield [1911–2003]). Although no catalogue for the 1849 school year has yet been found to verify Devereux's attendance, the context of Day's letter leaves room for the possibility that Devereux briefly attended this work-study school before joining his siblings in Massachusetts. *Annual Catalogue & Circular of Terms of Comer's Commercial College of Boston* (Boston: Damrell & Moore, 1857), frontispiece. Cook's diary shows that he and Pittsburgh abolitionist J. B. Vashon were in constant communication. Vashon's son George had received a B.A. from Oberlin in 1844 and was its first African American graduate. Cook's own sons, John and George, would later go there, too. John also attended New York Central College, where his father's friend Charles Reason was professor of Greek, Latin, French, and mathematics. Cook recorded the arduous twelve-day round trip between Philadelphia to McGrawville and back to Washington from August 31 to September 11, 1851, in his diary.

63. The U.S. Federal Census of 1850 lists Devereux in Milton at the same time Mary Ann and Thomas were enumerated in Wilbraham. They are listed in the Wesleyan catalogues of 1849–1850, 1850–1851, and 1851–1852. Devereux is listed only in the catalogues of 1850–1851 and 1851–1852. Thomas Day to Mary Ann Day, November 27, 1851. The transcribed copy from the collection of Mary Satterfield (1911–2003), Milton, N.C., in the archives of the Thomas Day Education Project has periods after the "R" and the "M," while an undated copy of a fragment of the mimeographed original letter owned by Satterfield and William A. Robinson before her does not.

64. Sherman, *History of the Wesleyan Academy*, pp. 196, 225. Josephine F. Pacheco, *The Pearl: A Failed Slave Escape on the Potomac* (Chapel Hill: University of North Carolina Press, 2005), pp. 180–82. Two sources indicate that Day delivered and retrieved his children from boarding school: the November 27, 1851, letter to Mary Ann in which he openly worries about Devereux's health and tells her he will go to see him in Boston in the summer of 1852; and John Cook's diary entry of May 12, 1850, which suggests that Day was on his way from Milton to Wilbraham with Thomas Jr. and Mary Ann. From Washington City, they could have taken trains to Baltimore and Philadelphia and from Philadelphia a steamship to New York and from there to Boston, the port nearest to Wilbraham. From Boston he could have taken a train to Springfield and then a stagecoach to Wilbraham, which was and is a Springfield suburb. Sherman, *History of the Wesleyan Academy*, p. 238: "one of the great enterprises of the time was the building of the Boston & Albany railroad which was completed from Boston to Springfield in 1839." The debate leading to the passage of the Fugitive Slave Act is vividly depicted by historian Pacheco, *The Pearl: A Failed Slave Escape on the Potomac*.

65. "Black codes were enacted for the convenience of the white majority who applied them in times of . . . stress and slave unrest but ignored them when it was in their interest" (Rodney Barfield, "Thomas and John Day and the Journey to North Carolina," in *Thomas Day: African American Furniture Maker*, p. 9). "The Cook Family in History," *Negro History Bulletin* 9, no. 9 (June 1946): 195–96. The article focuses on the Cook family of Fredericksburg, Virginia, which included John Hartwell Cook, a student of the Reverend John F. Cook's in Washington and later dean of Howard University Law School.

66. Lewis Tappan reported Sheridan's trip in the *Colored American*, December 8, 1838. Kathleen Housley, "Yours for the Oppressed: The Life of Jehiel C. Beman," *Journal of Negro History* 7, no. 1 (Winter 1992): 17–29. Beman, a shoemaker and preacher from Middletown, Connecticut, reported his experience on the train in a letter to the editor for the August 16, 1844, edition of the *Emancipator*. After attending a conference in Baltimore, he and another minister visited several black leaders in Washington, including "Rev. Mr. Cook and his school for black children." A facsimile of Day's original insolvency indenture lists "Seymore & Co." of New York, P. E. Brenan of Baltimore, and Pannell and Son of Petersburg as creditors (Caswell County Deed Book II, March 11 [1858], p. 508, Caswell County Court House, Yanceyville, N.C.).

67. Wilbur H. Siebert, *The Underground Railroad from Slavery to Freedom: A Comprehensive History* (1898; reprint, Mineola, N.Y.: Dover, 2006), p. 10. Franklin, *The Free Negro in North Carolina*, pp. 211–12. John C. Calhoun, *A Disquisition on Government and A Discourse on the Constitution and Government of the United States*, edited by Richard K. Cralle (Columbia, S.C.: A. S. Johnson, 1851), pp. 37–38, online version accessed on Google Books.

68. John Day, "Sentiments of Colonization in Liberia," *Colonization Herald*, p. 145.

69. Later, Grimes raised the funds to buy the freedom of Anthony Burns, who was apprehended by slave catchers in Boston in 1854 under the Fugitive Slave Law.

70. John Marsh, *Marsh's New Diary or Daily Rememberancer* (Boston: John Marsh, 1850. Cook Family Papers, Collection 20, box 3, Moorland-Spingarn Research Center, Howard University, Washington, D.C. Cook recorded the Days' visit on May 12 and May 13, 1850.

71. William A. Robinson to Carter Woodson, May 20, 1927, Carter G. Woodson Papers, Library of Congress. In this letter, Robinson reported that he has received a letter from Caroline Pell Gunter, whom he describes as "some white woman I don't know" and has begun to research his family. In her letter, dated May 16, 1927, Gunter requested that Robinson send a picture of "Tom Day, Sr." and asked what became of his children. Goodwin, *History of Schools of the Colored People*, pp. 206–11, 216–17, states that Anie Washington was "educated chiefly under Rev. John Francis Cook and Miss Myrtilla Miner." Miner, a white abolitionist from New York State, opened her "genteel school for missus of color" in 1851 to train black female teachers with seed money from Harriet Beecher Stowe.

72. The credit ledger identifies Thomas Day as a "Milton Cabinetmaker" (North Carolina

Credit Ledger, vol. 5, p. 187, R. G. Dun & Co. Credit Report Volumes, Baker Library, Harvard University Business School, Boston, Mass.). Founded by Lewis Tappan in 1841, the Mercantile Agency was later known as R. G. Dun & Co. of New York. Day sold 206.38 of his 270 acres in 1856. See Caswell County Deeds, Book II, March 19, September 2, and May (undated, 1856), pp. 238, 423, 355. Edward J. Balleisen, *Navigating Failure: Bankruptcy and Commercial Society in Antebellum America* (Chapel Hill: University of North Carolina Press, 2001), p. 3. Prown, "The Furniture of Thomas Day: A Reevaluation" p. 218. North Carolina Credit Ledger 5, p. 187. Caswell County Deeds, Book II, March 11, 1858, pp. 508–9, 778. Day's presumed 1861 death date may derive from the date on the chimney of the James Malone House, but his 1858 letter to former Governor Reid of North Carolina concerning a furniture order makes it clear that he was seriously ill. It is possible that the elaborate interior (and exterior trim) at the Malone House in the Caswell County town of Leasburg is the work of Thomas Jr. An excellent house carpenter in his own right, he would later fabricate the beautiful woodwork in the summer home of Zebulon Vance near Asheville.

73. "A Few Strange Incidents from the South: Through the Carolinas," *Christian Recorder*, April 15, 1865. The author, identified only as "Arnold," describes the fall of the city to federal troops, the state of its schools, and identifies a number of free black citizens, including "Mr. Thomas Day." The *Christian Recorder* also noted that "Misses Day, Sampsons and Cowan" had been teaching in Wilmington's "underground" schools for "a number of years." A letter from "Miss Mary A. Day," datelined Wilmington and describing her teaching experience there, establishes her presence in the city at the same time as her brother. See Mary Ann Day, correspondence to the American Missionary Association, August 1865, American Missionary Association Archives, no. 10027, Amistad Research Center, Tulane University, New Orleans, La. Meeting of October 9, 1864, Records of the Presbyterian Church of Milton, N.C., Historical Foundation of the Presbyterian and Reformed Churches, Montreat, N.C. The church's records show that on this date, Mrs. A. Day "requested a "letter of dismission to the First Presbyterian Church of Wilmington, North Carolina." Martha Spencer's transcription of the church minutes appears online at www.rootsweb.ancestry.com/~nccaswel/misc/milton-ses2.htm (accessed August 10, 2008).

74. The fate of Devereux is unknown, although Robinson asserts in his article that he "ran away with the white daughter of one of the best families" in Milton. *Christian Recorder*, April 15, 1865. The article noted that Mary Ann, the Sampson sisters, and Miss Cowan had helped Brigadier General Hawley organize the enormous school for nearly seven hundred children, and that it was in "splendid running order" at the time of the meeting. "A Few Strange Incidents from the South," *Christian Recorder*, September 30, 1865, described a steamship trip to Wilmington via Philadelphia, New York, and New Bern, where the reporter arrives at "Bro. Chresfield's." After preparing for the Presbyterian ministry at the Ashmun Institute (later Lincoln University), Chresfield dropped out to teach in Wilmington during the Civil War. The article describes the progress made by the students in a school held in the First Presbyterian Church, the one that Aquilla asked to join. The author appears to be describing Chresfield when he writes, "The children reflected great credit on their preceptor, a colored man of considerable education."

75. *Christian Recorder*, April 15, 1865. James D. Sampson Papers, North Carolina Room, New Hanover County Public Library, Wilmington, N.C. Beverly Tetterton, former archivist for the Wilmington library system and editor of William M. Reaves, *Strength Through Struggle: The Chronological and Historical Record of the African-American Community in Wilmington, North Carolina, 1865–1950* (Wilmington, N.C.: New Hanover County Public Library, 1998), surmises that the Days were in Wilmington through the auspices of the Sampson family.

76. Mary Ann Day, correspondence to the American Missionary Association, August 1865, American Missionary Association Archives, no. 10027, Amistad Research Center, Tulane University, New Orleans, La.

77. Thomas Day's Bible lists Mary Ann's death date as September 6, 1870. Her infant son, James Day Chresfield, died in January 1871. Annie Day Shepard's husband, Dr. D. A. Robinson, a graduate of Shaw University Medical School in Raleigh, North Carolina, was a physician in Danville, Virginia.

Figure 1   Side chair attributed to Richard
Parkin, Philadelphia, Pennsylvania, 1834–1840.
Walnut and walnut veneer with tulip poplar.
H. 32¼", W. 18", D. 18". (Courtesy, Carswell
Rush Berlin, Inc.; photo, Gavin Ashworth.)

Carswell Rush Berlin

"A Shadow of a Magnitude": The Furniture of Thomas Cook and Richard Parkin

▼ THE NAMES OF THOMAS COOK and Richard Parkin are not typically listed alongside those of Anthony G. Quervelle, Joseph B. Barry, Michel Bouvier, and other renowned Philadelphia furniture makers of the classical period. Yet, at the time, that is precisely the company Cook and Parkin kept. *Niles' Weekly Register*'s review of the Franklin Institute's second annual exhibition of manufactures in 1825 listed "beautiful and otherwise remarkable specimens of manufacture" by the city's leading cabinetmakers, including "White, Bouvier, . . . Quervyl [Quervelle], . . . [and] Cook and Parkins [*sic*]."[1]

The stenciled and printed trademark of Cook and Parkin's firm and the printed label of Richard Parkin are found on some of the most avant-garde pieces of American classical furniture, but many unmarked objects of comparable importance have escaped the attention of scholars and collectors. Thanks to the recent discovery of a pair of side chairs, one of which is illustrated in figure 1, Parkin's name can now be associated with seating in the collections of the Metropolitan Museum of Art, the Philadelphia Museum of Art, and the Yale University Art Gallery. These new findings have provided the impetus to reexamine the lives and work of Cook and Parkin, to raise questions about their training and design influences, and to return them to their former place in the firmament of Philadelphia's nineteenth-century cabinetmaking community.

Richard Parkin was born in England circa 1787, died in Philadelphia on September 16, 1861, and was buried in the American Mechanics Cemetery on Islington Lane at Twenty-Seventh Street. Family tradition maintains that he emigrated from Sheffield, England, and it is likely that he served his apprenticeship before coming to the United States. John and Hannah (Padley) Parkin of Sheffield had a son named Richard in 1791, but no definitive connection between that family and the émigré cabinetmaker has been established. Similarly, a family of Parkins arrived in Philadelphia from Liverpool on the ship *Lancaster* in September 1819, but the passenger manifest does not mention anyone named Richard. The cabinetmaker's absence in the 1810 and 1820 federal censuses suggests that he arrived shortly before his name began to appear in Philadelphia directories in partnership with Cook in 1819.[2]

On February 6, 1825, Parkin married Clara Stevens (1801–1875) in a civil ceremony performed by Philadelphia mayor Joseph Watson (1784–1841). Parkin may have had a business connection to Watson, who worked as a lumber merchant before taking office in 1824. Richard and Clara had six children. The eldest, Thomas, was born in Philadelphia in 1827, followed by

Sarah, born in 1831, twins Clara (d. 1860) and Anna in 1833, Henry (d. 1885) in 1835, and Richard Jr. two years later. All three sons became cabinetmakers, but none of their work has been identified.[3]

Thomas Cook's naturalization application, dated July 16, 1819, describes his trade as "cabinetmaker" and states that he was born in Yorkshire, England, on May 12, 1789, emigrated from London, and arrived in Philadelphia on April 29, 1817. His wife, Ann (ca. 1786–1871), also was born in England, and it is likely that they came to America together. Thomas was listed at 26 Bank Street in Dock Ward in the 1820 Philadelphia city directories. He and Ann had one child, a daughter, Mary (ca. 1823–187?). Cook retired from business at the age of forty-nine, younger than many of his contemporaries. He seems to have accumulated enough capital to invest in real estate, like his competitors Bouvier and Quervelle. Beginning circa 1835, Cook devoted his time to the acquisition of investment property and bought at least eight such lots. The 1860 U.S. census recorded his wealth at $10,000 and Parkin's at $1,000, a disparity that might be explained by the number of children they each raised. Cook died on May 13, 1868, at seventy-nine, after thirty-one years as a "gentleman," leaving his investments to his daughter, Mary Stell-wagen, and the income from rents and dividends from securities to his wife for her lifetime. Two years after his death, the 1870 census valued his widow's net worth at $15,000 and his daughter's at $24,000.[4]

Cook & Parkin

Thomas Cook and Richard Parkin were among the first generation of English cabinetmakers born during the classical revival of the late eighteenth century. Their birth dates nearly coincided with the publication of George Hepplewhite's *Cabinet-Maker and Upholsterer's Guide* (1788), the first broadly available design book in the classical taste, and their apprenticeships likely began just before the publication of Thomas Sheraton's *Cabinet Dictionary* (1803). The latter book and Thomas Hope's *Household Furniture and Interior Decoration* (1807) helped shift the focus of classical design from Robert Adam's abstract interpretations of ancient designs to furniture based on archaeological models. As furniture historian Joseph Aronson suggests, pattern books also heralded the final step in an "evolution from cottage handi-craft through the Factory System and the Industrial Revolution . . . the ultimate division of functions . . . aiming for greater output and efficiency to meet the demands of expanding markets and wealth." During their appren-ticeships, Cook and Parkin would have developed specialized hand skills while learning how to design furniture, create working drawings, and exploit the new industrialized systems of production. By the time they arrived in Philadelphia, both men were capable craftsmen with clear ideas about what furniture in the classical taste should look like and how it should be made.[5]

The Philadelphia directory listed Cook & Parkin first as "Chair Makers" at 26 Bank Street in 1819, then as "Cabinet Makers" at 56 Walnut Street from 1820 to 1833 (fig. 2). Cook also appeared alone, listed as a cabinetmaker at 4 Fromberger's Court in *Paxton's Directory*, in 1819, and in some directories he and Parkin were listed jointly as "Chair Makers" as late as 1824. In 1829,

while maintaining a business at 56 Walnut Street, both men began working at separate addresses, Parkin at 94 South Third Street and Cook at 7 Pear Street. Four years later, they dissolved their partnership when Parkin moved to Egyptian Hall, a building at 134 South Second Street, leased from cabinetmaker Joseph Barry; Cook remained at 56 Walnut Street.[6]

Cook and Parkin's separation in 1829 may have been an expedient way to gain production space while maintaining 56 Walnut Street as a showroom. Scholar Deborah Ducoff-Barone has noted that the central business district, which encompassed that area of Walnut Street, was a prestigious location and the epicenter of Philadelphia's furniture making industry (fig. 3). Rents were high, and only the most successful and well-capitalized firms could afford to set up and maintain businesses there. All but two of the cabinet-making enterprises mentioned in the October 15, 1825, issue of *Niles' Weekly Register* were located within two blocks of Cook and Parkin's Walnut Street address and Parkin's shop on South Second Street (after 1833): Quervelle at 126 South Second Street (1825–1848), Bouvier at 91 South Second Street (1825–1844), Charles H. White at 109 Walnut Street (1815–1854), and John Jamison at 75 Dock Street (1815–1829). These shop masters understood that location was key to securing wealthy local patrons and attracting foreign buyers and entrepreneurs engaged in the coastal trade.[7]

Cook maintained a business at 56 Walnut until 1837, when he retired from the cabinetmaking trade. City directories referred to him as a "gentleman" until 1860, eight years before his death. Parkin's forty-one-year career was even more extensive, among the longest of any Philadelphia cabinetmaker of the period. Similarly, Cook and Parkin's fourteen-year partnership was longer than 90 percent of all cabinetmaking businesses recorded in Philadelphia between 1800 and 1840.[8]

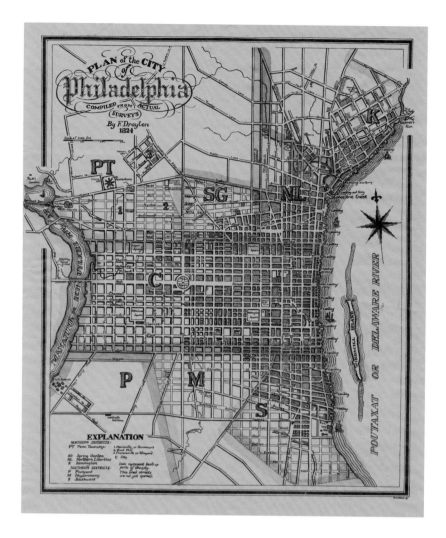

Figure 3 Joseph Drayton, *Plan of the City of Philadelphia*, published by H. C. Cary and I. Lea, Philadelphia, Pennsylvania, 1824. Hand-colored engraving on paper. 15½" x 17¼". (Courtesy, Historical Society of Pennsylvania.) This detail shows the central business district and the locations of businesses maintained by Cook & Parkin, Thomas Cook, and Richard Parkin.

In the absence of documentation, the size of Cook and Parkin's manufacturing business can be extrapolated through comparison with other firms. Barry advertised "employment for six journeymen cabinetmakers" while working at 134 South Second Street, a building he subsequently leased to Joseph Aiken and then to Richard Parkin. While at that location, Aiken's shop had "five turning lathes and a number of workbenches." During Barry's tenancy, 134 South Second Street was a shop and wareroom as well as a dwelling, but advertisements for the sale of Aiken's stock in 1829 indicate that the space was entirely dedicated to selling furniture. It is reasonable to assume that the workforce and scope of Parkin's business was larger than Barry's and at least as large as Aiken's, but smaller than that of Cook and Parkin.[9]

Maintaining a large business between 1819 and 1833 was a notable accomplishment for Cook & Parkin because that period was as difficult and unstable as the American cabinet trade had ever known. Their firm survived two major depressions, damage to the local economy caused by President Andrew Jackson's struggle with the Second Bank of the United States, wild fluctuations in the price of mahogany, and worker strikes precipitated by two technological advancements—the introduction of the steam-powered lathe and the circular saw.

In 1826 confrontations between master cabinetmakers and journeymen forced a revision of piecework prices and, by extension, the cost to produce various furniture forms. Working with a three-man "Committee of Journeymen," the "Committee of Employers," composed of Parkin, White, and Jamison, issued a broadside detailing the "per centage upon start prices of jobs" in the 1826 reissuing of the 1811 *Journeyman Cabinet and Chairmaker's Pennsylvania Book of Prices*. Parkin's leadership position on the committee reflects his high stature as a cabinetmaker as well as Cook & Parkin's importance as an employer of numerous journeymen.[10]

Like many of Philadelphia's most successful firms, Cook & Parkin consigned furniture to agents in southern cities and ports in the Caribbean and South America. Outbound coastal manifests for the port of Philadelphia beginning in 1823 recorded multiple shipments by the firm to Charleston, South Carolina; Savannah, Georgia; Baltimore, Maryland; Petersburg, Virginia; and St. Thomas in the Virgin Islands. As was the case with Cook & Parkin, cabinet- and chairmaking firms that exported furniture tended to be among the most long-lived in Philadelphia.[11]

Figure 4 W. H. Rease, engraver, "George Mecke Cabinet Maker and Upholsterer," published by Wagner and McGuigan, Philadelphia, Pennsylvania, 1846. Lithograph. 20" x 13". (Courtesy, Arader Galleries, Philadelphia.) This lithograph shows the shop of cabinetmaker George Mecke at 355 North Second Street. The building is a typical Philadelphia row house with a cabinet shop in the front.

Egyptian Hall

In 1809 Barry built and occupied a row house at 134 South Second Street. Typical of many Philadelphia town houses (figs. 2, 4), this two-storey brick building had a showroom on the street side of the first floor and shop space at the back and on the second floor. Barry may have eliminated the wall that usually separated the first-floor rooms, since his space—22 by 80 feet—was much longer than most warerooms. Furniture warerooms like Barry's typically had large windows so clients and pedestrians could view the stock-in-trade. His featured "two plain Bulk windows glass 12 by 20 inches & a square head door with a fan sash."[12]

When Barry relocated his business in 1825, he rented the building at 134 South Second Street to the Pennsylvania Society of Journeymen Cabinetmakers for use as a wareroom. Aiken took over the lease in 1827, followed by Parkin six years later. During Parkin's tenancy, the front door and bulk windows were replaced with "2 large cased posts & 3 folding sash front doors" framed by "4 large Square boxed open Egyptian Columns . . . crowned by a large Carved Human Bust, Square Capt . . . surmounted by a plain Egyptian entablature and cornice," thereafter being known as Egyptian Hall (fig. 5).

Parkin's occupancy during and after this redesign advertised his status as a leader of fashion and a beacon of new taste. The façade must have created

Figure 5   A Shop Front in the Egyptian Style
(Courtesy, Sir John Soane's Museum, London.)
The façade of Parkin's shop may have resembled
this storefront in the Egyptian style. In addition
to a new façade, the redesign of Parkin's shop
opened the show room to the street, making it
more inviting and conducive to display.

Figure 6   Egyptian Hall, designed by Peter
F. Robinson for George Bullock, Piccadilly,
London, 1811–1812. (Courtesy, Sir John Soane's
Museum, London.)

a striking architectural tableau juxtaposed with Benjamin Latrobe's Bank of
Pennsylvania on South Second Street, which was the first Greek revival
building in the United States. Both buildings were testaments to the era's
fascination with ancient cultures.[13]

Parkin's wareroom was not the first or the only Philadelphia furniture
shop to undergo refurbishment during this period, but the modifications
made by him and his landlord Barry, were exceptionally elaborate and
uniquely "Egyptian," which explains Parkin's reference to that taste on his
label and trade card. It is likely that both men were familiar with Egyptian
Hall, the widely known showroom maintained by English cabinetmaker
George Bullock (1782/83–1818) in Piccadilly, London (fig. 6). In 1811 Barry
traveled to that city and Paris to buy furniture and other "fashionable articles," which he offered in the *Aurora General Advertiser* the following year—
"the newest and most fashionable Cabinet Furniture, superbly finished in
the rich Egyptian and Gothic style." The construction of Egyptian Hall
began in 1810 and would have been open when Barry was in London.[14]

Parkin remained at Egyptian Hall for about sixteen years until relocating
to Lewis Street below Thompson, where he was joined in 1853 by his son
Thomas, who died unexpectedly in 1855. From 1856 to 1860 Parkin operated
a steam sawmill, first at 399 Broad Street, then at 683 North Broad, and
finally at Spring Garden, where he was joined by another son, Richard Jr.
In 1860, which was Richard Sr.'s last directory appearance, their firm was
referred to as Richard Parkin & Son.[15]

The Furniture of Cook & Parkin
On December 10, 1819, Cook & Parkin submitted their earliest known bill
to Zaccheus Collins (1764–1831) for a mahogany breakfast table valued at
$25.00.[16] Collins was a Philadelphia merchant, botanist, and member of the
American Philosophical Society and the Philadelphia Society of Natural
Sciences. Earlier in his career, he was a partner in his father's business,

Stephen Collins & Son. They bought and sold a variety of goods, including Windsor chairs. Zaccheus's patronage shows that Cook and Parkin developed a reputation among elite members of Philadelphia society shortly after establishing their firm.[17]

One of the most significant examples of Cook & Parkin's work is a sideboard bearing the firm's engraved paper label: "COOK & PARKIN / Cabinet and Chair Makers / No. 58 / Walnut Street / Between Dock & Third Streets / South Side / PHILAD" (figs. 7, 8). The sideboard probably dates to the early 1820s, because Cook & Parkin are described as "cabinet and chair makers" in directory entries before 1824 and only as "cabinetmakers" thereafter. The stenciled ink text on other labels refers to "Cabinetware" and "mahogany seating." The design of the sideboard was adapted from the "large library or writing-table flanked with paper presses, or escrutoirs" illustrated in plate 11 in Hope's *Household Furniture and Interior Decoration*

Figure 7 Sideboard bearing the label of Cook & Parkin, Philadelphia, Pennsylvania, 1819–1824. Mahogany and mahogany veneer with white pine, tulip poplar, and oak. H. 63¼", W. 98½", D. 24¾". (Courtesy, Baltimore Museum of Art; purchase fund with exchange funds from gift from estate of Margaret Anna Abell, gift from Mr. and Mrs. Warren Wilbur Brown, gift of Jill and M. Austin Fine, bequest of Ethel Epstein Jacobs, gift of William M. Miller and Norville E. Miller II, 1989.26.)

Figure 8 Detail of the label on the sideboard illustrated in fig. 7.

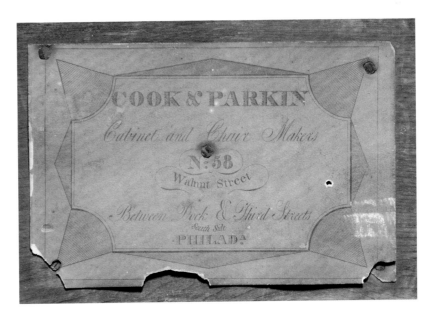

Figure 9 Design for a "large library or writing-table flanked with paper presses, or escrutoirs," illustrated in pl. 11 in Thomas Hope, *Household Furniture and Interior Decoration* (London, 1807).

Figure 10 Detail of a Pergamene capital on the sideboard illustrated in fig. 7.

(fig. 9). Many cabinetmakers were inspired by Hope's designs, but American copies of his archaeologically based designs are rare.[18]

Among the many exceptional characteristics of this sideboard is the use of Pergamene capitals surmounting the pillars flanking the upper cabinets (fig. 10). This variation on the Corinthian capital, identified with the ancient city of Pergamum near the Aegean coast of Asia Minor, has palm fronds issuing from a basket of acanthus leaves. Examples of this capital are extremely uncommon and not used in London work until the late 1820s, when they were adapted for table base designs by George Smith and Peter and Michael Angelo Nicholson. There are two plausible explanations for the use of Pergamene capitals on Cook & Parkin furniture made prior to the appearance of those capitals in London design books. They may have seen the example Lord Elgin brought to England with the Elgin marbles before they emigrated, or they had access to Giovanni Battista Piranesi's *Della magnificenza ed architettura de' Romani* (1761).[19]

A sideboard documented to Cook & Parkin and visible in a 1930s photograph of the dining room in the house of Anthony Wayne in East-town Township, Paoli, Pennsylvania, is more in keeping with conventional Philadelphia classical styles (fig. 11). Isaac Wayne purchased the piece in 1823, when he was redecorating the house and beginning his first term as a U.S. senator. On August 7 of that year, his brother-in-law and agent William Atlee wrote:

> I fear not that the article will please you, for I think it handsome, this the opinion of a good workman who accompanied me it is pronounced of good workmanship & the best materials & well *seasoned* stuff. . . . I have however exceeded your limit as to price, ten dollars, but I believe in the end you will be a gainer—I will challenge this City to produce a better, or one so gentile for that sum.[20]

A slightly later pier table with Cook & Parkin's stenciled label (figs. 12, 13) has a cavetto frieze rather than a flat and shaped frieze like those often used by Quervelle and other Philadelphia cabinetmakers who worked in the classical style. Published examples include the mantelpiece and table shown in plates 10 and 12, respectively, in Hope's *Household Furniture* (fig. 14) and an "Egyptian Chimney-Front" illustrated in Rudolph Acker-

Figure 11 Photograph showing the dining room of the Anthony Wayne House, Easttown Township, Paoli, Pennsylvania, 1930–1940. The sideboard has later brass drawer pulls.

Figure 12 Pier table bearing the stenciled label of Cook & Parkin, Philadelphia, Pennsylvania, 1825–1830. Mahogany and mahogany veneer with white pine and tulip poplar; marble. H. 40¾", W. 47¾", D. 20". (Private collection; photo, Johnny Miller.) A molding with a cavetto frieze of similar profile is illustrated in pl. 1 in the *Philadelphia Cabinet and Chair Makers' Union Book of Prices* (1828).

Figure 13 Detail of the stenciled label on the pier table illustrated in fig. 12.

2

Figure 14 Design for a table illustrated in pl. 12 in Thomas Hope, *Household Furniture and Interior Decoration* (London, 1807).

Figure 15 Detail of the pier table illustrated in fig. 12, showing the dovetails used to attach the pilasters to the bottom board.

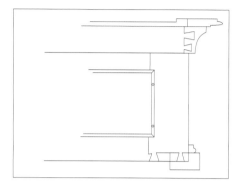

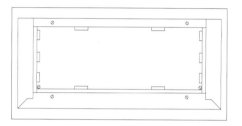

Figure 16 Detail of the pier table illustrated in fig. 12, showing the stepped miters of the boards above the frieze.

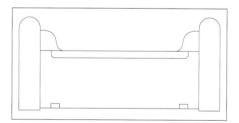

Figure 17 Detail of the pier table illustrated in fig. 12, showing the construction of the base.

mann's *Repository of Arts, Literature, Commerce, Manufactures, Fashions, and Politics.*[21]

The pilasters of the pier table are attached to the bottom board with two dovetails (fig. 15), and the molded boards of the frieze above have stepped miters at the front corners (fig. 16). By contrast, many Philadelphia pier tables of this period have pilasters attached with a single dovetail and cornice boards joined at the front corner with conventional miters, lap joints, or blind dovetails. Even more distinctive is Cook & Parkin's incorporation of a dust board under the frieze (fig. 17).

The labeled pier table is related to three unmarked examples similar to the one illustrated in figure 18. Each has a cavetto frieze below a Gothic astragal, or knife-edge molding; identical stenciling at the center and corners of the frieze; and the same bronze mounts. Although the construction of these objects differs, it is possible that all are from Cook & Parkin's shop. Structural variations are common in the work of large cabinetmaking enterprises, which typically employed several apprentices and journeymen.[22]

Cook and Parkin's entrepreneurial spirit and embrace of avant-garde design are reflected in their decision to offer faux-gilded metal furniture. An article in the *Franklin Journal and American Mechanics' Magazine* of 1827 referred to an *artimomantico* bedstead among the stock-in-trade in the firm's "cabinet wareroom." Although the journal erroneously reported that a gentleman from Leghorn (Livorno), Italy, had recently invented that alloy, the article correctly stated that *artimomantico* had been used for buttons and tableware sold by Louis Vernon Company, a Philadelphia mercantile firm specializing in luxury goods. Metal bedsteads became popular in the second quarter of the nineteenth century, largely because they were perceived as being more hygienic and insect-resistant than wooden examples. J. C. Loudon described the virtues of cast-iron bedsteads, dining tables,

Figure 18 Pier table possibly by Cook & Parkin,
Philadelphia, Pennsylvania, 1824–1833. Mahogany
and mahogany veneer with tulip poplar; marble.
H. 38", W. 38", D. 20". (Courtesy, President
James Buchanan's Wheatland, Lancaster, Penn-
sylvania; photo, Lancaster County Historical
Society.)

Figure 19 Center table bearing two stenciled labels of Cook & Parkin, Philadelphia, Pennsylvania, 1824–1833. Mahogany and mahogany veneer with white pine and ash; marble. H. 29", Diam. 38". (Courtesy, Carswell Rush Berlin, Inc.; photo, Richard Goodbody.)

Figure 20 Design for *table à thé* illustrated in pl. 515 in Pierre de la Mésangère, *Collection de meubles et objets de goût* (Paris, 1821). (Courtesy, Carswell Rush Berlin, Inc.)

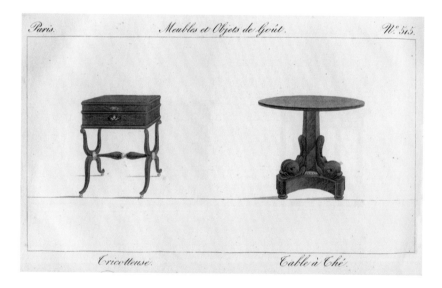

sideboards, and seating (hall, lobby, and porch chairs) in his *Encyclopaedia of Cottage, Farm and Villa Architecture and Furniture* (1833) and noted that iron bedsteads "are to be found in houses of people of wealth and fashion in London; sometimes even for best beds." The *artimomantico* bedstead offered by Cook & Parkin six years earlier was at the vanguard of this new fashion in domestic furniture.[23]

Contemporary Philadelphia cabinetmakers viewed Cook & Parkin as leaders in style and technological innovation. After Joseph Aiken and Company received the right to manufacture Daniel Powles's patent bed in 1827,

Figure 21 Drum table attributed to Cook & Parkin, Philadelphia, Pennsylvania, 1824–1833. Rosewood and rosewood veneer with unidentified secondary woods. Dimensions not recorded. (Allison Boor and Jonathan Boor, *Philadelphia Empire Furniture* [West Chester, Pa.: Boor Management, 2006], p.129).

the firm solicited Cook & Parkin's endorsement along with that of Joseph Barry, William Brown, Michel Bouvier, Lewis Costens, John Jamison, Jacob Jarret, Anthony G. Quervelle and Charles H. White. All of these men were at the summit of the cabinet trade in early nineteenth-century Philadelphia.[24]

The center table illustrated in figure 19 may have been inspired by Pierre de la Mésangère's 1821 design for a *table à thé* published in his *Collection de meubles et objets de goût* (1802–1830) (fig. 20). The center table has two ink stencils reading, "COOK & PARKIN / Cabinetware / Mahogany seating / No. 56 Walnut St. / Philadelphia" and depicting what appears to be a sofa. Three nearly identical, marble-top center tables are known, one bearing a stencil like those on the example shown here, as well as a rosewood drum table with an identical base and a radial inlaid top (fig. 21). A sixth center table of the same design but with a wooden top, was in the second-floor parlor of the George Eveleigh House at 39 Church Street, Charleston, South Carolina, when it appeared in the *Octagon Library of Early American Architecture* (1927) (fig. 22). By family tradition, the table can be traced to 1875, when Richard Maynard Marshal (1845–1894) purchased the Eveleigh House from Mary Ann Love, widow of Charles Love. Whether the table was in the house when Marshal acquired it or was inherited from his father,

Figure 22 Photograph showing the second-floor parlor of the George Eveleigh House, 39 Church Street, Charleston, South Carolina, ca. 1927.

Alexander W. Marshal, it is likely that it had been in Charleston since the late 1820s. Cook & Parkin consigned furniture to Charleston agents Thomas H. Deas in 1825 and James Dick in 1830.[25]

A mechanical chair can also be attributed to Cook & Parkin's shop based on its arm supports (figs. 23, 24), which relate directly to the acanthus-carved scrolls on the center tables (see fig. 19). Thomas King's *Modern Style of Cabi-*

Figure 23 Mechanical easy chair attributed to Cook & Parkin, Philadelphia, Pennsylvania, 1824–1833. Mahogany with white pine. H. 46½", W. 27¼", D. 29". (Courtesy, Carswell Rush Berlin, Inc.; photo, Gavin Ashworth.)

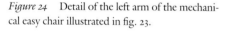

Figure 24 Detail of the left arm of the mechanical easy chair illustrated in fig. 23.

net Work Exemplified (1829) shows several mechanical and easy chairs, including examples with "inclining backs" (plate ten in the supplement) and construction features identical to those of the attributed chair (fig. 25). The crest on the Cook & Parkin chair may also have been inspired by details in one of King's illustrations. The S-scrolls, leafage, and anthemion are similar to those on the back on the "Sideboard Table" shown in plate 45 (figs. 26, 27). Variations of this design also appear on the bottom edge of the tablet back on side chairs from Parkin's shop (see figs. 50–52) and on a "Drawing Room Chair" illustrated in plate 3 of Smith's *Cabinet Maker and Upholsterer's Guide*.

American mechanical chairs are exceedingly rare. A few Boston examples are known, including one bearing the partial label of Boston upholsterer William Hancock (act. 1820–1835). In 1833 his brother's upholstery firm, John Hancock and Company, Philadelphia, placed an advertisement in *DeSilver's City Directory and Stranger's Guide*, touting "easy chairs of every description." John's advertisement also featured an engraving of a Grecian couch with a tubular drawer at one end identical to a couch illustrated in

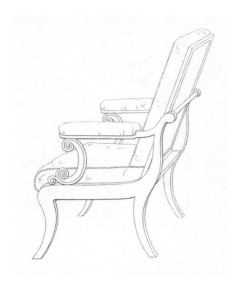

Figure 25   Detail of "Chairs with inclining backs" illustrated in pl. 10 in Thomas King, *Modern Style of Cabinet Work Exemplified* (London, 1829).

William's advertisements and on his label. John's advertisement and his 1835 estate inventory reveal that "Self Acting Chairs" and "Recumbent chairs" (easy chairs with seats that slide forward as the back reclines) were among his stock-in-trade as well. His estate inventory also reveals that Cook and Parkin owed him $77.95 and $188.40, respectively, and that Cook Thomas was one of the appraisers. Because the Hancock brothers were in the mechanical chair business, this financial connection and the close proximity of John Hancock's and Cook & Parkin's shops suggest that Hancock commissioned and upholstered the mechanical chair illustrated in figure 23. Upholsterers and decorators often ordered seating from cabinetmakers and chairmakers.[26]

Consumers often bought furniture directly from upholsterers, decorators, cabinetmakers, and other suppliers, including those in distant cities. Maria Hull Campbell of Savannah, Georgia, commissioned furniture from Cook & Parkin or Cook working independently while visiting Philadelphia. The firm had shipped furniture to Savannah during the 1820s, and it is likely that their products had developed a good reputation among her family and friends. In 1830 Maria wrote her friend George Jones Kollock (1810–1894) in Philadelphia, complaining about a repair made to a wardrobe she had purchased earlier:

> I requested to put a "ketch" on my wardrobe, similar to your Aunts, & showed him that, which he promised to do. He put a hook instead—and in attempting to hook the wardrobe, the hook flies off—This has always been the case. But now the wood has shrunk so much, that neither lock nor hook is of any use—for the doors do not meet. I must trouble you to ask [Cook & Parkin] . . . to send me a ketch . . . & I will get it fixed I hope by a Cabinet maker in this place.[27]

Campbell's dismay at the inadequately seasoned wood of her wardrobe does not seem to have shaken the loyalty other Savannah clients felt to Cook, nor did his high prices dissuade them. In August 1831 Dr. Phineas

Figure 26   Detail of the crest of the mechanical easy chair illustrated in fig. 23.

Figure 27   Detail of a sideboard table illustrated in pl. 45 in Thomas King, *Modern Style of Cabinet Work Exemplified* (1829). (Courtesy, Carswell Rush Berlin, Inc.)

Miller Kollock (1804–1872) wrote his brother and agent George:

> I am very much surprised . . . concerning the sofa—Aunt Harriet did not give more than $50.00 for both of hers exclusive of cushions, & I cannot imagine how these last can cost more than $15.00 or $20.00—If you cannot however, procure a Sofa of the description I mention (which I do not think Cook could have understood) I will thank you to . . . procure one of any cheaper pattern which Aunt Jones may like—If it will not be giving Aunt too much trouble, I wish you would consult her in regard to every thing which you purchase, inasmuch as the people with whom you have to deal will be very apt to impose upon one whom they may think not much experienced in such matters. In regard to the Sofa, if you cannot do better, I should like a Lounge like those which Aunt used to have in her rooms, which I should suppose were not quite as expensive—Whatever you get, desire the man to keep a particular description of it, as I may at some future period desire to get a match for it—If possible I do not wish the Sofa & cushions to cost more than $50.00.[28]

The following year Dr. Kollock asked his brother to procure

> at Cooke's [sic] a small sized center table, of a size suitable for such a room as Aunt's front parlor . . . of the best bird's eye maple, perfectly plain, without black moulding, the pedestal exactly after the pattern of that of my dining tables. Mr. Wm. W. Gordon of this City has one exactly of the description which I wish—I think he purchased it in Philadelphia, probably at Cooke's [sic], & I think I have understood that it cost about $30.00. I wish you would charge Cooke [sic] to be very sure, that the wood of which he makes the furniture is well seasoned; for the maple furniture which he has sent me has warped in some places, & opened at the joints.[29]

Parkin's involvement with Kollock's purchases is ambiguous. What is clear, however, is that Savannah's climate created problems with furniture purchased by both those patrons and that Cook, probably in collaboration with Parkin, made maple furniture for several prominent Savannah families. Margaret Telfair, a close friend of the Kollocks, ordered a mahogany dining table from Cook in 1836 (fig. 28), which suggests that his shop may have been responsible for the maple pieces owned by her and her husband, Alexander. The latter include a set of eighteen extraordinary curule-base, cane seat, curly-maple chairs (fig. 29), a pair of figured maple Grecian couches, and a bird's-eye maple center table.[30]

Figure 28   Thomas Cook, extension dining table, Philadelphia, Pennsylvania, 1836. Mahogany and mahogany veneer with white pine and oak. H. 28¼", Diam. 85½" (with large leaves). (Courtesy, Telfair Museum of Art, Savannah, Georgia.)

Figure 29 Side chair, possibly Thomas Cook, Philadelphia, Pennsylvania, ca. 1830. Curly or figured maple. H. 33", W. 19", D. 22". (Courtesy, Telfair Museum of Art, Savannah, Georgia.)

The Telfair table's masterful design was inspired by plate 31 in Thomas Sheraton's *Designs for Household Furniture* (1812) (fig. 30) and plate 8 in Richard Brown's *The Rudiments of Drawing Cabinet and Upholstery Furniture* (1820) (fig. 31), and the scrolled supports were derived from those shown in supplementary plate 17 in King's *Modern Style of Cabinet Work Exemplified* (fig. 32). Although American cabinetmakers occasionally adapted details from different plates in the same design book, the maker of the Tel-

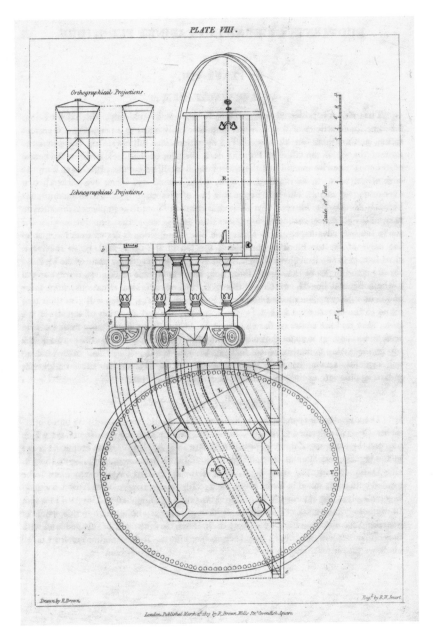

Figure 30 Design for a dining table in pl. 31 in Thomas Sheraton, *Designs for Household Furniture* (London, 1812).

Figure 31 Design for a dining table in pl. 8 in Richard Brown, *The Rudiments of Drawing Cabinet and Upholstery Furniture* (London, 1820). (Courtesy, Carswell Rush Berlin, Inc.)

Figure 32 Designs for "Supports for Sideboard Tables" illustrated in pl. 17 in the supplement of Thomas King, *The Modern Style of Cabinet Work Exemplified* (London, 1829). (Courtesy, Carswell Rush Berlin, Inc.) The center design relates to the supports of the table illustrated in fig. 28.

fair table's reliance on three design books is highly unusual. This attests to the depth of Cook's library and knowledge of British classical style and his ability to work within that idiom.

Cook & Parkin's favorable reputation in the South is further confirmed by Louisiana senator Josiah Stoddard Johnston's (1784–1833) patronage. On January 16, 1826, Cook and Parkin wrote, "This being the season of the

Figure 33 Richard Parkin, washstand, Philadelphia, Pennsylvania, 1833–1840. Mahogany and mahogany veneer with white pine; marble. H. 37", W. 26", D. 20½". (Courtesy, Neal Auction Company, New Orleans, La.)

Figure 34 Detail of the label on the washstand illustrated in fig. 33.

Figure 35   Carter Hall, Millwood, Virginia, 1814.

Figure 36   Sofa bearing the stenciled label of Cook & Parkin, Philadelphia, Pennsylvania, ca. 1830. Mahogany and mahogany veneer with unidentified secondary woods. H. 35", W. 89", D. 24½". (Private collection; photo, Bob Godwin, RGB Photography, Santa Fe.)

year we have to pay our bills, if you [Johnston] make it convenient to remit us the amount of your bill it would relieve us very much at present $677 = oo. The bill of the last Furniture was duly paid." Judging from the amount owed, Johnston must have been one of Cook & Parkin's most important clients. His debt would have been sufficient to furnish an entire house, not to mention the furniture for which payment had been received.[31]

George Harrison Burwell (1799–1873) of Millwood, Virginia, was also a customer of Cook & Parkin. On December 1, 1831, the firm charged Burwell $455.00 for a dressing table, a set of dining tables, two sofas, a wardrobe, a ladies' worktable, and a sideboard. The invoice was accompanied by a note indicating that Cook & Parkin had erred in sending Burwell a marble-top basin stand and asked that he send $15.00, which was a 25 percent discount of the retail price.[32] Although the basin stand has not been identified, it may have resembled a marble-top washstand bearing Parkin's Egyptian Hall label (figs. 33, 34). Burwell's furniture was intended for Carter Hall, a house on 5,800 acres inherited from his father in 1814 (fig. 35). He redecorated Carter Hall after the death of his first wife and his remarriage to Agnes Atkinson (1810–1885) in August 1831.[33]

A Grecian sofa bearing the stencil mark of Cook & Parkin is roughly contemporaneous with Burwell's order, and it descended in families living on the north fork of the Shenandoah River near Millwood (fig. 36). Unlike much formal furniture of the age, which was inspired by engravings in English or French pattern books, the sofa's design is distinctively Philadelphia. Local cabinetmakers who made related sofas with low scrolled backs, shell-shaped armrests, and squat turned legs included Joseph Barry, Charles and John White, and David Fleetwood. Cook & Parkin's version of this form is as stylish and well made as any of their competitors' products.[34]

During the late 1820s the "Grecian" or "Plain" style began supplanting the more architectonic French Empire. Inspired by the forms of Greek

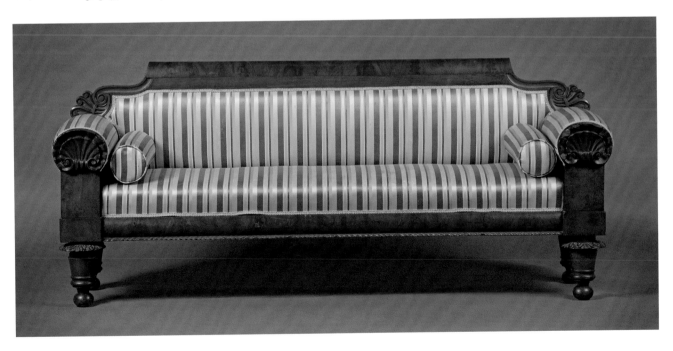

antiquity and influenced by French Restoration tastes (1815–1830), the Grecian style was sleeker, more streamlined, and more curvilinear than its predecessors. Through the furniture export trade, Cook & Parkin contributed to the dissemination of the Grecian style, which became ubiquitous in American furniture design by 1833.[35]

At the time of their manufacture, the wardrobes illustrated in figures 37 and 38 would have been considered avant-garde examples of the Grecian style. Composed entirely of abstracted geometric forms, Cook & Parkin's were more streamlined and "modern" than any contemporaneous published designs for that form. With a base price of $30.00, winged wardrobes were the most expensive furniture form described in the *Philadelphia Cabinet and Chair Makers' Union Book of Prices for Manufacturing Cabinet Ware* (1828). The wardrobe George Harrison Burwell purchased from Cook & Parkin in 1831 cost $65.00.[36]

Design features that occur in later examples of Cook & Parkin's work, as well as furniture made by Parkin working independently, include the use of distinctive demilune panels (figs. 37–41), large flat bosses with ovolo-molded edges (figs. 40, 41, 46, 52, 53, 57), bosses with prominent convex centers surrounded by ovolo molding (see figs. 50, 53), and a variety of individualistic carved and gilded details (see figs. 1, 39). When any of these details appears alone or in combination on the same object, it is likely that Cook & Parkin or Richard Parkin working independently was the maker.

Figure 37 Wardrobe bearing the stenciled label of Cook & Parkin, Philadelphia, Pennsylvania, 1827–1833. Mahogany and mahogany veneer with unidentified secondary woods. H. 84½", W. 80¾", D. 23¼". (Private collection; photo, Richard Sexton.) This example has five stenciled labels.

Figure 38 Wardrobe attributed to Cook & Parkin, Philadelphia, Pennsylvania, 1827–1833. Mahogany, mahogany veneer, maple, and maple veneer with white pine and tulip poplar. H. 87½", W. 81½", D. 23". (Courtesy, Charles and Rebekah Clark, Woodbury, Connecticut; photo, Gavin Ashworth.)

Figure 39   Bookcase attributed to Cook & Parkin or Richard Parkin, Philadelphia, Pennsylvania, 1825–1835. White pine; paint. H. 102", W. 71¾", D. 16½". (Courtesy, Carlton Hobbs, LLC, New York.) Demilune panels like those on the cornice occur on other furniture attributed to Cook & Parkin (see figs. 37, 38). The beaded Romanesque panel of the base is a larger version of that on the door of the washstand illustrated in fig. 33. The pediment is virtually identical to that of the wardrobe illustrated in fig. 38, and both designs relate to the "large library or writing-table" shown in pl. 11 in Thomas Hope, *Household Furniture* (1807) (fig. 9).

Figure 40 Dressing table attributed to Cook & Parkin or Richard Parkin, Philadelphia, Pennsylvania, 1829–1835. Maple and maple veneer with unrecorded secondary woods. H. 67", W. 48", D. 21½". (Courtesy, Gates Antiques, Ltd., Midlothian, Virginia.) The design of this object may have been inspired by "A Toilet" illustrated in pl. 92 of Thomas King, *The Modern Style of Cabinet Work Exemplified* (1829). The demilune cutouts relate to the panels on the case pieces illustrated in figs. 37–39, and the large flat bosses on the mirror brackets are identical to those on the scrolls of the couch, chairs, occasional table, and sideboards illustrated in figs. 45, 51, 56, 59, and 60.

Furniture by Richard Parkin

A benchmark for identifying seating made by Parkin is a set of eleven chairs (probably at least twelve originally), all labeled "RICHARD PARKIN / CABINET − MAKER / EGYPTIAN HALL / 134 South Second Street / Philadelphia" (fig. 41). Their stay rails are triangular in shape, decorated with a carved anthemion, and surmount the rear seat rails. These features are unique in American seating but have precedents in Brown's *Rudiments of Drawing Cabinet Furniture* (fig. 42) and a group of drawings inscribed "Tracings from Thomas Wilkinson from Designs of the late Mr. George Bullock, 1820" (fig. 43). Bullock was an ingenious artist of great renown and influence whose surviving work is unsurpassed in Regency furniture. His innovative use of indigenous material, inlays inspired by native plants and classical designs placed him at the forefront of British cabinetmakers of the period and garnered him important commissions from Sir Walter Scott, the Duke of Atholl, Matthew Robinson Bolton, and the Prince Regent for

Napoleon Bonaparte's residence on St. Helena. Bullock was active during the period when Cook and Parkin served their apprenticeships and worked as journeymen in England. It is likely that both of the future partners were familiar with Bullock's furniture, an assertion supported by the similarity of chairs attributed to Parkin (fig. 41) and one illustrated in the Wilkinson Tracings. Another chair on the same page (upper right) could be the model for many sets of Philadelphia chairs, both with and without brass inlay (see fig. 43). Cook and Parkin's apparent knowledge of Bullock's designs suggests that they may have been the source for some of the Klismos-type chairs popular in Philadelphia throughout the 1820s.[37]

A number of Philadelphia chairs possibly made by Cook & Parkin or Richard Parkin working independently have die-stamped brass inlay, which is significant because Bullock was the most important exponent of Boulle work in English Regency furniture. Side chairs like the Parkin example illus-

Figure 41 Side chair from a set of at least eleven with one bearing the label of Richard Parkin, Philadelphia, Pennsylvania, 1834–1840. Mahogany, black walnut, and mahogany veneer with walnut. H. 32", W. 18", D. 18". (Landis Valley Farm Museum, Lancaster, Pennsylvania; photo, Gavin Ashworth.) Elements of these chairs may have been inspired by designs in several pattern books, but the overall composition is original and unlike any published chair design. The form and crest rail relate to a chair illustrated in pl. 194 in Pierre de la Mésangère, *Collection de meubles et objets de goût* (Paris, 1805), and the legs relate to those on chairs shown in pl. 143 in George Smith, *Cabinet-Maker and Upholsterer's Guide* (London, 1828), and pl. 18 in Thomas King, *The Modern Style of Cabinet Work Exemplified* (1829).

Figure 42   Design for a library chair illustrated in pl. 7 in Richard Brown, *The Rudiments of Drawing Cabinet and Upholstery Furniture* (1820). (Courtesy, Carswell Rush Berlin.) The chair on the left may have been inspired by a George Bullock design as indicated by the Wilkinson Tracings (fig. 43).

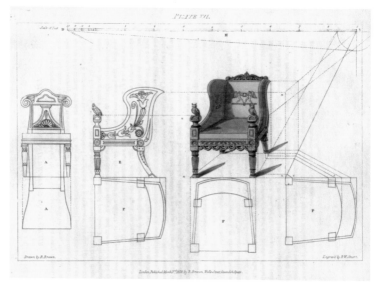

Figure 43   Chair designs on p. 8 in "Tracings from Thomas Wilkinson from Designs of the late Mr. George Bullock, 1820." (Courtesy, Birmingham Museums Trust.) Several sets of Philadelphia chairs have details similar to those depicted in these "tracings." The example on the left of the second row has a back design that relates to those on chairs documented and attributed to Parkin.

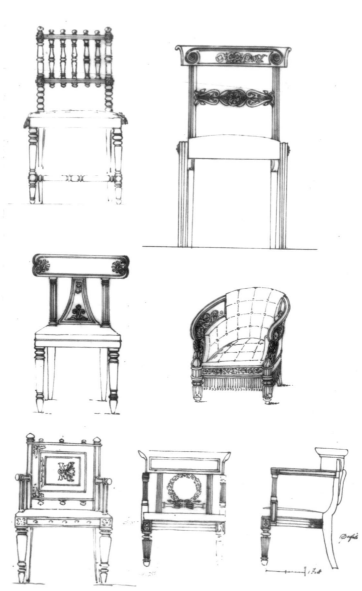

Figure 44 Drawing depicting the entrance to George Bullock's Grecian Rooms at Egyptian Hall, Piccadilly, London, 1812–1814. (Courtesy, Birmingham Museums Trust.)

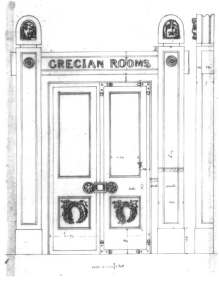

Figure 45 Armchair attributed to Richard Parkin, Philadelphia, Pennsylvania, 1833–1840. Rosewood and rosewood veneer with unrecorded secondary woods. Dimensions not recorded. (Private collection; photo, Johnny Miller.) This chair is one of three identical armchairs and six related chairs, including the example illustrated in fig. 51.

trated in figure 41 indicate that he and Cook were familiar with Bullock's designs (see fig. 43). Barry's association with brass inlay can be traced in part to his September 11, 1824, notice in the *American Daily Advertiser*, where he offered for sale "2 Rich sideboards, Buhl work and richly carved." Barry would have had the opportunity to study Boulle work while visiting London and Paris in 1811 and may have seen examples of Bullock's furniture in his Grecian rooms at Egyptian Hall in Piccadilly, London, or Liverpool (fig. 44). If Barry was another conduit for Bullock's designs, stylistic transfer

Figure 46   Designs for "Drawing Room and Dining Room Gothic Chairs" illustrated in pl. 143 in George Smith, *Guide* (1828). (Courtesy, Carswell Rush Berlin.) The chair on the left has legs similar to those on seating documented and attributed to Richard Parkin.

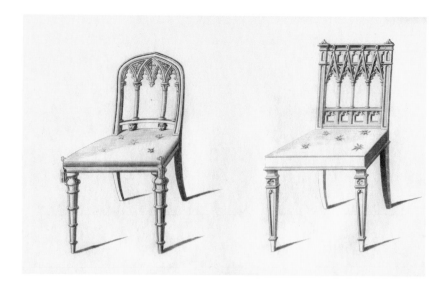

Figure 47   Design for a "Drawing Room State Chair" illustrated in pl. 58 in George Smith, *Household Furniture* (London, 1808). (Courtesy, Carswell Rush Berlin.)

Figure 48   Side chair attributed to Richard Parkin, Philadelphia, Pennsylvania, 1834–1840. Mahogany and mahogany veneer with ash. H. 33⅛", W. 17¾", D. 21½". (Courtesy, Philadelphia Museum of Art; gift of Andrew Jones and George Celio, 1996.)

Figure 49   Side chair attributed to Richard Parkin, Philadelphia, Pennsylvania, 1834–1840. Mahogany and mahogany veneer with tulip poplar. H. 33½", W. 17½", D. 21". (Courtesy, Yale University Art Gallery.)

could have occurred through collaboration with Parkin or through journey-men who may have worked for both men. Barry and Parkin are the only Philadelphia cabinetmakers known to have used cross-braces on the back upholstery frames of their chairs (fig. 45).

A pair of side chairs made of highly figured walnut and walnut veneer (fig. 1) provides a link between the set bearing Parkin's label (fig. 41) and several undocumented chairs in public and private collections. The walnut chairs have legs identical to those on the labeled examples and rear stiles that terminate in stylized Ionic capitals with molded edges and paneled tablets like the chairs illustrated in figure 49. This leg design may have been inspired by a Gothic chair illustrated in plate 143 in Smith's *Guide* (fig. 46), and the capitals are similar to those on a "Drawing Room State Chair"

Figure 50 Side chair attributed to Richard Parkin, Philadelphia, Pennsylvania, 1834–1840. Mahogany, mahogany veneer, and walnut with white pine. H. 35¼", W. 18¼", D. 20¾". (Private collection; photo, Gavin Ashworth.)

Figure 51 Side chair attributed to Richard Parkin, Philadelphia, Pennsylvania, 1834–1840. Rosewood and rosewood veneer with ash. H. 35¼", W. 18¼", D. 20½". (Private collection; photo, Gavin Ashworth.)

shown in plate 58 of his *Household Furniture* (fig. 47). Parkin is the only Philadelphia cabinetmaker known to have used these capitals, which appear on the chairs illustrated in figures 1, 45, and 50–52.[38]

The chairs illustrated in figures 48–52 have additional features indicative of Parkin's work. The chair illustrated in figure 50 has large bosses with molded edges attached to the inner and outer faces of the front leg volutes, and all three chairs have small bosses glued to the round corners of the rectangular appliqués on their backs. Bosses similar to those on the chair shown in figure 51 also occur on a pair of footstools bearing Parkin's Egyptian Hall label (fig. 53).[39]

A side chair possibly from Parkin's shop (fig. 54) and a related example in maple with ebonized details represent a genre of seating traditionally attributed to Michel Bouvier, yet the turned and faceted legs relate closely to those on a pair of armchairs attributed to Parkin, and the tablet back is nearly identical to that on the chair illustrated in fig. 48. No documented Bouvier chairs share those details.[40]

As the occasional table illustrated in figure 56 suggests, furniture made by

Figure 52   Side chair attributed to Richard Parkin, Philadelphia, Pennsylvania, 1834–1840. Rosewood and rosewood veneer with ash. H. 35¼", W. 18¼", D. 20½". (Private collection; photo, Gavin Ashworth.)

Figure 53   Footstool from a pair bearing the label of Richard Parkin, Philadelphia, Pennsylvania, 1834–1840. Woods not identified. (William MacPherson Horner Jr., "Some Early Philadelphia Cabinetmakers," *Antiquarian* 16, no. 3 [March 1931]: 76.) Parkin's design is similar to that of a footstool illustrated in Rudolph Ackermann, *The Repository of Arts, Literature, Commerce, and Manufactures*, ser. 1, vol. 10 (October 1813): 232, pl. 25. This publication was very influential, particularly in Philadelphia.

Figure 54 Side chair, possibly from the shop of Richard Parkin, Philadelphia, Pennsylvania, 1834–1840. Mahogany and mahogany veneer with ash. H. 33", W. 19", D. 20". (Courtesy, Carswell Rush Berlin, Inc.; photo, Richard Goodbody.) This chair is from a set of at least twelve seating forms. Its crest rail is related to that on the side chair illustrated in fig. 49, and its faceted legs are similar to those on the armchair illustrated in fig. 55.

Figure 55 Armchairs attributed to the shop of Richard Parkin, Philadelphia, Pennsylvania, 1834–1840. Walnut and walnut veneer. Secondary woods not recorded. H. 35", W. 19¼", D. 16¾". (Private collection; photo, Johnny Miller.)

Figure 56 Occasional table bearing the Egyptian
Hall label of Richard Parkin, Philadelphia, Pennsylvania, 1835–1840. Mahogany and mahogany
veneer with white pine. H. 29½", W. 44", D. 22".
(Private collection; photo, Gavin Ashworth.)

Figure 57 Design for a table illustrated in pl. 12
in Thomas Hope, *Household Furniture and Interior Decoration* (1807). This form is referred to as
an "occasional table" in Peter Nicholson and
Michael Angelo Nicholson, *The Practical Cabinet
Maker, Upholsterer and Complete Decorator* (London, 1826), George Smith, *Cabinet Maker and
Upholsterer's Guide* (1828), and Thomas King, *The
Modern Style of Cabinet Work Exemplified* (1829).

Parkin working independently and in partnership with Cook demonstrates a much stronger affinity with Hope's designs than work by other American cabinetmakers. The design of this object appears to be inspired by a table illustrated in plate 12 of Hope's *Household Furniture* (fig. 57), which had its roots in an ancient Roman marble bench drawn and published by Charles Heathcote Tatham in 1799 (fig. 58). The table, which bears Parkin's label, has scrolled legs, an "Egyptian" marble top, and large flat bosses with molded edges.[41]

An unmarked sideboard with elaborate stenciled decoration may also be from Parkin's shop (fig. 59). The original owners were probably Charles Henry Fisher (1814–1862) and his wife, Sarah (Atherton), who lived at Brookwood near Germantown, Pennsylvania. The supports of the sideboard are similar to those on the occasional table (fig. 56), the central stencil on its frieze is very closely related to that on the pier table bearing Cook &

Figure 59 Sideboard attributed to Richard Parkin, Philadelphia, Pennsylvania, ca. 1835. Rosewood and rosewood veneer with mahogany, white pine, tulip poplar, and cedrela; marble. H. 40¾", W. 60¼", D. 22". (Courtesy, Philadelphia Museum of Art, 1976-17-1.)

Figure 60 Sideboard probably by Richard Parkin, Philadelphia, Pennsylvania, 1835. Mahogany and mahogany veneer with white pine; marble. H. 43", W. 60", D. 24". (Courtesy, Rosedown Plantation Historic Site, St. Francisville, Louisiana.) Made for Rosedown Plantation and invoiced by Anthony G. Quervelle, exhibiting distinctive flat bosses.

Parkin's label (fig. 12), and the piece is decorated with bosses like those commonly used by their firm and Parkin working independently.[42]

The design of the Fisher sideboard is similar to that of an example that Quervelle sold Daniel and Martha Turnbull of St. Francisville, Louisiana, in 1830 (fig. 60). Although the Turnbulls' sideboard was part of a suite, it bears no relation to the other forms. Indeed, the distinctive turned bosses on the sideboard suggest that Parkin was the maker. Quervelle may have needed assistance to complete his commission in a timely fashion and turned to Parkin, whose shop was less than a block away from his on South Second Street. Collaborations of this type were relatively common in the period. Alternatively, Quervelle could have simply retailed a sideboard

Figure 61 David Bodensick, sofa table, Baltimore, Maryland, 1833. Mahogany and mahogany veneer with white pine and tulip poplar. H. 29⅛", W. 57¾ (open)", D. 26". (Courtesy, Maryland Historical Society, 1990.3.) The table is inscribed, "Made by / David Bodensick From Baltimore / And Sold By Mr. Cook & Perkins / Philadelphia, PA."

made by Parkin, as Cook and Parkin did with a sofa table made by David Bodensick of Baltimore (fig. 61).[43]

Legacy

The furniture made by Thomas Cook and Richard Parkin reflects a thorough knowledge of English and French pattern-book designs and a level of patronage that allowed both men to work at the cutting edge of fashion. Unlike many of their competitors, who copied design book engravings, Cook and Parkin used published details selectively and combined them with their own innovative features. Cook and Parkin's success at the beginning of the industrial age may have been predicated on size and volume, but it is clear from documented objects that their standard of quality was high and, in the finest pieces, as structurally and stylistically sophisticated as Philadelphia cabinetmakers had to offer. The shops where these men worked no longer stand, but their record of accomplishment remains in the novel and beautiful classical furniture that survives today.

ACKNOWLEDGMENTS For assistance with this article, the author thanks Gavin Ashworth, Peter M. Kenny, and Alexandra A. Kirtley. I am especially grateful to Deborah Ducoff-Barone for her detailed research on Philadelphia cabinetmakers working in the classical style and Thomas Gordon Smith for his pioneering work on Cook & Parkin.

1. *Niles' Weekly Register*, October 15, 1825, p. 107.

2. He was listed as being sixty years old in the 1850 census and sixty-eight in the 1860 census (U.S. Bureau of the Census, 1869, 14th Ward, 2nd Division, City of Philadelphia, Pennsylvania, roll M653-1164, p. 405). Parkin's death notice in the September 18, 1861, issue of the *Philadelphia Public Ledger* and his city death certificate state that he was seventy-four (Philadelphia City Death Certificates, 1803–1915, City Archives, Philadelphia, Pennsylvania). At the time of his death, Parkin lived at 1336 Brown Street. His gravesite, in Division B, Section 5, lot 30, grave 4, was moved in the mid-1950s, when the cemetery was closed. The location of his remains and those of many family members is unknown. The Sheffield directory listed a Thomas Parkin "cutler" on Scotland Street in 1787, the probable year of Richard Parkin's birth (*Directory of Sheffield* [Sheffield: Gales and Martin, 1787], p. 17). The first British census, taken in 1841, listed 531 Parkins in Sheffield (David Hay, *A History of Sheffield* [Carnegie Publishing, 1998]). The *Sheffield General & Commercial Directory* listed seventeen Parkins, many of whom were in the steel knife, file, and metals business (*Sheffield General & Commercial Directory*, edited by R. Gell [Manchester, Eng.: Albion Press, 1825]). The Yorkshire directory of 1817 listed a man named Thomas Cooke and two men named Thomas Parkin in Leeds. All were in the metal business (*Directory, General and Commercial of the Town and Borough of Leeds for 1817* [Leeds, Eng.: Edward Baines, 1817]).

3. For the marriage announcement, see *Poulson's American Daily Advertiser*, February 8, 1825. Clara's year of birth is also uncertain. The 1850 census listed her age as forty-five, the 1860 census listed her age as sixty-two, and her death notice in 1875 listed her age as seventy-four. Richard Jr., who would have been about twenty in 1856, was probably working with his father by that date. After Richard Sr.'s death in 1861, Richard Jr. moved in with his older brother Henry at 540 North Twelfth Street. Richard Jr. was listed at 1627 Poplar Street in 1865 and 1866 and as a cabinetmaker at 206 Lagrange Street in 1870 and 1872 (*McElroy's Philadelphia City Directory* [Philadelphia: McElroy, 1870]). Henry S. Parkin, Richard Sr.'s second son, is listed separately as a cabinetmaker at 540 North Twelfth Street beginning in 1860 (*McElroy's Philadelphia City Directory*). Richard Jr. was living with him at that date but working on Spring Garden Street, north of Broad, in 1865 and 1872. A Sarah Stevens is listed in the 1825 city directory as a widow in Goforth Ally. She was probably Clara's mother.

4. Naturalization Petitions for the Eastern District of Pennsylvania, 1795–1930, National Archives and Records Administration (hereafter NARA), Publication M1522, National Archives Catalog ID 573414, compiled 1795–1991, Record Group 21, Pennsylvania 1819. If the birth date on Cook's petition is correct, he was three years younger than his Philadelphia death notice states. Ann Cook's death notice is in the April 28, 1871, issue of the *Philadelphia Public Ledger*. 1820 U.S. Census, Philadelphia Dock Ward, Philadelphia, Pennsylvania, p. 26, NARA, roll M33-108, image 37. Philadelphia City Archives, Deeds AM 64-400, 70-411, 47-270, SHF 6-704, GS 35-128, 48-568, RLL 16-473, 25-125. On May 16, 1868, the *Philadelphia Public Ledger* reported that Cook had died two days earlier at the age of eighty-two, and his city death certificate stated that he was eighty-one (Philadelphia City Death Certificates, 1803–1915). Cook was buried at Ronaldson's Cemetery at Tenth and Wharton Streets, but his remains appear to have been removed to Forest Hills, Bensalem Turnpike, Bucks County, Pennsylvania. His will was dated August 25, 1866, and probated on May 29, 1868 (Thomas Cook Will, 1868.312, City and County of Philadelphia and Administrations, City Archives repository, Philadelphia).

5. George Hepplewhite, *The Cabinet-Maker & Upholsterer's Guide*, introduction by Joseph Aronson (3rd ed., 1794; reprint, New York: Dover Publications, 1969), pp. vii–viii.

6. 56 and 58 Walnut Street was owned and formerly occupied by merchant and Pennsylvania state treasurer Peter Baynton (1754–1821) and inherited by his wife, Elizabeth Bullock Baynton. The Philadelphia Contributionship Survey 301660 for George and Elizabeth Bullock dating to 1773 indicates that there were two houses, each three stories with two rooms per floor and each 17' wide and 34' deep. This explains why some Cook & Parkin labels say 58 Walnut Street and suggest that the firm occupied both houses but used only one address, #56. Fromberger's Court does not appear on period or modern maps, but *O'Brien's Wholesale Business Directory* of 1849 indicates that it ran west from 34 North Second Street, probably north of Church Street; Fromberger's Court may have been what is now Filbert Street (Philadelphia: O'Brien, 1849). *Robert DeSilver's Philadelphia Directory and Stranger's Guide* (Philadelphia: Robert DeSilver, 1833). It is possible, albeit unlikely, that these are residences. 7 Pear Street (Thomas today), which ran one block between Dock Street and South Third south of Walnut, may have been the back or residential entrance to 56 Walnut Street. For the move to Egyptian Hall, see *DeSilver's Philadelphia Directory*.

7. Deborah Ducoff-Barone, "The Early Industrialization of the Philadelphia Furniture Trade, 1800–1840" (Ph.D diss., University of Pennsylvania, 1985), pp. 15–21. J. Drayton, *Plan of the City of Philadelphia* (Philadelphia: H. C. Carey and I. Lees, 1824).

8. Cook is listed at 16 Pine Street until 1857 and 104 Pine Street until 1860. Cook's house at 16 Pine Street was surveyed by the Philadelphia Contributionship in 1836, 1840, and 1848 (505157). 16 and 104 Pine may reflect a renumbering rather than a change of location. His daughter, Mary, her husband, Henry C. Stellwagen, and the couple's children, Thomas and Catherine, were living with Cook in 1850. The final directory listing for Cook was in 1862 at 1627 Chestnut Street, the Stellwagens' home (*McElroy's Philadelphia City Directory* [Philadelphia: McElroy, 1862]). The Thomas R. Cook who was described in the 1839 directory as a carver and gilder at 35 Plum Street emigrated from Edinburg, Scotland, and was not a relative. His son, Thomas A. Cook, also became a carver and gilder in Philadelphia (Ducoff-Barone, "Early Industrialization of the Philadelphia Furniture Trade," p. 80).

9. Deborah Ducoff-Barone, "Philadelphia Furniture Makers, 1816–1830," *Antiques* 145, no. 5 (May 1994): 742–55. Thomas Whitecar's shop had seven workbenches (1822), Benjamin Thompson's, eight (1819), Jacob Super's, nine (1820), Thomas Nossitter's, nine (October 12, 1825), T. B. Emery's, eleven (1825), and David Fleetwood's, twenty-two (1833–1837) (Ducoff-Barone, "Early Industrialization of the Philadelphia Furniture Trade," p. 110). Isaac Pippitt advertised for four journeymen (April 26, 1826); Robert West employed five journeymen, three boys, and a woman (1830); Thomas Whitecar had "four persons with little work to keep them busy and twenty persons within the last 12–18 months" (1820), and John Jamison employed eight men and four boys (1830) (Ducoff-Barone, "Philadelphia Furniture Makers," pp. 744–55).

10. Ducoff-Barone, "Early Industrialization of the Philadelphia Furniture Trade," pp. 65–79. The broadside is dated March 9, 1826, and is bound into a copy of the price guide owned by cabinetmaker Stephen Noblitz (act. 1826–1840) (Joseph Downs Collection of Manuscripts and Printed Ephemera, Henry Francis du Pont Winterthur Museum, Winterthur, Delaware). Cook & Parkin's copy of *The Philadelphia Cabinet and Chair Makers' Union Book of Prices for Manufacturing Cabinet Ware* (1828), one of the very few to survive, is in the collection of the

Library Company of Philadelphia. Of the 187 chair- or cabinetmakers who were signatories to the Constitution of the Pennsylvania Society of Journeymen Cabinetmakers in either 1825 or 1829, only ten remained listed in the Philadelphia city directories for fifteen years or more. None of the most prominent furniture makers—including Joseph B. Barry, Joseph Beal, Michel Bouvier, Henry Connelly, Thomas Cook, Otto James, John Jamison, Isaac Jones, Anthony G. Quervelle, Richard Parkin, I. Pippitt, Charles H. White, John F. White, or Thomas Whitecar—signed the agreement (Ducoff-Barone, "Philadelphia Furniture Makers," pp. 744–55).

11. Ducoff-Barone, "Philadelphia Furniture Makers," pp. 744–55.

12. Ducoff-Barone, "Early Industrialization of the Philadelphia Furniture Trade," pp. 116, 123. A building behind the house was used for domestic purposes.

13. Ibid., p. 128.

14. *Aurora General Advertiser*, January 12, 1812. *George Bullock Cabinetmaker*, edited by Clive Wainwright (London: H. Blairman and Son, Ltd., 1988), p. 23.

15. *O'Brien's Wholesale Business Directory* listed Parkin at 134 South Second Street in 1849. The Richard Parkin listed at other addresses in 1853 and 1854 must have been his son. The elder Parkin lived with Richard Jr. at 540 North Twelfth Street in those years.

16. Historical Society of Pennsylvania, Daniel Parker Papers, Zaccheus Collins receipted bills 1819, HSP Coll. 1587. The author thanks Anne Verplank for bringing the receipt to his attention.

17. Nancy Goyne Evans, *Windsor-Chair Making in America: From Craft Shop to Consumer* (Hanover, N.H.: University Press of New England, 2006), pp. 160, 210, 213, 214, 234, 247, 248, 327, 328, 454.

18. Only one other paper label is known. On that example, the address was corrected in ink to read "56" rather than "58" Walnut Street. This label appears on a photocopy along with an image of a Restoration pier table, presumably the object on which the label is found. Regrettably, the location of the pier table is not known (acc. file 1989.26, Baltimore Museum of Art). The author thanks David Park Curry and Dawn Krause for making the sideboard and the museum's file available for study. Wendy A. Cooper, *Classical Taste in America, 1800–1840* (Baltimore, Md.: Baltimore Museum of Art, 1993), p. 56.

19. This distinctive capital was also used at Ephesus, near Pergamum. James Stuart and Nicholas Revett discuss and illustrate the Tower of the Winds at Athens, which supposedly featured Pergamene capitals, in volume 1 of *Antiquities of Athens* (1762), but there is no useful depiction of the structure's capitals. See Thomas Gordon Smith, *Vitruvius on Architecture* (New York: Monacelli Press. 2003), fig. 218, for an image of the Pergamene capital Lord Elgin brought to England. The British Museum acquired the Elgin marbles in 1816 and may have put them on view shortly thereafter. In 1817 John Keats published his poem "On Seeing the Elgin Marbles for the First Time."

20. Allison Boor and Jonathan Boor, *Philadelphia Empire Furniture* (West Chester, Pa.: Boor Management, 2006), p. 53. William Atlee to Isaac Wayne, August 7, 1823, Wayne Family Papers, William L. Clements Library, University of Michigan, Ann Arbor. A copy of Cook & Parkin's receipt for $55.00 is in the files at Waynesborough, Anthony Wayne Foundation. The sideboard's location is currently unknown. Isaac Wayne served in the Pennsylvania House of Representatives and Senate between 1799 and 1810 and the U.S. Senate from 1823 to 1825. The author thanks Donna Lynne Anderson of the Anthony Wayne Foundation for her assistance.

21. Decorative Arts Photographic Collection (hereafter DAPC), file no. 2000.0240, Winterthur Library, Winterthur, Delaware. A jelly jar label on the bottom of the pier table is inscribed "Gertrude Dun / her Grand Mother / James left her by her mother / 1898." The dust board is inscribed "Dun West Jefferson." The author thanks Jeanne Solensky at the Winterthur Library, John R. Tompkins, Tom Halverson of New Orleans Auction Gallery, and the table's current owners for their assistance. Rudolph Ackermann, *Repository of Arts, Literature, Commerce, Manufactures, Fashions, and Politics*, ser. 2, vol. 14 (December 1822): 367.

22. Boor and Boor, *Philadelphia Empire Furniture*, pp. 233–35. Oral tradition maintains that the table illustrated in figure 18 descended from Henry Eichholtz Leman (1812–1887) to his son Henry Leaman Jr. to his daughter Delia Leaman, who donated it to the James Buchanan Foundation in 1942. For more on this table, see Nicholas Vincent, "Philadelphia Pier Tables and Their Role in Cultures of Sociability and Competition," in *American Furniture*, edited by Luke Beckerdite (Easthampton, Mass.: Antique Collector's Club, Ltd. for the Chipstone Foundation, 2008), p. 118, fig. 27. The original owner of the table may have been artist Jacob Eichholtz, Henry Eichholtz Leman's uncle. Jacob mentioned a pier table in a letter dated 1832, but it is not clear that he was referring to the example illustrated here. The author thanks Jennifer

L. Walton, assistant director of President James Buchanan's Wheatland, for information on this table.

23. *Franklin Journal and American Mechanics' Magazine* 3 (1827): 54, 55. According to Richard D. Hoblyn, *Dictionary of Terms Used in Medicine and the Collateral Science* (Philadelphia, Pa.: Henry C. Lee, 1865), *artimomantico* was patented in France in 1814 and is an alloy composed of tin, sulfur, bismuth, and copper. It was reputed to have the visual appearance of gold and not tarnish. J. C. Loudon, *An Encyclopaedia of Cottage, Farm and Villa Architecture and Furniture: Selections* (1833) (1839; reprint, East Andsley, Yorkshire: S. R. Publishers, 1970), pp. 654, 1065. In the March 5, 1840, issue of the *Evening Post*, New York cabinetmaker Alexander Roux advertised "iron frame Sofas and Chairs, being the first of the kind ever introduced into this country, which for comfort and durability, place them superior to any thing now in use."

24. *Freeman's Journal and Philadelphia Mercantile Advertiser*, August 15, 1827. Daniel Powles's invention was first publicized in the *Journal of the American Institute of the City of New York* 1 (October 1836): 2, 374. A Baltimore, Maryland, inventor, Powles patented a bed and sacking bottom "which can be put up and taken down by any person owing to the peculiar construction of the joints and is proof against insects." The patent was issued on October 31, 1821, and expired on the same day in 1835. Powles's invention won the John Scott Award in 1827. With the award, the city council of Philadelphia acknowledged his contribution to the "comfort, welfare and happiness of mankind" and awarded him $20.00 and a copper medallion inscribed "To the Most Deserving" (www.garfield.Library.upenn.edu/johnscottaward/js1822-1830.html).

25. Ducoff-Barone, "Philadelphia Furniture Makers," pp. 744–46. The stencil is the same as the one on the pier table illustrated in figure 12. Plate 3 of the 1828 *Philadelphia Cabinet and Chair Makers' Union Book of Prices* shows feet for Loo Tables that are of the same profile as those on the center table, indicating that this foot design was already in use when that book was published. One of the tables bearing a stencil like the example illustrated in figure 19 is illustrated in Boor and Boor, *Philadelphia Empire Furniture*, p. 129, and is in the Sewell Biggs Museum, Dover, Delaware. An identical, unmarked table has a Savannah provenance and is in a private collection in Pine Mountain, Georgia. A fourth, unmarked table was offered for sale at New Orleans Auctions, New Orleans, Louisiana, September 20–October 2, 2011. The author thanks Brandy Culp and Karen Emmons at Historic Charleston Foundation, Lynn Hanlin of Carriage Properties, Charleston, Albert Simons III, and G. Dana Sinkler for assistance in finding the table illustrated in *The Octagon Library of Early American Architecture*, vol. 1, *Charleston, South Carolina*, edited by Albert Simons and Samuel Lapham Jr. (New York: Press of the American Institute of Architects, 1927), n.p. The table was in the same location in the Eveleigh house in 1954 (*Charleston Evening Post*, March 19, 1954). The table is partially visible in a photograph published two years later (Samuel Chamberlain and Narcissa Chamberlain, *Southern Interiors of Charleston* [New York: Hastings House, 1956], p. 60). Thomas Deas was located on East Bay in the 1820s. James Dick, operating after 1813 at 341 King Street, was a dry goods merchant. He closed this business in 1820 and subsequently went into partnership with Sandiford Holmes. The author thanks Bridget J. O'Brien of Historic Charleston Foundation for investigating the activities of these merchants.

26. For a Boston example, see Barry Tracy, Marilyn Johnson, and Marvin D. Schwartz, *19th Century American Furniture and Other Decorative Arts* (New York: Metropolitan Museum of Art, 1970), fig. 66. *DeSilver's Philadelphia Directory*. For the labeled sofa, see Tracy, Johnson, and Schwartz, *19th Century American Furniture and Other Decorative Arts*, fig. 65. John Hancock Will, 1835: 172, City and County of Philadelphia Wills and Administrations. For more on the Hancocks, see David H. Conradsen, "The Stock-in-Trade of John Hancock & Company," in *American Furniture*, edited by Luke Beckerdite (Hanover, N.H.: University Press of New England, 1993), p. 54; and David H. Conradsen, "Ease and Economy: The Hancock Brothers and the Development of Spring-Seat Upholstery in America" (M.A. thesis, University of Delaware, 1998). The author thanks David Conradsen for bringing this information to his attention. Cook & Parkin's shop was at 56 Walnut, and John Hancock & Company was across Third Street at Walnut and Third Streets.

27. Ducoff-Barone, "Philadelphia Furniture Makers," pp. 744–46. Outbound Coastal Manifests, Port of Philadelphia, October 16, 1823, December 1824, July 5, 1828, December 9, 1830, Record Group 36, NARA. Page Talbott, *Classical Savannah* (Savannah, Ga.: Telfair Museum of Art, 1995), p. 16. Maria Campbell to George J. Collock, March 5, 1830, in "The Kollock Papers, Part III," *Georgia Historical Quarterly* 31, no. 1 (January 1947): 41–42. Cook and Parkin consigned furniture to several Savannah agents, including R. and J. Habersham, J. J. Middleton, and cabinetmaker Isaac W. Morrell (Ducoff-Barone, "Philadelphia Furniture

Makers," pp. 744–76; and Outbound Coastal Manifests, Port of Philadelphia, October 16, 1823, December 1824, July 5, 1828, December 9, 1830, Record Group 36, NARA). Morrell often traveled north to buy furniture on speculation and was the Savannah agent for many New York cabinetmakers, including Joseph Brauwers, John Hewitt, and Duncan Phyfe. Talbott, *Classical Savannah*, p. 14.

28. Talbott, *Classical Savannah*, pp. 145, 146n72.

29. Ibid., pp. 146, 147n73.

30. For the table, see Mary Telfair to Margaret Telfair, October 25, 1836, Manuscript Collection 793, Georgia Historical Society, Savannah. Feay Shellman Coleman, *Nostrums for Fashionable Entertainments: Dining in Georgia, 1800–1850* (Savannah, Ga.: Telfair Academy, 1992), pp. 65, 66; Boor and Boor, *Philadelphia Empire Furniture*, p. 163. Talbott notes that the Telfairs and Kollocks were friends and that members of both families were in Philadelphia in 1831 and 1832, when Cook & Parkin were executing orders for maple furniture for Savannah clients (Talbott, *Classical Savannah*, p. 168nn74, 77). Thomas Graham was a journeyman in Cook's shop when Margaret Telfair ordered the table. Graham was born in Ireland in 1817, began serving his apprenticeship with Cook & Parkin in 1828, and left the former's employ as a journeyman in 1837 (*Philadelphia & Popular Philadelphians*, edited by Col. Clayton McMichael [Philadelphia: North American, 1891], p. 286).

31. Cook & Parkin to Josiah Johnston, January 16, 1826, Johnston Collection, Historical Society of Pennsylvania, Philadelphia. Johnston served in the Seventeenth Congress from 1821 to 1822 and in the U.S. Senate from 1823 until his untimely death in 1833 from an explosion on the steamboat *Lioness* on the Red River in Louisiana (Biographical Directory of the United States Congress, http://bioguide.congress.gov/scripts/biodisplay.pl?index=j000194).

32. George was the son of Colonel Nathaniel Burwell and grandson of Carter Burwell, owner of Carter's Grove Plantation. Correspondence of George Harrison Burwell, 1820–1871, Mss 1 B9585 a 40-384, Burwell Family Papers, 1770–1965, Sec. 6, Department of Manuscripts and Archives, Virginia Historical Society, Richmond. The invoice notes that payment was received from the tailors Robb & Winebrenner, who were located at the northeast corner of South Third and Pear Streets on the same block as Cook & Parkin. The author thanks Eileen Parris and Katherine Wilkins of the Virginia Historical Society for retrieving this manuscript.

33. Ibid. Neal Auction, *Winter Estates Auction*, New Orleans, Louisiana, February 24, 2008, lot 835. www.rootsweb.ancestry.com/deschart/z0000594.html. Burwell bought, at the same time, forty-four chairs from Joseph Burden (act. 1793–1839), a successful Philadelphia Windsor and fancy chairmaker and exporter, whose shop at 95–97 South Third Street was around the corner from Cook & Parkin's (*DeSilver's Philadelphia Directory*). Photographs of Carter Hall in 1932 by Samuel H. Gettscho show a Philadelphia sideboard in the dining room. That object may be the sideboard listed on Cook & Parkin's invoice to George Burwell for $70.00 (Gettscho-Schleisner Collection, Library of Congress).

34. Boor and Boor, *Philadelphia Empire Furniture*, pp. 378, 379. DAPC, file no. 80.483. A related sofa by Barry is inscribed, "G. W. Pickering, Maker, September 5, 1833, Barry" (ibid., p. 377). The sofa's history can be traced to the Rev. Joseph Layton Mauzé and his wife, Eleanor (Harmon), but it is not clear from which of their families it descended. Their respective grandfathers, William Burbridge Yancy (1803–1858), a landholder along the North Fork of the Shenandoah River, and Michael G. Harmon (1823–1887), a stagecoach and hotel owner and planter of Staunton, Virginia, are likely owners. The author thanks Chet Breitwieser for information on the provenance, and Charles MacKay and Cameron McCluskey for making the sofa available for photography.

35. Cook and Parkin's southern market also consisted of furniture made by other cabinetmakers. They sold a sofa table made by Baltimore cabinetmaker David Bodensick (act. 1833–1860) to Dr. William Newton Mercer in Natchez, Mississippi, circa 1833 (Gregory R. Weidman, *Classical Maryland, 1815–1845* [Baltimore, Md.: Maryland Historical Society, 1993], p. 132).

36. The "wardrobe" and "dwarf wardrobe" illustrated in plates 133 and 134 in Smith's *Household Furniture* influenced Cook & Parkin's work. Those designs presaged the "Ladies Dwarf Wardrobe" illustrated in plate 31 in Smith's *Cabinet Maker and Upholsterer's Guide* and influenced the wardrobe shown on page 83 in King's *Modern Style of Cabinet Work Exemplified*. Jason T. Busch, "Furniture Patronage in Antebellum Natchez," *Antiques* 157, no. 5 (May 2000): 804–13. The wardrobe was all but destroyed by fire on September 17, 2002. The author thanks Mimi Miller of the Natchez Historical Foundation for pictures of this object taken both before and after the fire.

37. The label, now separated from the chair, has a corrected address changed from 123 (South Second Street) to 134 and is inscribed "Whitfield," a family name in the provenance of this set. The set descended in the Reigart family of Lancaster, Pennsylvania. The original owner was probably Emanuel Carpenter Reigart (1796–1869) and his wife, Barbara (Swarr) (1800–1838). Their granddaughter Mary Catherine Reigart married William V. Whitfield in 1874. This distinctive, anthemion-carved stay rail also appears on a chair design in plate 17 in King's *Modern Style of Cabinet Work Exemplified*, but the rail is set at the traditional height.

38. A set of chairs with these capitals in the collection of the Teackle Mansion in Princess Anne, Somerset County, Maryland, is identical to the chairs at the Metropolitan Museum of Art and at the Yale University Art Gallery. The history of the Teackle Mansion and chairs is unrelated, and no history of the chairs is known. I thank antiquarian John R. Tompkins for bringing the Teackle chairs to my attention. A single side chair closely related to this group but with an upholstered back is in a private collection.

39. For the footstools, see William MacPherson Horner Jr., "Some Early Philadelphia Cabinetmakers," *Antiquarian* 16, no. 3 (March 1931): 76. The stools' design was inspired by footstools illustrated in Rudolph Ackermann, *Repository of Arts, Literature, Commerce, and Manufactures*, ser. 1, vol. 10 (October 1813): 232, pl. 25. This publication was influential in America, particularly in Philadelphia. Bosses similar to those on the footstools and legs of the chair illustrated in figure 51 also occur on a center table and a set of chairs made by George Bullock for Great Tew Park, Oxfordshire, England, in 1818 (Christie's, *Great Tew Park*, Oxfordshire, England, May 27–29, 1987, lots 33, 53). Thomas Cook appears to have owned a copy of Brown's *The Rudiments of Drawing Cabinet and Upholstery Furniture* (London, 1820). Brown's office was close to Bullock's workshop, and the former published a number of the latter's designs in *Rudiments of Drawing* (*George Bullock: Cabinet-Maker*, introduction by Clive Wainwright [London: H. Blairman & Son, 1988], pp. 16, 17).

40. *George Bullock: Cabinetmaker*, p. 79, fig. 17.

41. Boor and Boor, *Philadelphia Empire Furniture*, p. 145. Carswell Rush Berlin, "'Solid and Permanent Grandeur': The Design Roots of American Classical Furniture," in *International Fine Art and Antique Dealer's Show* (New York, 2002), pp. 17–26. Charles Heathcote Tatham, *Etchings Representing the Best Examples of Ancient Ornamental Architecture; Drawn from the Originals in Rome* (London, 1799).

42. Philadelphia Museum of Art, acc. file 1976-17-1, Gift of Mr. and Mrs. C. Jared Ingersoll. The underside of this sideboard is marked "Rev Purviance Baltimore," referring to the Reverend George D. Purviance (ca. 1812–1873). Charles Henry Fisher's (1814–1862) father was James Logan Fisher, a prominent financier who helped capitalize the Reading Rail Road and the Philadelphia, Wilmington and Baltimore Rail Road. Sarah's sister Emily J. Atherton married the Reverend Purviance. The sideboard appears to have descended through the family of Charles Henry Fisher's eldest brother's wife, Elizabeth (Ingersoll) Fisher, and her brother Charles Jared Ingersoll Jr.

43. Thomas Gordon Smith, "Quervelle Furniture at Rosedown, in Louisiana," *Antiques* 159, no. 5 (May 2001): 770–79. The sideboard appears on Quervelle's invoice at $85.00 (Boor and Boor, *Philadelphia Empire Furniture*, p. 276). The author thanks Polly Luttrull, Curator of Rosedown Plantation State Historic Site, St. Francisville, Louisiana, for making her photography of this sideboard available for study.

*Figure 1   Prospect Of the new Lutheran Church in
Philad^n which was on the 26th of Dec. 1794 in the
evening from the hour of eight till twelve Consumed
by Fire*, engraved by Frederick Reiche, Philadelphia, Pennsylvania, 1795. (Courtesy, Historical
Society of Pennsylvania.)

Lisa Minardi

Philadelphia,
Furniture, and the
Pennsylvania
Germans: A
Reevaluation

▼ FIRE! JACOB HILTZHEIMER heard the alarm while visiting a neighbor on the evening of December 26, 1794. About eight o'clock, the wife of Quaker merchant Henry Drinker was sitting in her back parlor when she heard "the noise of a Fire Engine, and the ringing of Bells." Both Hiltzheimer and Drinker went to investigate and learned the fire was in the back of Zion Lutheran Church at Fourth and Cherry Streets in Philadelphia, where a steeple was under construction. By nine o'clock, the church was thought safe. Soon, however, the bells began ringing again. The fire had spread to the roof (fig. 1). Elizabeth Drinker climbed to the third floor of her house and watched while a "mighty blaze" consumed the church, a "great and superb building . . . said to be one of the most splendid in the Union." When the sun came up the next day, she found pieces of burned shingles in her yard. The fire had caused the church roof to collapse, gutting the interior and destroying its magnificent new organ, built by David Tannenberg and completed just four years earlier. Only the brick walls remained.[1]

Zion was one of two German Lutheran churches in Philadelphia at the time, which together with St. Michael's formed one congregation. Construction began on the first church, St. Michael's, following the arrival of Lutheran minister and German émigré Henry Melchior Muhlenberg (1711–1787) in November 1742 (fig. 2). Appalled by the "leaky slaughterhouse" in

Figure 2   Detail of a portrait of Henry Melchior Muhlenberg, from Justus Heinrich Christian Helmuth, *Denkmal der Liebe und Achtung . . . dem Herrn D. Heinrich Melchior Mühlenberg* (Philadelphia: Melchior Steiner, 1788). (Courtesy, Lutheran Archives Center, Philadelphia.)

which the members of the congregation had been worshipping, Muhlenberg led them to acquire a lot on Fifth Street at Appletree Alley and embarked on the construction of a church. Dedicated in 1748, St. Michael's was an impressive brick edifice that cost a substantial £1,607 to build and measured 45 by 70 feet (fig. 3). It was also the first church in Philadelphia to have a steeple tower, although the weight of the tower caused the walls to bow and it had to be removed in 1750. Although the church had a seating capacity of eight hundred, it was soon overcrowded. A brick schoolhouse was built in 1761 to provide additional space, and in October 1765 the front pews were altered to accommodate more people. The congregation was becoming so large that these measures proved insufficient, even with the use of a third building (Whitefield Hall or New Building at the College of Philadelphia), so they acquired a nearby lot at Fourth and Cherry Streets on which to build a new church (fig. 4). Robert Smith was hired as the architect, and construction began in 1766. When completed, Zion measured 108 by 70 feet and had seating capacity for twenty-five hundred; it was one of the largest public buildings in the country and cost more than £9,500. The church was dedicated on two successive days in June 1769, with services held in German the first day and in English on the second. Inside, eight large fluted columns supported the arched ceiling, while the galleries were ornamented with a Doric entablature. The brick exterior was also grand, with Venetian windows, brick pilasters, and ornately carved pediments and cornices. A balustrade of urns ran along the roof. Less than ten years after it was completed, Zion was taken over during the British occupation of Philadelphia and used as a hospital, service that wreaked havoc on the interior. It was repaired and a service of thanksgiving held there on December 21, 1781, following Cornwallis's surrender at Yorktown.

In 1786 the congregation hired David Tannenberg (1728–1804), a Moravian, to make what would be the largest and finest organ built in eighteenth-century America. With three manuals (or keyboards) and thirty-four stops, it was Tannenberg's masterpiece and cost the congregation a staggering £1,500 — not including the case. Master joiner George Vorbach/Forepaugh (ca. 1741–1817), who was a member of the congregation, built the case. Measuring 24 feet wide, 27 feet high, and 8 feet deep, the case had five towers and more than one hundred pipes. On the central tower was a painting of the sun rising above the clouds, flanked by gilded eagles and trumpeting angels on the side towers. A skilled craftsman, Vorbach was a member of the Carpenters' Company of Philadelphia and in 1787 oversaw the construction of the senate gallery in Congress Hall. The dedication of the organ in October 1790 was held over three days to accommodate the large crowds who attended, and Michael Billmeyer of Germantown printed a special pamphlet in German for the occasion. Although the organ was lost in the fire of 1794, some sense of its scale and grandeur can be found in the organ of Trinity Lutheran Church at Lancaster (fig. 5).[2]

In an impressive campaign of one-upmanship, Trinity Lutheran commissioned an organ with twenty stops from Tannenberg in 1771; two years earlier, the German Reformed church in Lancaster had hired him to build them an organ with fifteen stops. Whereas the latter organ had a case made for £50 by local cabinetmaker George Burkhardt (d. 1783), the Lutherans hired Peter Frick (1743–1822), who had recently moved to Lancaster from Germantown, to build the case. A masterpiece of cabinetwork for which the church paid £210, the case has fluted columns on the lower half, elaborate moldings, carved and pierced overlays, and ornate finials on each of the five towers. The carving is strongly reminiscent of Philadelphia workmanship, and some of it may even have been executed there, as a payment was made in January 1774 for transporting "wood or wooden parts" for the organ from Philadelphia (fig. 6). The organ was dedicated in December 1774 and

Figure 5   Peter Frick, organ case, Lancaster, Pennsylvania, 1771–1774. (Courtesy, Holy Trinity Lutheran Church, Lancaster, Pa.; photo, ca. 1880.)

Figure 6 Detail of the carved plaque at the base of the central tower on the organ illustrated in fig. 5. (Courtesy, Holy Trinity Lutheran Church, Lancaster, Pa.; photo, Lloyd Bull.)

Figure 7 Photograph of Zion Lutheran Church interior, Philadelphia, Pennsylvania, 1866. (Private collection; photo, Winterthur Museum.)

at the time was the largest built in America. Four years later, it overwhelmed a British lieutenant who saw the church interior. He wrote: "the large galleries on each side, the spacious organ loft, supported by Corinthian pillars, are exceedingly beautiful . . . . The church, as well as the organ, painted white with gilt decorations, which has a very neat appearance . . . the organ is reckoned the largest and best in America. . . . It is the largest, and I think the finest I ever saw, without exception."[3]

Following the devastating fire at Zion Church in 1794, the congregation decided to rebuild and hired master builder William Colladay to oversee the project. The organ, which Tannenberg offered to rebuild for £3,000, was postponed for financial reasons and not completed until 1811. On November 27, 1796, the rebuilt church was consecrated. Three years later, on December 26, 1799, some four thousand people crowded into Zion to attend the state memorial service for George Washington, following a funeral procession that began at the Pennsylvania State House (Independence Hall). Bishop William White, rector of Christ Church, led the service, and General Richard Henry Lee of Virginia delivered his famous eulogy from the pulpit. Eight years earlier, on March 22, 1791, a large crowd had gathered at Zion for Benjamin Franklin's memorial service. A photograph of Zion taken in 1866 during the church's centennial celebration shows the post-1794 interior, with its elegant wineglass pulpit and sounding board topped with a gilt blaze finial and neoclassical ornament on the galleries (fig. 7). Little else is known about the interior, as Zion was torn down in 1869; three years later, St. Michael's would suffer the same fate.[4]

Ethnicity and Identity

With the loss of these two buildings, the most tangible vestiges of Philadelphia's German-speaking community disappeared and its heritage was increasingly forgotten. Scholarship on the mid-Atlantic region has long since operated under a pervasive myth of English-speaking dominance. Most studies of Philadelphia have perpetuated this problem by emphasizing the city's Quakers and Anglicans to the near-total exclusion of its sizable German-speaking population. Monolithic stereotypes of Philadelphia as the "Quaker City" obscure the German presence, and the oft-repeated

2 O O   L I S A   M I N A R D I

description of Quaker decorative arts—"of the best Sort, but Plain"—continues to hold sway. There is also a corresponding assumption that German-speaking people were all peasant farmers who furnished their houses with nothing but painted chests, colorful pottery, and other folk art (figs. 8, 9).

Figure 10 Birth and baptismal certificate for Anna Sara Huett, Berks County, Pennsylvania, ca. 1782. Watercolor and ink on laid paper. 16" x 12½". (Courtesy, Steve and Susan Babinsky; photo, Gavin Ashworth.)

Figure 11 Chest-over-drawers, Manheim area, Lancaster County, Pennsylvania, ca. 1780. Cherry with walnut and yellow pine. H. 19", W. 29¼", D. 15¾". (Private collection; photo, Winterthur Museum, Laszlo Bodo.) The brasses are replaced.

The notion of sophisticated, urban objects made or owned by people of German heritage is rarely considered, a misconception revealed in statements such as "in the Germanic communities of Pennsylvania, rococo ornament was seldom employed, and then usually only on special commission." Surviving objects—including long rifles, stove plates, silver, furniture, and even some fraktur—reveal that, on the contrary, Pennsylvania German artisans and status-conscious consumers both made and acquired objects with rococo designs (figs. 10, 11). Lancaster in particular became a center of rococo-inspired furniture, initiated by "Germanic craftsmen working for Germanic patrons, under the influence of Philadelphia-oriented taste setters." Pennsylvania German entrepreneurs also made goods that appealed to a wide range of consumers, such as ironmaster and glassmaker Henry William Stiegel of Manheim. Some of the most elaborate rococo ornament made in Pennsylvania was on iron stoves cast at his Elizabeth Furnace (fig. 12). Although some of these stoves were made from molds carved in Philadelphia, it would be a mistake to assume that only English-speaking customers bought them, as stoves for heating were by far preferred by Germans and no examples made by Stiegel are known with a history of ownership in a non–German Pennsylvania family. Indeed, Stiegel may have been targeting wealthy Pennsylvania German customers by combining their preferred heating technology with the most fashionable ornament.[5]

Figure 12 Ten-plate stove, Elizabeth Furnace, Elizabeth Township, Lancaster County, Pennsylvania, 1769. Iron. H. 63¼", W. 15", D. 44¼". (Courtesy, Hershey Museum; photo, Metropolitan Museum of Art, David Allison.) The front plate depicts Aesop's fable of the dog and its reflection.

A common misconception about German furniture craftsmen in Philadelphia is that those who "did well were assimilated to some degree into the dominant English community, either through business connections, kinship ties, or religious affiliation," because "in order to be tied into the city's economic base, German woodworkers needed an English clientele." The Pennsylvania Germans, especially those living in Philadelphia, are generally assumed to have "rapidly assimilated," thus implying a declension model in which Germanic identity gradually lessened and was ultimately subsumed by a dominant Anglo-American culture. Many historians and material culture scholars have clung to a tripartite model of immigrants' adaptation to life in America: rejection of the new culture, rapid assimilation, or a "controlled acculturation" that attempted to moderate between assimilation and rejection. As Bernard L. Herman and others have argued, the problem with such interpretations is that they assume the dominance of Anglo-American culture and ignore the significant impact that German-speaking immigrants had on their non-German neighbors. Historian Steven Nolt argues that during the early national period, German-speaking immigrants and their descendants developed a distinctive Pennsylvania German identity in a process he terms "ethnicization-as-Americanization." The latter viewpoint enables us to consider the Pennsylvania Germans as active participants in the construction of American identity, rather than as merely reacting against it or being absorbed within it. This is strongly supported by the material evidence in Philadelphia, which reveals that German-speaking people played a vital role in the formation of the city's multicultural, cosmopolitan identity. Fashioning themselves as "representative Americans," the Pennsylvania Germans became Americanized without having to assimilate, retaining distinctive traditions and "alternate, ethnic visions" of what it meant to be an American.[6]

Figure 13 George Heap, *The East Prospect of the City of Philadelphia in the Province of Pennsylvania* (*London Magazine*, 1761). (Courtesy, American Philosophical Society.)

Philadelphia's Germans

Founded in 1682 by William Penn, Philadelphia was the capital of the most culturally diverse of the thirteen British colonies in North America. By 1750 it was the largest city in the colonies and one of the major seaports. Settlement grew rapidly along the banks of the Delaware and Schuylkill Rivers

Figure 14 Map of southeastern Pennsylvania. (Artwork, Wynne Patterson and Tom Willcockson.)

(figs. 13–15). Although New York would surpass it in size by 1810, Philadelphia remained the country's most important hub of manufacturing, finance, and international trade—some seven hundred ships arrived each year—well into the 1800s. It was also the social capital of the region and the political capital of the United States during the 1790s.

German-speaking immigration began in 1683 with the establishment of Germantown, about seven miles northwest of Philadelphia, by a group of German Quakers and Mennonites. For the next twenty years, relatively few Germans, probably no more than three hundred, arrived, but a severe winter in Germany in 1709 prompted a second wave of immigration (initially to New York). The third and largest influx of Germans to America began

Figure 15 *Plan of the City of Philadelphia*, drawn and engraved by William Russell Birch and Thomas Birch, Philadelphia, Pennsylvania, 1800, and published in *Birch's Views of Philadelphia* (Philadelphia: W. Birch, 1800) (Courtesy, Winterthur Library, Printed Book and Periodical Collection; photo, James Schneck.)

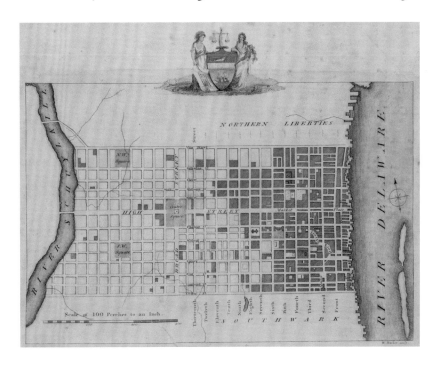

Figure 16 Looking glass labeled by John Elliott Sr., Philadelphia, Pennsylvania, 1762–1767. Walnut with white cedar. H. 13¼", W. 7", D. ¾". (Private collection; photo, Winterthur Museum, Laszlo Bodo.)

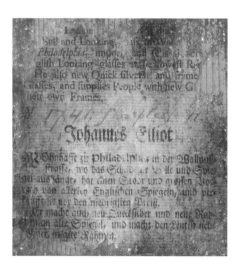

Figure 17 Detail of the label on the reverse of the looking glass illustrated in fig. 16.

in the 1720s and continued until the outbreak of the Revolution, peaking from 1749 to 1754, when some 35,000 Germans arrived in Pennsylvania. About 81,000 of the estimated 111,000 Germans who immigrated to America before 1783 settled in Pennsylvania.[7]

As early as 1717 Quaker merchant Jonathan Dickinson of Philadelphia predicted, "We shall have a great mixt multitude." The increasing German population during the 1740s led Benjamin Franklin to fear that they would "shortly be so numerous as to Germanize us instead of our Anglifying them." In 1751 he complained that the "Palatine Boors . . . swarm into our Settlements and, by herding together, establish their Language and Manners, to the Exclusion of ours." Perhaps Franklin was disgruntled that his efforts to establish a German-language newspaper in 1732 had failed, outdone by Christopher Saur Sr. (1693–1758) of Germantown, who began printing in 1738 and started a German-language newspaper the following year. One German immigrant writing about Philadelphia in 1754 reported, "in this city and in this part of the country one can see people from every part of the entire world, especially Europeans. . . . The greatest number of inhabitants of Pennsylvania is German." To serve this diverse population, savvy businessmen such as the looking glass retailer John Elliott used labels printed in both English and German (figs. 16, 17). This bilingual tradition continued to the end of the century. In 1772 Godfreyd Richter offered his services "to those Gentlemen who incline to learn the GERMAN LANGUAGE; and as it has been his chief study, they may depend upon due care, and the true pronunciation." Pamphlets printed in both English and German were distributed to the crowd of onlookers who attended the Grand Federal Procession in Philadelphia on July 4, 1788.[8]

The ethnic and cultural identity of these German-speaking immigrants was complicated by a number of factors. German-speaking Europe was then subdivided into hundreds of territories under the rule of semi-autonomous kings, bishops, dukes, margraves, and others. This political fragmentation tended to promote regional rather than national identity, which was compounded by the presence of multiple dialects and religious beliefs (fig. 18). Most Lutheran and Reformed immigrants came from the Palatinate, Kraichgau, and Württemberg regions of southwestern Germany as well as the Alsatian region of eastern France. The Mennonites and Amish came primarily from the German-speaking cantons of Bern and Zurich in Switzerland, the Moravians from Bohemia and Moravia, and the Schwenkfelders from Silesia (modern-day Poland). Before these immigrants could become Pennsylvania German, they had to develop a shared sense of German identity. This process began during their shared migration experiences and was fostered by participation in German-speaking churches and organizations such as the German Society of Pennsylvania (est. 1764) or the German-speaking Hermann Masonic Lodge no. 125 (est. 1811). German-speaking craftsmen also sought patronage from other Germans, such as Philadelphia clock- and watchmaker Frederick Dominick, who in 1768 encouraged his "Landesleute, die Deutschen" (countrymen, the Germans) to patronize him. A sense of common German identity was also promoted

Figure 18 Map of European origins of German-speaking immigrants to Pennsylvania (in blue). (Courtesy, Winterthur Museum; artwork, Tom Willcockson, Mapcraft.com.)

by English-speaking Philadelphians, who routinely lumped the immigrants together by referring to them all as "Germans" or "Palatines." Under these circumstances, linguistic and other differences quickly "faded into the background as the distinctions between them and their English-speaking neighbors moved into the foreground." The blending of Germanic dialects, religious faiths, and cultural traditions combined with New World realities led by the early nineteenth century to the formation of a hybrid Pennsylvania German culture.[9]

Although most German-speaking immigrants who arrived in Philadelphia soon settled in the surrounding backcountry, a sizable number stayed in the city. In 1730 approximately 15 percent of Philadelphia's population was German; by 1740 this grew to 25 percent and in 1750, 35 percent. Spurred by massive waves of immigration and natural increase, Philadelphia's German population reached a height of 45 percent in 1760. Immigration was disrupted by the Seven Years' War and the American Revolution, but in 1800 people of German heritage vied with those of English ancestry as the largest ethnic group in Philadelphia, with both populations estimated at 32 to 35 percent of the total 68,000 residents. The single largest religious denomination in 1800 was German Lutheran, at 12.6 percent of the city's entire population. German Reformed comprised 8 percent, while Episcopalians measured 10.5 percent and Quakers only 6.6 percent. A small percentage was Mennonite, Moravian, Catholic, Jewish, or Schwenkfelder.

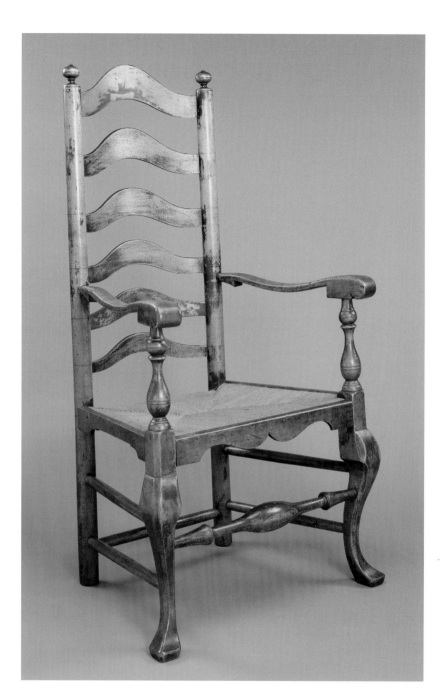

Figure 19   Armchair attributed to the shop of Solomon Fussell, Philadelphia, Pennsylvania, ca. 1740. Maple. H. 45", W. 25½", D. 21¼". (Courtesy, Winterthur Museum; photo, James Schneck.)

These numbers differed only slightly from the regional concentration of German-speaking people in southeastern Pennsylvania, which in 1790 was approximately 40 percent German, 30 percent English, and 18 percent Scots-Irish. At the same time, estimates of religious affiliation in southeastern Pennsylvania are about 30,000 Quakers (9 percent), 60,000 Presbyterians (19 percent); and 85,000 German Lutherans or Reformed (26 percent). By 1815 Philadelphia's population had grown to approximately 100,000 but remained 20–30 percent German. More immigration following the end of the Napoleonic Wars increased these numbers; in 1847 it was estimated that one-third of Philadelphians were of German origin and 80,000 understood the German language. The presence of so many German-speaking people—

Figure 20 Christopher Witt, *Johannes Kelpius*, Germantown, Pennsylvania, ca. 1705. Watercolor and ink on laid paper. 9⅛" x 6⅜". (Courtesy, Historical Society of Pennsylvania.)

who largely did not settle in ethnic enclaves within the city but wherever space permitted—had a profound effect on the ethnic, cultural, linguistic, and religious balance of the city.[10]

This German-speaking population also had a tremendous impact on Philadelphia's material culture. Many of the leading craftsmen in Philadelphia were of German birth or heritage, including clockmaker Jacob Godschalk, pewterers William Will and Johann Philip Alberti, and silversmith Christian Wiltberger. Jacob Knorr, a master carpenter from Germantown, was the builder of Cliveden, the country house of Benjamin Chew, as well as the Germantown Academy in 1760–1761. Most scholarship, however, has focused on nonurban Pennsylvania German material culture. Benno Forman complained of this problem more than thirty years ago, writing, "virtually no recognition has been accorded the German craftsmen who disembarked from the ships in Philadelphia and never left the town, and their influence on the most sophisticated furniture-producing community in eighteenth-century America has never been considered a possibility." He continued, "No one has even suggested that it might have been the presence of German craftsmen or German ideas in Philadelphia that made the furniture of that metropolis unique in colonial America." Before his death in 1982, Forman argued persuasively that the ubiquitous slat-back chairs made by Solomon Fussell (d. 1762), his apprentice William Savery (1721/22–1787), and others were a direct result of German influence (fig. 19). He found that although slat-back chairs were made in other regions, those from southeastern Pennsylvania differed in having tapered stiles, slats that were arched on both the top and bottom, and arms that were undercut at both ends, rather than just at the front. Forman attributed these features to the German presence, citing related German chairs as well as an early portrait of Germantown resident Johannes Kelpius (1673–1708) seated in a slat-back armchair (fig. 20). Forman also contended that Fussell may have been of Germanic heritage, as the surname can be documented in both Germany and Switzerland in the early 1700s but not in England. He hypothesized that the distinctive seat-framing techniques used to make compass seat chairs in Philadelphia could also be traced to the influence of émigré German craftsmen. Building on his work, Désirée Caldwell concluded that these chairs were a combination of Germanic construction techniques and English design principles.[11]

The period from 1740 to 1820, however, remains largely unexplored in terms of German furniture in Philadelphia. A complex web of language, ethnicity, religious beliefs, and family ties helped shape the contours of a world that was neither German nor English but, rather, American. Many of the resulting objects were an amalgam of Continental and British forms, construction techniques, and ornament within the locally specific context of Philadelphia taste and patronage. Through a detailed investigation of three distinct groups of furniture made by German cabinetmakers in the Philadelphia area, the following article will attempt to resurrect some of this lost history while reevaluating our understanding of Philadelphia and its furniture in the process.

Early Inlay

Although the first permanent German settlement in Pennsylvania was established in 1683, few examples of Pennsylvania German furniture made before 1740 are known to survive. Chests brought over by immigrants were a common early storage form, but fewer than ten documented ones are extant. Among the earliest known surviving examples of Pennsylvania German furniture is a walnut chair that descended in the family of John Bernhard Reser (ca. 1685–1761) of Germantown, who emigrated from Schwarzenau in the late 1720s. With its raised panel back and elongated baluster turnings, the chair likely dates to the 1730s or 1740s (fig. 21). The

Figure 21 Side chair, probably Germantown, Pennsylvania, 1730–1740. Walnut. H. 43¾", W. 18½", D. 15½". (Courtesy, Winterthur Museum; photo, James Schneck.)

base of the chair—turned legs, stretchers, and plank seat set within a frame—resembles that of some wainscot chairs made in Chester County, Pennsylvania, including one owned by Irish Quaker Joseph Pennock (fig. 22), but the turned rear stiles and raised panel back distinguish the Germantown chair as a more fully developed example. The narrow, vertical shape of the paneled back is also unlike the broad, horizontal back of a typical wainscot chair. It may be the work of a turner such as Johannes Bechtel (1690–1777), who trained in Heidelberg, Germany, before settling in Germantown in 1726. He later joined the Moravian church and in 1749 moved to Bethlehem.[12]

Figure 22   Side chair, probably West Marlborough Township area, Chester County, Pennsylvania, 1730–1750. Walnut. H. 40½", W. 17¾", D. 16½". (Courtesy, Primitive Hall Foundation; photo, Winterthur Museum, Laszlo Bodo.)

Figure 23   Chest, Philadelphia, Pennsylvania, ca. 1750. Walnut veneer and maple and mahogany inlay with yellow pine. H. 8¼", W. 12¼", D. 8". (Courtesy, Krauth Memorial Library, Lutheran Theological Seminary at Philadelphia; photo, Gavin Ashworth.) Two slots were inserted at a later date to convert the chest into an alms box or ballot box. The veneer was identified as American black walnut by microanalysis.

Figure 24   Detail of the lid of the chest illustrated in fig. 23. (Photo, Gavin Ashworth.)

Figure 25   Lewis Miller, drawing of the altar in Christ Lutheran Church, York, Pennsylvania, ca. 1811. (Courtesy, York County Heritage Trust; photo, Gavin Ashworth)

Another early object, probably built in Philadelphia by a German émigré craftsman, is a small, domed-lid chest made for St. Michael's Lutheran Church (fig. 23). The main body of the chest is inlaid with flowers on all four sides, and the lid bears an image of the Agnus Dei, or Lamb of God (fig. 24). Clearly intended for display in the round, the chest may have been used for the storage of communion wafers on an altar. A ciborium with figure of the Agnus Dei on the lid was among the early furnishings of Christ Lutheran Church in York, Pennsylvania (est. 1733). A drawing of the church altar by York artist Lewis Miller (1796–1882) shows the ciborium, with a paten, wafers, serving spoon, two flagons, and a chalice nearby (fig. 25). The right end panel of the St. Michael's chest slides up to reveal a shallow compartment at the bottom, about the right size for storing a spoon (fig. 26). Several other Lutheran and Reformed churches in southeastern Pennsylvania had pewter communion vessels with the Agnus Dei engraved on them.[13]

The earliest dated example of Pennsylvania German furniture is a clock case with "1740" inlaid on the top rail of the bonnet door, flanked by applied columns (fig. 27). The initials "I M C" are inlaid on the pendulum door along with flowering vines and a ruffled cartouche around the oculus.

Figure 27   Tall-case clock, Philadelphia area, Pennsylvania, 1740. Walnut and mixed-wood inlay with tulip poplar and red oak. H. 90", W. 20½", D. 13". (Courtesy, Rocky Hill Collection; photo, Gavin Ashworth.) The movement is probably British and dates 1680–1700.

Figure 28 Schrank, Philadelphia area, Pennsylvania, 1741. Walnut and mixed-wood inlay with yellow pine, tulip poplar, walnut, and oak. H. 76", W. 75¼", D. 27½". (Courtesy, Rocky Hill Collection; photo, Gavin Ashworth.)

Closely related inlay is also found on a *Kleiderschrank*, or clothes cupboard, dated 1741 (fig. 28). This magnificent example of German baroque furniture has flat pilasters inlaid with flowering vines and large shells, flanked by ornately carved capitals and bases modeled after the Corinthian order (figs. 29–32). Together with the plain Tuscan-style columns on the clock hood, this carving indicates that the maker was familiar with academic design principles and the five orders of architecture, which were readily available in German translation. The inlay reflects the work of an émigré craftsman trained in traditional Continental marquetry, in which tech-

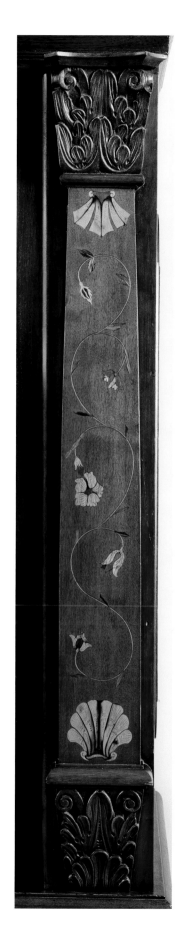

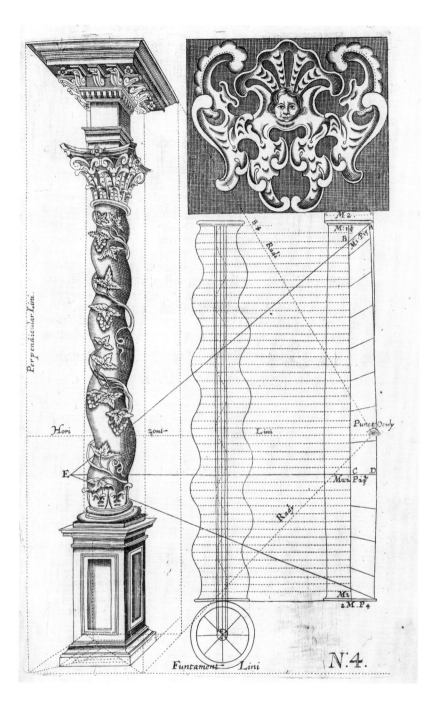

Figure 29   Detail of an inlaid pilaster on the schrank illustrated in fig. 28. (Photo, Gavin Ashworth.)

Figure 30   Detail of a column with carved floral decoration, in Georg Caspar Erasmus, *Seulen-Buch Oder Gründlicher Bericht von der Fünff Ordnungen der Architectur-Kunst welche solche von Marco Vitruvio, Jacobo Barrozzio, Hans Blumen C. und Andern . . .* (Nuremberg, 1688). (Courtesy, Winterthur Library, Printed Book and Periodical Collection; photo, James Schneck.)

Figure 31 Detail of the Ionic and Corinthian orders, in Georg Caspar Erasmus, *Seulen-Buch Oder Gründlicher Bericht von der Fünff Ordnungen der Architectur-Kunst welche solche von Marco Vitruvio, Jacobo Barrozzio, Hans Blumen C. und Andern . . .* (Nuremberg, 1688). (Courtesy, Winterthur Library, Printed Book and Periodical Collection; photo, James Schneck.)

Figure 32 Detail of the inlaid shell and carved capital on the schrank illustrated in fig. 28. (Photo, Gavin Ashworth.)

niques such as scorching and line engraving are used to create detail and shading; this is particularly evident in the shells as well as the birds inlaid on the two raised panel doors (fig. 33). The bird on the left may represent the Carolina parakeet. The only parrot species native to North America, it was noted for its brilliant green body with red and yellow markings on the head and wings (fig. 34). Now extinct, the birds were common in Pennsylvania during the mid-1700s, when German immigrant Gottlieb Mittelberger described them as "grass-green ones, with red heads." By the 1820s Carolina parakeets were increasingly rare, as farmers who considered them a pest decimated their flocks. Noted for their colorful plumage, these parrots were

Figure 33 Details of the inlaid birds on the schrank illustrated in fig. 28. (Photo, Gavin Ashworth.)

Figure 34 *The Parrot of Carolina*, in Mark Catesby, *Natural History of Carolina, Florida and the Bahama Islands* (London, 1729–1747). (Courtesy, Winterthur Library, Printed Book and Periodical Collection; photo, James Schneck.)

Figure 35 Drawing of a parrot, bird, and flowers, attributed to Henrich Otto, Lancaster County, Pennsylvania, ca. 1780. Watercolor and ink on laid paper. 7⅞" x 6½". (Collection of Dr. and Mrs. Donald M. Herr.)

Figure 36 Desk, Philadelphia area, Pennsylvania, ca. 1750. Walnut and mixed-wood inlay with walnut and tulip poplar. H. 42¾", W. 42", D. 21¼". (Private collection; photo, Gavin Ashworth.)

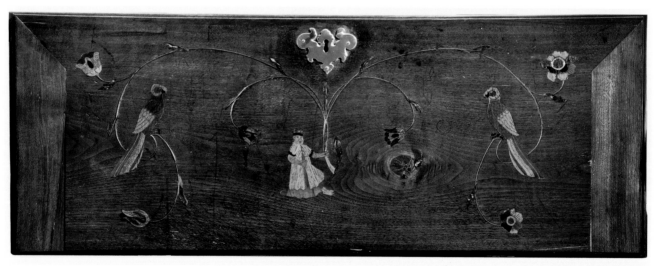

Figure 37 Lid of the desk illustrated in fig. 36. (Photo, Gavin Ashworth.)

an inspiration to many Pennsylvania German artisans who put them on everything, from painted chests to fraktur drawings (fig. 35). The parrot on the right door is nearly identical to those on the lid of a slant-front desk, which also has closely related vines and flowers (figs. 36, 37). At the center of the lid is an inlaid human figure who grasps the base of the vine in his left hand; the inlay is so minutely detailed that even his individual curled fingers are discernible. The use of multiple woods for the inlaid flowers also yields a polychrome effect (figs. 38, 39). By comparison, the inlaid birds on two Lancaster County clocks, both dated 1755, appear rather crude and unsophisticated even though both were embellished with sand shading and engraving (fig. 40).[14]

Figure 38 Detail of the figure inlaid on the desk illustrated in fig. 36. (Photo, Gavin Ashworth.)

Figure 39 Details showing two flowers inlaid on the desk illustrated in fig. 36. (Photo, Gavin Ashworth.)

Figure 40 Details showing the birds inlaid on the pendulum doors of a clock made for George Yunt, Ephrata, Lancaster County, Pennsylvania, 1755 (left), and a clock, Lancaster County, Pennsylvania, 1755 (right). (Courtesy, Earle H. and Yvonne Henderson; photo, Winterthur Museum, Laszlo Bodo [left]; courtesy, Pook & Pook [right].)

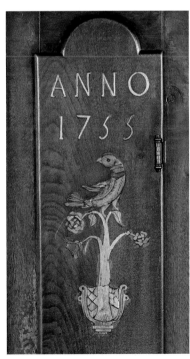

Figure 41   Valuables cabinet or spice box, Philadelphia area, Pennsylvania, ca. 1740. Walnut and mixed-wood inlay with walnut and pine. H. 16", W. 14¼", D. 10⅛". (Private collection; photo, Gavin Ashworth.)

Figure 42   Detail of the inlay on the cabinet illustrated in fig. 41. (Photo, Gavin Ashworth.)

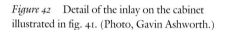

Figure 43   Detail of the interior of the cabinet illustrated in fig. 41. (Photo, Gavin Ashworth.)

   Related inlay and structural details also appear on the door of a diminutive valuables chest or spice box, essentially a cabinet with small drawers for storing items such as coins and spices (fig. 41). The applied columns on either side of the paneled door resemble those on the clock hood, while the tiny inlaid bird relates closely to the parrots on the schrank—in particular, the use of line engraving to add detail to the feathers and tree stump (fig. 42). The cove molding that surrounds the raised panel door is also nearly identical to the doors of the schrank. Small brass knobs are on each of the seven interior drawers; the entire cabinet rests on four turned feet, all of which are original (fig. 43). Although this form is generally thought of in Pennsylvania as an English and typically Philadelphia or Chester County Quaker object, the inlaid ornament and its relation to the clock and schrank suggest that this example is of Pennsylvania German origin. The bold projecting cornice and base molding, use of large iron tulip-shape hinges, and drawer construction with tiny wedges driven into the pins of the dovetails are indicative Germanic craftsmanship. Small valuables chests were made in Britain as well as Continental Europe, which is likely where the maker of this box originated.[15]

Between 1700 and 1740, exotic birds were popular motifs for painted and inlaid furniture in Continental Europe (fig. 44). In Württemberg and Hohenlohe, bird motifs were so common that the term *Papageieinschrank* (parrot cupboard) came into use. Craftsmen did not have to work from live

Figure 44   Desk-and-bookcase, Kirchheim unter Teck, Baden-Württemberg, Germany, 1720–1730. Walnut, maple, and plum with poplar and yew. H. 62½", W. 44¼", D. 30". (Courtesy, Landesmuseum Württemberg, 1977/106.)

Figure 45　*A Parroqueet from Angola*, in Eleazar Albin, *A Natural History of Birds*, vol. 3 (London, 1740). (Courtesy, Teylers Museum.)

birds, as publications such as Mark Catesby's *Natural History of Carolina, Florida and the Bahama Islands* (London, 1729–1747) and George Edwards's *A Natural History of Uncommon Birds* (London, 1743–1751) provided illustrations of both native and exotic species, including macaws, toucans, cockatoos, and various parrots. Many of the birds were depicted perched on a branch—like the taxidermy specimens from which they were typically drawn—and closely resemble their inlaid and painted counterparts. The parrot on the right door of the schrank and those on the lid of the desk appear to be based on the engraving "A Parroqueet from Angola" in Eleazar Albin's *A Natural History of Birds* (fig. 45). Published in three volumes between 1731 and 1740, the book was widely popular in Europe and would have been available before the 1741 date of the schrank. Little is known of Albin himself. He is thought to be of German heritage, although by 1708 he was in London and counted both Catesby and Edwards as friends. The work of these three naturalists provided artistic inspiration for media other than furniture, including needlework, such as a pair of silkwork pictures made in 1752 by Sarah Wistar (1738–1815), daughter of German émigré Caspar Wistar (fig. 46).[16]

Figure 46　Pair of silkwork pictures, by Sarah Wistar, Philadelphia, 1752. Silk on silk moiré. 9½" x 7" (unframed). (Courtesy, Winterthur Museum.)

Figure 47 Tall-case clock with movement by Augustin Neisser, Philadelphia area, Pennsylvania, ca. 1745. Walnut and mixed-wood inlay with tulip poplar and pine. H. 93½", W. 22½", D. 12½". (Courtesy, Historical Society of Berks County, Reading, Pa.; photo, Gavin Ashworth.) The feet, waist door hinges, and bottom section of waist molding are replaced.

Figure 48 Tall-case clock with movement by Joseph Wills, Philadelphia, Pennsylvania; case, Philadelphia area, Pennsylvania, ca. 1745. Walnut and mixed-wood inlay with tulip poplar and pine. H. 86", W. 22¼", D. 12". (Courtesy, York County Heritage Trust; photo, Gavin Ashworth.) The waist door hinges are replaced.

A Philadelphia-area attribution for these four objects is supported by the use of related motifs on the pendulum doors of two tall clocks, one with a movement by Augustin Neisser (1717–1780) of Germantown and the other by Joseph Wills (1700–1759) of Philadelphia (figs. 47, 48). The door of the Neisser clock case is inlaid with a bird perched on a flowering branch. A nearly identical bird is inlaid on the Wills clock, above a pastoral vignette complete with buildings, agricultural fields, and a fence (fig. 49); the wood has been dyed to achieve a polychrome effect. The elaborate foliate inlay surrounding the oculus (fig. 50) bears a strong relation to the work of French

Figure 49   Details of the inlaid birds on the
clocks illustrated in fig. 47 (left) and fig. 48
(right). (Photo, Gavin Ashworth.)

Figure 50 Detail of the cartouche on the clock illustrated in fig. 48. (Photo, Gavin Ashworth.)

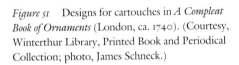

Figure 51 Designs for cartouches in *A Compleat Book of Ornaments* (London, ca. 1740). (Courtesy, Winterthur Library, Printed Book and Periodical Collection; photo, James Schneck.)

designer Jean Bérain (1637–1711), whose published engravings were highly influential in western Germany, Switzerland, the Low Countries, and London during the first half of the eighteenth century. A page of Bérainesque designs for cartouches is extremely similar to the cartouche on the clock (fig. 51). Comparable, albeit more elaborate, Bérainesque motifs also appear on German furniture at this time, including a Rhenish *tabernakelschrank* made by Johann Georg Wahl (1702–1773) in 1743 (fig. 52). Although the Neisser and Wills clock cases appear to have been made by a different craftsman than the other inlaid group (see figs. 27, 28, 36, 41), the inlaid decoration, robust moldings, and ample use of wooden pegs in their construction suggest that all were built by craftsmen of Germanic heritage. The presence of Wills clock movements in several closely related clock cases, including

Figure 52 Johann Georg Wahl, *tabernakelschrank* Osthofen, Germany, 1743. Oak with maple and walnut veneer and mixed-wood, ivory, and ebony inlay. H. 81½", W. 47", D. 26". (Courtesy, Newark Museum; photo, Robert Crabb, 1929)

one in the Yale collection whose cornice is nearly identical to that of the clock in figure 48, indicates that the maker was from the Philadelphia area.[17]

Both Neisser and Wills had close ties to the German-speaking community. Neisser was born in Schlen, Moravia, in 1717 and moved as a young boy to the estate of Count Nicholas von Zinzendorf in Herrnhut, where he joined the Moravian faith. He immigrated to America in 1736 and three years later settled in Germantown, where he worked as a clock- and watchmaker until his death in 1780. Wills was a native of South Molton Parish in Devonshire, England. Although many sources claim that he was in Philadelphia by the mid-1720s, the recent discovery that "Joseph Wills, clockmaker" of South Molton took an apprentice in 1729 suggests that he did not immigrate until the 1730s. Despite his English heritage, Wills was closely allied with Philadelphia's German-speaking community. The records of St. Michael's and Zion Lutheran Church list the death of his wife,

Maria Dorothea, in 1757, along with the notation, "Her husband requested that they be buried in our churchyard." The executors of Wills's estate were Thomas Say and Maria Sophia Cogen/Gogen; Say was married to a German woman, Susannah Catharine Sprogell, and Maria Sophia Cogen/Gogen's name is clearly also German. Because Wills had only one witness sign his will and not the required two, affidavits made by several acquaintances to confirm its validity reveal that Wills spent significant time in the area of New Hanover (now part of Montgomery County), where Lutheran schoolmaster Michael Walter and innkeeper Caspar Singer both knew him. Wills likely trained clockmaker Jacob Godschalk (d. 1781), who inventoried Wills' estate and bought the time of his indentured mulatto servant, Benjamin. Born in Towamencin Township, in what is now Montgomery County, Jacob was probably the son of German immigrant Herman Godschalk.[18]

Although these objects appear to have been made by two different artisans, all exhibit a deep familiarity with Continental marquetry traditions and imply that they are the work of émigré German craftsmen. Multiple woods were used to achieve a polychrome effect, while a surface application of stain or dye was used to tint the leaves and birds' plumage. This painterly technique may be an indication of the makers' origins, as furniture from Württemberg and Hohenlohe from the early-to-mid 1700s is especially noted for using colored inlay as well as parrot motifs. In the second half of the eighteenth century, German Moravian cabinetmaker Abraham Roentgen (1711–1793) of Neuwied and his son David (1743–1807) would develop more vibrant and colorfast pictorial inlays with the use of penetrating dyes.[19]

Unfortunately, none of these objects has a firm provenance. Given the Neisser and Wills clock movements, together with the early dates, refined construction, and sophisticated inlay techniques, a Philadelphia-area origin is likely. Because Wills also had ties in the New Hanover area, which before 1784 was part of Philadelphia County, it is possible their origin may extend into what is now Montgomery County. The presence of inlaid initials on the 1740 clock and 1741 schrank (figs. 27, 28) enables further investigation and a tentative identification of the original owner in the case of the latter. The initials on the clock, "I ^{M} c," stand for a married couple such as Johannes or Jacob and Catharina or Christina M   ; numerous couples, however, fit these initials even at this early date. The initials on the schrank can be arranged as "AM MI" or "MI AM" because the drawers are interchangeable. Since it was common for full names to be abbreviated on furniture with initials (one schrank bears the initials "DV HS" for David Hottenstein), and since nearly all known documented schranks with initials or a name represent either the husband or both spouses, the original arrangement of the initials on this schrank was likely "MI AM." Only one likely person has been found whose name fits these initials, Michael Amenzetter (1696–1784), a German immigrant who settled in Philadelphia and was a member of St. Michael's and Zion Lutheran Church. His name does not appear in the lists of arrivals that Philadelphia began requiring in 1727, which means that either he immigrated before that year or he arrived in

Figure 53 Library bookcase attributed to Martin Pfeninger, Charleston, South Carolina, 1770–1775. Mahogany, mahogany and burl walnut veneer, mixed-wood inlays and ivory with cypress. H. 128¾", W. 99", D. 20½". (Courtesy, Charleston Museum; photo, Museum of Early Southern Decorative Arts, Gavin Ashworth.)

a different city. In 1741 Michael would have been forty-five, which is in keeping with the fact that schranks were typically acquired for established households rather than young couples. Unfortunately, although Michael's death is recorded in the church records, no estate papers have been located.[20]

The accomplished carving and sophisticated figural inlay (which predates its use on federal furniture such as that by Bankson and Lawson of Baltimore by nearly fifty years) on these objects reveal the high level of craftsmanship that was executed by some German émigré woodworkers in America. This practice was not limited to Pennsylvania. Charleston, South Carolina, was also home to a sizable population of German émigré craftsmen, including cabinetmaker Martin Pfeninger (d. 1782), to whom is attributed a spectacular mahogany library bookcase with inlaid baroque strapwork and ivory husks (fig. 53). Given the elaborate pictorial inlay on furniture made by German craftsmen such as the Roentgens or Johann Friedrich Hintz, a Moravian working in London who in 1738 advertised furniture "inlaid with fine Figures of Brass and Mother of Pearl," this should come as little surprise, but it is in sharp contrast with the furniture typically associated with the Pennsylvania Germans. Unlike the stereotypical painted chests, plank-bottom chairs, and other readily identifiable forms made by German-speaking craftsmen throughout southeastern Pennsylvania, the work of German craftsmen in Philadelphia can be difficult to recognize without documentation. Such is the case with a tall clock accompanied by a hand-written label inscribed, "This Clock Case Was made and Sould by William Bomberger 1765 In the Reign of King George the thirt anno domeny 1765 germantown all work and no play makes [illeg.] bould would you [illeg.] your plan [illeg.]; on the other side is written, "Made in Germantown 1765" (figs. 54, 55). The walnut case retains its original ogee feet and sarcophagus top with compressed ball finials and closely resembles several earlier clock cases housing movements by Joseph Wills and John Wood Sr.

Little is known about Bomberger beyond this label. In 1783 a "William Bomberger, carpenter" paid tax on a rented dwelling from turner Jacob Shoemaker's estate. Three years later, Bomberger was described as a joiner and paid an occupational tax of £50. In the city directories he is listed variously as a carpenter or house carpenter, residing at 5 Elbow Lane (also known as White Horse Alley), from 1791 until 1801, with the exception of 1796, when he is listed as a joiner, and 1797, when his occupation is given as "sharpener of saws." Starting in 1802 Bomberger is listed on Bank Street, which was another name for the north–south portion of Elbow Lane, where he remained through at least 1809. Without the label identifying this clock case as the work of William Bomberger, the ethnic identity of the cabinetmaker would be nearly impossible to determine. The following two case studies will explore this issue in more detail.[21]

Figure 54 Tall-case clock with movement by George Miller and case by William Bomberger, Germantown, Pennsylvania, 1765. Walnut with tulip poplar, and yellow pine. H. 98", W. 20¾", D. 11¼". (Private collection; photo, Winterthur Museum, Laszlo Bodo.)

Figure 55 Details of the label inside the clock illustrated in fig. 54. (Photo, Laszlo Bodo.)

Leonard Kessler

One of the leading German cabinetmakers in Philadelphia during the second half of the eighteenth century was Leonard Kessler, a member of St. Michael's and Zion Lutheran Church. Born on September 4, 1737, Kessler emigrated from Germany circa 1750. His marriage to Anna Maria Ritschauer (1736–1825) on October 3, 1758, was witnessed by Reinhardt Uhl and his wife, Jacob Shoemaker, and the brothers Scheubele/Scheuffele. Both Reinhardt Uhl and Jacob Scheubele/Scheuffele (later Schieffelin) were Kessler's brothers-in-law, married to his wife's sisters, Christina Catharina and Regina Margaretta Ritschauer. The Schieffelin family Bible notes Regina's birthplace as Mühlhausen an der Enz, a town in Württemberg; presumably all three sisters were born there and immigrated to Philadelphia. The name of the third party who attended the wedding, Jacob Shoemaker, is an important clue as to Kessler's training as a cabinetmaker. No Jacob Shoemaker appears in the records of St. Michael's and Zion Lutheran Church or the German Reformed Church in Philadelphia as a baptismal sponsor, communicant, or witness to a wedding except for this one instance, implying a relationship with Kessler other than that of a family member or coreligionist. Given that Kessler emigrated from Germany as a young man and would have apprenticed in Philadelphia, Shoemaker is very likely the man who trained him and can thus reasonably be identified as the turner Jacob Shoemaker Jr. (1692–1772), father of cabinetmaker Jonathan Shoemaker (1726–1793) of Philadelphia.[22]

Three generations of Schumachers/Shoemakers were woodworkers, beginning with Jacob Sr., who emigrated from Mainz in 1683 and was one of the original settlers of Germantown. A Quaker, he moved to Philadelphia circa 1715 and worked there approximately five years. In 1722 he bequeathed all of his "turning tools and all the other timber materials utensils and Tools belonging to the Trades of Turning and Wheel Making" to his son Jacob Jr., whose shop was located on Market Street next to that of Caspar Wistar, another German émigré. Jacob Jr. probably trained his son Jonathan, who signed the walnut chest-on-chest with shell-carved drawer and fluted quarter columns illustrated in figures 56 and 57. Jonathan was working as a joiner by 1750 and in 1752 acquired a shop on the west side of

Figure 56   Jonathan Shoemaker, chest-on-chest, Philadelphia, Pennsylvania, ca. 1765. Walnut with tulip poplar and white cedar. H. 97", W. 44", D. 23". (Courtesy, © Christie's Images Ltd.)

Figure 57 Detail of the carving on the chest-on-chest illustrated in fig. 56.

Second Street. In 1767 he relocated to Third Street near Arch. One of his apprentices, Samuel Mickle (1746–1803), made a series of furniture drawings that indicates his shop produced a variety of sophisticated furniture, including large case pieces and cabriole-leg chairs. An armchair that

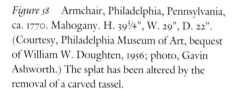

Figure 58 Armchair, Philadelphia, Pennsylvania, ca. 1770. Mahogany. H. 39¾", W. 29", D. 22". (Courtesy, Philadelphia Museum of Art, bequest of William W. Doughten, 1956; photo, Gavin Ashworth.) The splat has been altered by the removal of a carved tassel.

descended in the family of Jonathan Shoemaker has also been attributed to him, although attributions based solely on descent can be problematic (fig. 58).[23]

No signed or labeled furniture by Kessler is known, but the journals of Lutheran minister Henry Muhlenberg offer significant insight into his work. A member of St. Michael's and Zion Lutheran Church, Kessler was the only cabinetmaker the Muhlenbergs are known to have patronized while they lived in Philadelphia from 1761 to 1776. In October 1762 Kessler was hired to build a chimney door for the parsonage; for this and other cabinetwork he was paid more than £12, some of which he returned to Muhlenberg as a contribution to the pastor's salary. When five-year-old Johann Enoch Samuel Muhlenberg died in February 1764, Kessler built the coffin. On October 22, 1765, the church council passed a resolution that charged "Mr. Ehwald and Mr. Kessler, two master carpenters . . . with supervising the alterations in the pews in the front section of St. Michael's Church" (an attempt to add more seating until Zion Church was built). On January 21, 1763, Muhlenberg paid Kessler £10.2.6 for "new chairs." At least six chairs from this set are known, one of which is marked "XII," indicating that it was a set of twelve or more (fig. 59). Made of mahogany, the chairs have

Figure 59 Pair of side chairs attributed to Leonard Kessler, Philadelphia, Pennsylvania, 1763. Mahogany. H. 40½", W. 21½", D. 17". (Private collection; photo, Gavin Ashworth.)

through-tenoned side rails, two-part vertical glue blocks, and compressed ball-and-claw feet typical of Philadelphia chairs. They are ornamented with an interlaced scroll splat, fluted rear stiles, a ruffled shell on the crest, and carved shells on the knees and front seat rail. Although £10.2.6 seems a low price for twelve mahogany chairs with this level of embellishment (which, according to the 1772 Philadelphia price book should have cost more than £25), Philadelphia was in a postwar economic depression in the early 1760s and artisans struggled to make ends meet. Kessler may have charged Muhlenberg a lower price for the chairs simply because he needed the work, or he may have given his pastor a discount. Muhlenberg paid for the chairs in January, the time of year when parishioners often contributed toward his salary. Although much more elaborate chairs were available in Philadelphia, these chairs do have a number of embellishments and would have been well suited to Muhlenberg's relatively modest means. A large set of chairs would have been a necessity for the minister, who frequently hosted sizable groups of visitors at his home. Muhlenberg was also keenly aware of the need for keeping up appearances, remarking that when in the city he "would not

Figure 60 Detail of the cartouche on the crest of one of the chairs illustrated in fig. 59. (Photo, Gavin Ashworth.)

Figure 61 Detail of the cartouche on the chair illustrated in fig. 62. (Photo, Gavin Ashworth.)

dare" wear the clothing his wife made for him "unless I wanted the children on the streets to laugh at me behind my back."[24]

The Muhlenberg chairs have a number of distinctive features, including structural details that identify seating from Kessler's shop and, likely, that in which he trained. At the rear inside corners of the seat frame, thin strips of wood occupy the space created by the overlapping shoe and serve as a foundation for larger glue blocks. The chairs are also distinguished by having flared, scrolled ears decorated with four pairs of crescent-shaped chip cuts, the topmost pair being located on the apex of the ear and not visible from the front; pierced splats with large scroll volutes and high, straight plinths; scallop shells with unusually small flanges on the front seat rail; and the ball-and-claw feet with pronounced knuckles. The cartouche on the crest rail was derived from those on chairs with carving attributed to Nicholas Bernard, but subtle differences help distinguish his work from Kessler's (figs. 60–62). On the Muhlenberg chairs, the volutes flanking the leaf at the bottom are slightly overscale, like those on the splat, and the concave

Figure 62   Side chair, Philadelphia, Pennsylvania, ca. 1765. Mahogany. H. 41", W. 21½", D. 15½". (Courtesy, Leslie Miller and Richard Worley; photo, Gavin Ashworth.) The carving is attributed to Nicholas Bernard.

Figure 63 Side chair attributed to Leonard Kessler, Philadelphia, Pennsylvania, ca. 1765. Mahogany. H. 40½", W. 21½", D. 17". (Courtesy, Yale University Art Gallery, Mabel Brady Garvan Collection.)

Figure 64 Detail of the cartouche on the chair illustrated in fig. 63.

Figure 65 Side chair attributed to Leonard Kessler, Philadelphia, Pennsylvania, ca. 1765. Mahogany. H. 41", W. 21", D. 16½". (Courtesy, H. L. Chalfant.)

sides of the cabochons are gently curved, rather than sharply peaked, at the waist. Using the Muhlenberg chair as a basis for identification, it can be seen that Kessler made less ornate chairs, including a mahogany one with plain rear stiles and no carving on the knees (figs. 63, 64). This format is identical to that of six walnut chairs from another set. Similarly, a mahogany side chair with comparable carving and a solid splat descended in the Morris family of Philadelphia (fig. 65). As will be discussed below, significant evidence suggests that Kessler was both a cabinetmaker and a carver, making it plausible that he made and carved the Muhlenberg chairs and those illustrated in figures 63–65.[25]

Documentary evidence sheds light on Kessler's interactions with other cabinetmakers, both German and English. In 1769 he witnessed the will of joiner John Gaul. Eleven years later, Kessler and Anthony Leckler inventoried the stock of Johann Michael Barendt/Behrendt, a joiner and musical-instrument maker. Behrendt's will had stipulated that "all my Tools of my Trade shall be particularly mentioned in the Inventory or Appraisement of my Estate and be put up and carefully kept . . . for the use of my beloved son John." Thus, Kessler was likely selected for this task because of his knowledge of woodworking tools. The following year, carpenter George Adam Pfister appointed as executors of his estate "my worthy and Esteemed Friends Leonerd Kessler of the said City Cabinetmaker and Michael Bowes of the same Place Victualler," together with his wife. When Benjamin Randolph's tools, lumber, hardware, and other shop equipment were dispersed in 1778, Kessler was paid "for a lot of carved work to be sold at auction" by the vendue master, John Ross.[26]

Starting in October 1779, Kessler began working for David Evans (1748–1819), a Quaker cabinetmaker who lived and worked at 115 Arch Street. In 1780 Evans paid him £228 for walnut boards and glue along with "12 Back feet Walnut—£47.6," "2 Pillars Walnut—£7.10," and "12 Chair Legs—£26.5." The following year, Evans owed Kessler £285 for "Framing Slate" and making coffins that ranged from £22.10 for a poplar one to £37.10 in walnut and £75 in mahogany. Evans also owed Kessler £75 for four days' work on three separate occasions in 1780. Even with price inflation due to the war, this amount is remarkably high and may reflect the fact that Kessler was being paid master's rather than journeyman's wages. The payments for tea table pillars and chair legs, together with the carving work that Kessler did for Randolph, clearly indicate that he was both a carver and a cabinetmaker. In February 1782 Kessler made "1 Corded bonnet bedstead." He also built significant case pieces, as indicated by a payment of £22 for a desk made for Friederich Schenckel, a maker of leather breeches in Philadelphia. It was described as a mahogany desk-and-bookcase and valued at $25 when Schenckel died in 1810. A final indication of Kessler's range of work is suggested by the inventory taken when he died in 1804. In addition to "One lot Joiner's Tools (very old)," valued at fifty cents, there was an extensive list of furniture, including an eight-day clock and case, desk-and-bookcase, six chairs, a chest of drawers, two bureaus, two tea tables, a stand, fire screen, and chest—all of mahogany—together with twelve chairs, a bureau, table, and tea table in walnut. Likely most, if not all, of this furniture was made by Kessler, as it made good business sense for a cabinetmaker to make pieces for his own household rather than pay someone else to do it. One of Kessler's sons, Michael (1764–1793), became a cabinetmaker, but little is known of his work. Michael is listed in the 1791 Philadelphia City Directory as a joiner, residing at his father's address of 125 Arch Street; he died in 1793 during the yellow fever epidemic.[27]

One way to measure Kessler's success as a craftsman is to compare his occupational tax, which was based on yearly income, with that of other cabinetmakers. Topping the list in 1783 was Thomas Affleck at £250, followed by Benjamin Randolph and George Claypoole at £200 each. Kessler was one of eleven woodworkers who paid a tax of £100; others include David Evans, Jonathan Gostelowe, and Francis Trumble. Daniel Trotter was taxed at £75, while the majority of woodworkers were taxed at £30 to £50. Kessler paid additional tax on his dwelling and lot, a cow, and five ounces of silver plate. With the exception of Trumble, a Windsor chairmaker who in 1783 was sixty-seven years old, this cadre of woodworkers was relatively close in age: the youngest, David Evans, was thirty-five; Affleck was forty-three; Randolph and Kessler were both forty-six; and Claypoole was fifty. By 1786 Kessler's business had apparently declined, since he paid a tax of £50, the same as Evans, while Gostelowe and Trotter were both now taxed at £100. Affleck's business was also down significantly, taxed at £122, and Randolph was not even listed.[28]

Another method of assessing Kessler's success is to compare the insurance records for his house with those of other cabinetmakers. In 1765 Kessler took out an insurance policy with the Philadelphia Contributionship, established in 1752 by Benjamin Franklin, for his "Dwelling house, Kitchen and Work Shop" located on the north side of Arch (or Mulberry) Street between Third and Fourth Streets. The house was three stories tall and measured 15 feet wide by 25½ feet deep. On the first floor, the front room was "partitioned off for a Shop with Bord partition," while the back room had a "Brest Sirbace and washbord." The second storey, accessed by stairs of the "Common winding sort," had a front room with "Brest wash bord Sirbace & Single Cornish Round the Room." This concentration of carpentry work, together with a notation that the second storey was painted, indicates that this was the best room. Behind a plaster partition was a small back room "without any Carpentry." The third storey had a "Brest & Washbord," and the garret had one room that was plastered and had a board partition. Behind the house was a kitchen that measured 11 by 16 feet, two and a half stories high; there was also a two-storey frame workshop of 19 feet 6 inches by 15 feet. The three buildings were together insured for £200, the house at £150, kitchen at £35, and shop at £15. By the time the property was resurveyed in 1772, wainscoting had been added to one of the rooms and the kitchen expanded to 27 feet 6 inches by 11 feet. The house and kitchen totaled 1,752 square feet of living space (not counting the attic), with an additional 588 square feet for the workshop. This puts Kessler squarely in the category of middling-to-wealthy families, who on average occupied three-storey houses of approximately 2,000 square feet. By way of comparison, the average Philadelphia laborer occupied a two-storey house of about 500 square feet.[29]

In 1763, only two years before Kessler took out his policy, chairmaker and joiner William Savery insured his new, three-storey brick house on Third between Walnut and Spruce. Measuring 18 by 33 feet, the house—together with a two-storey kitchen of 17½ feet by 11 feet—were insured for £400 and measured a total of 2,167 square feet. Savery's old two-storey house, on Second between High and Chestnut, measured 12 feet 3 inches by 37 feet and was described as having "No Sirbase Washboard or Chimney Except Belo" (probably in the front parlor); it also had a two-storey kitchen of 16 by 9 feet. The policy also noted Savery's "Cheer Makers Shop," which measured 26 by 9½ feet; it was three stories tall, the first of brick, the other two levels of wood. Thus, Kessler's house and kitchen in 1765 were both larger and more highly finished than Savery's old house, but not quite as large as his new house. Savery's workshop was also slightly larger than Kessler's, totaling 741 versus 588 square feet. The footprint of their two workshops was quite different, Savery's being long and narrow, whereas Kessler's was nearly square, likely owing to the difference in their trades as chairmaker and joiner respectively. Savery probably used the upper levels of his three-storey shop as spaces for allowing chair lists and rungs to dry while turning took place on the ground floor. Although the layout of Kessler's workshop is unknown, its two-storey construction provided a space for lumber storage above the main work floor. The first-floor front room of Kessler's house, which was "partitioned off for a shop," provided additional space for him to interact with customers, tend to his accounts, and display examples of his work.[30]

As relatively few Philadelphia cabinetmakers had insurance with the Contributionship, it is rare to have this level of detail for their buildings and work spaces. Two other policyholders were Benjamin Randolph and Daniel Trotter. One of the leading cabinetmakers in Philadelphia, Randolph owned a large, three-storey brick house, located on the north side of Chestnut Street between Third and Fourth, which measured 25 by 40 feet. It was finished with wainscot paneling, cornices, pilasters, and "Tabernakles," or overmantels on the chimneybreasts. In 1772 his policy valued the house together with a two-storey kitchen and washhouse at £1,000 and included the addendum, "No Carved Work, Gilding or History Painting ensured"—implying that such luxuries were present. By contrast, the 1784 survey of Trotter's property on Elfreth's Alley described his house as two stories high and measuring only 19½ feet wide by 17 feet deep. It was finished in a manner similar to Kessler's house but included "Newell Stairs." There was also a two-storey kitchen of 11 by 15 feet, giving Trotter a total of 993 square feet of living space versus Kessler's 1,752.[31]

The insurance surveys shed light on the physical spaces in which cabinetmakers ate, slept, and worked. Although Kessler's house was not nearly as grand as Randolph's, it was nearly quadruple the size of the average artisan's dwelling in Philadelphia and provided his family with comfortable, well-outfitted living quarters. Here Leonard and Mary raised six children: Leonard Jr. (b. 1759), John (b. 1761), Michael (b. 1764), Elizabeth (b. 1766), Rachel (b. 1768), and Anna Maria/Hannah (b. 1770); a seventh child, Jacob (b. 1772) died in infancy. Details about Kessler's personal life found in the journals of his pastor, Henry Muhlenberg, reveal that he was an active participant in congregational life. On November 7, 1761, Muhlenberg recorded his first visit from "Mr. Kessler, the joiner." The Muhlenbergs had just moved to the city on October 29, relocating from Trappe in what is now Montgomery County. This was the first of many visits the pastor would receive from Kessler, as the congregation was in the midst of a bitter controversy over church leadership and the cost of building a new schoolhouse. Kessler was one of the chief complainants against the current trustees and elders, who were accused of mismanaging church funds and trying to avoid annual elections. Muhlenberg paid a visit to Kessler's home on December 30 to discuss the situation. The controversy soon worsened, and after church on January 10, 1762, Muhlenberg recorded that "two dissatisfied members, Messrs. Leonhard Kessler and Enderle, delivered written complaints to my house." Two weeks later, Muhlenberg was invited to dine at the home of Kessler's brother-in-law, Reinhard Uhl. When he arrived, he found "Messrs. Fuchs and Kuhn, former elders, together with Leonhard Kessler and their wives." The church controversy gave Kessler cause for concern about his spiritual state. On a Tuesday in early February 1762, Muhlenberg noted in his journal, "Toward evening had a visit from the joiner, Mr. Kessler, who conferred with me concerning his spiritual condition and requested me to pray with him." Later that week Muhlenberg was visited in the evening by "Messrs. Kessler and Enderle, with whom I conferred and prayed, for they were awakened—Mr. Enderle by Pastor Völcker and Pastor Starck in Frankfurt, Mr. Kessler here." The three men also discussed a religious tract that Kessler had brought along, which Muhlenberg denounced as "papistic abominations."[32]

When these fragments of information are woven together with extant furniture, tax records, insurance policies, and other sources, a more complete picture of Leonard Kessler emerges. In addition to being a craftsman, he was a father, husband, neighbor, and Lutheran preoccupied not just with work but also with his family, friends, and spiritual matters. By the 1790s Kessler had profited enough from his trade that he began to invest in land, acquiring several rental properties. He also began to make potash (used in soapmaking, textile bleaching, and glassmaking), advertising for sale in 1790 "a quantity of POTASH, of the first quality." And he acquired a hearse, which he advertised as a "commodious Carriage for the conveyance of the Dead either out or into town." Since Kessler also made coffins, this was a logical expansion of his existing business. This combination of property investments, potash works, and funerary activities may have helped Kessler escape the repetitiveness of working at a single trade. As he grew older, these diverse investments provided income that was not as physically demanding as cabinetmaking. Beginning in 1798 Kessler is listed in the Philadelphia city directories as a "gentleman," indicating that he had retired. By the time of his death on January 27, 1804, at the age of sixty-six, he had achieved a substantial degree of material comfort. In addition to the extensive assortment of mahogany and walnut furniture previously enumerated, he owned thirty-three books and two German Bibles, twelve silver spoons and sugar tongs, a silver pocketwatch with shagreen case, silver shoe buckles, three looking glasses, and a ten-plate stove. Kessler left his entire estate to his wife, Mary, who continued to live in their house at 125 Arch Street until her death in 1825.[33]

Beyond Philadelphia
In July 1776 Henry Muhlenberg and his wife moved to Trappe, about twenty-five miles northwest of Philadelphia in what is now Montgomery County, bringing the chairs that Kessler had made thirteen years earlier to their new house (fig. 66). A scalloped-top mahogany tea table that

Figure 66 House of Henry and Mary Muhlenberg, Trappe, Montgomery County, Pennsylvania, built ca. 1750–1755. (Photo, Glenn Holcombe.)

Figure 67 Tea table, Philadelphia, Pennsylvania, ca. 1766. Mahogany. Dimensions unrecorded. (Photo reproduced from Henrietta Meier Oakley and John Christopher Schwab, *Muhlenberg Album* [New Haven, Conn.: the authors, 1910].)

descended in the family of the Muhlenbergs' eldest daughter, Eve Elisabeth (1748–1808), also left Philadelphia soon after it was made (fig. 67). The present location of this table is unknown, but a photograph of it in 1910 shows its elaborate scalloped top as well as acanthus carving on the knees. According to family tradition, the table was a wedding present from Eve Elisabeth's brother Peter Muhlenberg (1746–1807) when she married Christopher Emanuel Schultze on September 23, 1766. A Lutheran minister, Schultze emigrated from Germany in 1765. The couple lived in Philadelphia for five years but in 1771 moved to the Tulpehocken region of western Berks County, where Schultze was pastor of Christ Lutheran Church near Stouchsburg. When Schultze died in 1809, he owned both a "Mohockony Table" valued at £3.15 (likely a dining table) as well as a "round Table" worth 11s. 3d. He also owned a clock valued at £14, a desk-and-bookcase worth £6, and a set of armchairs. Philadelphia furniture was available in the backcountry in a variety of ways beyond being taken there by former city dwellers. Wealthy nonurban residents often acquired Philadelphia-made furniture for their homes, such as Lancaster, Pennsylvania, attorney Jasper Yeates (1745–1817), who bought looking glasses from John Elliott, chairs from Benjamin Randolph, and a sofa and easy chair from Plunket Fleeson. In late 1776 John Cadwalader of Philadelphia asked permission to send Yeates "part of his most valuable Furniture" for safekeeping. Writing to his wife from Philadelphia, Yeates instructed her to have the furniture "put up in the Garret & have the Room locked up."[34]

Nonurban residents commissioned, in addition to furniture, clocks, portraits, silver, and even tavern signs from Philadelphia artisans. In April 1788 John Penn spent the night in Trappe at George Brooke's tavern, located across the road from Frederick Muhlenberg's house and store (fig. 68). Built circa 1763, the house had a long, narrow plan like a Philadelphia town house, with a large second-floor drawing room and rear kitchen ell. The store, which was attached to the east side of the house, offered a variety of goods, including candles, ink, and soap; flour, salt, tea, coffee, sugar, and molasses; rum, wine, and tobacco; readymade clothing, fabric, and sewing notions;

Figure 68 House of Frederick Muhlenberg, Trappe, Montgomery County, Pennsylvania, built ca. 1763. (Courtesy, The Speaker's House; photo, Gavin Ashworth.) The roofline of the store is visible on the right side; the mansard roof is a later addition.

Figure 69 Augustus Lutheran Church, Trappe, Montgomery County, Pennsylvania, built 1743. (Photo, Gavin Ashworth.) The stucco is a later addition.

Figure 70 Communion flagon attributed to Johann Philip Alberti, Philadelphia, Pennsylvania, ca. 1760. Pewter. H. 13". (Courtesy, Augustus Lutheran Church; photo, Glenn Holcombe.)

and imported creamware, white salt-glazed stoneware, and brass hardware. Before calling on Muhlenberg the next day, Penn paused to admire the tavern's sign, a likeness of Benjamin Franklin, which he noted was made by George Rutter, an ornamental painter and gilder in Philadelphia. Among Rutter's best-known works is the Pennsylvania coat of arms that he made in 1785 for the State House, its frame carved by Martin Jugiez. Some of the best-documented objects made by German craftsmen in Philadelphia for nonurban customers are church pewter vessels. When Henry Muhlenberg administered communion at Augustus Lutheran Church in Trappe, he used a flagon made by Johann Philip Alberti (d. 1780) of Philadelphia (figs. 69, 70). Another German immigrant, William Will (1742–1798) of Philadelphia, made prodigious amounts of pewter for German Lutheran and Reformed churches throughout southeastern Pennsylvania, such as the extraordinary flagon and chalice given in 1795 by Andreas and Catharina Elisabetha Morr to the Zion Lutheran Church in Penn Township, Northumberland (now Snyder) County (fig. 71).[35]

The presence of Philadelphia-made furniture outside the city, whether taken there when families moved or commissioned by nonurban residents, served as inspiration to rural cabinetmakers and joiners, as demonstrated by a set of six walnut chairs that descended in the Hiester family of Reading, Berks County (figs. 72, 73). The pierced splats and carved cartouches are similar to those on the Muhlenberg chairs, but there is no shell carving on the knees or seat rail; the crests have flat ears with simple volutes; and the stiles are plain rather than fluted. Family tradition maintains that Joseph Hiester (1751–1829), one of Reading's most prominent citizens (fig. 74), was the original owner of the chairs illustrated in figures 72 and 73, but since those objects probably date from the late 1750s or early 1760s, they were more likely purchased by his father-in-law, Adam Witman, a wealthy Reading merchant. Joseph apprenticed to Witman and in 1771 married his only daughter, Elizabeth (fig. 75). The couple came into a sizable fortune when Adam Witman died in 1781, leaving an estate valued at £16,909.2.4. Joseph became involved in public service and was a member of the Philadelphia

Figure 71 Communion flagon and chalice attributed to William Will, Philadelphia, Pennsylvania, 1795. Pewter. H. 13¾" (flagon), 7⅞" (chalice). (Courtesy, Yale University Art Gallery, The Dobson Foundation; Friends of American Arts Acquisition Fund; Mr. and Mrs. Frank J. Coyle, LL.B. 1943, Fund, Peter B. Cooper, B.A. 1960, LL.B. 1964, M.U.S. 1965, and Field C. McIntyre American Decorative Arts Acquisition Fund; Friends of American Arts Decorative Arts Acquisition; and Lisa Koenigsberg, M.A. 1981, M.Phil. 1984, Ph.D. 1987, and David Becker, B.A. 1979 Fund [flagon]; Winterthur Museum [chalice].)

Figure 72 Side chair, Philadelphia, Pennsylvania, ca. 1760. Walnut with hard pine slip seat frame. H. 40½", W. 24", D. 21". (Private collection; photo, Colonial Williamsburg Foundation, Craig McDougal.)

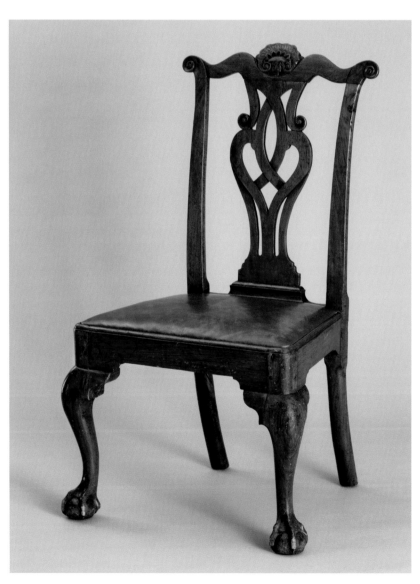

Figure 73   Detail of the crest on the chair illustrated in fig. 72. (Photo, Craig McDougal.)

Figure 74   *Joseph Hiester*, attributed to Jacob Witman, Reading, Berks County, Pennsylvania, 1795. Oil on canvas. 36" x 30½". (Courtesy, Historical Society of Berks County, Reading, Pa.; photo, Gavin Ashworth.)

convention in June 1776; served in the Revolutionary War, was taken prisoner at the Battle of Long Island, and was promoted to major general in 1807; and was a member of the Pennsylvania Assembly (1787–1790), Pennsylvania Senate (1790–1794), U.S. Congress (1797–1805 and 1815–1820), and governor of Pennsylvania (1820–1823). The portrait of Elizabeth Hiester

Figure 76   Bergère attributed to George Bright, Boston, Massachusetts, 1797. Mahogany with white pine. H. 33½", W. 24", D. 23¾". (Courtesy, Winterthur Museum; photo, Laszlo Bodo.)

depicts her in a modest brown silk dress and seated in a Windsor chair. Joseph, by contrast, sits in an upholstered armchair with a low back known as a bergère. This distinctive style of chair became fashionable in the 1790s and was particularly appropriate for men engaged in business and politics. A set of thirty was made in 1797 by Boston cabinetmaker George Bright (1726–1805) for the new Massachusetts State House (fig. 76). Elizabeth's elbow rests on top of a circular tea table, no doubt the one that descended in the Hiester family (fig. 77). Probably made in Reading rather than Philadelphia, the walnut table has a circular top with reverse-dish edge, identical to the one in the portrait. The Hiesters also owned an impressive silver teapot, coffeepot, and creamer engraved with their conjoined initials, made by Philadelphia silversmith Joseph Richardson Jr.[36]

The Hiesters were among Reading's most affluent, status-conscious tastemakers. Not only were their houses well furnished, but the architecture

Figure 77   Tea table, probably Reading, Berks
County, Pennsylvania, ca. 1775. Walnut. H. 28⅛",
Diam. 33⅞".(Historical Society of Berks County,
Reading, Pa.; photo, Gavin Ashworth.)

Figure 78   House of Daniel Hiester, Montgomery County, Pennsylvania, built 1757. (Photo,
Gavin Ashworth.)

Figure 79 Paneled wall with built-in schrank and corner fireplace in the Daniel Hiester House. (Photo, Gavin Ashworth.)

Figure 80 Detail of the staircase in the Daniel Hiester House. (Photo, Gavin Ashworth.)

itself was equally impressive. Joseph's uncle Daniel Hiester (1713–1795) built a large brick house in Montgomery County before moving to Reading in 1774. Constructed of Flemish bond, glazed header brick on all four sides, the house contained two built-in schranks and an elaborate staircase with Germanic flat-sawn balusters (figs. 78–80). Many affluent, status-conscious Pennsylvania Germans turned to local craftsmen for their furniture. Peter Stichter (1761–1843), a merchant whose father emigrated from Germany in 1750 and was one of the first settlers in Reading, owned a walnut chair with pierced splat, claw-and-ball feet, and carved shell on the seat rail (fig. 81). Made by a local craftsman but clearly inspired by a Philadelphia model, the carving of the cartouche on the crest (fig. 82) lacks the detail of that on the Hiester or Muhlenberg chairs. The flatness of the leaf at the bottom conveys only a vague sense of reality, while the cabochons around the ruffled edge are not nearly as crisp and well defined as those on the Philadelphia chairs. Nonetheless, compared with other locally made chairs such as one with straight legs, no carving, and a yoke crest that was owned by the Bertolet family of Berks County (fig. 83), Peter Stichter had a much more stylish and expensive chair.[37]

The discovery of Leonard Kessler—a heretofore unknown carver and cabinetmaker working in Philadelphia from the late 1750s through the mid-1790s—and the evident success and importance of his shop underscore the vital contribution made by German-speaking craftsmen to the production of Philadelphia furniture. In light of this information, the search for unidentified carvers should not overlook German craftsmen. Although it is easy to interpret the chairs Kessler made for the Muhlenberg family as English-style chairs and therefore as evidence of assimilation, it is less clear what contemporary Philadelphians thought of them. Rather than being seen as a product of one ethnic group succumbing to the influence of another, the chairs were likely seen as fashionable seating furniture. Now that chairs by Kessler have been identified, it remains to be determined what, if any, case furniture from his shop survives. While the task of resurrecting the output

Figure 81   Side chair, Reading, Berks County, Pennsylvania, ca. 1765. Walnut. H. 39½", W. 21¾", D. 20". (Courtesy, Historical Society of Berks County, Reading, Pa.; photo, Gavin Ashworth.)

Figure 82   Detail of the cartouche on the chair illustrated in fig. 81. (Photo, Gavin Ashworth.)

Figure 83   Side chair, Berks County, Pennsylvania, ca. 1770. (Courtesy, Pook & Pook.)

of Kessler's shop is challenging in the absence of signed or labeled pieces, the next case study focuses on a maker who produced a significant body of clearly marked furniture.

Charles Albrecht, Joiner and Instrument Maker

Music was a vital part of everyday life in early American cities. Bells called people to worship, announced the time, and marked important events. When the infamous Stamp Act was reported in 1765, Philadelphia's ministers were asked to muffle their church bells and toll them in mourning as a sign of protest. After George Washington's death on December 14, 1799, the bells of Christ Church, which he had attended while residing in Philadelphia, were muffled for three days. Because the Quakers largely eschewed music, German-speaking immigrants were among the first and most enthusiastic promoters of both sacred and secular music in colonial Pennsylvania. Due to its large Germanic population, Philadelphia soon became the leading center of musical-instrument making in colonial America and the early republic. One of the earliest known portraits of a German resident of Pennsylvania is a self-portrait by Germantown artist and musician John Meng (1734–ca. 1754), who painted himself with a sheet of music held prominently in his right hand (fig. 84). Philadelphia was particularly noted for the production of keyboard instruments and dominated the manufacturing of pianos in America from 1775 until the 1830s, when New York and Boston took over. The oldest surviving dated American piano was built in 1789 by Charles Albrecht, a German immigrant (see fig. 88).[38]

One of the first keyboard instrument makers in the colonies was Johann Gottlob Klemm (1690–1762), a German Moravian. In 1733 he immigrated

Figure 84 John Meng, *John Meng*, Germantown, Pennsylvania, ca. 1750. Oil on canvas. 43¼" x 32½". (Courtesy, Philadelphia History Museum at the Atwater Kent, The Historical Society of Pennsylvania Collection.)

Figure 85 Johann Gottlob Klemm, spinet, Philadelphia, Pennsylvania, 1739. Walnut, maple, yellow pine, and white cedar. H. 33½", W. 73¼", D. 27". (Image copyright © Metropolitan Museum of Art, Rogers Fund, 1944; image source, Art Resource, NY.) The keyboard is replaced.

to Philadelphia, where he made and signed a spinet six years later that is the earliest American-made keyboard instrument (fig. 85). Also in 1739 Klemm completed an organ for the Swedish Lutheran Church (Gloria Dei) of Philadelphia. In 1741 New York's Trinity Church acquired an organ from Klemm, which was his principal stock-in-trade. Music was an expected part of German Lutheran, Reformed, and Moravian worship, and their churches were among the first to acquire an organ. The earliest known use of an organ in the American colonies was in Philadelphia in 1703 at the ordination of Justus Falckner (1672–1723) at Gloria Dei. Other musical instruments played during the service included trumpets, drums, a viol, and hautboy (oboe). By 1742 St. Michael's Lutheran Church in Germantown owned a small organ, as did First Moravian in Philadelphia by 1743. Trinity Lutheran Church in Lancaster acquired its first organ before 1744. St. Michael's Lutheran Church of Philadelphia dedicated an organ in May 1751, built by Johann Adam Schmahl of Heilbronn, Germany; that same year Augustus Lutheran Church in Trappe acquired an organ built by Klemm. The Moravians were especially noted for their love of music. Bethlehem, founded in 1741, had organized a trombone choir by 1754 and could boast of "an active and sophisticated musical life, fully European in its tastes, standards, and repertoire" by 1757.[39]

Due to the nature of their construction, keyboard instruments were a highly specialized area of cabinetmaking. In addition to technical expertise, instrument makers needed a detailed knowledge of many different types of wood and their properties relative to the special needs of musical instruments. For example, the tuning pins of a piano are inserted into a wrest plank, which in America is typically made of maple and may be up to 1½ inches thick; it is often of laminated construction with alternating grain to prevent splitting. The soundboard, which produces the tone of the piano, is a thin sheet of wood (often spruce or white pine) that covers about one-third of the right side of the piano interior. To this is affixed the bridge, which transmits the vibrations to the soundboard that are caused by the hammer striking the piano wires. The keys also had to be cut from wood; in America basswood or tulip poplar was preferred. The naturals were then covered in ivory and the black keys in ebony or dyed wood. Many instrument makers were first trained as joiners and later specialized in instruments or developed it as a sideline trade. Demand was an important factor, since in many areas there were not enough people or churches to support instrument making as a full-time occupation. Instruments were also complicated to build; a large organ could take a single craftsman a year or more to finish, while a piano might take anywhere from 57 to 143 working days, depending on its complexity.[40]

Both Klemm and his protégé—David Tannenberg of Berthelsdorf, Germany—worked as joiners. After Klemm died in 1762, Tannenberg was directed by the Moravian authorities to return to cabinetmaking, likely because another Moravian, Philip Feyring (1730–1767), had arrived in Philadelphia and built several instruments, including a clavichord for Henry William Stiegel in 1762 and an organ for Christ Church in 1766. Tannenberg began building organs again by 1765, however, and would become the most prolific and renowned organ builder in early America—producing nearly fifty organs before his death in 1804. He also built stringed keyboard instruments, including a clavichord dated 1761. Tannenberg's son David Jr. followed his father in the cabinetmaking trade and later worked in the shop of organ builders John and Andrew Krauss. In Lancaster, Conrad Doll (1772–1819) was described in the tax lists from 1799 to 1814 as a "spinet and organ maker" and in an 1805 deed as a "joiner and cabinetmaker." George Burkhardt, the cabinetmaker who built the case of the Tannenberg organ for Lancaster's First Reformed Church in 1770, was Doll's nephew. When Johannes Scheible of New Holland, Lancaster County, died in 1793, the inventory of his estate included an unfinished fortepiano, an unfinished house organ, as well as patterns for clock cases, a painted chest, one chest "not painted without hindges," and "1 unfinished Wallnut Chest." Scheible also had walnut, cherry, and poplar boards; a workbench and lathe; seven new spinning wheels, spinning wheel parts, and bedsteads; tea-table tops and feet; carpenter's tools and unspecified carpentry books; saws, files, bits, chisels, gouges, and thirty-seven molding planes, in addition to four "Croofing" or grooving planes, two plough planes, paintbrushes, and one "Sea Cow Tooth," probably a walrus tusk. When piano maker George Albrecht of Baltimore died in 1802, his inventory included six pianos, ranging in value from $70 to $110, along with twenty-five feet of half-inch mahogany boards, a piece of "purple wood," ivory, and a box of music wire. Items in his "Worck Shop" included two stoves, sixteen planes, four saws, seventeen hand screws (probably used to clamp veneer), a piece of ebony, two workbenches, sundry tools, a glue pot, three boxes with lathes, and a "Frame & unfinished case for a Forte Piano." Samuel Ache (1764–1832) of Schaefferstown, Lebanon County, Pennsylvania, owned pieces of ebony and ivory; piano patterns and piano wire; three hundred feet of cherry boards; two carpenter's benches; chisels, planes, augers, files, clamps, saws, and other tools; gold leaf and "2 Sets wooden Alphibets" (possibly for laying out inscriptions on piano nameboards). Ache also owned a "Forte Piano and a House Organ" and is thought to be the maker of a paint-decorated zither that bears his name and the date 1788 as well as a group of painted chests—including two made for his sisters. Because of the close connection between the makers of musical instruments and furniture, objects such as harpsichords and pianos (which typically bear the maker's name and location) can be very useful in the study of American furniture because they document the appearance of particular styles of casework, inlay, and other types of ornament.[41]

With the exception of the rare house or chamber organ, most keyboard instruments in colonial American homes were harpsichords and other related instruments (spinets, virginals, or clavichords), which use plectra (often made of quills) to pluck the wire strings. Mechanical devices such as stops and dampers helped vary the instrument's tone and volume, but in a limited fashion. By the end of the eighteenth century, harpsichords were rapidly becoming obsolete owing to the rising popularity of the piano—generally

Figure 86 Mather Brown, *Portrait of a Young Woman*, Boston, Massachusetts, 1801. Oil on canvas. 50" x 40¼". (Image copyright © Metropolitan Museum of Art, gift of Caroline Newhouse, 1965; image source, Art Resource, NY.)

Figure 87 Music stool, possibly Pennsylvania, ca. 1810. Mahogany, tulip poplar, hickory (screw); paint. (Courtesy, Winterthur Museum; photo, James Schneck.) The black horsehair upholstery and brass nails are original.

credited as being invented by Bartolomeo Cristofori (1655–1731) of Florence in the late 1600s. Distinguished by the use of small hammers to strike the strings, a piano enabled the player to control the sound to a much greater extent simply by varying the pressure applied to the keys. Although keyboard instruments were referred to by many names, often incorrectly or inconsistently, the term "fortepiano" (*pianoforte* in French), literally meaning "loud-soft," was introduced by the early 1700s and was widely used to differentiate hammered from plucked string keyboard instruments. Most pianos made for a domestic setting were of an oblong, rectangular shape that resembled the harpsichord; the form was called a square piano or, in German, a *Tafelklavier*. The piano quickly became popular with German musicians and instrument makers, who introduced it to England in the mid-1700s. One of these émigré craftsmen, Johannes Zumpe (1726–1790), settled in London and by 1766 is said to have built the first square piano made in England. Another German instrument maker, Johannes Geib (1744–1818), moved to London, where he received several patents for his inventions, including the so-called English double or grasshopper-action piano movement in 1786. He immigrated in 1797 to New York, where he made pianos well into the 1800s.[42] The square piano was ideal for household use, having "a pleasing tone that was neither too loud nor too harsh."[43] It was typically played in the parlor, although some homes had designated music rooms. The undecorated back of the piano was placed against the wall, and the player sat with her back to the room. A small, upholstered stool was typically used for seating, like that in the portrait of a young woman with her square piano (fig. 86). The top of her round stool is covered in red upholstery, secured with a row of brass nails. Music stools typically swiveled so the player could easily rotate back and forth between her audience and her instrument, and the height on some was adjustable by means of a large screw (fig. 87).[44]

The earliest known reference to a piano made in America was in Philadelphia by Johann Michael Behrent (d. 1780), "Joiner and Instrument Maker," who in March of 1775 announced that he had "just finished for sale, an extraordinary instrument, by the name of PIANOFORTE, of Mohogany, in the manner of an harpsichord, with hammers." Eight years later, James Juhan moved to Philadelphia and advertised "that he makes the great North American forte pianos, the mechanical part of them being entirely of his own invention." In 1789 Charles Albrecht built what is the oldest known dated American-made piano (fig. 88). Constructed of highly figured mahogany with square tapered legs and string inlay, it is also the earliest known piece of dated federal furniture from Philadelphia and possibly even America. The nameboard of the piano bears a long, horizontal oval plaque on which the phrase "Charles Albrecht Philadelphia 1789" was carefully inscribed, then infilled with a black substance, possibly mastic, to contrast with the satinwood veneer (figs. 89, 90). The lettering, particularly the "C" and the "A," is rendered in an elaborate font resembling the German *Fraktur* typeface. The piano, which employs Broadwood's single action and has the tuning pins along the back, once had two pedals that raised the dampers and controlled an overhead mute.[45]

Figure 88 Charles Albrecht, square piano, Philadelphia, Pennsylvania, 1789. Mahogany, mahogany and satinwood veneer, black mastic, ivory, ebony, and brass. H. 31½", W. 61¾", D. 21½". (Courtesy, Philadelphia History Museum at the Atwater Kent, The Historical Society of Pennsylvania Collection; photo, Gavin Ashworth.)

Figure 89 Detail of the nameboard on the piano illustrated in fig. 88. (Photo, Gavin Ashworth.)

A German native, Carl or Charles Albrecht (ca. 1760–1848), immigrated to Philadelphia in the mid- to late 1780s and may have been the "Jno Carl Allbrink" (as the ship captain spelled it) who arrived on the *Hamburgh* on October 11, 1785. On June 17, 1787, he married the widow Mary Fox (1752–1837), née Knies, at St. Michael's and Zion Lutheran Church. Mary, who was eight years older than Charles, had two children from her first marriage but none with Charles. Her first husband, John Fox/Fuchs (1746–1780), was a cabinetmaker; he is likely the "John Fox, cabinetmaker" listed as one of the original subscribers to the Philadelphia edition of Abraham Swan's *British Architect*, printed by Robert Bell in 1775. Fox left a sizable estate when he died, including £80 of lumber, two "Carpenter or Joyners

Benches," a "Chest & Joyners Tools" valued at £800, and "Sundries in the Shop," probably unfinished furniture, worth £200. His output included coffins, as "Sundery Coffen Furniture" worth £80 was also noted. Among his household furnishings were a "Low Case of Wallnut Drawers," a high case of drawers and dressing table, mahogany stand, eight-day clock, tea table, silver spoons, a globe, and a fiddle. The entire estate was valued at £5,960.10.0. No evidence of these items being sold after John Fox's death has been found; thus, Charles Albrecht may have gained access to Fox's shop contents and tools in addition to his well-furnished home when he married Fox's widow.[46]

For a recent immigrant, marriage was a quick way to gain the support of a family network. By all appearances Charles became quite close with his in-laws, who introduced him to a larger circle of German-speaking craftsmen. His wife, Mary, was the daughter of John and Maria Barbara Knies, who were members of First Reformed Church in Philadelphia. Her younger sister, Elizabeth Knies (b. 1765), married storekeeper Jacob Deal in 1787. In 1793 Elizabeth and Jacob named one of their children Charles Albrecht Deal (he later worked for Charles), and in 1808 Jacob appointed his "esteemed Friend Charles Albrecht" as co-executor of his estate. Peter Deal Jr. (ca. 1751–after 1830), Jacob's brother, was a house carpenter. A third brother, Daniel Deal, was a blacksmith. The patriarch of the Deal family, Peter Sr., lived at 130 Vine Street in the Northern Liberties section of Philadelphia. Charles and Mary Albrecht lived next door at 128 Vine Street after their marriage before moving to 95 Vine Street in 1793. During the 1790s Joseph Fox, a house carpenter, lived at 132 Vine Street; he may have been related to John Fox, Mary's first husband. In September 1792, Charles Albrecht's brothers, George and Henry, emigrated from Germany on the *Columbia*. George (ca. 1767–1802) worked with Charles for a time in Philadelphia before moving to Baltimore, where he married Ann Scriver in 1800 but died only two years later without issue. Henry Albrecht went back to Germany to rejoin his family but returned to Pennsylvania in 1804 together with his wife, Margaret, and two children. Soon more relatives emigrated from Germany, including Charles's nephew Philip Albrecht (ca. 1777–1860) in 1805 and his niece Carolina Scheib, her husband, Henry, and sons Cassimer and William Scheib. Philip was a cabinetmaker and settled in Reading; the Scheibs were carpenters and both settled in Berks County.[47]

Albrecht's Pianos

Charles Albrecht was a prolific maker. By 1798 his shop had produced at least ninety-three pianos. More than twenty examples survive, including one with the serial number 166 (see fig. 98). The piano dated 1789 is Albrecht's earliest known instrument; three others with similar nameboards survive, all inscribed "Charles Albrecht Fecit Philadelphia" in elaborate lettering (fig. 91). Although probably rendered by a professional calligrapher, the alphabet chosen closely resembles one identified as "German Text" in George Bickham's popular writing manual, *The Universal Penman* (London, 1743). The decoration on Albrecht's nameboards evolved over time

Figure 90 Detail of the letter "C" on the nameboard of the piano illustrated in fig. 88. (Photo, Gavin Ashworth.)

Figure 91 Detail of the nameboard on a square
piano by Charles Albrecht, Philadelphia, Pennsylvania, ca. 1790. Mahogany, mahogany and satinwood veneer, and black mastic (infill). (Courtesy,
National Museum of American History, Smithsonian Institution.)

Figure 92 Charles Albrecht, square piano,
Philadelphia, Pennsylvania, ca. 1790. Mahogany,
mahogany and satinwood veneer, mixed-wood
inlay, ivory, ebony, and brass. H. 33", W. 63",
D. 22½". (Courtesy, E. Milby Burton Memorial
Trust and The Charleston Museum, photo, Sean
Money.)

Figure 93 Detail of the inlay on the nameboard of the piano illustrated in fig. 92.

Figure 94 Detail of the nameboard on the piano illustrated in fig. 92.

and is one means of determining the relative sequence of his pianos. From the earliest examples with incised and filled lettering, the ornament shifted to being inlaid and then gilded and painted, reflecting the growing popularity of fancy decoration by the turn of the nineteenth century. Three Albrecht pianos with inlaid nameboards are known; they feature a small oval plaque at the center, surmounted by a bowknot and flanked by undulating, flowering vines that terminate in a kylix urn at either end and two paterae (figs. 92, 93). The inscriptions within the plaques vary slightly; one is inscribed in Roman lettering "CHARLES ALBRECHT / *MAKER* / Philadelphia" (fig. 94); another is inscribed in German-style lettering "Charles Albrecht / *Philadelphia*"; and one is inscribed in italicized Roman font "*CHARLES ALBRECHT* / Philadelphia." A fourth piano with related inlay was made by Charles Albrecht's brother George and is the only known example of his work (fig. 95). Inscribed "George Allbright / *Philadelphia*" on the central plaque, the nameboard has a smaller flowering vine and a different, more leafy paterae at either end of the key well (figs. 96, 97). Nearly identical patera appear on a piano signed and dated by Charles Taws of Philadelphia in 1794, indicating that the inlay was likely acquired from a specialist outside the Albrecht workshop. It is also noteworthy that George spelled

Figure 95 George Albrecht, square piano, Philadelphia, Pennsylvania, ca. 1797. Mahogany with mahogany veneer and mixed-wood inlay; ivory, ebony, brass. H. 33⅞", W. 64⅝", D. 22¼". (Courtesy, State Museum of Pennsylvania, Pennsylvania Historical and Museum Commission; photo, Gavin Ashworth.) The only known piano signed by George Albrecht, it may date to 1797, when Charles is absent from the Philadelphia city directory and was likely in Chester County.

his surname as "Allbright," whereas Charles consistently spelled his "Albrecht" (although the compilers of the Philadelphia city directories often Anglicized it to Albright).[48]

The third and most common style of nameboard decoration features a small, pointed oval cartouche flanked by a swagged floral garland and bowknots. It appears that Albrecht switched to this nameboard style early on and then continued using it, as it is found on pianos with the serial numbers 24 and 166 (figs. 98, 99). The inscription is typically rendered in gilt lettering as "CHARLES ALBRECHT / *MAKER* / Philadelphia," though on some his first name is abbreviated "CHA'S." These nameboards were likely decorated by an ornamental painter, who could also do the ornamental lettering

Figure 96 Detail of the nameboard on the piano illustrated in fig. 95. (Photo, Gavin Ashworth.)

Figure 97 Detail of the key well inlay on the piano illustrated in fig. 95. (Photo, Gavin Ashworth.)

of Albrecht's name. The piano illustrated in figure 98 is noteworthy, as it is inscribed with both the serial number 166 and the signature "Joshua Baker Maker" on the key bed. Born in 1773, Baker was almost certainly trained by Albrecht; Baker's wife, Mary Deal, was the daughter of Albrecht's sister-in-law, Elizabeth Knies, and her husband, Jacob Deal. Two other Albrecht pianos are known that Baker signed on the interior. From 1810 until 1816 Baker is listed in the Philadelphia city directories as an instrument or piano maker at 130 Vine Street (previously the residence of his wife's grandfather); he died in 1821. A rare variation on Albrecht's typical painted nameboards uses oak leaves rather than flowers for the swagged ornament (fig. 100). Another variant that appears on two known examples has the pointed oval cartouche, but rather than swags of flowers it is flanked by a long, flowering vine of pink roses that extends across most of the nameboard (fig. 101).[49]

Figure 98 Charles Albrecht, square piano, Philadelphia, Pennsylvania, 1800–1805. Mahogany, mahogany and satinwood veneer, ivory, ebony, and brass. H. 31½", W. 63", D. 22¼". (Courtesy, Colonial Williamsburg Foundation, gift of Mrs. Jeannette S. Hamner; photo, John Watson.) This piano has the serial number 166 and is signed on the key bed "Joshua Baker Maker." The music shelf is replaced.

Figure 99 Detail of the nameboard on the piano illustrated in fig. 98.

Figure 100 Detail of the nameboard on a square piano by Charles Albrecht, Philadelphia, Pennsylvania, ca. 1800. (Courtesy, Blennerhassett Historical Foundation; photo, Donald H. Prior.)

Although the nameboard decoration on the pianos varies, in general the cases are similar. This began to change by 1813, when Albrecht's shop produced a piano with six round, reeded legs and matching foot pedal, shallow drawers, and rounded front corners (fig. 102). This piano is signed on the interior: "C. Deal Philadelphia [illeg.] 1813 / No 71." Deal was Albrecht's nephew and namesake, born Charles Albrecht Deal in 1793. He was also the brother-in-law of Joshua Baker, another member of Albrecht's shop. The

Figure 101   Charles Albrecht, square piano, Philadelphia, Pennsylvania, ca. 1800. Mahogany, mahogany and satinwood veneer; ivory, ebony, and brass. H. 33¾", W. 62¾", D. 22¼". (Courtesy, Christie's Images, Ltd.)

Figure 102 Charles Albrecht and Charles Deal, square piano, Philadelphia, Pennsylvania, 1813. Mahogany, mahogany and satinwood veneer; ivory, ebony, and brass. H. 35¼", W. 69", D. 25". (Courtesy, Freeman's; photo, Elizabeth Field.) This piano has the serial number 71 and is signed on the inside by Charles Deal.

piano contains a handwritten note that was concealed underneath a board covering the wedge-shaped hollow area between the tuning pin block and inside corner of the frame. Placed there during construction, the note reads, "The Person who first casts his eye on this may know that this Piano was made in the year 1813 about the time Bonaparte was defeated by the Russians. Charles Deal." The serial number 71 inscribed below Deal's signature is likely a reference to how many pianos Deal had made, as an Albrecht piano dated 1798 is labeled number 93. In 1815 Deal worked on a piano owned by Andrew Law (1749–1821), then one of the leading music instructors and composers in the country. A letter sent in December 1815 from Deal to Law, who was then in Newark, New Jersey, describes the renovations under way to Law's piano. The nameboard of the piano signed by Deal continues to have a pointed oval cartouche and floral swags, but the roses are now much larger and painted with brushier strokes. The inscription has also changed slightly to include an address: "CHA^S ALBRECHT / N° 9^5 Vine S^t / Philadelphia" (fig. 103).[50]

Figure 103 Detail of the nameboard on the piano illustrated in fig. 102. (Photo, Daniel C. Scheid.)

Noted for their excellent craftsmanship and elegant design, Albrecht's pianos are typically built of mahogany with lightwood stringing and satinwood nameboards. All known examples are of the square piano form in what is generally considered an English style, though it bears repeating that many of the piano makers in England at this time were Germans. A contrasting satinwood veneer banding was sometimes used to frame the nameboard and front of the case, which was finished with a linseed oil polish or varnish to produce a high sheen on the wood. Most have four, square, tapered legs, although the two latest examples each have six reeded legs. The tapered legs are outlined in lightwood stringing, terminating in cuffs and small brass casters. Stretchers at either side help reinforce the delicate legs and add stability to the frame, which is attached with large bolts. Some models have a wooden shelf running from side to side, beneath the mechanism, to hold sheet music. Mitered dovetail joints were typically used to conceal all evidence of the joinery in the frame, which was usually built of solid rather than veneered mahogany because of the enormous strain exerted by the tension of the strings. Heavy bases and diagonal braces made of oak, tulip poplar, or other local woods were often used within the frame. The piano lid was usually segmented to enable only a small panel covering the key well area to be opened, which could be folded back and used to prop up sheet music. Like most square pianos, Albrecht's are made with the keyboard at the left side, but when the lid is fully closed, it has a symmetrical appearance. The entire lid could be propped open if more sound was desired; some pianos even had an internal folding music rack that could be deployed to help hold the lid open as well.

The actions of Albrecht's pianos were of a very high quality and had a range of five to five and one half octaves (fig. 104). The action is the mechanism by which the force applied to the keys sets the hammers in motion, causing them to strike the wire strings. The action must have an escapement that disengages it from the hammer once it is set in motion; numerous action types were developed and some patented during the late 1700s

Figure 104   Detail of the action in the piano illustrated in fig. 98. (Photo, John Watson.)

and 1800s. Albrecht built pianos with a variety of mechanisms, including single action, double action, and the Viennese *Prellmechanik*, which may reflect the size of his workshop and indicate that he had assistants of varying backgrounds. In some cases it is difficult to know how the original action functioned, as the moving parts of pianos wear out, break, or get updated over time, and many have suffered from insensitive restorations. Albrecht's pianos also employed a variety of damper mechanisms, knee levers, foot pedals, hand stops, and swells as options for moderating sound and tone. These features were more gimmicks than necessity, but their presence reveals that he was capable of producing pianos with a wide variety of options to meet the demands of his clientele. That said, pianos 24 and 166 both have rather old-fashioned features, including a hand stop to raise the dampers, rather than a pedal or knee lever, and the placement of the tuning pins at the right along a diagonal block. This suggests that Albrecht's pianos do not follow a technological progression, perhaps an indication of customer preferences, since he clearly was capable of making more advanced actions.[51]

A comparison of pianos made by Albrecht and John Huber of Harrisburg, Pennsylvania, reveals, at first glance, remarkably similar exterior cases (figs. 105, 106). The lid of the Huber piano, however, has battens applied at either end—a common technique in the construction of Pennsylvania German chest lids and tabletops to keep them from warping but one that is unknown on pianos of British origin. Both have a single-action English movement, but the dark color of the bridge and the ogee terminal of the hitch pin rail extension (near the curved or treble end of the bridge) on the

Figure 105 John Huber, square piano, Harrisburg, Pennsylvania, 1805–1809. Mahogany with satinwood veneer; ivory, ebony; paper, glass. H. 33⅛", W. 65⅝", D. 23⅛". (Colonial Williamsburg Foundation, The Friends of the Colonial Williamsburg Collections Fund; photo, John Watson.)

Figure 106 Detail of the action in the piano illustrated in fig. 105. (Photo, John Watson.)

Huber piano are Germanic features that do not appear on the Albrecht movement (see fig. 104). The black keys of the Huber piano are made of ebony veneer over a black-stained hardwood, whereas those on the Albrecht piano are of solid ebony. The label on the Huber piano is a paper insert printed from a copperplate engraving (fig. 107) rather than an inlaid or painted one like those used by Albrecht—indicating that Huber probably lacked access to an ornamental painter.[52]

Documenting Albrecht

Charles Albrecht is listed in the 1791 Philadelphia city directory as a joiner, residing at 128 Vine Street between Third and Fourth. He began advertising in March of that year, offering for sale an "Elegant Double Key'd Harpsichord, Also a Piano Forte Harpsichord," and informing readers that in addition he "makes and repairs Harpsichords, Piano Forte's and Spinnet's and also tunes the same at a moderate rate." By January 28, 1792, he had moved to 95 Vine Street, where he described himself as a "Musical Instrument-Maker" and offered for sale "TWO new and elegant PIANO FORTES which he will warrant to be good." He may have struggled to sell them, since he ran the same ad through June 12, 1792. By March 1796 Charles was joined in business by his brother George, when he advertised that they "continue to carry on business . . . [and] have now for sale, two Piano Fortes, which they will warrant to be good." The 1797 Philadelphia city directory lists George Albrecht at 95 Vine Street, but Charles is absent, having moved out of the city to Vincent Township, Chester County, where he acquired a 23-acre woodlot (primarily of chestnut and oak) and a 175-acre farm. In February 1797 he offered the two tracts for sale and sold them in June to George Hubener, an earthenware potter (see fig. 9). In November Charles Albrecht announced that "he has commenced business again, and makes in the newest stile, all kinds of Forte Piano's and Harpsichords, which he will warrant to be good—and has now on hand several of an excellent quality and workmanship." By August 1798 George moved to Baltimore, where he advertised himself as a "Piano Forte Maker, From Philadelphia," noting that he "TURNS Piano Fortes, Harpsichords, and spinnets, by the quarter or single time" as well as repairs them. On October 17, 1798, he advertised, "FOR SALE, A new Piano Forte MADE in this city by the subscriber, who tunes and repairs Pianos, Harpsichords and Spinnets." George was one of only two piano makers in Baltimore before 1800, the other being John Harper.[53]

On February 15, 1798, Charles Albrecht officially became a citizen of the United States. In November 1799 he began advertising pianos imported from London "of the latest patent . . . with additional keys, of the neatest workmanship and first quality, for sale on the most reasonable terms." In March 1800 he advertised, "JUST ARRIVED . . . from London, Piano Fortes, Of superior quality, new patent, with and without additional keys, and also common." Apparently the pianos sold well, as later that year, in October, he advertised a shipment of "Common, new patent, elegant patent with and without additional keys—Also new patent with six octaves, superior to any hitherto imported, and from the first workman in London." The same ad also offered for sale a "very good Hand Organ with four stops and three barrels, and plays thirty choice tunes." In May 1802 he advertised "Piano Fortes, Of a superior quality, LATELY imported from London . . . Likewise, patent Hand-Organs, with drum and triangle, playing the most modern tunes." The following year, "Charles Albright" advertised for the return of books and notification of claims against the estate of Frederick Whitesecker, "late teacher of Musick, of Philadelphia." Then ensued a long hiatus in Albrecht's advertising, part of which coincided with his ownership of a house and farm in Trappe formerly owned by Frederick Muhlenberg (see fig. 68), which Albrecht bought from Muhlenberg's sister, Mary, and her husband, Francis Swaine, in November 1803. Although Albrecht likely knew the Muhlenbergs already, earlier that year he sold a piano to Peter Muhlenberg, which may have been the occasion of his learning about the Trappe property. Albrecht appears on the Montgomery County tax lists from 1804 to 1807 as an instrument maker; he may have used the 20-by-40-foot general store built by Frederick Muhlenberg as his workshop. On December 1, 1807, he advertised the property for sale in the German-language Reading newspaper, describing it as the "plantation on which the undersigned lives" and referring to himself as "Carl Albrecht." In 1808 he is listed in the tax records as a "farmer," but the entry is crossed out, indicating he had already returned to Philadelphia.[54]

Albrecht did not commence advertising again until January 1813, when he offered for sale "a handsome assortment of elegant Piano Fortes, made of the best materials and workmanship, equal to any imported or made here," at his "Manufactory" at 95 Vine Street. In October of that year, he advertised a wide range of pianos for sale, including "upright, grand, portable—organised, circular front, square, &c." He retired from piano making by 1825, when he is listed in the Philadelphia city directory as a "gentleman." In 1841 he acquired a farm in Montgomery Township, Montgomery County, where he moved in 1844 and resided until his death on June 28, 1848.

Albrecht's obituary described him as "in the 88th year of his age . . . for seven years a resident of Montgomery township, Montgomery county, for fifty-eight years, a citizen of Philadelphia." Friends were directed to join his funeral procession starting from the house of Charles Deal, 22 Palmyra Row on Vine Street. Albrecht's will, written in 1844, identified him as a "Piano Forte Manufacturer" and included bequests to many of his relatives. His nephew Philip Albrecht/Albright (ca. 1777–1860), a cabinetmaker who immigrated from Germany in 1805 and settled in Reading, was bequeathed $2,000 and all of Charles's clothes and wearing apparel. He left a gold watch to Charles Deal, and to Mary (Deal) Baker, his wife's niece and the widow of his former employee Joshua Baker, he left $1,000 and all of his "Household Furniture, Beds, Bedding, Bedsteads and Plate." Also named in the will are Cassimer and William Scheib, the grandsons of Charles's late sister, Elizabeth, who both immigrated from Germany and settled in Berks County, where they worked as carpenters. The inventory of his estate included farm equipment and household furnishings, including a mahogany breakfast table, mahogany desk, eight-day clock; a tea table and silver spoons, cream jug, and sugar tongs; and an organ but no piano.[55]

Figure 108 Anna Kliest, *The Birthday Wish*, made for Jacob van Vleck, Bethlehem, Pennsylvania, 1795. 9" x 7½". Watercolor and ink on laid paper. (Courtesy, Moravian Historical Society, Nazareth, Pa.)

Pianos and Patrons

Only the wealthiest Americans could afford pianos. Virginia planter Robert Carter of Nomini Hall was one of the first in the colonies to own a piano, which he acquired in 1771. Philip Vickers Fithian, the tutor of the Carter children, noted many occasions on which Carter entertained guests by playing the piano during supper. Thomas Jefferson was another early owner of a piano, which he ordered from London in 1771 while simultaneously canceling an order for a harpsichord. In 1789 George Washington ordered a piano for his step-granddaughter, Nelly Custis, from "Mr. Dodd," likely Dodd & Claus of New York. Square pianos were primarily used by young women, who learned to play them and other musical instruments to entertain family and friends within the home. The mother-in-law of Nancy Shippen (b. 1763) of Philadelphia, who played the harpsichord and guitar, told her that "A little music at the age of 12 or 14, sufficient to entertain herself and friends," was enough. Women were not expected to make a career of music nor to perform in concerts or other public events. Church organists, professional musicians, and even music teachers were almost exclusively male. At the Moravian Seminary for Young Ladies in Bethlehem, founded in 1742 and opened to non-Moravian students in 1785, music and needlework were major parts of the curriculum. A rare view of a music lesson at Bethlehem shows four young women standing at a square piano, which is being played by their male instructor (fig. 108). By 1792 the seminary owned seven pianos and clavichords. The previous year, Joseph and Elizabeth Hiester of Reading sent their two youngest daughters, Rebecca and Mary Elisabeth, to the school (fig. 109). One twelve-year-old girl, writing home from Bethlehem in 1787, reported, "Here I am taught music, both vocal and

Figure 109   Tunebook, probably Bethlehem, Pennsylvania, 1791. (Courtesy, Winterthur Library, Joseph Downs Collection of Manuscripts and Printed Ephemera; photo, James Schneck.) This book may have been shared with Rebecca Hiester's sister, Mary Elisabeth, whose name is inscribed within.

instrumental, I play the guitar twice a day—am taught the spinet and forte-piano; and sometimes I play the organ."[56]

Only five of Charles Albrecht's clients are known, and in just three cases can the actual pianos associated with them be identified. In 1803 he sold a piano to Peter Muhlenberg, the older brother of Speaker Frederick Muhlenberg, shortly before buying a property from the Muhlenberg family in Trappe. The Muhlenbergs were musically inclined; Frederick Muhlenberg owned both a violin and "Spinet," valued at £7.10.0, when he died in 1801. The Seibert family of Philadelphia also purchased an Albrecht piano before 1807, according to family lore. Another piano was made for Catherine Naylor Brearley of New Jersey; its nameboard has a pointed oval cartouche with swagged roses. A fourth piano (see fig. 100) was owned by Colonel Abner Lord (1760–1821), a native of Connecticut who moved to Marietta, Ohio, circa 1800; it supposedly then resided in the home of Harman Blennerhassett (1764–1831), located on an island in the Ohio River. Peter and Anna Catharine Dieffenbach of Tulpehocken Township, Berks County, acquired the fifth piano for their daughter Esther (1793–1851). That piano also has the pointed oval cartouche. This sale is particularly noteworthy, as Peter Dieffenbach (1755–1838) was the younger brother of Jacob Dieffenbach (1744–1803), a cabinetmaker who by 1787 took up organ building. It is unknown how Jacob learned to make instruments, although family tradition claims that he went to Philadelphia in 1774 to study an organ and returned home with measurements and notes. David Tannenberg, who by then was living in Lititz, Pennsylvania, about twenty miles from the Dieffenbach farm, may have influenced him. Jacob's son, Christian Dieffenbach, continued the trade and built at least seven organs before 1820; the next two generations of the family also built organs.[57]

Other Instrument Makers

Although Charles Albrecht may have been one of the first piano makers in Philadelphia, by the 1790s he faced increasing competition from a number of recent arrivals. One of his major competitors was Charles Taws (ca. 1742–1836), who emigrated from Scotland in 1786 and settled initially in New York. By late 1787 he relocated to Philadelphia, where the following year he married Elizabeth Bucher/Butcher, a German Catholic, at St. Joseph's Church. Taws began advertising in 1790, when he offered for sale "of his own manufacture, a few elegant and well toned Piano Fortes." In 1791 he is listed in the Philadelphia city directory as an "organ builder" and in subsequent years as a musical-instrument maker or instrument maker. In February 1792 Taws and Albrecht placed dueling advertisements that appeared directly next to one another. In what may have been a dig at Albrecht, Taws noted that the "unfair practice of making an allowance to Musicians, for their influences with Ladies and Gentlemen in recommending particular Instruments, shall not be adopted by him . . . it is recommended to purchasers to apply in the first instance to the Maker." The following year, Taws advertised "a few fine toned FORTE PIANOS which he will warrant superior to any imported," warning readers against the "great number of Forte-Pianos lately imported from London and Dublin," which he derided as "inferior, and including repairs, cost twice their purchase price." In 1799 he complained that music teachers, "when they find a Lady or Gentleman wanting an instrument of Music," brought them to his shop to inspect the wares, then afterward demanded a 10 or 15 percent commission in return for the business or threatened to take their client elsewhere. By 1805 Taws began advertising imported London pianos, which he now praised as superior to local products. In 1813 he derided "certain instrument makers (calling themselves such) in this city, [who] vainly pretend they can make Forte Pianos from 50 to 200 dollars cheaper than those of Clementi and Company, but such assertion is an error and a silly pretension, for their HOME MADE instruments will by no means, bear a comparison."[58]

Taws found clients both near and far. Sarah Whipple Sproat (1782–1851), who learned to play while a student at the Bethlehem Seminary, owned one of his instruments. Her father, Colonel Ebenezer Sproat, helped found Marietta, Ohio, in 1788. Sarah married Solomon Sibley (1769–1846), a Marietta attorney who became the first mayor of Detroit; her piano was transported from Bethlehem to Marietta and then to Detroit and is claimed to be the first piano in the Northwest Territory. In 1791 Richard Butler of Pittsburgh, Pennsylvania, acquired a piano from Taws for his daughter Mary and had it transported across the state. Another Taws piano, dated 1794, was purchased by Henley Chapman (1779–1864) of Giles County, Virginia. Taws built organs in addition to pianos, including one for St. Augustine's Catholic Church in 1800 and one for St. Mary's in 1805. In 1802 and 1803 he also bid on the new organ for Zion Lutheran Church, to replace the one by Tannenberg that was lost in the 1794 fire, but John Lowe was awarded the contract and completed the organ in 1811. Two of Charles Taws's sons, James and Lewis, also made pianos.[59]

Another rival of Albrecht was Charles Trute, who had worked in London since the 1760s and made harpsichords and pianos. Trute immigrated to Philadelphia by 1794. Together with a man named Wiedberg, he established a shop at 25 Filbert Street, and in January 1794 advertised that they had "just finished a Grand-Piano Forte . . . and a double key'd Harpsichord." A two-manual harpsichord, dated 1794, is in a private collection and is likely the one mentioned in the ad. In September 1795 Trute and Wiedberg sold a piano for £41.5 to the Moravians, likely for use at the Young Ladies Seminary in Bethlehem. During the mid-1790s they moved to Wilmington, Delaware, where they continued to make pianos; Trute also became a tavern keeper. Wiedberg died in 1803 and Trute in 1807. Thomas Loud Evenden was another London émigré; he arrived in 1811 in Philadelphia and went into business with Joshua Baker, who previously had worked for Albrecht and was married to Albrecht's niece Mary Deal. The partnership lasted only briefly, however, for in March 1812 Baker announced that it was being dissolved and "business will be carried on solely by the said J. Baker" at 130 Vine Street. After leaving Baker, Evenden continued in the piano-making and importing business and was joined by his son Thomas Jr. and two of his brothers. By 1817 the Evenden name was dropped and the company became known as Loud & Brothers. The firm dominated the Philadelphia piano trade during the 1820s and 1830s, exporting pianos to South America and the West Indies by 1821; in 1824 it reportedly made an astonishing 680 pianos. One of the Louds' chief rivals was Christian Frederick Lewis Albrecht (1788–1843), who emigrated from Germany in 1822 and opened a piano shop in Philadelphia the following year. Although many have speculated that he was related to Charles Albrecht, no connection between the two men has been found. Philadelphia continued to dominate the piano trade, and in 1830 the city could boast of eighty piano makers. Even Alpheus Babcock (1785–1842), the renowned Boston piano maker, worked in Philadelphia from circa 1830 to 1837. New York and Boston were gaining ground, however. In 1829 approximately 2,500 pianos were built in America: 900 in Philadelphia, 800 in New York, and 700 in Boston. German immigrants such as John Geib (1744–1818) and his sons, followed by Heinrich Engelhard Steinweg (1797–1871) and the establishment of Steinway & Sons in 1853, would soon shift the locus of the piano industry to New York; Boston would also become a major production center.[60]

Figure 110   Detail of the nameboard on a square piano by John Haberacker, Reading, Berks County, Pennsylvania, ca. 1805. Satinwood. (Courtesy, Marlowe A. Sigal.)

By the early 1800s even smaller urban centers throughout Pennsylvania began to have piano makers. Lancaster, Pennsylvania, which in 1776 was the largest inland town in North America, was home to instrument maker John Wind (1783–1858). Wind was at work by March 1810, when Jacob Eichholtz (who was also a portrait painter) charged him fifteen shillings for "painting a frontis piece," or nameboard. Eichholtz also charged organ builder Conrad Doll for a "frontispiece" and clockmaker George Hoff for "painting his name," no doubt on a white painted dial. Starting in 1815 Wind is listed as a "spinnetmaker" and, later, a cabinetmaker in the Lancaster tax records. In Reading, the seat of Berks County, John Haberacker (1780–1846) was active as a piano and instrument maker. At least four of his pianos are known to survive. The earlier models have satinwood nameboards with elaborate painted decoration of Grecian scrolls, anthemion, and acanthus leaves that closely resemble elements in plate 36, "Ornament for a Frieze or Tablet," of Sheraton's *Drawing Book* (figs. 110, 111). Classical ornament was popular not just with English-speaking Americans; many leaders in the "antique" movement were German, including art historian and archaeologist Johann

Figure 111   Design for a frieze or tablet illustrated in plate 36 in Thomas Sheraton's *The Cabinet-Maker and Upholsterer's Drawing Book* (London, 1791–1794). (Courtesy, Winterthur Library, Printed Book and Periodical Collection; photo, James Schneck.)

Figure 112 John Haberacker, square piano, Reading, Berks County, Pennsylvania, ca. 1805. Mahogany with mahogany and satinwood veneer, ivory, and ebony. H. 33⅝, W. 64, D. 22⅝". (Courtesy, Historic RittenhouseTown; photo, Gavin Ashworth.)

Joachim Winckelmann (1717–1768), author of *Geschichte der Kunst des Alterthums* (*History of Art in Antiquity*), published in 1764 and soon translated into French, English, and Italian. Neoclassical architect-designer Benjamin Henry Latrobe was also of German heritage; his mother was the daughter of Moravian master builder Henry Antes.[61]

One of Haberacker's pianos descended in a branch of the Rittenhouse family of Philadelphia (figs. 112, 113). Built of highly figured mahogany, the piano has inlaid bellflowers on the front legs that relate to those found on several tall-case clocks with Reading movements dating circa 1805–1810. Frederick Christopher Bischoff (1771–1834), a German émigré artist who

Figure 113 Detail of the nameboard on the piano illustrated in fig. 112. (Photo, Gavin Ashworth.)

Figure 114 Birth and baptismal certificate of Maria Magdalena Meyer, decoration attributed to Frederick Christopher Bischoff, Reading, Berks County, Pennsylvania, ca. 1800. Watercolor and ink on laid paper. 13" x 14". (Courtesy, Rare Books Department, Free Library of Philadelphia.)

arrived in Reading circa 1799, may have been responsible for the elaborate script of John Haberacker's name as well as the painted decoration on the nameboard. Bischoff is known to have used delicate floral imagery and a palette of pastel colors on birth and baptismal certificates that he decorated, most of which were printed in Reading between 1802 and 1804 (fig. 114). In 1809 he advertised in the Reading newspaper that he painted portraits on wood for $1 and on paper for 25¢. One of his oil portraits depicts a young man in profile holding a music book. Bischoff is also known to have painted fire buckets (figs. 115, 116). He was a founding member of the Readinger Deutsche Lese-Gesellschaft (Reading German Reading Society), begun in 1803. Reading's first subscription library was founded in 1764; it went defunct in 1774 but was revived in 1808 as the Library Company of Reading. Bischoff may have had access to design books such as Sheraton's through one or both of these resources.[62]

Two later Haberacker pianos have a different style of classical ornament on the nameboard, including a painted floral swag surrounding a pointed oval cartouche with the gilt inscription "JOHN HABERACKER / READING" and a trophy of musical instruments including a lyre and oboe together with an open book of music (fig. 117). The frame of one of these pianos has rounded front corners and is on six turned legs; it is labeled as serial number 104. Haberacker probably trained his son, John W. Haberacker (1804–1833), as a cabinetmaker. In 1824 John W. advertised the opening of a new shop in 1824 beside his house on East Penn Street in Reading, by the name of John W. Haberacker & Co.," where they will be ready and are determined to execute every description of cabinetwork at the most reduced

Figure 115 Portrait of John Stump, attributed to
Frederick Christopher Bischoff, Reading, Berks
County, Pennsylvania, ca. 1805. Oil on panel.
10" x 8". (Courtesy, Historical Society of Berks
County, Reading, Pa.; photo, Gavin Ashworth.)

Figure 116 Frederick Christopher Bischoff, fire
bucket, Reading, Berks County, Pennsylvania,
ca. 1805. Leather. H. 13". (Courtesy, Historical
Society of Berks County, Reading, Pa.; photo,
Gavin Ashworth.)

Figure 117 Detail of the nameboard on a square
piano by John Haberacker, Reading, Berks
County, Pennsylvania, ca. 1820. (Courtesy, John
Watson.)

prices." He also noted "highest prices will at all times be given for good walnut, cherry, poplar and other stuff used in the like of their business." In 1829 he advertised for a runaway named Abraham Meyers, "indented apprentice to the Cabinet-making business."[63]

Conclusion

When the sun came up on the smoldering ruins of Zion Lutheran Church on the morning of December 27, 1794, the situation must have looked bleak. Gone was the beautiful interior, with its eight fluted columns and Doric entablature, along with the Tannenberg organ for which the church had paid a small fortune (£3,500 total, according to Elizabeth Drinker). When the trustees of St. Michael's and Zion met and decided to rebuild, they were led by Frederick Augustus Muhlenberg, son of the late pastor Henry Muhlenberg. Born in Trappe, Montgomery County, on January 1, 1750, Frederick was an all-American success story (fig. 118). Sent to Germany in 1763 for his education—which included Latin, Greek, Hebrew, French, theology, general and ecclesiastical history, biblical criticism, and logic—Frederick returned in 1770 and was ordained a Lutheran minister.

Figure 118 Joseph Wright, *Frederick Augustus Conrad Muhlenberg*, New York, 1790. Oil on canvas with applied wood strip. 47" x 37" (including frame). (Courtesy, National Portrait Gallery, Smithsonian Institution / Art Resource, NY.) A 1⅜" strip of wood was added to the canvas at the left edge and painted by Wright.

Figure 119 *Brettstuhl* (board chair), southeastern Pennsylvania, ca. 1775. Pine and oak. H. 32", W. 18", D. 18". (Courtesy, Winterthur Museum; photo, Laszlo Bodo.)

Figure 120 Chair attributed to Johann Friedrich Bourquin (1762–1830), Bethlehem, Northampton County, Pennsylvania, 1803–1806. Maple; paint. H. 39¼", W. 18½", D. 18". (Courtesy, Moravian Archives, Bethlehem, Pa.; photo, Winterthur Museum, Laszlo Bodo.)

After serving congregations in Pennsylvania and New York for nine years, in 1779 he left the ministry and joined the Continental Congress. The following year, he was elected to the Pennsylvania Assembly and made speaker. When Montgomery County was established in 1784, he was the first president judge, recorder of deeds, and register of wills. Three years later, Frederick was president of the Pennsylvania Constitutional Convention. On November 26, 1788, he was elected to the U.S. House of Representatives along with his brother Peter and friend Daniel Hiester. While waiting for enough delegates to arrive in New York to make a quorum, Frederick wrote a letter to Benjamin Rush in Philadelphia: "My friends here . . . think of me as a Candidate for the Speakers Chair. . . . Never did I dread a Business more." He continued, "I feel the want of Abilities & knowledge to such a Degree that the Thought of it makes me tremble & yet on the other Hand to refuse . . . those who have honoured me with their Confidence & a Seat in the Legislature would in my opinion be a Crime which I hope never to be guilty of." On April 4, 1789, Frederick was elected speaker by a landslide vote of 23 to 7. The *Pennsylvania Packet* announced "the German gentleman has been honored with the chair of speaker of the legislature," while the *Philadelphische Correspondenz* proclaimed that "the blood of the grandchildren of our grandchildren will proudly well up in their hearts when they will read in the histories of America that the first Speaker . . . was a German, born of German parents in Pennsylvania."[64]

Unfortunately, Muhlenberg has rarely made the history books. His unpopular tie-breaking vote to fund the Jay Treaty in 1796 led to a fall from political power, followed by his early demise in 1801 at the age of fifty-one, likely have something to do with this. But the larger reason returns to the issue of how Pennsylvania German culture has come to be defined. For generations, we have been taught to think of the *Brettstuhl* as a Pennsylvania German chair but not the oval-back one made by Johann Friedrich Bourquin; the redware teapot as Pennsylvania German but not the silver sugar bowl made by Christian Wiltberger (figs. 119–122). As a result, our understanding of Pennsylvania German culture has been flattened and compressed into a heavily skewed perception of what in reality was an extraordinarily diverse and dynamic society. People such as Frederick Muhlenberg—along with other influential, affluent, and successful Pennsylvania Germans who were merchants, doctors, scientists, educators, lawyers, ministers, and so on—do not conform to the rural peasant stereotype to which we have been accustomed. Nor does Frederick Muhlenberg fit within the exalted ranks of the Founding Fathers or the English-

Figure 121 Teapot, southeastern Pennsylvania, 1779. Lead-glazed red earthenware. H. 5⅝". (Courtesy, Winterthur Museum; photo, Laszlo Bodo.)

Figure 122 Christian Wiltberger (1766–1851), sugar bowl. Philadelphia, Pennsylvania, ca. 1800. Silver. H. 10¼". (Courtesy, Winterthur Museum.)

speaking, Quaker mythology that characterizes most studies of the mid-Atlantic. Thus, when it is discovered that Frederick furnished his house with stylish mahogany furniture, silver, china, and other expensive "English" goods, it becomes all too easy to interpret his actions as assimilation. Yet clearly his contemporaries continued to identify him as German. Why the distinction?

Being Pennsylvania German in early America has come to be defined as being ethnically distinctive, a boundary that during this period was much less rigid or clear than we think of it today. As these case studies have demonstrated, Pennsylvania German material culture was sometimes not ethnically specific, as in the chairs made by Leonard Kessler or the pianos by Charles Albrecht. Ethnicity could also be expressed through language, religion, heating preferences, foodways, and other less tangible means. Status-conscious, affluent Pennsylvania Germans such as Frederick Muhlenberg were probably first and foremost concerned with acquiring fashionable furnishings for their homes. It did not matter much to them whether the dovetails were wedged or the drawer bottoms pegged up, so long as the object was well built and the overall appearance suited. The objects made and owned by elite German-speaking people in southeastern Pennsylvania helped them become active participants in the formation of national identity and a *sensus communis* of sociability and refinement. A chair made by a German Lutheran cabinetmaker for his pastor in the rococo style had multiple meanings; it cannot simply be read as evidence of ethnicity. By furnishing their houses with fashionable goods, elite Pennsylvania Germans allied themselves with other elites, not as a rejection of their German heritage. Connected variously by marriage, politics, language, ethnicity, religion, and commerce, both urban and nonurban Pennsylvania Germans sought to fashion themselves not as Germans or Englishmen but as Americans (figs. 123, 124).

In Philadelphia's multicultural, multiethnic society, identity was a much more fluid, multivalent concept. Working from both British and Continental sources, English Protestants, German Lutherans, French Catholics, Welsh Quakers, and others produced an astonishing range of furniture. Together, they formed a furniture tradition that was more specific as to region than it was to any one ethnic group. The work of many German émigré craftsmen in Philadelphia is unknown. In her study of early Philadelphia seating furniture, Désirée Caldwell identified sixty-six Germanic woodworkers in Philadelphia and Germantown between 1681 and 1755. The church records of St. Michael's and Zion note the occupations of some members, such as Jeremias Schoenbach (d. 1757), a "master scribe, singer, engraver, [and] woodcarver." We can only wonder what his carving and engraving looked like. Newspapers carried advertisements announcing the arrival of craftsmen seeking indentures to pay for their voyage; one notice in 1784 highlighted "several German Tradesmen, among whom are joiners, cabinet-makers, Bookbinders, engravers, taylors, and tanners . . . desirous of engaging themselves in their respective branches, for a stipulated time, on the most reasonable terms." Beginning in the 1820s, a new influx of

Figure 123   Chest-over-drawers, southeastern Pennsylvania, ca. 1815. Pine; paint; brass. H. 29⅜", W. 51", D. 23". (Courtesy, Winterthur Museum; photo, Laszlo Bodo.)

Figure 124   Detail of the eagle on the chest illustrated in fig. 123. (Courtesy, Winterthur Museum; photo, Laszlo Bodo.)

German immigrants included cabinetmakers who brought the Biedermeier style with them. Twenty years later, German émigré Johann Heinrich Belter would establish himself as one of the leading makers of rococo-revival furniture. By the 1850s more than one-third of Philadelphia's cabinetmakers and nearly two-thirds of their New York counterparts were German-born.

From the city's founding in 1682 through the nineteenth century, Philadelphia's German-speaking craftsmen and their patrons contributed to the rise of a furniture tradition that may have been derived from European sources but ultimately became American.[65]

ACKNOWLEDGMENTS For assistance with this article, the author thanks Gary Albright; Gavin Ashworth; Steve and Susan Babinsky; Luke Beckerdite; Blennerhassett Museum, Ray Swick; Philip Bradley; Ray Brunner; H. L. Chalfant; Charleston Museum, Grahame Long and Jennifer Scheetz; Christie's, Andrew Holter and Hillary Mazanec; Colonial Williamsburg Foundation, Ron Hurst, Angelika Kuettner, Margaret Pritchard, Kate Teiken, and John Watson; Phil Cooper; William K. du Pont; Don Fennimore; Freeman's, Lynda Cain; Ritchie Garrison; Chip and Vonnie Henderson; Don Herr; Hershey Museum, Valerie Seiber; Historic Rittenhouse Town, Chris Owens; Historical Society of Berks County, Joshua Blay, Kim Richards Brown, and Kim Longlott; Historical Society of Pennsylvania, Hillary, Kativa; Holy Trinity Lutheran Church, Peter Brown and Andrea Collins; Charlie Hummel; Louise Kale; Alan Keyser; Joe Kindig; Ed LaFond; Landis Valley Museum, Mike Emery; Frank Levy; Laurence Libin; Lutheran Theological Seminary at Philadelphia, Karl Krueger; Mennonite Heritage Center, Joel Alderfer; Metropolitan Museum of Art, Nick Vincent; Ken Milano; Alan Miller; Leslie Miller and Richard Worley; Rick Mones; Moravian Archives, Paul Peucker; Museum of Fine Arts, Boston, Nonie Gadsen and Darcy Kuronen; National Museum of American History, Smithsonian Institution, Cynthia Adams Hoover and Stacey Kluck; Newark Museum, Ulysses Dietz and Andrea Hagy; Oberlin College, Barbara Lambert; Old Barracks Museum, Rebecca Heiliczer; Pennsylvania Governor's Residence, Tammy McClenaghan; Pennsylvania Historical and Museum Commission, Beatrice Hulsberg and Mary Jane Miller; Pennsylvania State Archives, Jonathan Stayer; Philadelphia History Museum, Susan Drinan; Philadelphia Museum of Art, Alexandra Kirtley; Pook & Pook, James Pook and Deirdre Magarelli; Jamie Price; Reading Public Museum, Ashley Hamilton; Becky Roberts; Merri Lou Schaumann; Margaret Schiffer; Marlowe A. Sigal; John J. Snyder Jr.; Sotheby's, Erik Gronning and Kristin Nottebohm; Teylers Museum, Martijn Zegel; University of Pennsylvania, Jim Duffin; Vassar College Department of Music, Kathryn Libin; Fred Vogel; Charlie Wilson; Winterthur Museum, Mark Anderson, Laszlo Bodo, Emily Guthrie, Brock Jobe, Susan Newton, Lauri Perkins, Tom Savage, Jim Schneck, and Jeanne Solensky; Bob Wood; Yale University Art Gallery, Patricia Kane, Nancy Yates; Don Yoder; and York County Heritage Trust, Cindy Brown, Lila Fourhman-Shaull, and Joan Mummert.

1. Jacob Cox Parsons, *Extracts from the Diary of Jacob Hiltzheimer, of Philadelphia, 1765–1798* (Philadelphia: Wm. Fell & Co., 1893), p. 210. *The Diary of Elizabeth Drinker*, edited by Elaine Forman Crane, 3 vols. (Boston: Northeastern University Press, 1991), 2: 634–35. Many of the organ pipes, along with the church's records and library, were saved before the roof collapsed;

see Raymond J. Brunner, *That Ingenious Business: Pennsylvania German Organ Builders* (Birdsboro, Pa.: Pennsylvania German Society, 1990), p. 87.

2. Charles E. Peterson, *Robert Smith: Architect, Builder, Patriot, 1722–1777* (Philadelphia: Athenaeum of Philadelphia, 2000), p. 76. *The Journals of Henry Melchior Muhlenberg*, translated and edited by Theodore G. Tappert and John W. Doberstein, 3 vols. (1942; reprint, Camden, Maine: Picton Press, 1980), 2: 277. Dimensions are from the 1788 fire insurance survey; The Philadelphia Contributionship Digital Archives (hereafter PCDA), policy no. 2423. Independence Hall was 107 by 44½ feet; Christ Church in Philadelphia was 87 by 61½ feet; Faneuil Hall in Boston was 100 by 40 feet before its 1805 expansion; Nassau Hall in Princeton was 177 feet by 53 feet 8 inches; see Peterson, *Robert Smith*, p. 49. On the Zion organ, see Brunner, *That Ingenious Business*, pp. 85–87; also Raymond J. Brunner, "The Historical and Cultural Importance of David Tannenberg and Other Pennsylvania German Organ Builders, in *"Pleasing for Our Use": David Tannenberg and the Organs of the Moravians*, edited by Carol A. Traupman-Carr (Bethlehem, Pa.: Lehigh University Press, 2000), p. 73; and William H. Armstrong, *Organs for America: The Life and Work of David Tannenberg* (Philadelphia: University of Pennsylvania Press, 1967), pp. 44–45. Specifications do not survive for the organ of St. Michael's Lutheran Church in Charleston, S.C., acquired in 1768, built in London by Johann Snetzler; see Louis P. Nelson, *The Beauty of Holiness: Anglicanism & Architecture in Colonial South Carolina* (Chapel Hill: University of North Carolina Press, 2008), p. 231; also Maurie D. McInnis et al., *In Pursuit of Refinement: Charlestonians Abroad, 1740–1860* (Columbia: University of South Carolina Press, 1999), p. 57. Relatively little is known about Vorbach's work. In 1776 he executed £181.13.3 worth of woodwork for the new house of Jacob Graff (1727–1780), a German émigré bricklayer and master builder, at the corner of Seventh and Market Streets in Philadelphia. That same year, Thomas Jefferson rented two rooms in this house, where he wrote the Declaration of Independence. Jacob Graff to George Forepaugh, April 25, 1774, Graff Family Papers, col. 388, Downs Collection of Manuscripts and Printed Ephemera, Winterthur Library. Vorbach's obituary in 1817 gives his age as seventy-six, putting his birth date about 1741; see *Poulson's American Daily Advertiser*, Philadelphia, December 26, 1817, Early American Newspapers Database (hereafter EAND). On June 23, 1768, he married Anna Margreth Binghardt. Their sons Andreas (b. 1769) and George Jr. (b. 1774) were baptized at St. Michael's and Zion; the latter's entry notes his father's name as "Georg Vorbach (also known as Forepaugh)." *18th-Century Records of the German Lutheran Church at Philadelphia, Pennsylvania (St. Michael's and Zion)*, translated by Robert L. Hess and edited by F. Edward Wright, 5 vols., *Pennsylvania German Church Records*, CD-ROM, 1: 257, 2: 348, 4: 922 (hereafter SM&Z). Karl John Richard Arndt and Reimer C. Eck, *The First Century of German Language-Printing in the United States of America*, vol. 1, *1728–1807* (Göttingen: Hubert & Co., 1989), p. 311. On the Muhlenbergs, see Lisa Minardi, *Pastors & Patriots: The Muhlenberg Family of Pennsylvania* (Collegeville, Pa.: Berman Museum of Art, 2011).

3. John J. Snyder Jr., "Carved Chippendale Case Furniture from Lancaster, Pennsylvania," *Antiques* 107, no. 5 (May 1975): 964–69; Brunner, *That Ingenious Business*, pp. 71–72, quotes the lieutenant. The Tannenberg organ for Trinity Lutheran was replaced in 1885, but the case was retained. Two more towers were added at either side in 1893 and remain today.

4. Crane, ed., *Elizabeth Drinker*, 3: 1250. Peterson, *Robert Smith*, pp. 89–93.

5. Huguenot material culture has been subject to similar prejudices; see Neil Kamil, "Hidden in Plain Sight: Disappearance and Material Life in Colonial New York," in *American Furniture*, edited by Luke Beckerdite (Hanover, N.H.: University Press of New England for the Chipstone Foundation, 1995), pp. 191–249; Luke Beckerdite, "Religion, Artistry, and Cultural Identity: The Huguenot Experience in South Carolina, 1680–1725," in *American Furniture*, edited by Luke Beckerdite (Hanover, N.H.: University Press of New England for the Chipstone Foundation, 1997), pp. 196–227. On Quaker plainness, see J. William Frost, "From Plainness to Simplicity: Changing Ideals for Quaker Material Culture," in *Quaker Aesthetics: Reflections on a Quaker Ethic in American Design and Consumption*, edited by Emma Jones Lapsansky and Anne A. Verplanck (Philadelphia: University of Pennsylvania Press, 2003), pp. 16–40; also Susan Garfinkel, "Quakers and High Chests: The Plainness Problem Reconsidered," in ibid., pp. 50–89. Morrison H. Heckscher and Leslie Greene Bowman, *American Rococo, 1750–1775: Elegance in Ornament* (New York: Harry N. Abrams, 1992), p. 59. Snyder, "Carved Chippendale Case Furniture," p. 965. On rococo influence on long rifles, see Joe K. Kindig III, *Artistic Ingredients of the Longrifle* (York, Pa.: George Shumway, 1989), esp. pp. 50–53. A silver tureen with rococo ornament by Lancaster silversmith Peter Getz (1764–

1809) is in the collection of the Wadsworth Atheneum Museum of Art, Hartford, Connecticut; see Beatrice B. Garvan and Charles F. Hummel, *The Pennsylvania Germans: A Celebration of Their Arts, 1683–1850* (Philadelphia: Philadelphia Museum of Art, 1982), pl. 23. On stoves, see Heckscher and Bowman, *American Rococo*, pp. 223–28; also Henry C. Mercer, *The Bible in Iron*, rev. ed. (1914; Doylestown, Pa.: Bucks County Historical Society, 1961), esp. figs. 283–320.

6. Désirée Caldwell, "Germanic Influences on Philadelphia Early Georgian Seating Furniture" (master's thesis, University of Delaware, 1985), pp. 54–55. "[R]apid assimilation" is in David Hackett Fischer, *Albion's Seed: Four British Folkways in America* (New York: Oxford University Press, 1989), pp. 428–33. On the tripartite model, see Scott T. Swank, "The Germanic Fragment," in *Arts of the Pennsylvania Germans*, edited by Catherine E. Hutchins (New York: W. W. Norton for the Henry Francis du Pont Winterthur Museum, 1983), pp. 4–5. See also Cynthia G. Falk, *Architecture and Artifacts of the Pennsylvania Germans: Constructing Identity in Early America* (University Park: Pennsylvania State University Press, 2008), esp. pp. 13–29. Steven M. Nolt, *Foreigners in Their Own Land: Pennsylvania Germans in the Early Republic* (University Park: Pennsylvania State University Press, 2002), pp. 3, 5–9.

7. On Philadelphia's economy, see Thomas M. Doerflinger, *A Vigorous Spirit of Enterprise: Merchants and Economic Development in Revolutionary Philadelphia* (Chapel Hill: University of North Carolina Press, 1986); the information on ship arrivals is on p. 292; Mary M. Schweitzer, *Custom and Contract: Household, Government, and the Economy in Colonial Pennsylvania* (New York: Columbia University Press, 1987); and James T. Lemon, *The Best Poor Man's Country: A Geographical Study of Early Southeastern Pennsylvania* (Baltimore: Johns Hopkins University Press, 1972). On immigration, see Marianne S. Wokeck, *Trade in Strangers: The Beginnings of Mass Migration to North America* (University Park: Pennsylvania State University Press, 1999), pp. 37–46, 53. On Germantown, see Stephanie Grauman Wolf, *Urban Village: Population, Community, and Family Structure in Germantown, Pennsylvania, 1683–1800* (Princeton: Princeton University Press, 1980).

8. Jonathan Dickinson to John Askew, October 24, 1717, Jonathan Dickinson Copy Books of Letters, pp. 163–64, quoted in Wendy A. Cooper and Lisa Minardi, *Paint, Pattern & People: Furniture of Southeastern Pennsylvania, 1725–1850* (Winterthur, Del.: Henry Francis du Pont Winterthur Museum, 2011), p. xiv. Benjamin Franklin, quoted in Falk, *Architecture and Artifacts*, pp. 53–54. On Saur, see Arndt and Eck, *The First Century of German Language-Printing*, 1: 6. Christopher Saur Jr. (1721–1784) and Saur III (1754–1799) continued the business; other German printers include Michael Billmeyer (1752–1838) of Germantown, and Henrich Miller (1702–1782) and Carl Cist (1738?–1805) of Philadelphia. *Journey to Pennsylvania by Gottlieb Mittelberger*, translated and edited by Oscar Handlin and John Clive (Cambridge, Mass.: Harvard University Press, 1960), p. 38. *The Pennsylvania Packet; and the General Advertiser*, May 11, 1772, EAND. A. Kristen Foster, *Moral Visions and Material Ambitions: Philadelphia Struggles to Define the Republic, 1776–1836* (New York: Lexington Books, 2004), p. 46.

9. A. G. Roeber, "'The Origin of Whatever Is Not English Among Us': The Dutch-Speaking and the German-Speaking Peoples of Colonial British America," in *Strangers within the Realm: Cultural Margins of the First British Empire*, ed. Bernard Bailyn and Philip D. Morgan (Chapel Hill: University of North Carolina Press, 1991), pp. 245–47; also A. G. Roeber, "In German Ways? Problems and Potentials of Eighteenth-Century German Social and Emigration History," *William & Mary Quarterly*, 3rd ser., 44 (1987): 750–74. *Pennsylvanische Staatsbote*, Philadelphia, July 12, 1768, quoted in J. Carter Harris, *The Clock & Watch Maker's American Advertiser* (Sussex, U.K.: Antiquarian Horological Society, 2003), no. 453; see also George H. Eckhardt, *Pennsylvania Clocks and Clockmakers* (New York: Devin-Adair Company, 1955), p. 175. Marie Basil McDaniel, "Processes of Identity Formation among German Speakers, 1730–1760," in *A Peculiar Mixture: German-Language Cultures and Identities in Eighteenth-Century North America*, edited by Jan Stievermann and Oliver Scheiding (University Park: Pennsylvania State University Press, 2013), pp. 189, 191, 193. Friederike Baer, *The Trial of Frederick Eberle: Language, Patriotism, and Citizenship in Philadelphia's German Community, 1790 to 1830* (New York: New York University Press, 2008), p. 12. See also Philip Otterness, *Becoming German: The 1709 Palatine Migration to New York* (Ithaca, N.Y.: Cornell University Press, 2004), esp. pp. 1–6.

10. Population estimates for 1730–1760 are from McDaniel, "Processes of Identity Formation," p. 189. Information on Philadelphia's population in 1800 by ethnicity and religion is based on tables 1 and 2 in Robert J. Gough, "The Philadelphia Economic Elite at the End of the Eighteenth Century," in *Shaping a National Culture: The Philadelphia Experience, 1750–1800*,

edited by Catherine E. Hutchins (Winterthur, Del.: Henry Francis du Pont Winterthur Museum, 1994), pp. 18–19. For 1790, see Lemon, *Best Poor Man's Country*, pp. 14, 18. For 1815, see Baer, *Trial of Frederick Eberle*, p. 19. For 1847, see Franz Löhrer, *History and Status of the Germans in America* (1847), cited in Charles L. Venable, "Germanic Craftsmen and Furniture Design in Philadelphia, 1820–1850," in *American Furniture*, edited by Luke Beckerdite (Hanover, N.H.: University Press of New England for the Chipstone Foundation, 1998), p. 45.

11. On Knorr, see *Philadelphia: Three Centuries of American Art* (Philadelphia: Philadelphia Museum of Art, 1976), pp. 81–83. Benno M. Forman, "German Influences in Pennsylvania Furniture," in Hutchins, ed., *Arts of the Pennsylvania Germans*, pp. 102–3. Benno M. Forman, "Delaware Valley 'Crookt Foot' and Slat-Back Chairs: The Fussell-Savery Connection," *Winterthur Portfolio* 15, no. 1 (1980): 47, 50–54. Caldwell, "Germanic Influences on Philadelphia Early Georgian Seating Furniture," pp. 40, 62–63. Venable, "Germanic Craftsmen and Furniture Design in Philadelphia, 1820–1850," pp. 41–80. For research on German cabinetmakers in Philadelphia from 1820 to 1850, see Charles L. Venable, "Philadelphia Biedermeier: Germanic Craftsmen and Design in Philadelphia, 1820–1850" (master's thesis, University of Delaware, 1986).

12. On immigrant chests, see Cooper and Minardi, *Paint, Pattern & People*, pp. 28–29. A note that accompanied the Reser chair states, "This chair when fitted up in 1851 was 105 yrs old. It belonged to Grandmother Reasor." A mate to this chair descended to the Twaddell sisters of Germantown, from the Ashe-Davis family, and is illustrated in Jack L. Lindsey, *Worldly Goods: The Arts of Early Pennsylvania, 1680–1758* (Philadelphia: Philadelphia Museum of Art, 1999), cat. no. 125. On wainscot chairs, see Cooper and Minardi, *Paint, Pattern & People*, pp. 11, 27; also Joseph K. Kindig III, *The Philadelphia Chair, 1685–1785* (York, Pa.: Historical Society of York County, 1978), figs. 1–7. On Bechtel, see Caldwell, "Germanic Influences," pp. 57–58; also John W. Jordan, "John Bechtel: His Contributions to Literature, and His Descendants," *Pennsylvania Magazine of History and Biography* 19, no. 2 (1895): 137–51. Bechtel worked in the Bethlehem turner's shop after moving there in 1749. His daughter Mary Agneta married Cornelius Weygandt, another German émigré turner, who lived in Germantown, while daughter Mary Susan married John Levering, son of joiner Jacob Levering (d. 1753) of Germantown and Roxborough.

13. The Agnus Dei is engraved on the side of a communion flagon used by Trinity Lutheran Church in Lancaster, Pennsylvania, and a chalice used by Swamp Reformed Church in Reinholds, Lancaster County, Pennsylvania; see Donald M. Herr, *Pewter in Pennsylvania German Churches* (Birdsboro, Pa.: Pennsylvania German Society, 1995), p. 45.

14. The clock and schrank are also discussed in Cooper and Minardi, *Paint, Pattern & People*, pp. 30–31. Handlin and Clive, *Journey to Pennsylvania by Gottlieb Mittelberger*, p. 57. Carole Boston Weatherford, *The Carolina Parakeet: America's Lost Parrot in Art and Memory* (Minneapolis: Avian Publications, 2005), pp. 41, 50. The desk is illustrated in Margaret Berwind Schiffer, *Furniture and Its Makers of Chester County, Pennsylvania* (Philadelphia: University of Pennsylvania Press, 1966), figs. 140, 141. The interior relates to a group of desks from the Carlisle area of Cumberland County, Pennsylvania, where several Philadelphia-area cabinetmakers moved by the 1770s. One clock is inscribed "GORG IUNT ANNO 1755"; see Cooper and Minardi, *Paint, Pattern, & People*, pp. 136–37. The other is inscribed "ANNO 1755" and was sold at Pook & Pook, Downingtown, Pa., *The Collection of Richard and Joane Smith*, October 30, 2010, lot 210.

15. Lee Ellen Griffith, *The Pennsylvania Spice Box: Paneled Doors and Secret Drawers* (West Chester, Pa.: Chester County Historical Society, 1986); see also Cooper and Minardi, *Paint, Pattern & People*, pp. 12–14, 72, 129–30.

16. *Möbel zwischen Handwerk und Kunst: Die Möbelgestaltung Johann Michael Rößlers und ihre Ursprünge* (Schwäbisch Hall: Hohenloher Freilandmuseum, 1999), pp. 43–44; *Barockmöbel aus Württemberg und Hohenlohe, 1700–1750* (Ulm: Württembergisches Landesmuseum Stuttgart, 1985), pp. 28–29; Bernward Deneke, *Bauernmöbel: Ein Handbuch für Sammler und Liebhaber* (Munich, 1969), 314. Bird inlay was also used in Switzerland at this time; a commode inlaid with parrots, circa 1740, is illustrated in Walter R. C. Abeggeln and Sibylle E. Burckhardt, *Das Luzerner Möbel: Von der Spätrenaissance bis zum Biedermeier* (Lucerne: Pro Libro, 2011), p. 105. Albin was actually selected to come to America by the Royal Society to prepare a natural history but declined, and Catesby came in his place; see Amy R. W. Meyers and Margaret Beck Pritchard, eds., *Empire's Nature: Mark Catesby's New World Vision* (Chapel Hill: University of North Carolina Press for the Omohundro Institute of Early American History and Culture

and the Colonial Williamsburg Foundation, 1998), p. 6. With thanks to Margaret Pritchard and Kate Teiken at Colonial Williamsburg for their assistance in identifying this print source.

17. The *Tabernakelschrank* is illustrated and discussed at length in Robert C. Smith, "A Rhenish Cabinet of the Eighteenth Century," *Antiques* 87, no. 1 (January 1965): 68–72. For an illustration of the Yale clock, see Edwin A. Battison and Patricia E. Kane, *The American Clock, 1725–1865* (New Haven, Conn.: Yale University Art Gallery, 1973), pp. 110–13.

18. On Neisser, see William J. Murtaugh, *Moravian Architecture and Town Planning: Bethlehem, Pennsylvania, and Other Eighteenth-Century American Settlements* (Philadelphia: University of Pennsylvania Press, 1967), p. 5. North Devon Record Office, 814A/PO340, 1729, Barnstaple. The apprentice was John Hacche (son of John). Only one Joseph Wills is known to have been a clockmaker; see Brian Loomes, *Watchmakers and Clockmakers of the World*, vol. 2 (London: N.A.G. Press, 1976), p. 255. The translation of the church records describes her as the "English wife of Joseph Wills," but this is probably a mistake in the translation and the original intention was to identify Joseph, rather than his wife, as English; SM&Z, 5: 1096. She may have been his second wife, as the records of First Reformed Church, Philadelphia, note the marriage of Joseph Wills, widower, to Maria Brand on October 8, 1750; see F. Edward Wright, *Early Church Records of the First Reformed Church of Philadelphia*, 2 vols., on *Pennsylvania German Church Records*, CD-ROM (hereafter FR), 1: 124. Will of Joseph Wills, written August 12, 1758, proved May 24, 1759, Philadelphia will books microfilm 1759, no. 261, Winterthur Library, Downs Collection. Further corroboration that Wills came from South Molton is a bequest to Giles and Grace Tucker of South Molton made in his will. "Maria Sophia Cogen, Executrix" advertised that Wills's debtors and creditors make themselves known to her in the *Pennsylvania Gazette*, Philadelphia, July 19, 1759, EAND. Thomas Say (b. 1709) married Susannah Catharine Sprogell (1713–1749) in 1734 at Christ Church in Philadelphia; see "Genealogical Records Copied from the Bible of Thomas Say," *Pennsylvania Magazine of History and Biography* 29 (1905): 217–18. She is likely the daughter of Ludwig Christian Sprogel, who represented Philadelphia County in the colonial assembly from 1725 to 1729 and in 1728 sold an organ to Christ Church in Philadelphia for £200; see Brunner, *That Ingenious Business*, p. 48. On the Godschalk genealogy, see Joel D. Alderfer, "New Discoveries in Godshalk-Godshall-Gottschall Family Research," *Newsletter of the Mennonite Historians of Eastern Pennsylvania* 10, no. 2 (May 1983): 1–4; also Bruce Ross Forman, *Clockmakers of Montgomery County, 1740–1850* (Norristown, Pa.: Historical Society of Montgomery County, 2000), p. 17.

19. Common woods used for making stained or dyed inlay were the European or black poplar (*Populus nigra*), maple (*Acer pseudoplatanus* in particular), and holly (*Ilex aquifolium*)—all fast-growing, clear woods that were easy to color; see Heidrun Zinnkann, *Furniture Woods* (Munich: Prestel Verlag, 2002), p. 58. Hans Michaelsen, "Painting in Wood: Innovations in Marquetry Decoration by the Roentgen Workshop," in Wolfram Koeppe, *Extravagant Inventions: The Princely Furniture of the Roentgens* (New York: Metropolitan Museum of Art, 2012), pp. 228–33.

20. The Wills clock was donated to the York County Heritage Trust by Mrs. Frederick Dempwolf, a native of York. The Neisser clock was acquired by the Historical Society of Berks County from the estate of Lewis Kraemer in 1944. The 1740 clock is said to have come from the area of East Greenville, Montgomery County, Pennsylvania; the 1741 schrank was formerly owned by Donald Shelley. "AM" does not correspond to a German male first name; it could represent the female name Anna Maria, but that would be highly unusual given that schranks almost always use either the husband's name/initials alone or those of both spouses. The most likely arrangement, therefore, is "MI AM" for a Michael Am . This surname is spelled Amensetter/Omensetter/Umensetter and variations thereof. Michael died on September 19, 1784, and was identified in the St. Michael's and Zion church records as "Michael Ummensetter, from Germany. Age 88 yrs, 8 months, and 2 days," putting his birth in January 1696; see SM&Z, 5: 1262. There were actually two Michael Amenzetters. Both are listed in the 1779 Pennsylvania tax lists, one in Germantown and the other in the Mulberry Ward of Philadelphia; see Ancestry.com, from the Pennsylvania Historical & Museum Commission, Records of the Office of the Comptroller General, RG-4, *Tax & Exoneration Lists, 1762–1794*, microfilm roll 333. The one who died in 1784 lived in the Mulberry Ward of Philadelphia; the other immigrated in 1751 with his son Jacob and settled in Germantown, where he had a mill along Cresheim Creek next to John Rittenhouse; see Ralph Beaver Strassburger and William John Hinke, *Pennsylvania German Pioneers: A Publication of the Original Lists of Arrivals in the Port of Philadelphia from 1727 to 1808*, 3 vols. (Norristown, Pa.: Pennsylvania German Society, 1934), 1: 475.

21. On Bankson and Lawson, see Sumpter Priddy III, J. Michael Flanigan, and Gregory R. Weidman, "The Genesis of Neoclassical Style in Baltimore Furniture," in *American Furniture*, edited by Luke Beckerdite (Hanover, N.H.: University Press of New England for the Chipstone Foundation, 2000), pp. 59–99. On Pfeninger, see J. Thomas Savage, "The Holmes-Edwards Library Bookcase and the Origins of the German School in Pre-Revolutionary Charleston," in *American Furniture*, edited by Luke Beckerdite (Hanover, N.H.: University Press of New England for the Chipstone Foundation, 1997), pp. 106–26. Helene M. Reiley, "Michael Kalteisen and the Founding of the German Friendly Society in Charleston," *South Carolina Historical Magazine* 100, no. 1 (January 1999): 29–48. On the Roentgens, see Koeppe, *Extravagant Inventions*; also Petra Krutisch, *Weltberühmt und heiß begehrt: Möbel der Roentgen-Manufaktur in der Sammlung des Germanischen Nationalmuseums* (Nuremberg: Germanisches Nationalmuseums, 2007). On Hintz, see Lanie E. Graf, "Moravians in London: A Case Study in Furniture-Making, c. 1735–65," *Furniture History: The Journal of the Furniture History Society* 40 (2004): 1–52; also Christopher Gilbert and Tessa Murdoch, *John Channon and Brass Inlaid Furniture, 1730–1760* (New Haven, Conn.: Yale University Press in association with Leeds City Art Galleries and the Victoria & Albert Museum, 1993), p. 21. The Bomberger clock is also discussed in Cooper and Minardi, *Paint, Pattern & People*, p. 33. A Joseph Wills clock with related case and ogee feet is currently owned by Philip H. Bradley Co., Downingtown, Pennsylvania; a John Wood Sr. clock with related case and ball feet of circa 1730–1740 in date is illustrated in Lindsey, *Worldly Goods*, p. 146. Another John Wood Sr. clock in related case with ball feet is in a private collection; it is inscribed "9/6/1748" on the inside of the backboard, possibly when it was cleaned and oiled rather than made. The 1783 tax list is in William Henry Egle, ed., *Proprietary, Supply, and State Tax Lists of the City and County of Philadelphia*, Pennsylvania Archives, 3rd ser., vol. 16 (Harrisburg, Pa.: Wm. Stanley Ray, 1897), p. 795; Bomberger is listed in the extract of the 1786 list printed in William Macpherson Hornor Jr., *Blue Book: Philadelphia Furniture, William Penn to George Washington, with Special Reference to the Philadelphia-Chippendale School* (Philadelphia: printed for the author, 1935), p. 321.

22. Kessler's obituary gives his date of birth as September 4, 1737. Three men by the name of Johann Leonard Kessler emigrated from Germany to Philadelphia, arriving on September 9, 1749, November 30, 1750, and October 26, 1754; see Strassburger and Hinke, *Pennsylvania German Pioneers*, 1: 397, 449, 661. One married a Maria Catharina and died before April 1753; see SM&Z, 1: 35. Witnesses at Leonard Kessler's marriage are named in *Pennsylvania German Church Records of Births, Baptisms, Marriages, Burials, Etc., from the Pennsylvania German Society Proceedings and Addresses*, 3 vols. (Baltimore, Md.: Genealogical Publishing Co., 1983), 1: 658. Jacob Schieffelin (1732–1769) was a Württemberg immigrant and entrepreneur; in 1760 he relocated his family to Montreal. His son Jacob Schieffelin Jr. (1757–1835) became a noted merchant in Philadelphia, while son Thomas Schieffelin married Leonard Kessler's daughter Hannah (his first cousin); see Susan S. Lukesh, "Jacob Schieffelin," in *Immigrant Entrepreneurship: German-American Business Biographies, 1720 to the Present*, edited by Marianne S. Wokeck, German Historical Institute, vol. 1, last modified November 08, 2012, http://immigrantentrepreneurship.org/entry.php?rec=124.

23. Forman, "Fussell-Savery Connection," p. 54. *Philadelphia: Three Centuries*, p. 87. The chest-on-chest is illustrated in David H. Conradsen, *Useful Beauty: Early American Decorative Arts from St. Louis Collections* (Saint Louis: Saint Louis Art Museum, 1999), pp. 72–73; see also Christie's, New York, *The Collection of Mr. and Mrs. E. J. Nusrala*, January 21, 2006, lot 683. The armchair was a bequest of William M. Doughten, who was a direct descendant of Jonathan Shoemaker through the line of his son Joseph (b. 1765); it is illustrated in Hornor, *Blue Book*, pl. 159; also *Philadelphia: Three Centuries*, pp. 87–88.

24. Muhlenberg, *Journals*, 1: 280, 564, 581–82, 590, 727; 2: 35, 276–77, 766; 3 :13. Five of the Muhlenberg chairs were sold at Pennypacker Auction Centre, Reading, Pa., *Collections from the Estates of Minnie T. Nicolls and Frederick W. Nicolls Jr.*, June 25–26, 1962, lot 525. Accompanying those five were three chairs made circa 1845–1855 in Lancaster, Pennsylvania, to form a set of eight (lot 526). These chairs were from the estate of Frederick W. Nicolls Jr., who was a Muhlenberg descendant. Two chairs were sold at Pook & Pook, Downingtown, Pa., October 1, 2010, lot 99; that pair had previously been donated by a Muhlenberg descendant to the Historical Society of Berks County benefit auction on October 12, 2002. The eighth chair is in the collection of the Historical Society of Berks County (acc. no. 61.24) and was donated by Katharine Muhlenberg Schmucker (1884–1966), a descendant of Henry Melchior Muhlenberg through his son Henry Jr.

25. A side chair with carving attributed to Bernard is illustrated in Luke Beckerdite and Alan Miller, "A Table's Tale: Craft, Art, and Opportunity in Eighteenth-Century Philadelphia," in *American Furniture*, edited by Luke Beckerdite (Hanover, N.H.: University Press of New England for the Chipstone Foundation, 2004), p. 20. The Yale chair is illustrated and discussed in Patricia E. Kane, *300 Years of American Seating Furniture: Chairs and Beds from the Mabel Brady Garvan and Other Collections at Yale University* (Boston: New York Graphic Society, 1976), p. 136, no. 115. The six walnut chairs are illustrated in *American Antiques from Israel Sack Collection*, vol. 4 (Washington, D.C.: Highland House Publishers, 1974), p. 880.

26. Will of John Gaul, dated January 16, 1769, proved February 1, 1769, Philadelphia will books microfilm 1769, no. 239, Downs Collection, Winterthur Library. Will of John Michael Barendt, dated August 31, 1780, proved October 15, 1780, Philadelphia will books microfilm 1780, no. 331, Downs Collection, Winterthur Library. Unfortunately, the inventory itself has not been located. Will of George Adam Pfister, dated July 16, 1781, proved September 24, 1793, Philadelphia will books microfilm 1793, no. 268, Downs Collection, Winterthur Library. The payment by John Ross is cited in Nancy Ann Goyne, "Furniture Craftsmen in Philadelphia, 1760–1780: Their Role in a Mercantile Society" (master's thesis, University of Delaware, 1963), p. 65.

27. On Evans, see Eleanore P. Gadsden, "When Good Cabinetmakers Made Bad Furniture: The Career and Work of David Evans," in *American Furniture*, edited by Luke Beckerdite (Hanover, N.H.: University Press of New England for the Chipstone Foundation, 2001), pp. 65–87; also Eleanore Parker Gadsden, "From Traditional Cabinetmaking to Entrepreneurial Production: David Evans (1748–1819)" (master's thesis, University of Delaware, 2000). Daybooks of David Evans, microfilm, Downs Collection, Winterthur Library. The bedstead reference is in Hornor, *Blue Book*, p. 163. Hornor, ibid., p. 237, claimed to have "absolute knowledge of at least one article of furniture" made by Michael Kessler but did not specify the form. The desk purchase is noted in Friederich Schenckel's account book of 1770 to 1775: "Bought a desk from carpenter Leonhart Köseler on February 24, 1773 for 22 pounds." The account book is in the Pennsylvania German Archives, Myrin Library, Ursinus College; with thanks to Alan Keyser for this information and translation.

28. Life dates for some of the major Philadelphia cabinetmakers are (in chronological order): George Claypoole Jr. (1733–1793), Benjamin Randolph (1737–1792), Leonard Kessler (1737–1804), Thomas Affleck (1740–1795), Jonathan Gostelowe (1744–1806), Daniel Trotter (1747–1800), and David Evans (1748–1819). The 1783 and 1786 tax lists are in Hornor, *Blue Book*, pp. 317–26.

29. "Brest," for "breast," probably refers to wainscot paneling, and "Sirbace" means "surbase," a molding above a base, such as a baseboard. The initial survey is dated July 1, 1765, the resurvey is dated August 4, 1772, policy no. 1018, PCDA. Information about workers' housing is from Bernard L. Herman, cited in Amy Hudson Henderson, "Furnishing the Republican Court: Building and Decorating Philadelphia Homes, 1790–1800" (Ph.D. diss., University of Delaware, 2008), p. 88.

30. Policy no. 846, PCDA; see also Forman, "Fussell-Savery Connection," p. 45.

31. Benjamin Randolph, policy no. 1580, PCDA. Daniel Trotter, policy no. 2147, PCDA.

32. SM&Z, 1: 115, 143, 188, 252, 291; 5: 1190. Muhlenberg, *Journals*, 1: 467, 471, 475, 481, 486, 488, 490.

33. Ned Cooke has called for the study of "nonwork relationships" to create a "richer, more comprehensive understanding of the craftsman and his world"; see Edward S. Cooke, "The Study of American Furniture from the Perspective of the Maker," in *Perspectives on American Furniture*, edited by Gerald W. R. Ward (New York: W. W. Norton & Co. for the Henry Francis du Pont Winterthur Museum, 1988), pp. 120–21, 125. *Pennsylvania Packet, and Daily Advertiser*, Philadelphia, October 4 and 22, 1790, EAND. Will of Mary Kessler, written November 24, 1815, proved December 2, 1825, Philadelphia will books microfilm 1825, no. 146, Downs Collection, Winterthur Library.

34. Inventory of Emanuel Schultze, taken April 11, 1809, Berks County Register of Wills. Snyder, "Carved Chippendale Case Furniture from Lancaster," p. 964. The Cadwalader request is quoted in Nicholas B. Wainwright, *Colonial Grandeur in Philadelphia: The House and Furniture of General John Cadwalader* (Philadelphia: Historical Society of Pennsylvania, 1964), p. 65.

35. John Penn, "John Penn's Journal of a Visit to Reading, Harrisburg, Carlisle, and Lancaster, in 1788," *Pennsylvania Magazine of History and Biography* 3 (1879): entry for April 7, 1788, 285. On the store, see Lisa Minardi, "'An Excellent Stand for Business': Frederick Muhlen-

berg's General Store," *Bulletin of the Historical Society of Montgomery County* 36, no. 4 (2013): 2–18. On the coat of arms, see Luke Beckerdite, "Philadelphia Carving Shops, Part II: Bernard and Jugiez," *Antiques* 128, no. 3 (September 1985): 512–13. Herr, *Pewter in Pennsylvania German Churches*, esp. pp. 32, 40–41, 89.

36. The Hiester chairs are numbered I through VI and were sold as part of the estate of Frederick W. Nicolls at Pennypacker Auction Centre, Reading, Pa., June 25–26, 1962, lot 525. Nicolls was a descendant of both the Muhlenberg and Hiester families. The chairs were acquired by the Sacks, who erroneously published them as having descended in the family of General Peter Muhlenberg; see *Antiques* 96, no. 4 (October 1969): 446. This was subsequently corrected when they were published in *American Antiques from Israel Sack Collection*, vol. 3 (Washington, D.C.: Highland House Publishers, 1981), p. 615. On the Hiester family, see Henry Melchior Muhlenberg Richards, "Governor Joseph Hiester: A Historical Sketch" and "The Hiester Family," in *Proceedings of the Pennsylvania German Society*, vol. 16 (Lancaster, Pa.: Pennsylvania German Society, 1907), pp. 3–51 and 5–42; see also V.E.C. Hill, *A Genealogy of the Hiester Family* (Lebanon, Pa.: Report Publishing Company, 1903). Adam Witman (1723–1781) was the eldest son of German immigrant Christopher Witman Sr. He married Catharina Barbara Gansert (1730–1808) on June 2, 1747; see F. Edward Wright, *Berks County Church Records of the 18th Century*, vol. 4 (Lewes, Del.: Colonial Roots, 2009), p. 66. They had only two children: John (b. 1752) and Elizabeth, who married Joseph Hiester. Some sources give John's death date as 1832; he is not mentioned in Adam's will of 1781 and was likely estranged or deceased. Inventory of Adam Witman, taken September 28, 1781, Berks County Register of Wills. The tea table was donated to the Historical Society of Berks County by Helen Brooke Wittman (b. 1862), a direct descendant of Joseph and Elizabeth Hiester via their eldest daughter, Catharine (1772–1833), who married John Spayd; their daughter Catharine Spayd (1801–1871) married John Brooke; their son John (1834–1898) was the father of Helen Brooke (b. 1862), who married Noel B. Wittman in 1884 and later donated the table; acc. no. 54-39-14. On this genealogy, see Hill, *Genealogy of the Hiester Family*, pp. 7–8. The silver is in the collection of the Reading Public Museum, acc. nos. 1969.417.1, 1969.418.1, and 1969.419.1.

37. Lisa Minardi, "Palladian Architecture, Germanic Style: The Hiester House of Montgomery County, Pennsylvania," *Antiques* 180, no. 5 (September–October 2013): 140–47. On Stitcher, see *The Biographical Encyclopedia of Pennsylvania of the Nineteenth Century* (Philadelphia: Galaxy Publishing Co., 1874), pp. 274–75. The Bertolet chair was sold at Pook & Pook, Downingtown, Pa., *Charming Forge Mansion: The Collection of Earle and Yvonne Henderson*, October 1, 2010, lot 362.

38. Daniel Spillane, *History of the American Pianoforte* (New York: the author, 1890), 72. Some sources contend that Philadelphia's dominance in piano making could be extended as late as 1860; see Robert A. Gerson, *Music in Philadelphia* (Philadelphia: Theodore Presser Co., 1940), p. 44.

39. On Klemm, see Brunner, *That Ingenious Business*, pp. 60–67; Barbara Owen, "Brother Klemm, Organ Builder," in Traupman-Carr, ed., *David Tannenberg and the Organs of the Moravians*, pp. 24–39. A spinet made by John Harris of Boston in 1769 is in the collection of the Metropolitan Museum of Art, acc. no. 1976.229. The Gloria Dei organ has often been attributed to Swedish Moravian painter Gustavus Hesselius (1682–1755), but a letter dated April 12, 1739, documents Klemm as the maker of that organ and indicates that Hesselius was only the agent for this commission. No evidence of Hesselius actually making instruments has been found. His son John Hesselius, also a painter, owned a harpsichord, chamber organ, guitar, flute, and three violins when he died in 1778, but it is unknown who made them; see Brunner, *That Ingenious Business*, p. 63. On Falckner's ordination, see John Ogasapian, *Music of the Colonial and Revolutionary Era* (Westport, Conn.: Greenwood Press, 2004), p. 86. Brunner, *That Ingenious Business*, pp. 49–54, 64–65; Ogasapian, *Music*, pp. 89–91. On Moravian music, see also Cooper and Minardi, *Paint, Pattern & People*, pp. 47–49.

40. On piano construction and function, see Walter Edward Mann, "Piano Making in Philadelphia before 1825" (Ph.D. diss., University of Iowa, 1977), pp. 15, 18–86.

41. On Feyring, see Brunner, *That Ingenious Business*, pp. 55–59. On Tannenberg, see ibid., pp. 69–97; Brunner, "Historical and Cultural Importance of David Tannenberg and Other Pennsylvania German Organ Builders," pp. 68–75. The Tannenberg clavichord is in the collection of the Moravian Historical Society, Nazareth, Pennsylvania, and contains a paper label inscribed (in translation): "David Tannenberg in June 1761 at Bethlehem"; see Jewel A. Smith, "The Piano among the Moravians," in *The Music of the Moravian Church in America*, edited by Nola Reed Knouse (Rochester, N.Y.: University of Rochester, 2008), p. 242. Armstrong,

Organs for America. On Doll, see Snyder, "Carved Chippendale Case Furniture," p. 967; Brunner, *That Ingenious Business,* pp. 157–62. On Scheible, see ibid., pp. 166–67; also inventory of John Sheibly, Earl Township, Lancaster County, taken January 7, 1793, Lancaster County Historical Society. Inventory of George Albright, Baltimore, taken August 5, 1802, Baltimore County Inventories, 22: 269–70, Maryland Hall of Records, Annapolis, Md. On Ache, see Lisa Minardi, "From Millbach to Mahantongo: Fraktur and Furniture of the Pennsylvania Germans," in *American Furniture,* edited by Luke Beckerdite (Hanover, N.H.: University Press of New England for the Chipstone Foundation, 2011), pp. 40–46.

42. Martha Novak Clinkscale, *Makers of the Piano, 1700–1820* (Oxford: Oxford University Press, 1993), pp. 397–98, 400, 402. Alfred Dolge, *Pianos and Their Makers* (Covina, Calif.: Covina Publishing Comp., 1911; reprint, New York: Dover Publications, 1972), pp. 48–49.

43. Jewel A. Smith, *Music, Women, and Pianos in Antebellum Bethlehem, Pennsylvania* (Bethlehem, Pa.: Lehigh University Press, 2008), p. 63.

44. A Baltimore piano stool of circa 1830–1850 in date, retaining its original black horsehair upholstery and brass tacks, is illustrated in Gregory R. Weidman, *Furniture in Maryland, 1740–1940* (Baltimore: Maryland Historical Society, 1984), p. 172. A piano by William Geib of New York that retains its original round upholstered stool is illustrated in Charles L. Venable, *American Furniture in the Bybee Collection* (Austin: University of Texas Press, 1989), p. 111.

45. *Dunlap's Pennsylvania Packet,* Philadelphia, March 13, 1775, EAND. *Freeman's Journal: or, the North-American Intelligencer,* July 2, 1783, EAND. Charles F. Montgomery, *American Furniture: The Federal Period* (New York: Viking Press, 1966), p. 133; Morrison H. Heckscher, "The Organization and Practice of Philadelphia Cabinetmaking Establishments, 1790–1820" (master's thesis, University of Delaware, 1964), p. 140. The 1789 Albrecht piano was previously in the collection of the Historical Society of Pennsylvania; see James E. Mooney, "Furniture at the Historical Society of Pennsylvania," *Antiques* 113, no. 5 (May 1978): 1042.

46. Strassburger and Hinke, *Pennsylvania German Pioneers,* 3: 12. Also on the ship were Julias Augustus Albrecht, Maria Elizabeth Albrecht, and Henry Vinsalous (Wenceslaus) "Allbrink." This may not be Albrecht the piano maker, as his obituary in 1848 described him as "for seven years a resident of Montgomery township, Montgomery county, for fifty-eight years, a citizen of Philadelphia," which would put his arrival circa 1783. *North American and United States Gazette,* Philadelphia, June 30, 1848, EAND. The obituary also may not be accurate, however, as tax lists show him living in Montgomery Township for only four years, although he owned the property for seven. Albrecht's marriage is in SM&Z, 4: 1011. Mary Albrecht's obituary gives her age as eighty-five when she died on July 7, 1837; *Poulson's American Daily Advertiser,* Philadelphia, July 12, 1837, EAND. This would put her birth in 1752. Mary was the daughter of John and Maria Barbara Knies; her younger sister, Elizabeth, was born on September 1, 1765, and baptized at First Reformed in Philadelphia on October 20, 1765; FR, 1: 43. On June 1, 1774, John and Barbara Knies were the sponsors at the baptism of Andrew, son of John and Mary/Maria Fuchs, at First Reformed; FR, 1: 142. Elizabeth Knies married Jacob Diehl/Deal on April 22, 1787, at First Reformed; FR 2: 74. In 1788 Charles and Mary Albrecht were the sponsors at the baptism of Jacob and Elizabeth's daughter, Maria; FR 2: 71. In 1793 "Carl Albrecht and Maria" were the sponsors for Jacob and Elizabeth's son, named Carl; FR, 2: 120. Will of John Fox, written June 31, 1779, proved May 2, 1780. Inventory of John Fox, taken May 17, 1780, Philadelphia will book 1780, no. 282, Downs Collection, Winterthur Library. John Fox names his children, John and Mary Fox, in his will and also names his wife Mary "and her Father John Knies" as executors; the witnesses were Charles Snyder and Michael Knies. John and Mary Fox probably died young, as no further record of them is known. Apparently Charles and Mary retained ownership of John Fox's three-storey brick house and lot at 41 North Fourth Street, as it was not advertised for sale until May 1797, when Charles also asked those with claims against John Fox's estate to send him their accounts. *Philadelphia Gazette & Universal Daily Advertiser,* May 24, 1797, EAND. The ad notes that the house had been rented in October 1796.

47. Will of Jacob Deal, written September 29, 1808, proven September 25, 1815, Philadelphia county will book 1815, no. 113, Downs Collection, Winterthur Library. The will notes that Jacob was a storekeeper in Kensington and names his wife, Elizabeth, and eight children: Mary, wife of Joshua Baker, Michael, Charles, John, Simon, Peter, Anna, and Susannah. Strassburger and Hinke, *Pennsylvania German Pioneers,* 3: 52. George Albrecht bequeathed money to his brother Henry and money paid to Charles for their siblings Philip, Jacob, Elizabeth, and Margaret in Germany. Henry Albrecht (ca. 1763–ca. 1833) immigrated in 1804 on the

Rebecca together with his wife, Margaret (d. 1837), and children Daniel (1791–1878) and Margaret (b. 1792). According to Daniel's naturalization papers, he was a native of Württemberg. They may have lived in Philadelphia with Charles but then moved to Upper Milford Township, Northampton (now Lehigh) County, Pennsylvania, where they lived until 1828. In that year Daniel Albrecht purchased a farm in Hilltown Township, Bucks County, from his uncle Charles, with the stipulation that he provide for his parents. Philip Albrecht's naturalization papers identify him as coming from "Creutznach" (Bad Kreuznach), a city along the Rhine in the Palatinate; he was the son of either Jacob or Philip Albrecht, who remained in Germany. Carolina Scheib (1792–1869) was the daughter of Charles Albrecht's sister, Elizabeth; Carolina married Henry Scheib (1790–1859) and had three children: Cassimer, William, and Carolina. Henry and Carolina Scheib are buried at the Hinnershitz (Good Shepherd) Church in Tuckerton, Muhlenberg Township, Berks County. A marriage record for Heinrich Scheib and Carolina Eilers in 1812 in Odernheim, in the Palatinate, is known, also a birth record for Heinrich Scheib, son of Johann Casimir Scheib and Maria Angelica Weber, born 1790, in "Odernheim, Pfalz, Bayern." Cassimer Scheib (1814–1882) lived in Alsace (now part of Muhlenberg Township) and William Scheib (1820–1899) in Ontelaunee Township, near the town of Hamburg, Berks County. William immigrated to America in 1840 via New York. Many of these relationships are detailed in Charles Albrecht's will, written June 20, 1844, proved July 14, 1848, Montgomery County will book 8, p. 607. With thanks to Gary Albright for his help with the Albrecht/Albright genealogy.

48. Twelve Albrecht pianos are listed in Clinkscale, *Makers of the Piano*, pp. 3–5; those and other examples are in the online database at www.earlypianos.org. At least twenty-one of Albrecht's pianos survive, including four at the National Museum of American History, Smithsonian Institution (one is serial no. 21), for which see Helen R. Hollis, *Pianos in the Smithsonian Institution* (Washington, D.C.: Smithsonian Institution Press, 1973), fig. 15; also C. Malcolm Watkins, "American Pianos of the Federal Period in the United States National Museum," *Antiques* 59, no. 1 (January 1951): 59; and one each at the Blennerhassett Historical Foundation, Charleston Museum, and Colonial Williamsburg (serial no. 166; acc. no. 2004-20); see John R. Watson, *Changing Keys: Keyboard Instruments for America, 1700–1830* (Williamsburg, Va.: Colonial Williamsburg Foundation, 2013), p. 62; Independence National Historic Park, see *Treasures of Independence: Independence National Historical Park and Its Collections*, edited by John C. Milley (New York: Main Street Press, 1980), p. 146; Philadelphia History Museum (formerly at the Historical Society of Pennsylvania); Philadelphia Museum of Art (acc. no. 1909-361); Metropolitan Museum of Art (serial no. 24; acc. no. 89.2.185), see Laurence Libin, *American Musical Instruments in The Metropolitan Museum of Art* (New York: Metropolitan Museum of Art, 1985), pp. 163–65; The Speaker's House; Vassar College Department of Music; State Museum of Pennsylvania (on loan to the Bradford House Historical Association, acc. no. 77.195.4); University of South Dakota–National Music Museum; and six or more in private collections (including serial no. 93, which is dated 1798). One Albrecht piano was previously in the collection of the Old Barracks Museum but was deaccessioned and sold at Alderfer's, Hatfield, Pa., September 29, 1994, lot 318. George Bickham, *The Universal Penman* (London, 1743; reprint, Mineola, N.Y.: Dover Publications, 1941), pl. 210. The piano at the Charleston Museum was advertised by Ginsburg and Levy in *Antiques* 75, no. 3 (March 1959): 229. Another was advertised by David Stockwell in *Antiques* 91, no. 6 (June 1967): 671. The Taws piano is in the collection of the Daughters of the American Revolution Museum, Washington, D.C.

49. Watson, *Changing Keys*, p. 62. At least seven Albrecht nameboards with painted floral swags are known, including two at the Smithsonian and one each at Colonial Williamsburg, Independence National Historic Park, The Metropolitan Museum of Art, Philadelphia Museum of Art, and The Speaker's House. The two pianos with long flowering vines include one in the Department of Music at Vassar College, inscribed "CHA^S ALBRECHT / Maker / PHILADELPHIA"; the other is inscribed "CHA^S ALBRECHT / Philadelphia" and was sold at Christie's, New York, January 21, 2011, lot 261 (fig. 101).

50. The Albrecht piano signed by Charles Deal was sold at Freeman's, Philadelphia, April 14, 2008, lot 350; it is also illustrated in *American Antiques from Israel Sack Collection*, vol. 6 (Washington, D.C.: Highland House Publishers, 1979), pp. 1618–19. With thanks to the Harpsichord Clearing House of Rehoboth, Massachusetts, and Dale Munschy for sharing information and photographs of the inscriptions inside this piano. Deal's letter to Law is cited in Charles H. Kaufman, *Music in New Jersey, 1655–1860: A Study of Musical Activity and Musicians in New*

Jersey from Its First Settlement to the Civil War (Rutherford, N.J.: Fairleigh Dickinson University Press, 1981), p. 126.

51. Information about Albrecht's piano actions is based on Clinkscale, *Makers of the Piano*, pp. 3–5; Watson, *Changing Keys*, pp. 62, 118; and Libin, *American Musical Instruments*, p. 164.

52. Watson, *Changing Keys*, pp. 63, 118; see also Laurence Libin, "John Huber Revisited," *AMIS Journal* 20 (1994): 73–83; Laurence Libin, "John Huber's Pianos in Context," *AMIS Journal* 19 (1993): 5–37.

53. *Dunlap's American Daily Advertiser*, Philadelphia, March 19, 1791, and January 28, 1792, EAND. *Claypoole's, American Daily Advertiser*, Philadelphia, March 29, 1796, EAND. The Vincent Township property included a stone house of 40 by 28 feet, log house, stone spring house, and stone-and-log barn of 60 by 23 feet, together with two fruit orchards; *Claypoole's American Daily Advertiser*, Philadelphia, February 4, 1797, EAND. Deed, Charles and Mary Albrecht to George Heebner (Hubener/Hübner), Chester County deed book I-3, 57: 139–40, Chester County Archives, West Chester, Pa. *Philadelphia Gazette & Universal Daily Advertiser*, November 23, 1797, EAND. *Federal Gazette & Baltimore Daily Advertiser*, Baltimore, August 3, 1798. Weidman, *Furniture in Maryland*, pp. 89, 265. *The New Baltimore Directory, and Annual Register, for 1800 and 1801* (Baltimore: Warner & Hanna, 1800).

54. Ancestry.com. *Philadelphia, 1789–1880 Naturalization Records* (database online); from P. William Filby, ed., *Philadelphia Naturalization Records* (Detroit: Gale Research Co., 1982). *Philadelphia Gazette & Universal Daily Advertiser*, November 26, 1799, March 6, 1800, October 22, 1800, and May 6, 1802, EAND. *Poulson's American Daily Advertiser*, Philadelphia, February 4, 1803, EAND. Daybook of Peter Muhlenberg, private collection. It is likely the "forte piano" that Peter bequeathed to his daughter Hetty in his will of 1807 together with his silver plate, a set of mahogany chairs ("six common & two arm chairs"), a pair of large looking glasses, a mahogany table, and two new bureaus; will of Peter Muhlenberg, written July 18, 1807, proved October 6, 1807, Philadelphia will book 1807, no. 104, Downs Collection, Winterthur Library. Hetty apparently did not want the piano, as a "well toned Forte Piano" was advertised in the auction notice of Peter Muhlenberg's estate; *Poulson's American Daily Advertiser*, Philadelphia, October 15, 1807, EAND. The property advertisement was in *Der Readinger Adler*, Reading, Pa., December 1, 1807, EAND.

55. *Poulson's American Daily Advertiser*, Philadelphia, January 25, 1813, and October 27, 1813, EAND. The term "organised" refers to a combination piano-organ that enjoyed only brief popularity in England and America; Libin, *American Musical Instruments*, p. 166. Albrecht bought the Montgomery Township property in 1841 but is listed in the Philadelphia city directories until 1844. The Greek revival house on the farm still stands and is now the rectory of the Mary, Mother of the Redeemer Catholic Church in Montgomeryville. Charles also owned land in Hilltown Township, Bucks County, which he sold in 1828 to his nephew Daniel, son of Henry. *North American and United States Gazette*, Philadelphia, June 30, 1848, EAND. It is unknown whom Charles Albrecht's sister, Elizabeth, married. On her daughter Carolina (1792–1869), who married Henry Scheib (1790–1859), see note 47 above. Will of Charles Albrecht, written June 20, 1844, proved July 14, 1848, Montgomery County will book 8, p. 607.

56. Hunter Dickinson Farish, ed., *Journal and Letters of Philip Vickers Fithian: A Plantation Tutor of the Old Dominion, 1773–1774* (Charlottesville: University Press of Virginia, 1968), pp. 22, 26, 30, 41, 55, 66, 69. Washington's order from Dodd is cited in Watkins, "American Pianos of the Federal Period," 60. In 1793 Washington also purchased a harpsichord from London; see Carol Borchert Cadou, *The George Washington Collection: Fine and Decorative Arts at Mount Vernon* (Manchester, Vt.: Hudson Hills Press, 2006), pp. 14, 16. Ethel Armes, comp. and ed., *Nancy Shippen: Her Journal Book* (Philadelphia: J. B. Lippincott Co., 1935), p. 283. On the seminary, see Smith, *Music, Women, and Pianos*, esp. p. 63. William C. Reichel and William H. Bigler, *A History of the Moravian Seminary for Young Ladies, at Bethlehem, Pa. with a Catalogue of Its Pupils, 1785–1870* (Bethlehem, Pa.: the Seminary, 1901), pp. 344–45. Their cousin Elizabeth Hiester, daughter of Gabriel Hiester of Reading, also appears to have attended in 1791; it is also possible that the Elizabeth Hiester who attended was their older sister, as her husband is identified as Levi Pawling, who married Elizabeth Hiester, daughter of Joseph Hiester, not Gabriel. The 1787 letter is quoted in Lou Carol Fix, "The Organ in Moravian Church Music," in Knouse, ed., *Music of the Moravian Church in America*, p. 148.

57. Inventory of Frederick Muhlenberg, taken June 18, 1801, Lancaster, Pa., Lancaster County Historical Society. The Brearley piano is in the collection of Independence National Historical Park; it is thought to have descended from Catherine Naylor Brearley to her daugh-

ter Alice Naylor Brearley; Alice married a Mr. Molton and moved to Germantown, Pa.; she gave the piano to her daughter Alice Naylor Molton (Mrs. John Earle), later of Danville, Virginia, and by 1966 it entered the collection of Independence National Historic Park. The Lord/Blennerhassett piano is said to have been taken to Marietta by Colonel Abner Lord and was used at Blennerhassett's mansion; it then passed to Nathaniel Gates, secretary to Blennerhassett, and was moved to Gallipolis in 1820. It was then owned by General and Mrs. Margaret Newsom of Marietta, Ohio; see *Gallipolis Bulletin*, March 1889. This piano then became the property of the Ohio Historical Society's Our House Museum in Gallipolis, Ohio, and was returned in 1999 via long-term loan to the Blennerhassett mansion. With thanks to Ray Swick for this information. The Dieffenbach piano was formerly in the collection of Mr. and Mrs. Joseph Wiederspohn and is illustrated in *Antiques* 95, no. 6 (June 1969): 835. As of 1974 it was in a private collection in South Carolina. On the Dieffenbachs, see Brunner, *That Ingenious Business*, pp. 109–14.

58. *Federal Gazette*, Philadelphia, November 6, 1790, EAND. *Dunlap's American Daily Advertiser*, Philadelphia, February 3, 1792, EAND. *Aurora General Advertiser*, Philadelphia, March 27, 1799, EAND. *Poulson's Daily Advertiser*, Philadelphia, September 24, 1813, EAND.

59. *Marietta Times*, February 14, 1889; Clarence M. Burton, *History of Detroit, 1780 to 1850* (Detroit, 1917), p. 357. The Butler piano is in the collection of the Historical Society of Western Pennsylvania. The Henley Chapman piano is in the collection of the Daughters of the American Revolution Museum, Washington, D.C.; for an illustration, see *Antiques* (April 1976): 756, fig. 16. Brunner, *That Ingenious Business*, p. 87. Biographical information about Taws is from Edward Taws Jr. and Helen Taws, *Charles Taws, ca. 1743–1836: Musical Instrument Maker, His Career, His Progeny, and Some of His Descendants* (Philadelphia: the authors, 1986), pp. 1–9.

60. *Philadelphia Gazette*, January 17, 1794, EAND. Laurence Libin, "Music-Related Commerce in Some Moravian Accounts," in Traupman-Carr, ed., *David Tannenberg and the Organs of the Moravians*, pp. 92–93; see also Deborah Dependahl Waters, "Delaware Furniture, 1740–1890," *Antiques* 127, no. 5 (May 1985): 1149. See also Charles G. Dorman, "Delaware Cabinetmakers and Allied Artisans, 1655–1855," *Delaware History* 9, no. 2 (October 1960): 212–13. *Aurora*, Philadelphia, March 24, 1812, quoted in Mann, "Piano Making," p. 184. On Thomas Loud Evenden, see Libin, *American Musical Instruments*, pp. 177–80. Pianos made by C.F.L. Albrecht include both upright and square models. Pianos continued to be made after his death under the company name Charles Albrecht, which was acquired by the Blasius & Sons piano company of Philadelphia in 1887 and continued into the 1920s; see Venable, "Philadelphia Biedermeier," pp. 238–50. On Geib and Steinweg/Steinway, see Libin, *American Musical Instruments*, pp. 169–73, 186–88. For piano production in 1829, see J. Leander Bishop, *A History of American Manufactures from 1608 to 1860*, 3 vols. (Philadelphia: Edward Young and Co., 1866), 2: 339.

61. Thomas R. Ryan, ed., *The Worlds of Jacob Eichholtz: Portrait Painter of the Early Republic* (Lancaster, Pa.: Lancaster County Historical Society, 2003), pp. 39, 88. One Haberacker piano dating circa 1820 is in the collection of the National Museum of American History, acc. no. 61285; it has six legs and a nameboard cartouche resembling the one in fig. 117. Three earlier pianos are known: one owned by Historic RittenhouseTown; one in a private collection; and one formerly in the collection of George Horace Lorimer that was sold at Sotheby's, New York, March 29–31 and April 1, 1944, lot 812. The whereabouts of the ex-Lorimer piano are unknown, but it does not appear to be either of the other two. These designs were especially popular on Baltimore painted furniture; see William Voss Elder III, *Baltimore Painted Furniture 1800–1840* (Baltimore, Md.: Baltimore Museum of Art, 1972), esp. pp. 61, 75–76. On the neoclassical tradition in the decorative arts, see Wendy A. Cooper, *Classical Taste in America, 1800–1840* (Baltimore, Md.: Baltimore Museum of Art, 1993).

62. Some sources claim the Haberacker piano was made for famed clockmaker and scientist David Rittenhouse in 1794; the same is said of a piano in a private collection, made by Charles Taws, that is dated 1794 on the nameboard. It is unlikely that David Rittenhouse would have owned a Reading- rather than a Philadelphia-made piano, but Haberacker's birth in 1780 makes it clear that he did not make this piano in 1794 and thus the Taws one is much more likely to have been David Rittenhouse's. The Haberacker piano descended in a branch of the Rittenhouse family that from 1833 to 1838 lived in Pottstown, Montgomery County—about eighteen miles southeast of Reading—which is likely when it came into their possession. According to the donor, Mrs. Theodore H. Steuber of Dallas, Texas, the piano was taken from

Philadelphia to Baltimore by Charles Rittenhouse, son of Nicholas Rittenhouse, in 1832. However, Charles (b. 1808) did not marry until 1833; he lived in Pottstown until 1838, then Germantown and Wissahickon for ten years, before moving to Baltimore about 1848. Charles was also only distantly related to David Rittenhouse; he was the son of Nicholas Rittenhouse (1774–1859) of Roxborough, Pennsylvania; Nicholas was the son of Martin Rittenhouse (1747–ca. 1828), a cousin of clockmaker David Rittenhouse (1732–1796); see Daniel Kolb Cassel, *History of the Rittenhouse Family* (Germantown, Pa., 1894), p. 20. Charles Rittenhouse married Amelia van Buskirk in 1833; the piano predates their marriage by about twenty years and may have first been owned by the van Buskirk family or acquired in some other way. On the piano, see Mary Rittenhouse Schwartzentruber, "The Square Piano: A RittenhouseTown Treasure," *RittenhouseTown: A Journal of History* 3 (2006): 3–6; see also a report by Bernice Graeter-Reardon, March 2000, Historic RittenhouseTown file. Richard S. Machmer and Rosemarie B. Machmer, *Berks County Tall-Case Clocks, 1750 to 1850* (Reading, Pa.: Historical Society Press of Berks County, 1995), pp. 59, 71. On Bischoff, see Russell Earnest and Corinne Earnest, "Fraktur-Fest II: A Tribute to Richard S. Machmer," *Der Reggboge* 41, no. 2 (2007): 11–12; also Alfred L. Shoemaker, "Reading's First Artist, a Painter of Butterflies," *Historical Review of Berks County* 13, no. 3 (April 1948): 89–90. Many of the forms were printed by Jacob Schneider and Johann Ritter of reading and bear the imprint "Verfertigt von FB" or "prepared by F[rederick] B[ischoff]" at the bottom of the central heart. The certificates have varying styles of writing on them, suggesting that Bischoff decorated them but other scriveners filled them out. Bruno J. Palmer-Poroner, "The Establishment of Libraries in Reading," *Historical Review of Berks County* 6, no. 4 (1941): 101.

63. *Berks and Schuylkill Journal*, Reading, November 27, 1824, and January 31, 1829, EAND.

64. Quoted in Minardi, *Pastors & Patriots*, pp. 27–28, 58.

65. Caldwell, "Germanic Influences," p. 24. SM&Z, 5: 1096. *Independent Gazetteer*, Philadelphia, June 5, 1784, EAND. Venable, "Germanic Craftsmen," pp. 73–75.

Book Reviews

Jennifer L. Anderson. *Mahogany: The Costs of Luxury in Early America*. Cambridge, Mass.: Harvard University Press, 2012. Xiii + 398 pp.; bw illus., map, index. $35.00.

In her acknowledgments, Jennifer L. Anderson states, "I conceived this work very much as a gathering of diverse perspectives and methodologies, which I hope may illuminate each other in some intriguing and thought-provoking ways." Mission accomplished. Anderson's *Mahogany: The Costs of Luxury in Early America* is about mahogany in the same way that Mark Kurlansky's *Cod* is about seafood. Her title subject is merely an entrée into an industry whose mission of extracting trees has a ripple effect far beyond the sound of the woodcutter's ax. The associated information on colonial shipping, the pitfalls of buying logs sight unseen, the legal battles over what really constitutes "San Domingan" mahogany, the myth of technological decadence, the effect of veneers on social status, and why Jamaican and not Cuban was considered the best wood are some of the subjects associated with the vast business of the tropical hardwood trade covered in the book.

Despite this wide range of topics, Anderson resists the historian's pitfall of straying too far from the subject. The reader will not forget that this is a history of the tree and its journey from tropical forest to table. No matter how much fascinating material she turned up in her research (her fifty-nine pages of notes attest to the amount and diversity of raw data she reviewed), she does not forget that the mahogany trade is her subject. The impediments to getting mahogany logs from the forest to the wharves of colonial America were numerous and subject to not only the whims of nature but also the problems of managing a labor force far from the control of the lumber merchants. Logs got irretrievably stuck in muddy trails, sunk in rivers, washed out to sea on their way to waiting boats, and lost at sea on the way to port. The trade was a seasonal one based on the annual swelling of the rivers to carry them out, and a dry season could strand a merchant's inventory far from the coast. In a trade dependent largely on slave labor it was not unusual for the population of an entire lumber camp to flee into the jungle and take their chances in another colonial territory. One slaveholder stated in 1765 that no Bayman, "however well disposed he may consider his Negroes, can think of his property safe for a single night. It is but a Week ago, since a whole gang of about Twelve . . . deserted in a body to the Spaniards" (p. 169). In the Bay of Honduras there was a constant skirmish over boundaries and labor between the Spanish and English colonies, where society was made up of the colonial mahogany cutters and their enslaved labor force. Anderson paints a Wild West scenario in which the rule of law was marginal and sneaking across the colonial border and cutting on your neighbor's land was often a cause for dispute. Tropical disease took a toll, and some made a good living augmenting the slave labor force with new workers from other colonies or Africa. Anderson's well-documented chapter devoted solely to slave labor and the mahogany trade leaves no doubt that, as Charles Dickens would characterize it in referring to a mahogany table, "[its] retrospective mirror quality . . . [reveals] in the depth of its grain, through all its polish, the hue of the wretched slaves" (p. 296).

Apart from Anderson's chronological tracking of the source of the best mahoganies from Jamaica to Honduras and Cuba, she pays considerable attention to it as an indicator of social position. As an expensive commodity beginning in the seventeenth century in the colonies, it served the same purpose as today's Ferrari in a land of Fords. As the Industrial Revolution and steam power, to which she devotes an entire chapter, made the sawing and transport of mahogany easier and consequently cheaper, the ability of the middling classes to have mahogany furniture expanded dramatically. By 1830 in England, William Cobbet worried that this new consumption led to "inappropriate displays of indulgence and vanity" and that the "want of frugality in the middle and lower ranks," especially among women, would lead them to be "full of admiration for the trappings of the rich and of desire to be able to imitate them" (p. 280). Ah, mahogany the great destroyer of class boundaries . . . Anderson then uses her historian's ability to deduce the meaning of Cobbet's comment, which is that he is troubled about this because the owning of mahogany still matters as an indicator of class. If everyone can have it, how will we tell who's who?

Many interesting "diverse perspectives" make their way into *Mahogany*. Anderson discusses the word itself as used in society to refer to people of color. She finds an eighteenth-century reference to sitting "around the mahogany," meaning to have dinner in a genteel setting. In recounting Jane Austen's comparison of writing novels to ivory painting, Anderson uncharacteristically strays from the path as she describes painting "pale English faces" on a material of "dead elephants and slave labor" (pp. 295). I see her point, but I nearly had a big yawn in the process. More mahogany, please.

As *Mahogany* nears present times, I was prepared for some finger-pointing and hand-wringing about the state of the trade and the commercial destruction of the forests. This is undeniable, and as someone who has a daily and tangible relationship with this magical material, I was prepared to accept my part of the blame. And although by no means an excuse for current behavior, the realization that the resource is finite and does not exist solely for the creation of nice sideboards has been going on for quite some time. Anderson gives us this news in a nice "history repeats itself" sort of way.

In 1774 a Jamaican planter advised that trees should be left for "the beauty arising from them around the estate" (p. 231). Another paper published by the Royal Society in 1772 postulated that the air was purified by "the immense profusion of vegetables . . . inhaling and exhaling" (p. 231).

Edward Long, another eighteenth-century thinker, noted that Indians and slaves were fond of living among trees and seemed to suffer no ill effects from doing so and that "congregations of trees are, in their growing state, far more friendly than inimical in the alterations which they produce on our atmosphere" (p. 232). Sound familiar?

Mahogany throughout follows the ongoing attempts of arborists over the centuries to cultivate commercially viable mahogany trees and their continuing failure to do so. This, as I see it, is Anderson's morality play for us as consumers. Do we really know where the mahogany in the lumberyard (an early nineteenth-century innovation, where for the first time cabinetmakers could actually see the boards they were buying) is coming from? Much of it is poached and untraceable once it is out of the country of origin. The moral of the story is that you really can't make these big and disappearing trees anymore. You are holding a publication filled with images of mahogany furniture and the chances are pretty good that you've been a consumer of the resource. After reading Anderson's fascinating history of mahogany, my opinion as a cabinetmaker is that apart from stopping the harvesting altogether, we should at least be charged a lot more for it.

Allan Breed
Allan Breed, Inc., South Berwick, Maine

Donald L. Fennimore and Frank L. Hohmann III. *Stretch: America's First Family of Clockmakers*. Winterthur, Del.: Winterthur Museum and Hohmann Holdings LLC, 2013. 343 pp.; 457 color illus., catalogue, 8 appendixes, bibliography, index. $75.00.

Great museum acquisitions sometimes have the ability to transform collections and to spark research projects and intellectual endeavors. Such is the case with the Winterthur Museum's purchase in 2004 of an extraordinary tall-case clock by Philadelphia clockmaker Peter Stretch (1670–1748). Heralded as a masterwork by Stretch, the clock set a record auction price, more than $1.68 million, for both this maker and a colonial American tall-case clock. The successful purchase by Winterthur and subsequent research on the clock brought together Winterthur's curator emeritus of metalwork Donald L. Fennimore and well-known clock collector and Winterthur trustee Frank L. Hohmann III for the first book-length treatment of Peter Stretch and his family, titled *Stretch: America's First Family of Clockmakers*. In it they position this group of craftsmen as not only worthy of careful study but also among the most accomplished and successful of American clockmakers in the early eighteenth century. "Measured against the norm," the authors state, the Stretches' most technically sophisticated clocks "appear to be singular for their time" (p. 91). Even among his contemporaries, Peter Stretch was considered the "most eminent" clockmaker in Philadelphia of his generation (p. 58).

Laudatory in tone and exhaustive in research, *Stretch* fits within a long line of publications on clockmaking in North America, which includes Hohmann's other major recent publication, *Timeless: Masterpiece American Brass*

Dial Clocks (2009). *Stretch* shares with *Timeless* a similar weighty catalogue format, boasting lavish, quite frankly stunning large-format color photographs, with introductory essays and concise catalogue entries. It adds to the monographic studies on American clockmakers, of which there are relatively few, beginning with the classic, filiopietistic *Simon Willard and His Clocks* (1911) by grandson John Ware Willard. This publication also calls to mind other recently published single-maker (or, rather, one should say, single-shop-tradition) studies, such as the Metropolitan Museum of Art's *John Townsend: Newport Cabinetmaker* (2005) by Morrison H. Heckscher and *Duncan Phyfe: Master Cabinetmaker of New York* (2011) by Peter M. Kenny and the late Michael K. Brown, both of which accompanied exhibitions. There are few household names in the field of colonial American decorative arts, but perhaps this publication will launch a new name into the canon. Like the Townsends of Newport, the Stretches were devout Quakers, who parlayed tight-knit familial and communal connections into commercial and political success. This Quaker community, as the authors would discover, would be key in establishing Stretch, an outsider in Philadelphia who emigrated from England, quickly within the highest political and mercantile circles in the city.

Peter Stretch was born in Harpers Gate, Staffordshire, England, and trained as a clockmaker with his older brother Samuel in Leek, later taking over his clockmaking business there around 1692. Fennimore and Hohmann include in their study a lantern, or wall-mounted, clock made by Stretch during this period, a fascinating comparison with the clocks he made in Philadelphia, where elite patrons generally preferred the taller, wood-encased, brass dial, 30-hour or 8-day clocks. Already an accomplished clockmaker in England, Stretch moved to Philadelphia with his family in 1703. His success in Philadelphia, aided by his active membership in the Friends Meeting and his election to the Common Council in 1708 (an important position he held in city politics until 1746), is duly evidenced by the 62 remarkable American clocks that bear his name catalogued in this book. The authors include an additional 22 clocks inscribed with the names of two of his sons—William and Thomas—who followed their father in the business. One marked Peter Stretch clock (cat. 12) bears the inscription "DS N 1" engraved on the front plate—evidently the first clock made by another son, Daniel Stretch, for his proud father, likely at the end of his apprenticeship circa 1714. The authors identified a total of 133 surviving clocks made by various members of the family in the eighteenth century, of which they published 84 in public and private collections that they had the opportunity to study.

The catalogue entries, which include basic information on the clock movements and cases and a short commentary on historical relevance, are further enlivened and contextualized by the essay "Stretch Clocks and the Philadelphia Clockmaking Community before 1750." This essay nicely situates the Stretch shop, which operated out of a 12-by-12-foot space in a three-storey brick house on the corner of Second and Chestnut Streets in Philadelphia, within the larger community of allied craftsmen in the city. One of those craftsmen was John Head, an English émigré furniture maker who created many of the elaborately carved wooden cases for Stretch and his sons. The authors include reproductions of pages from Head's account book that document charges for dozens of clock cases over a period of nearly two decades. In most instances, Head charged Stretch directly for the cases and Stretch delivered the final assembled product to his customers, presumably at retail prices. Stretch also undoubtedly was associated with Philadelphia carver Samuel Harding, whose distinctive carving style appears on the mahogany case of the Winterthur clock, including a rare instance of a coat of arms, those of the Plumstead family of Philadelphia, carved into the arch in the pediment (cat. 60). Truth be told, this is not a book about the casework, which often takes a backseat to detailed discussions of clock mechanics and biographical information. Furniture aficionados may wish for more detail about the cases, which are clearly so integral to the tall-case clock form; however, the authors do include excellent photographs of the cases, when original, and a discussion of noteworthy details, which make this book in the end a must for furniture scholars and collectors.

Further biographical detail on the Stretch family appears in the back matter of the book, as does a list of clock owners in Philadelphia (1682–1750) and a comprehensive checklist of all the known Stretch clocks in existence. The eight appendixes feature detailed comparative photographs of Stretch clockworks and representative signature plates bearing the names of the Stretch family of clockmakers. For those readers seeking even more information, the authors have generously made available in electronic form a further eight hundred images related to clocks in the book under the title "Photographic Essay Addendum to Stretch: America's First Family of Clockmakers." This can be obtained through the Decorative Arts Photographic Collection (DAPC) at Winterthur or by contacting the authors.

For the general reader, the first chapter of the book, "Time and Telling Time in Early Philadelphia," is especially enlightening and informative. In it we learn about the history of time-telling devices—sundials, watches, and clocks—during the seventeenth and eighteenth centuries in the city and the centrality of clocks in the life of the growing metropolis. Peter Stretch was hired by the city in the 1710s to maintain the town clock, which he continued to do until the 1740s, keeping the clock tolling the hour while Philadelphians went about their daily business. His son Thomas fulfilled a commission in 1753 for its replacement, a monumental architectural clock that stood like an oversize tall-case clock in rusticated wood attached to the side of the State House (Liberty Hall), seen in Thomas Birch's famous image of 1800 (fig. 2.14).

The publication of major studies of this nature, even those as exhaustive as this one, has a way of bringing additional objects and information out of the woodwork. One hopes this is also the case with this impressive book, as several important questions about Stretch's workshop and business practices, his professional relationships with other craftsmen in Philadelphia, and the role of his children and apprentices remain unanswered. Yet, the authors have done a commendable job of teasing out the historical record whenever possible and, when information was not at hand, of building a logical case with all the available evidence. What they have produced is a notable achievement documenting the history of, if not America's "first" family of clockmakers, then certainly the first in their class.

Dennis Carr

Museum of Fine Arts, Boston

David Nasby. *The Art of Thomas Nisbet, Master Cabinetmaker*. Guelph, Ont.: Macdonald Stewart Art Centre, 2012. 64 pp.; numerous color and bw illus.; glossary; bibliography. $15.00.

The Art of Thomas Nisbet, Master Cabinetmaker, featuring elegant classical revival furniture on its cover, rightly piques one's curiosity. To those interested in early nineteenth-century American cabinetmakers and their work, Nisbet's furniture looks familiar. Born and trained in Scotland, Thomas Nisbet (ca. 1777–1850) emigrated from Glasgow in 1812 to Saint John, New Brunswick. One of early Canada's best-known cabinetmakers, Nisbet is sometimes referred to as the "Duncan Phyfe of New Brunswick."

This catalogue accompanied a traveling exhibition that began in October 2011 at Maus Park Antiques in Paris, Ontario, moved to the Macdonald Stewart Art Centre in Guelph, Ontario, where it was on view from February 16 to April 22, 2012, and closed on August 10, 2012, following installations in Nisbet's home province at Government House in Fredericton, New Brunswick's capital, and the Kings Landing Historical Settlement in Prince William. Additional examples of Nisbet's furniture—not included in this volume—were drawn from public and private local collections for the last two venues. This small volume is handsomely designed but, unfortunately, its not-so-perfect binding has not stood up to this reviewer's steady use.

The title, *The Art of Thomas Nisbet, Master Cabinetmaker*, leads the reader to think she or he had discovered a large study documenting this important artisan's output. The reader will be disappointed. Instead, David Nasby highlights twenty-two examples of furniture labeled or attributed to Nisbet, featuring the private collection of William and Wynn Bensen, collectors of nineteenth-century furniture made in eastern Canada and sponsors of this exhibition and publication project. Six additional objects belong to the Kings Landing Historical Settlement in Prince William, a re-created village west of Fredericton. A short introduction by Judith Nasby, the director and curator of the Macdonald Stewart Art Centre, describes the history of the exhibition project and includes her acknowledgments.

In his essay "The Furniture of Thomas Nisbet," David Nasby, a former museum director now working as a decorative arts curator, limits the cabinetmaker's biography in favor of a general discussion of the design elements and the materials most often found in furniture labeled by or attributed to Nisbet. As a result, to gain a better understanding of Nisbet's life and output, readers must turn to the sources listed in the bibliography, some of which are difficult to find. While Nasby defines provenance and notes its importance to the study of New Brunswick furniture, he then tells us it will "not [be] addressed for the furniture under discussion in this essay" (p. 10). This is unfortunate because it limits one's understanding of the relative historical importance of the objects included here. He notes that "records of sale do exist for furnishings supplied by Nisbet for Government House in Fredericton" but does not discuss or illustrate them even, though they are, arguably, some of the finest examples of Nisbet's work. For example, for the new council chamber of 1840–1841, Nisbet designed armchairs based on plate 59 of Thomas Hope's *Household Furniture and Interior Decoration* (1807). Did he know of Thomas Constantine & Company's related designs for the United States Capitol, commissioned more than twenty years earlier? What resonance did Hope's classical designs have for Nisbet and his fellow New Brunswick citizens a third of a century after they were first published? For the selected catalogue entries, where not labeled, the furniture is "attributed to the workshop," "from the workshop," or has a "possible attribution to the workshop of Thomas Nisbet," but the distinctions between these definitions are not clear (pp. 23, 25, 27).

In the catalogue section, Nasby discusses twenty-two objects: nine tables (four card, one dining, two work, one center, and one sofa table), three sofas, one recamier, three side chairs, four chests of drawers, and two bureau secretaries (one with a bookcase). Each object is illustrated in color with an overall view and one or more details. Eight objects (five tables and three case forms) bear paper labels dating before 1834, when he took his son, Thomas Jr., as a partner and changed the firm's name to Thomas Nisbet & Son. Nisbet used imported mahogany and native birch, maple, and pine. A handy list of materials compiled with an object's catalogue data would have been preferable to making the reader scan the narrative for this information. The entries provide full descriptions of the "what" of the furniture design and the selection and placement of materials, but the "how" is missing. Nasby acknowledges the importance of "the careful measurement of labelled pieces . . . to compile benchmarks of 'common practice' that were used by the maker" (pp. 10–11), but this information is not discussed in the entries. Given Nisbet's large output, even a brief comparison of how the three labeled chests were constructed would have been instructive.

In Saint John, Nisbet's large furniture enterprise spanned the thirty-five years from 1813 to 1848. As a master cabinetmaker, he managed a shop full of apprentices, journeymen, joiners, turners, and carvers as well as a wareroom for clients. In his upholstery line, he offered "sophas and sopha beds" as well as bed and window curtains, imported fashionable textiles, cornices, and hardware. After his son joined his thriving furniture business in 1834, Nisbet diversified, leading the Saint John Hotel Company as president from 1837 to 1849 and investing in the Saint John Mechanic's Whaling Fishing Company from 1835 until his death in 1850.

Like Duncan Phyfe and many cabinetmakers in Great Britain, Canada, and the eastern seaboard of the United States, Nisbet drew inspiration from the pattern books of Thomas Sheraton and Thomas Hope, producing sophisticated furniture in the English neoclassical and Regency styles. Because Nisbet used paper labels, a body of his work has been readily identified. Hallmarks of his furniture include fine craftsmanship, high-quality materials, and decoration drawn from classical ornament with acanthus leaves, urns, reeded and rope-turned columns, animal legs and paws, dolphins, and Roman pinecones in regular use. Even with its limited scope, this volume reveals Nisbet's ability to meet the demands of his sophisticated Saint John clients, citizens of British North America's first incorporated city of 1785. When one considers the history and cultural development of New Brunswick, it is no surprise to find Nisbet, a well-trained Scottish émigré cabinetmaker, building furniture that looks as stylish as that made in major cities of the early American republic.

The links between New Brunswick and the eastern seaboard of the United States began when loyalists fled Connecticut, New York, Maryland, and other colonies at the end of the American Revolution and settled in Saint John. By the opening years of the nineteenth century, the rapid economic development of Saint John and the province of New Brunswick was under way. These Saint John citizens prospered in this large, ice-free harbor, continuing to pursue the successful enterprises as they had in their former homes in the mid-Atlantic and New England states: shipping, shipbuilding, lumbering, and transatlantic and West Indies trade. Also deserving consideration are the networks of trade and family that connected Saint John, removed as it seems on the north shore of the Bay of Fundy, to a vigorous transatlantic world.

Nisbet is regarded within and beyond the borders of New Brunswick as an exceptional and enduring cabinetmaker. He was, however, not the only skilled furniture maker and upholsterer in Saint John. The labeled pieces of Daniel Green, for example, reveal that he worked in the same style with the same materials as Nisbet. The fact that Nisbet offered "piece work" by his turners and carvers makes it even more difficult to ascribe furniture only to Nisbet. Knowing more about Nisbet's shop, practices, competitors, and clients would shed new, valuable light on his business networks, relationships with other artisans both in New Brunswick and abroad, the transmission of styles, and expectations of his consumers.

As an exhibition catalogue, *The Art of Thomas Nisbet, Master Cabinetmaker* presents a limited view of this accomplished artisan's life and work. It does, however, reveal that Nisbet deserves the scholarly effort required to compile his biography and documented furniture into one well-researched and produced volume. A more extensive investigation of furniture documented to Nisbet through labels, invoices, and other primary sources would ground the study in the objects he is known to have made rather than a larger group featuring numerous superficial similarities. This worthwhile future endeavor would contribute to a deeper understanding of early regional furniture in North America, including Canada, our friend to the north and east.

Laura Fecych Sprague
Bowdoin College Museum of Art

Lonn Taylor and David B. Warren. *Texas Furniture: The Cabinetmakers and Their Work, 1840–1880*. 1975. Vol. 1. Rev. ed. Austin: University of Texas Press, 2012. xi + 378 pp.; numerous bw and color illus., checklist of Texas cabinetmakers, appendix, glossary, bibliography, index. $60.00.

Lonn Taylor and David B. Warren, with a foreword by Don Carleton. *Texas Furniture: The Cabinetmakers and Their Work, 1840–1880*. Vol. 2. Austin: University of Texas Press, 2012. xi + 336 pp.; numerous color and bw illus., checklist of Texas cabinetmakers, glossary, bibliography, index. $65.00.

It is a cliché that "everything is bigger in Texas"—square miles, oil fields, barbeque, hair, hats, right-wing political extremism, and so on. That old saw applies to the new two-volume study of Texas furniture under review here, which contains some 736 pages, more than 350 illustrations, and weighs in at a hefty seven and a half pounds or so. It is a massive effort worthy of its subject's traditional reputation.

When Lonn Taylor and David B. Warren, inspired by the vision of Ima Hogg, compiled and published *Texas Furniture: The Cabinetmakers and Their Work, 1840–1880* in 1975, it was only the second book on the subject, following closely on the heels of the Witte Museum's *Early Texas Furniture and Decorative Arts*, issued in 1973. *Texas Furniture* gave us an in-depth look at the mid-nineteenth-century furniture produced in the Lone Star State, much of it in a Germanic fashion reflecting the second great wave of German immigrants to this country.

Now, thirty-seven years later, Taylor and Warren, with the assistance of the University of Texas Press and the university's Briscoe Center for American History, have done something unusual if not unprecedented in our field. They have reissued the 1975 volume in a revised format and have added a second volume of equal weight and depth to create a uniform, two-volume set that provides an encyclopedia of images and data that will be the standard source on the subject for at least another generation.

Volume 1 of the new set is essentially a reprint of the 1975 volume, which has long been out of print. Here, the contents are presented in an easier-to-use and -to-shelve vertical format, rather than the original horizontal design, and the black-and-white photographs of more than two hundred objects are larger. The revisions to the text consist of corrections and additions to the lengthy checklist of Texas cabinetmakers included as an appendix and cross-references to objects catalogued in the new volume 2.

More than 150 examples, derived from Taylor and Warren's ongoing research and new discoveries, are presented in volume 2, identical in format to the new volume 1 with the exception that this volume's objects are presented in color photographs. Each volume principally consists of a photo library of objects arranged by form into nine chapters: beds, wardrobes, chests of drawers, chairs, sofas, tables and stands, desks, cupboards, and safes (such as pie safes). (Volume 2 also contains a new section on miscellaneous objects.) Each section is preceded by a short introduction, written for the 1975 text and reprinted in both volumes here. The illustrated objects are identified as to maker, place, date, materials, dimensions, history, and current owner (although not necessarily updated for volume 1 objects), and are discussed in a short interpretative text. Each of the two new volumes contains the same list of some nine hundred Texas cabinetmakers and chairmakers, based largely on census records and other archival sources. At least one maker who made an object illustrated in the pictorial section, Henry Kuenemann, is not, somewhat inexplicably, included in the checklist. (This small oversight only came to my attention because the Museum of Fine Arts, Boston owns a large wardrobe of circa 1870 [1990.483] attributed to Heinrich Kuenemann II, and I was hoping to learn more about him.)

Two introductory chapters in volume 1 still remain the best overview of the regional nature of Texas furniture, covering "the coast and the hinterland" and the business and craft of cabinetmaking in the various areas at the time. Readers fresh to the subject, however, might find the new introduction to volume 2 (pp. 1–17) to be the best place to start navigating these books. There, the authors trace the evolution of collecting Texas furniture from the 1920s forward, highlighting the efforts of pioneer collectors over several generations to preserve the physical heritage of their state. From an art historical and material culture standpoint, they also discuss the dual Texas cabinetmaking traditions: the Anglo-American, based on immigration to Texas from the American South; and the Germanic, based on immigrants. German-born cabinetmakers were disproportionately represented in Texas, making up (for example) about one-third of the woodworking craftsmen in 1860 as opposed to a German-immigrant population of only about 6 percent. The Anglo-Texas furniture was largely in what the authors call a "Plain Grecian" (aka "pillar and scroll") style (p. 9), and objects in this tradition are more fully represented in volume 2. The Germans, in contrast, created furniture in the Biedermeier style that was, generally, more finely crafted and of higher-quality woods. Interestingly, although Spanish American and African American cultural traditions were significant in nineteenth-century Texas, the authors have been unable to locate any furniture by Hispanic or African American cabinetmakers (p. 11).

While the 1975 volume focused on the work of professional cabinetmakers, Taylor and Warren have added in volume 2 a number of works they classify as noncommercial furniture, such as a body of material by Christofer Friderich Carl Steinhagen (d. 1893), a wheelwright and wagon builder in Anderson, Texas, who made objects for his own family's use. The authors also bring to light in volume 2 additional examples of special-order marquetry furniture made as gifts or for display at state fairs and expositions. Much of the furniture they document is perhaps more reflective of a simple, sturdy way of life on the frontier, but some of the imposing case pieces, especially the wardrobes, safes, and cupboards, are also monumental objects that form a significant body of work worthy of consideration in any telling of the full story of American furniture from an aesthetic point of view.

Improved communication networks in the 1880s and onward, principally the extension of the railroad, largely brought to an end the small-shop, craft-based era of Texas furniture. Mass-market factory furniture from the North and East penetrated the local markets and provided an inexpensive option that overwhelmed the local craftsmen. As the authors note, "every piece of furniture illustrated and described in [these books] is the fossil of a conversation between craftsman and client, a conversation within a context that is gone forever" (2: 18). They are to be congratulated for their initial and ongoing, persistent efforts to recapture these conversations and to document this fascinating passage in American material life.

Gerald W. R. Ward
Museum of Fine Arts, Boston

Adam Bowett. *Woods in British Furniture-Making, 1400–1900: An Illustrated Historical Dictionary*. Kew, Eng.: Oblong Creative Ltd. in association with Royal Botanic Gardens, Kew, 2012. xxxiii + 360 pp.; numerous color illus., appendixes, bibliography, index of botanical names, index. $180.00.

In a number of articles and two books examining British furniture of the late seventeenth and early eighteenth centuries, Adam Bowett has brought welcome clarity and order to British furniture history. By clearly establishing navigable landmarks, Bowett is attempting a kind of hygiene very welcome to British furniture history that is also cleansing to the study of American furniture. Bowett's new book, *Woods in British Furniture-Making, 1400–1900: An Illustrated Historical Dictionary*, augments his previous work and surpasses it in effort, scope, and interpretative possibilities. This project was clearly dear to Bowett's heart, given the enormous amount of effort it required: much archival research, a prodigious number of field trips for personal examination of objects, the establishment of a multidisciplinary team including botanists from the Royal Gardens at Kew, and his journey to become proficient in the microanalysis of wood. *Woods in British Furniture-Making* documents the timber trade with its chronology of trade routes, colonial conquest and exploitation, and the availability of different species—sometimes leading fashion and sometimes following it pell-mell. It is a work of scholarship that will endure for centuries and that resonates with profound meaning for the study of American furniture.

Woods in British Furniture-Making starts with two introductory essays, the first an overview of timber and timber use in Britain that is the best thing ever written on the subject, clearly depicting how dependent British furniture makers were on imported wood and how the wood choices available were governed by colonial conquest and political alliances, import duties, bonuses, and treaties—themselves often subject to commercial pressures. The second essay is an overview of wood anatomy and identification written for a lay reader.

The body of the book, as suggested by the subtitle, is a list of entries on cabinet woods alphabetically arranged by common or trade name, first hardwoods and then softwoods. Four appendixes: a map of trade routes, a botanical family arrangement of the woods included, a geographic arrangement of the woods, and a photographic depiction of some of the woods (mostly from the collection at Kew) follow the body of the text. Latin botanical name and general information indexes conclude.

Even modern common names for woods are baffling and imprecise, and the addition of archaic names, often corruptions of words from many languages or based not on any wood name but on the port of shipping origin, results in the reader's occasional bewilderment. Bowett's experience as an archivist is evident in this possibly odd organizational choice. Most users of the book will probably be starting with an object and trying to comprehend it rather than starting with a period document and trying to understand the meaning of arcane wood names. A book of this type is not an ideal tool for trying to identify wood, and this book does not pretend to accomplish this. The Latin names for the trees harvested as wood are fully indexed and easily correlated to the common name headings but not listed in the headings unless they also are or were common names. A diligent reader will be able to locate the sometimes ephemeral common names associated with a known scientific name. The dictionary—or, perhaps more accurately, encyclopedia—format is not friendly to the casual general reader wishing to simply read the whole text in order. Since the entries reflect the frequently redundant and/or confusing names, sometimes for the same wood, some entries (for instance, for mahogany, madera, vinhatico, and canary wood) overlap and paraphrase one another to a degree unfortunate for through reading but essential for an alphabetic reference. The word "otiose" occurs twice in six pages; an editor of an essay might have insisted on "fruitless" for one instance, but, since each entry is a stand-alone piece, such a concern is irrelevant. Finding an editor, or editors, for the book must have been daunting. Copyediting a text with such diverse topics must have been difficult enough, but editing for content that includes botanic names and scientific terms, multiple foreign names often in pidgin or archaic versions, and art historical references is a task too complex for one content editor. A more widely versed editorial team would have been useful.

From a wood identification point of view the book is most important as a contextual tool. Bowett is not a trained wood identification scientist but a diligent and industrious amateur. If a professional anatomist were engaged for every sample, the book might be much more expensive, but it would be more accurate. The anatomic information will not aid the average reader to identify wood. Such a reader would learn that parenchyma and storied rays are anatomic structures useful in identifying wood genera and/or species, but it is unlikely that the reader would really understand what they are.

This reviewer consulted Harry Alden, Ph.D., of Alden Identification Services, about Bowett's wood identification assertions. Alden noted that he is very enthusiastic about Bowett's profound contribution to knowledge of the history of the timber trade but not pleased with Bowett's assertion, "wood identification is often a matter of educated guess work" (p. xxvi). It is true that wood anatomists compare microscopic samples to lists of salient keys that point them to a particular genus and sometimes species. These keys, especially for some tropical woods and uncommon species, may not take into account all the possible variations in a given genus or species; more minute or refined keys may one day be available. Also, as Bowett suggests, the salient features necessary to identify a wood may not be present in every sample available for examination. Veneer, for instance, may not be thick enough to contain an important identifying cell. Still, Bowett's contention that it is often guesswork is overly broad. A competent scientist will state what is known whether or not it is conclusive and merely allude to the possibilities if it is not. Microanalysis cannot specifically identify the white oak *Quercus alba*, the dominant eastern North American white group oak; it can identify only an oak of the white group—a group including oaks from all over the northern temperate world. Interpretation of style and date of the sample furniture source and timber trade information are rigors that should follow a completely dispassionate microanalysis and either could or could not reasonably point to *Quercus alba* as the likely white group oak candidate.

A number of technical errors of anatomic information scattered throughout the book were noticed by Dr. Alden and this reviewer. For example, *Swietenia mahogani* only occasionally has storied rays, although Bowett states that "most American mahogany" [that is, all three species] does (p. xxvii). It is this occasional feature that sometimes allows it to be distinguished from *S. macrophylla* and *S. humilis*, which do not have storied rays, a distinction Bowett states cannot reliably be done. The size of the early-wood pores of cherry (*Prunus*) are not significantly larger than the late-wood pores for the wood to be confidently called semi-ring porous, as Bowett does. Alder (*Alnus*) is native to the Americas as well as to Europe, something omitted in Bowett's range description of world alders, as is horse chestnut (*Aesculus*), with seven American species, although perhaps Bowett is asserting that only *A. hippocastanatum* was used in the British trade, something microanalysis cannot assert. "Spp." is the plural abbreviation for species and is not appropriate for describing a single unknown species of a known genus. So, unless the author is convinced that more than one unknown species of a known genus is present in an object—such as a case piece with both white and yellow group pine—the abbreviation for a single unknown species, "sp.," is the correct choice. Similarly, while "variety" and "family" are perfectly good words, they have specific botanical meanings to which Bowett does not adhere, for example, "the tupelo or gum family of North America comprises four species" (p. 239). Black gum and tupelo (*Nyssa*) are members of the family *Cornaceae* (dogwoods and their relatives) with more than 100 species, according to current taxonomy, which admittedly is a moving target. "There are 18 species and 7 varieties of ash native to North America"(p. 16). A variety of ash would be a reference to a horticultural selected clone or cultivar, the neologism for "cultivated variety," as in *Fraxinus americana* v. Autumn Blaze (the "v." stands for variety). Atlantic white cedar (*Chaemacyparis thyoides*) and northern white cedar (*Thuya occidentalis*) are certainly different species, as Bowett states (p. 278), but they further belong to different genera, and *Thuya occidentalis* can indeed be distinguished microscopically from its western relative *Thuya plicata*, as can butternuts from walnuts.

Many other examples of anatomic misinformation are present in *Woods in British Furniture-Making*, most of them very unimportant, but good copyediting by a competent botanist would easily overcome this minor flaw if the book gains another richly deserved edition. While creating a definitive taxonomic or anatomic reference was not really Bowett's goal, a book this important need not be tainted with misinformation. Readers attempting to learn more about tropical woods used for timber would be well served to consult *Tropical Timbers of the World* by Martin Chudnoff (1984) and *Present and Potential Commercial Timbers of the Caribbean* by Franklin R. Longwood (1962), both published by the U.S. Department of Agriculture and both missing from Bowett's bibliography.

The book is profusely illustrated, but many of the illustrations are not effective. The picture of the back of a white pine panel with red bricking (P5, p. 181) is intended to point out the ease of identification of white pine, even through the red stain, because of its prominent resin canals. The picture, however, is so small that the resin canals are hardly visible in the illustration even with magnification. One of the appendixes (4) is a series of photographs of historic samples of economically notable wood species, mostly from the Kew Gardens collection. Bowett is indebted to many at Kew, and that organization jointly published the book with Oblong Press, so it is entirely understandable that he wanted to publish this collection that no doubt figured strongly in the history of his study of wood. The resulting glossary, however, is not very effective; many of the samples are so discolored that they are useless as tools to recognize a wood. No one familiar with Brazilian or Indian rosewood (*Dalbergia nigra* and *Dalbergia latifolia*) would recognize those woods from the virtually black samples illustrated. The best use of photographs to depict the appearance of wood known to this reviewer remains *The Wood Book* by Klaus Ulrich Leistikow and Holger Thüs (2002), based on the work of Romeyn Beck Hough, employing large, clear pictures of transverse, tangential, and radial sections of the various species. *Woods of British Furniture-Making* is an expensive book and surely was expensive to produce. An online version of the book with illustrations that could be enlarged in high resolution would be a perfect adaptation of this fine work. Perhaps future scholars will be able to use the book in that format. The period illustrations, botanicals, graphs, maps, and tables all are quite clear in the book as it is.

Bowett is frank about clearing up previously published misinformation, some of it long and dearly held and useful to the trade, but in this work he is never sniping or disrespectful to previous authors even when they clearly could have known better. He also is very respectful of the conundrums and ambiguities of the subject and willing to fairly portray several sides of a disputed issue with grace and intellectual candor. The confusing and contradictory common names of some exotic woods as used in the literature can become baffling. Bowett's handling, for instance, of "horseflesh" and sabicu alone are worth the purchase price to this reviewer. We know by microanalysis when we encounter sabicu (*Lysiloma sabicu* or *L. sp.*), but we don't know for certain what "horseflesh" meant in the eighteenth-century wood trade. Alden identified a number of pieces of Boston furniture at Winterthur, most attributed to Benjamin Frothingham, as containing sabicu. Period shipping records indicate that "horseflesh" was shipped in some quantity to Philadelphia, but this reviewer knows of only one example of surviving sabicu Philadelphia furniture and that example does not strictly adhere to the anatomic keys for *Lysiloma sabicu*. Some entries are not as strong as others. The red cedar (*Juniperus*) entry overlooks the southern coastal American species *Juniperus salicicola*, which, while microscopically indistinguishable from *J. virginiana* or *bermudiana*, was probably the species most represented in the shipping map in the trade route glossary from Charleston, South Carolina, to England. It is the local *Juniperus* of the Charleston area and yields much better and clearer wood than its more northern cousin, and it was also shipped to northern American cities. Bowett's treatment of wainscot and deal—oak boards and softwood boards imported to England primarily from the Baltic, Germany, and Scandinavia—much surpasses anything previously published. The extensive entries on the major cabinet woods mahogany and walnut are exemplary.

Bowett has plowed through so many period documents researching this book that it is remarkable he has retained and organized them so thoroughly. He knows a gem when he finds one, as exemplified by the terse quotation he uses to end his entry on "walnut, satin," a onetime British trade name for the American red gum *Liquidamber styracifula*, "except for appearance, it possesses almost every bad quality which can be found in any wood." One can easily imagine woodworkers familiar with this unstable and uncooperative wood nodding in agreement. This statement coupled with the story of the fiasco in Whitehall in 1901, when red gum, in a confusion of common names with Australian gums, was used as street paving and lasted for about eight months before it was removed and lawsuits began, show Bowett's keen sense of the follies of human behavior when commerce is involved. He also is the first in what will no doubt be a long list of historians to employ his research in the interpretation of furniture history, as his entry on walnut demonstrates. Percy Macquoid's "Age of Mahogany"'s sudden eclipse of the "Age of Walnut" is belied by the information Bowett presents revealing the persistence of walnut in high-style London cabinetmakers' stock well into the 1750s and early 1760s.

Although Bowett appears to have consulted woodworkers to report their experience of working different woods, even including the smell of the wood being worked, his unfamiliarity with period tool use leads to the erroneous conclusion that walnut "mouldings were made in short grain sections, backed onto a deal or oak core. This was done to emphasize the figure; it may also have been easier to produce a crisp profile planing across the grain rather than along it" (p. 254). No one who uses molding planes, even those rare examples with skewed blades, could ever agree with the last part of that sentence. Cross-grain moldings were a design and aesthetic choice, and their manufacture required a great deal of difficulty and extra labor. Such moldings usually accompany the similarly vertical veneering of flat surfaces, even when those surfaces are horizontally configured, like drawers. This was a design choice. Simply planing the wood across the grain does not produce a crisp profile but a ripped-up mess. Bowett's occasional unfamiliarity with process does not devalue the book; it is typical of most academic-based writing on any craft or trade. His frequent successful efforts to understand technology, as in his description of Dutch gang-bladed sawmills, are a genuine boon to the understanding of furniture making.

This book is exploration, military, political, economic, art, shipping, cultural, and scientific history. It is not about the oppression of indigenous peoples to harvest the wood, nor about the resulting environmental degradation, as timbering was and is an extractive industry. It is not that Bowett is blind to this cost—several passages indicate otherwise—but that subject would be the province of a different book entirely, a sort of botanical version of Peter Matthiessen's *Wildlife in America* (1959). Such a book would be both welcome and heartbreaking, but that was not Bowett's mission.

Bowett's primary intent may well not have been to write a book that is important to the student of American furniture, but it is profoundly important to that field. A piece of furniture of typically British form can be worth ten or more times its British value in the American marketplace if it is provably of American origin. Thus, there are powerful market incentives to argue for American origins as long as the case being made is salable. A common method of establishing an American origin is the microanalysis of wood. This trend began to take hold in the 1960s and reached its academic apogee in Benno Forman's *American Seating Furniture, 1630–1730: An Interpretive Catalogue* (1988), with regional attributions based on microscopic wood identifications, frequently unsupportable by peer review or established wood anatomy. That work seemed to be the intellectual child of Joseph Downs's regionalism—then still very current as a working theory of the simultaneous development of every form in every style center—bolstered by more minute investigation of sources and construction techniques and by microscopic wood analysis done in-house at Winterthur by Gordon Saltar.

American Seating Furniture remains both an important intellectual contribution to furniture history and a monument to the misuse of microanalysis. Most of the entries other than those for seating furniture made entirely of black walnut include species identification, supposedly based on microanalysis, which is not possible: "all turned members American silver maple (*Acer saccharinum*) . . . red oak (*Quercus rubra*)" for plate 73, or "American ash (not *Fraxinus excelsior*)" for plate 5, or "American beech (*Fagus grandifolia*)" for plate 52—this is just a smattering. Microanalysis of wood cannot produce these species differentiations; maples can be divided only into hard and soft groups, oaks only into white, red, and live groups, and pines into the white, red, and yellow groups. *Fagus* (beeches), *Fraxinus* (ashes), *Aesculus* (buckeyes), *Populus* (poplars, cottonwoods, and aspens), *Prunus* (cherries, plums, apricots, peaches, and almonds), and *Ulmus* (elms) cannot be differentiated by species. *American Seating Furniture* is filled with plausible but hypothetical species identifications—red oak, white oak, white pine—as well as some just bizarre guesses, such as *Acer pensylvanicum* (moosewood, a small, high-altitude, and northern understory tree or shrub), *Quercus stellata* (post oak), or *Aesculus glabra* (Ohio or fetid buckeye). Even worse, many instances in which an American species is named are given apparently to help support an American attribution of the piece of furniture, sometimes of uncertain continent of origin. The list of impossible identifications and botanical/historical reckless error goes on and on.

Nonetheless, wood analysis was soon depicted in the trade as though it were a glossy scientific test akin to the introduction of fingerprints or DNA evidence in criminal court proceedings. The working theory that evolved in the trade and in academia was that, with some exceptions like imported exotic primary wood, the locality of the tree that produced the wood from which the furniture was made establishes the locality of the manufacture of the furniture. As Bowett makes very clear, if this theory were true, then after a certain date, perhaps as early as the seventeenth century, there would be almost no British furniture—certainly not urban furniture. What would exist would be German, Baltic, or Scandinavian furniture, since those areas were the sources of the secondary, core, and sometimes primary woods. After the establishment of trade in North American woods, British furniture would gradually become northern European/American. The problem with the "local tree means local manufacture" theory is that it overlooks the importance of an invention known to have been in use when the furniture was made. This mystery invention is the ship. It was cheaper to move goods by ship, sometimes for long distances, than to move them across swamps, mountains, forests, and rivers with no efficient system of roads. American black walnut was imported into Britain and used in quantity there. Most American cabinet woods also made their way to Britain in varying quantities and at various times. An understanding of the history of the timber trade is easily as important as genus and/or species identification in understanding which side of the Atlantic was responsible for the manufacture of a given piece of furniture.

The common genus used as secondary wood on both continents, pine (*Pinus*), is a perfect example of this complex relationship between species (or group, in this case) identification and the determination of the continent of origin of a given piece of furniture. The genus *Pinus* consists of more than one hundred species, which microscopic analysis can separate into only three groups: white group, red group, and yellow group. These groups roughly correspond to five-needle pines for the white group, two-needle pines for the red (and black) group, and three- or two- (or sometimes both) needle pines for the yellow group. American white pine (*Pinus strobus*) is a five-needle member of the white group widely used in furniture since the seventeenth century. Most other members of this group are American or Asian, along with the European alpine *Pinus cembra* and the Balkan *Pinus peuce*, which did not make their way into the larger timber trade in Europe. Thus, the working theory of thirty years ago regarding wood and furniture origin has been that white group pine in a piece of American or European antique furniture indicates American origin. Red group origin points to the pan-European Scotch pine *Pinus sylvestris* with occasional exceptions allowed for North American *Pinus resinosa*, according to the working theory. Although there are several western American and Asian members of the red pine group, they are eliminated by improbability. The eastern American red

Figure 1 Tall case clock with movement marked by James Crow, probably Liverpool, England, 1770–1780.

pine (*Pinus resinosa*) was not available to cabinetmakers of the American style centers of the eighteenth century because it was a tree of the high altitude Appalachians in what is now the United States (less so in cooler Canada) and too difficult to transport to cities to be economically viable, something that is slowly and grudgingly becoming understood in the antiques trade. The yellow group is primarily North and Central American, so this group was also thought to indicate American origin. The truth of the history of the timber trade as so tellingly presented by Bowett is that this theory is not only far from absolute but, in many instances, not even accurate. It is often the reverse argument that is most telling.

Thus, the presence of white or yellow group pine in eighteenth- or nineteenth-century furniture does not prove American origin since these woods were abundantly imported to England, something Bowett details by date and quantity as clearly as shipping records allow. But the presence of red pine, the primary constituent of yellow or red deal, as Bowett thoroughly explains, is usually an indication of British or other European origin because North American and Asian members of this group were not in the timber trade at the time. The same can generally be said of spruce and fir owing to the infrequent availability of the American species of these woods in early furniture manufacturing centers, again owing to transportation difficulties. Bowett's description of the importation of Canadian red pine somewhat displacing Baltic deal in the later nineteenth century does not alter the picture for seventeenth-, eighteenth-, and early nineteenth-century American and British furniture.

The meaning of the timber trade is complex, and it is not contended here that microanalysis be abandoned; rather, that its meaning should be understood in accurate historical context. Understanding antique furniture of uncertain continent of origin should actually require that it be subjected to much more thorough analysis. All the original softwoods should be analyzed with the recognition that it is not the presence of American wood that proves something American, it is the presence of European wood that proves something European. We were timber rich and had no need for imported secondary woods; the British were timber starved and relied almost entirely on imported wood. Several other European countries such as Holland also needed to import wood to manufacture furniture.

A clock case with an eight-day clock inscribed "Made by Thomas Crow, Wilmington" on a banner fastened to the dial arch (fig. 1) was part of Christie's American furniture sale of January 27, 1996. The mahogany case contains multiple American woods, including yellow group pine, tulip poplar, and Atlantic white cedar, as well as a white group oak determined by microanalysis. It looks like a case from the Liverpool, England, area, and, despite the Crow inscription, the movement and dial appear British and so unlike known Crow work as to strongly suggest that Crow was marketing a British clock and adding his name as the source. Perhaps what Thomas Crow *made*, according to the inscription, was the *sale* of a clock he imported. In 1996 the state of understanding about the importation of North American wood for use in British cabinetmaking was generally not sophisticated, since there was no accessible printed source of clear, accurate information; the only available avenue to a correct conclusion about this confusing subject was close observation and deep experience in the field.

The mahogany case of this clock is entirely foreign to local Wilmington cabinetmaking practice in the late eighteenth century or, for that matter, to any area near Wilmington. The auction catalogue entry suggesting the possible authorship of James McDowell is not plausible. The design of the case and the shop practices that produced it are entirely consistent with Liverpool, from the quoined corners of the base and surface treatment of book-matched mahogany veneer, to the shape of the waist door and the compact hood decorated with glass panels—presumably originally decorated with reverse painting. The stock of the case sides and other components is much thinner than is customary in any mid-Atlantic shop tradition and entirely consistent with those of Liverpool or other British areas. Clearly, either an immigrant maker traveled on a ship from Liverpool to Wilmington, bringing his stylistic and shop practice vocabulary along with a Liverpool clock for American relabeling, or else many species of American wood traveled by ship to Liverpool and then the clock and case were transported by ship back to Wilmington. Either explanation is possible. The "local wood means local manufacture" theory clearly favors the former. Christie's cataloguers were aware of this dichotomy but the "Made by Thomas Crow Wilmington" inscription and for them the existence of microanalyses proving the use of multiple American woods swayed the argument toward American manufacture. Furthermore, in 1996 the available wood analyses were somewhat erroneous and included more American woods than are present in the case and mistook northern white cedar for Atlantic white cedar.

If an understanding of the pattern of export to Britain of American wood in the late eighteenth century is coupled with the study of design, construction, and shop tradition on each side of the Atlantic, a different and clearer understanding can emerge. The mixture of woods in the case was an increasingly plausible option on the wood-starved west coast of Britain, as conditions strengthened favoring importation of American wood. Thus, a mixed lot of cheap North American imported secondary wood along with Caribbean mahogany for furniture making in a substantial port in this traffic is sensible; "Liverpool's position on the west coast made it a primary port of entry for American timber, second only to London" (Bowett, p. 153). The white group oak used in the base structure of the hood could well be wainscot. When the choice of who or what was on a transatlantic ship in the eighteenth century—a cabinetmaker who made one entirely Liverpool-derived sophisticated clock case in Delaware for a Liverpool manufactured clock and who then made no other known surviving American object, or secondary woods known to have been in international timber trade and then a clock of a type commonly made for export manufactured of those imported woods—is examined in this light, Liverpool manufacture becomes the logical conclusion.

A companion book to *Woods in British Furniture-Making* or a detailed extensive article dealing with the same subject in America to act as an adjunct to Bowett's book is easy to imagine since he has done the heavy lifting. The American story of wood use is largely implied by Bowett, even when it is not directly stated. Whether or not he considered how much his book would be of use to students of American furniture as he undertook this monumental work, we owe him a profound debt. Thank you, Adam Bowett. No collector, dealer, academic, or auctioneer of American or European furniture should overlook this work. It is essential for an understanding of the subject.

Alan Miller
Quakertown, Pennsylvania

Recent Writing on American Furniture: A Bibliography

Compiled by
Gerald W. R. Ward

This year's list primarily includes works published in 2012 and roughly through October 2013. As always, a few earlier publications that had escaped notice are also listed. The short title *American Furniture 2012* is used in citations for articles and reviews published in last year's edition of this journal, which is also cited in full under Luke Beckerdite's name.

This past year witnessed the long-awaited introduction of Winterthur Museum's online collections database, a major event for everyone interested in American furniture and decorative arts. The Metropolitan Museum of Art has also made many of its publications, starting in 1964, available online in a major initiative that provides a model for other institutions. The more focused website of the Four Centuries of Massachusetts Furniture consortium is also currently available.

Once again, many people have assisted in compiling this list. I am particularly grateful to Luke Beckerdite, Jonathan Fairbanks, Gary Albert, Mark Arnold, Dennis Carr, Meredith Crawford, Arthur Dion, Nonie Gadsden, Tom Hardiman, Steve Lash, Kelly H. L'Ecuyer, Johanna McBrien, Tom Michie, Richard Oedel, Phil Zea, Barbara McLean Ward, and Fronia W. Simpson, as well as to the scholars who have prepared reviews for this issue. I am also indebted to the librarians of the Museum of Fine Arts, Boston, the Portsmouth Athenaeum, and the Portsmouth Public Library for their ongoing assistance.

I would be glad to receive citations for titles that have been inadvertently omitted from this or previous lists. Information about new publications and review copies of significant works would also be much appreciated.

Ackermann, Daniel Kurt. "A Long and Winding S-Curve: American Vernacular Rococo in the Southern Backcountry." *Antiques* 180, no. 3 (May–June 2013): 134–43. 14 color illus.

American Period Furniture: Journal of the Society of American Period Furniture Makers 11 (2011): 1–114. Numerous color illus., line drawings. (See also individual articles cited elsewhere.)

American Period Furniture: Journal of the Society of American Period Furniture Makers 12 (2012): 1–120. Numerous color and bw illus., line drawings. (See also individual articles cited elsewhere.)

Arnold, Mark. "The Elliptical Journey: Retracing the Origins of Federal Paterae." *American Period Furniture: Journal of the Society of American Period Furniture Makers* 12 (2012): 76–91. 22 color illus.

Aslund, Jean, with contributions by Richard Oedel, Bill Garbus, Mitch Ryerson, and William E. Jewell. *Mind and Hand: Contemporary Studio Furniture.* Atglen, Pa.: Schiffer for the Furniture Society, 2012. 160 pp.; numerous color and bw illus.

Baker, Sarah Elsie. *Retro Style: Class, Gender, and Design in the Home.* London: Bloomsbury Academic, 2013. viii + 236 pp.; 25 bw illus., appendix, index.

[Balsbaugh, Richard, collection]. *The Richard Balsbaugh Collection of Vintage Radios.* New York: Bonhams, December 11, 2012. 52 pp.; color illus.

Barquist, David L. "'The Interior Will Be as Interesting as the Exterior Is Magnificent': American Period Rooms at the Philadelphia Museum of Art." *Winterthur Portfolio* 46, nos. 2–3 (summer/autumn 2012): 139–60. 20 color and bw illus.

———. "Kitchen from the Miller House, Millbach, Lebanon County, Pennsylvania, 1752." *Winterthur Portfolio* 46, nos. 2–3 (summer/autumn 2012): E1–E11. (Available as e-Book Edition from University of Chicago Press.)

———. "Period Room Architecture in American Art Museums." *Winterthur Portfolio* 46, nos. 2–3 (summer/autumn 2012): 113–15.

Barquist, David L., and Elizabeth Agro. "Cradle of Liberty, Cradle of Craft: Philadelphia's Heritage of Artist-Artisans." *Antiques* 180, no. 2 (March–April 2013): 98–107. Color and bw illus.

Barquist, David L., and Pauline K. Eversmann, guest editors. "Period Room Architecture in American Art Museums: A Special Issue." *Winterthur Portfolio* 46, nos. 2–3 (summer/autumn 2012): 113–212. Numerous color and bw illus. (See also individual articles, including e-Book Edition, cited elsewhere.)

Barter, Judith A., and Monica Obniski. *For Kith and Kin: The Folk Art Collection at the Art Institute of Chicago.* Chicago: Art Institute of Chicago, 2012. 120 pp.; numerous color illus. Distributed by Yale University Press.

———. "For Kith and Kin: The Folk Art Collection at the Art Institute of Chicago." *Antiques and Fine Art* 12, no. 3 (winter/spring 2013): 190–97. 10 color illus. (Includes a few pieces of furniture.)

Batley, Tania. "The Metamorphic Desk." 2 pp. www.morrisjumel.org (accessed November 1, 2013). (Re desk made in 1854 by Stephen Hedges of New York.)

[Bayou Bend]. "Rare Texas Desk and Pottery Donated to Bayou Bend." *Maine Antique Digest* 41, no. 1 (January 2013): 10A. 1 bw desk. (Re writing desk of ca. 1875 by Adolph Kempen [1844–1885].)

———. "Unique Kempen Desk and Early Texas Stoneware Gifted [sic] to Bayou Bend." *Antiques and the Arts Weekly* (December 7, 2012): 10. 1 bw illus. (Re writing desk of ca. 1875 by Adolph Kempen [1844–1885].)

Beach, Laura. "The Curator, the Cabinetmaker, and the Carver: An Exhibition at the Massachusetts Historical Society. . . ." *Antiques and the Arts Weekly* (October 18, 2013): 1, 30–32. bw illus.

———. "Furniture Masterworks: Tradition and Innovation in Western Massachusetts." *Antiques and the Arts*

Weekly (September 27, 2013): 1, 62–64. bw illus.

———. "Latest Chipstone Volumes Dig Deep and Venture Forward." *Antiques and the Arts Weekly* (April 19, 2013): 40. 2 bw illus. (Includes review of Luke Beckerdite, ed., *American Furniture 2012*.)

———. "Living with Antiques: Continental Congress." *Antiques* 180, no. 1 (January–February 2013): 142–53. 18 color illus.

———. "What's New at Colonial Williamsburg?" *Antiques and the Arts Weekly* (April 19, 2013): 48–49. 12 bw illus. (Mentions new furniture acquisitions, including a dressing table, ca. 1745–1750, from Norfolk, Virginia, and a corner cupboard, 1810–1830, from Hawkins County, Tennessee.)

Beckerdite, Luke, ed. *American Furniture 2012.* Milwaukee, Wis.: Chipstone Foundation, 2012. vii + 192 pp.; numerous color and bw illus., bibliography, index. Distributed by University Press of New England, Hanover.

Bias, Jerome. "A Carpenter's Testament: The John Brown Painted Corner Cabinet." *American Period Furniture: Journal of the Society of American Period Furniture Makers* 12 (2012): 92–100. 31 color and bw illus. (Re cupboard of 1818 attributed to Thomas Sheridan, Bladen County, North Carolina, recently acquired by MESDA.)

Binzen, Jonathan, and Arthur Dion. *GWOW! Hank Gilpin Loves Wood.* Boston: Gallery NAGA, 2013. 28 pp.; color illus., accompanying DVD.

Brown, Jeffrey. "Made in Massachusetts: Studio Furniture of the Bay State." *Antiques and Fine Art* 12, no. 6 (autumn/winter 2013): 144–49. 10 color illus.

Brown, Jeffrey, and Michael McMillan. *Across the Grain: Turned and Carved Wood.* Brockton, Mass.: Fuller Craft Museum, 2013. 48 pp.; color illus., checklist, bibliography.

Brown, Jeffrey, and Pat Warner, with the assistance of Michael McMillan and with essays by Jonathan L. Fairbanks and Gerald W. R. Ward. *Made in Massachusetts: Studio Furniture of the*

Bay State. Brockton, Mass.: Fuller Craft Museum, 2013. 104 pp.; numerous color illus., bibliography.

Brown, Michael K. "Duncan Phyfe & Sons Peremptory and Extensive Auction Sale." *Antiques and Fine Art* 12, no. 1 (summer 2012): 174–79. 6 color illus.

Brown, Rachael, and Lorraine Farrelly. *Materials and Interior Design*. London: Laurence King, 2012. 192 pp.; numerous color illus., glossary, bibliography, index.

Budwig, Judith, and Jeffrey Preston. *Redux: The Arts and Crafts Revival, 1972–2012*. Princeton, N.J.: Mercer Oak Publishing, 2013. 392 pp.; 734 illus.

Burks, Jean M. "Color, Collectors, and Connoisseurs." *Antiques* 180, no. 4 (July–August 2013): 126–28. Color illus. (Re Shelburne Museum collections.)

Burt, Owen H., and Jo Burt. "Walter H. Durfee and His Grandfather Clocks: Part 1." *Watch & Clock Bulletin* 55, no. 1 (January–February 2013): 14–28. 28 color and bw illus.

———. "Walter H. Durfee and His Grandfather Clocks: Part 2." *Watch & Clock Bulletin* 55, no. 2 (March–April 2013): 145–64. 67 color illus.

———. "Walter H. Durfee and His Grandfather Clocks: Part 3." *Watch & Clock Bulletin* 55, no. 4 (July–August 2013): 372–88. 69 color and bw illus.

———. "Walter H. Durfee and His Grandfather Clocks: Part 4." *Watch & Clock Bulletin* 55, no. 5 (September–October 2013): 486–500. 67 color and bw illus.

Busch, Jason T. "Continuing Currents of Change: Art, Life, and Culture along the Mississippi River, 1850–1861." In *The Civil War and the Material Culture of Texas, the Lower South, and the Southwest*, 1–31. The David B. Warren Symposium, vol. 3. Houston, Tex.: Bayou Bend Collection and Gardens, Museum of Fine Arts, Houston, 2012.

Busch, Jason, and Catherine L. Futter. "American Decorative Arts at the World's Fairs." *Antiques and Fine Art* 12, no. 2 (autumn/winter 2012): 132–41. Color illus.

Cape, Jonathan. *We Sit Together: Utopian Benches from the Shakers to the Separatists of Zoar*. New York: Princeton Architectural Press, 2013. 112 pp.; color and bw illus., line drawings, bibliography, research sources.

[Castle, Wendell]. "'Wendell Castle: Wandering Forms' on Display at SCAD Museum." *Antiques and the Arts Weekly* (October 18, 2013): 45.

Chicarda, Tara Gleason. "Keeping Time: Southern Tall Case Clocks." *Antiques and Fine Art* 12, no. 2 (autumn/winter 2012): 166–73. Color illus.

Cooper, Wendy A. "The Kaufman Collection: A Rare Glimpse of American Artistry, 1700–1830." *National Gallery of Art Bulletin*, no. 47 (fall 2012): 2–13. 15 color illus.

———. Review of *Duncan Phyfe: Master Cabinetmaker in New York* by Peter M. Kenny et al. In *American Furniture 2012*, 165–74.

Cuff, Dana. Review of *California Design, 1930–1965: Living in a Modern Way* by Wendy Kaplan et al. *Journal of the Society of Architectural Historians* 72, no. 1 (March 2013): 100–101.

Cunningham, Joseph. "New Light: Charles Rohlfs *Did* Show at the Louisiana Purchase Exposition." *Antiques* 180, no. 3 (May–June 2013): 56, 58. 4 color illus.

Curtis, Nancy. *Gropius House, Lincoln, Massachusetts*. Boston: Historic New England, 2011. 24 pp.; color illus.

[Dean, Peter]. "Wood, Design, Sustainability: An Interview with Peter Dean." *Be in Touch: A Magazine for Members of Fuller Craft Museum* (fall 2013): 4–6. 1 color illus.

Dervan, Andrew H. "Grand Rapids Clock and Mantel Company." *Watch & Clock Bulletin* 55, no. 5 (September–October 2013): 457–62. 13 bw illus., 1 table.

———. "John Polsey, Clockmaker: Working in the Shadow of Edward Howard." *Watch & Clock Bulletin* 55, no. 4 (July–August 2013): 407–10. 15 bw illus.

The Design Book. New York: Phaidon Press, 2013. 511 pp.; numerous color and bw illus., index.

DeSmith, Christy. "Populist Modern." *American Craft* 72, no. 2 (April–May 2012): 41–47. Color illus. (Re furniture by Scott McGlasson.)

Dibble, R. Ruthie. "The Hands That Rocked the Cradle: Interpretations in the Life of an Object." *American Furniture 2012*, 1–23. 17 color and bw illus.

Dickinson, Alice. "Hunter House and the Point: A Community of Consumers and Craftsmen in Eighteenth-Century Newport, Rhode Island." *Antiques and Fine Art* 12, no. 3 (winter/spring 2013): 244–49. 12 color illus.

Dietrich, Steven. "Charleston Queen Anne Easy Chairs: A Study in Their History and Construction." *American Period Furniture: Journal of the Society of American Period Furniture Makers* 11 (2011): 16–23. 35 color illus.

Dilbeck, April A., and Robert Scobie. "Barrister Bookcases: Expanding the Possibilities." *New England Antiques Journal* 32, no. 5 (November 2013): 42–45. 10 color and bw illus., list of manufacturers.

"Discoveries: Another Seymour Trait?" *Antiques and Fine Art* 11, no. 6 (spring 2012): 14. Color illus. (Re spherical "round loaf casters" used by Thomas Seymour.)

Düchting, Hajo, et al. *50 Designers You Should Know*. Munich: Prestel, 2012. 156 pp.; numerous color and bw illus., index.

[Dunlap, Samuel]. "Important Dunlap Cabinetmaking Records Acquired." *New Hampshire Historical Society Newsletter* 49, nos. 3–4 (spring 2013): 9–10. 5 color illus. (Re purchase by NHHS of account book of Samuel Dunlap of Henniker and Salisbury, 1780s–1820s.)

Durieux, Brigitte, Laziz Hamani, Elodie Palasse-Leroux, and Laura Bennett. *Industrial Chic: Cult Furniture, Design and Lighting*. London: Thames and Hudson, 2012. 239 pp.; color illus., bibliography.

Eaton, Peter. "Spectacular Vernacular." *Antiques and Fine Art* 12, no. 5 (summer 2013): 138–55. Numerous color illus.

Edwards, Robert. "William Lightfoot Price: His Furniture and Its Context."

American Furniture 2012, 116–53. 67 color and bw illus.

Esterly, David. *The Lost Carving: A Journey to the Heart of Making*. New York: Viking, 2012. 283 pp.; bw illus.

Eversmann, Pauline K. "Evidences of American Home Life: Henry Francis du Pont and the Winterthur Period Rooms." *Winterthur Portfolio* 46, nos. 2–3 (summer/autumn 2012): 179–93. 14 color and bw illus.

"Everson's Arts and Crafts Exhibition Focuses on Fashion, Art, and Stickley." *Antiques and the Arts Weekly* (May 24, 2013): 43. 1 bw illus.

Falk, Cynthia G. Review of *Paint, Pattern, and People: Furniture of Southeastern Pennsylvania, 1725–1850* by Wendy A. Cooper and Lisa Minardi. In *Pennsylvania History: A Journal of Mid-Atlantic Studies* 80, no. 4 (autumn 2013): 541–44.

Fauntleroy, Gussie. "West by Mid-West." *American Craft* 73, no. 4 (August–September 2013): 64–69. Color illus. (Re furniture by Geoffrey Keating.)

Fennimore, Donald L., and Frank L. Hohmann III. "Stretch: America's First Family of Clockmakers." *Antiques and Fine Art* 12, no. 5 (summer 2013): 105–11. 12 color illus.

———. *Stretch: America's First Family of Clockmakers*. Winterthur, Del.: Winterthur Museum and Hohmann Holdings LLC, 2013. 343 pp.; 457 color illus., catalogue, 8 appendixes, bibliography, index.

Findlen, Paula, ed. *Early Modern Things: Objects and Their Histories, 1500–1800*. London: Routledge, 2013. xxiv + 389 pp.; numerous bw illus., tables. (Of the sixteen essays here, see especially Amanda Vickery, "Fashioning Difference in Georgian England: Furniture for Him and for Her.")

Fiske, John. "Four Centuries of Massachusetts Furniture: The Massachusetts Historical Society Presents 'The Cabinetmaker and the Carver: Boston Furniture from Private Collections.'" *New England Antiques Journal* 32, no. 5 (November 2013): 58–60. 14 color illus.

———. "Four Centuries of Massachusetts Furniture: Old Sturbridge Village Presents the Furniture of Nathan Lombard." *New England Antiques Journal* 32, no. 4 (October 2013): 50–51. 1 color and 7 bw illus.

———. *When Oak Was New: English Furniture and Daily Life, 1530–1700*. Ipswich, Mass.: Belmont Press, 2013. xii + 266 pp.; numerous bw illus., bibliography, index.

Fleming, John A., and Michael J. Rowen. *Canadian Folk Art to 1950*. Edmonton: Canadian Museum of Civilization and the University of Alberta Press, 2012. 557 pp.; numerous color illus., bibliography, index.

Flynt, Suzanne, with a foreword by Wendy Kaplan. *Poetry to the Earth: The Arts and Crafts Movement in Deerfield*. Deerfield, Mass.: Pocumtuck Valley Memorial Association; Stockbridge, Mass.: Hard Press Editions; Easthampton, Mass.: Hudson Hills Press, 2013. 235 pp.; numerous color and bw illus., index.

"Foot for Penn's Desk Found." *Maine Antique Digest* 41, no. 5 (May 2013): 10A. 3 bw illus. (Re turned-elm foot for Penn's desk at the Library Company of Philadelphia found at Germantown Historical Society.)

Four Centuries of Massachusetts Furniture. www.fourcenturies.org. (Includes timeline, bibliography, highlight objects, and other features.)

"Four Centuries of Massachusetts Furniture." *International View* (spring/summer 2013): 49–51. 6 color illus. (An interview of Nancy Carlisle of Historic New England by Lynda A. Cain.)

Frank, Stuart M. *Ingenious Contrivances, Curiously Carved: Scrimshaw in the New Bedford Whaling Museum: A Comprehensive Catalog of the World's Largest Collection*. Boston: David R. Godine in association with New Bedford Whaling Museum, 2012. xv + 384 pp.; numerous color illus., 2 appendixes, bibliography, index.

Franklin, Adrian. *Retro: A Guide to the Mid-20th Century Design Revival*. 2011. 2nd ed. London: Berg, 2013. 256 pp.; 735 color illus., index.

Friary, Grace. "American Decorative Arts at the New England Historic Genealogical Society." *Antiques and Fine Art* 12, no. 4 (spring 2013): 150–57. Color illus.

Frishman, Bob. "Horology in Art: Part 10." *Watch & Clock Bulletin* 55, no. 5 (September–October 2013): 474. 1 color illus. (Re Edward Hopper's *Seven A.M.* (1948), depicting a clock; see earlier references by the author online to other Hopper works including clocks.)

———. Review of *Marking Modern Times: A History of Clocks, Watches, & Other Timekeepers in American Life* by Alexis McCrossen. In *Watch & Clock Bulletin* 55, no. 5 (September–October 2013): 529. 1 bw illus.

Gómez-Ibáñez, Miguel. Review of *The House That Sam Built: Sam Maloof and Art in the Pomona Valley, 1945–1985* by Harold B. Nelson et al. In *American Furniture 2012*, 154–58.

Gordon, Alastair. *Wendell Castle, Wandering Forms: Works from 1959–1979*. New York: Gregory R. Miller and Co. in association with Aldrich Contemporary Art Museum, 2012. 239 pp.; numerous color and bw illus.

Gordon, John Stuart. Review of *The Story of Eames Furniture* by Marilyn Neuhart with Jon Neuhart. In *American Furniture 2012*, 158–62.

Gorton, Gregory. "Seth Thomas Clock Company's Grand Office Calendar." *Watch & Clock Bulletin* 55, no. 3 (May–June 2013): 265–73. 25 color and bw illus.

Grant, Daniel. "Museums by the Numbers: 2012 in Review." *Antiques and Fine Art* 12, no. 3 (winter/spring 2013): 148–53. 8 color illus. (Includes acquisition of the "Fox and Grapes" Philadelphia rococo dressing table by the Philadelphia Museum of Art and a Kentucky chest of drawers acquired by MESDA.)

Green, Harvey. Review of *Mahogany: The Costs of Luxury in Early America* by Jennifer L. Anderson. In *New England Quarterly* 86, no. 2 (June 2013): 346–49.

Hand, Thomas P. "Allan Breed: 2012 Cartouche Award Recipient." *American Period Furniture: Journal of the*

Society of American Period Furniture Makers 12 (2012): 2–5. 8 color illus.

Harris, Neil. "Period Rooms and the American Art Museum." Winterthur Portfolio 46, nos. 2–3 (summer/autumn 2012): 117–37. 16 color and bw illus.

Heckscher, Morrison H. "The American Wing Rooms in the Metropolitan Museum of Art." Winterthur Portfolio 46, nos. 2–3 (summer/autumn 2012): 161–77. 17 color and bw illus., appendix.

Historic Deerfield, Inc. Historic Deerfield Annual Report 2012. Deerfield, Mass.: Historic Deerfield, 2012. 40 pp.; color illus. (Includes new acquisitions of furniture: a workbench attributed to Calvin Stearns, ca. 1805 and later; a chest of drawers attributed to Bates How, 1790–1800; and a bureau attributed to George Stedman, 1816–1822.)

[Historic Deerfield, Inc.]. "Historic Deerfield's Newest Exhibition." Antiques and the Arts Weekly (September 27, 2013): 40. 5 bw illus.

———. "New and Noteworthy: Landmark Book with Local Provenance Acquired." Up & Down the Street (spring/summer 2013): 4. 2 bw illus. (Re acquisition by Historic Deerfield of a copy of Asher Benjamin's The Country Builder's Assistant [1797] owned originally by William Mather [1766–1835] of Whately, a cabinetmaker and general carpenter. Deerfield also owns Mather's account book for the years 1808–1828.)

Hobbs, Calvin. "Native Son of Perquimans County: 2011 Cartouche Award Winner Ben Hobbs." American Period Furniture: Journal of the Society of American Period Furniture Makers 11 (2011): 30–34. 8 color illus. (See also Benjamin Hobbs, "Lessons from the Armchair," 24–29, in the same issue.)

Huerta, Dalila. "The Lure of Enameled Steel in the Interwar Period." Decorative Arts Trust [newsletter] 22, no. 2 (summer 2013): 8–9. 4 color illus.

Hummel, Charles F. Review of Make a Joint Stool from a Tree: An Introduction to 17th-Century Joinery by Jennie Alexander and Peter Follansbee. In American Furniture 2012, 158–65.

Humphreys, Nick. "A New Approach to Furniture: The Dr. Susan Weber Gallery at the Victoria and Albert Museum." Antiques and Fine Art 12, no. 3 (winter/spring 2013): 198–205. 11 color illus.

Jackson, Christie. "Delightfully Designed: The Furniture and Life of Nathan Lombard." Journal of Antiques and Collectibles 14, no. 7 (September 2013): 51–53. Color and bw illus.

———. "Nathan Lombard: A New Form and an Uncovered Family History." Antiques and Fine Art 12, no. 4 (spring 2013): 182–85. 6 color illus.

Jaye, Randy. "Revealing the Unique History of Lebanon County, Pennsylvania, Clockmakers." Watch & Clock Bulletin 55, no. 3 (May–June 2013): 242–52. 27 color illus., bibliography.

Jobe, Brock. "Bay State Riches: The Magazine Antiques and Four Centuries of Massachusetts Furniture." Antiques 180, no. 1 (January–February 2013): 166–75. 10 color illus.

Jobe, Brock, Philip Zea, and Joshua Lane. "Four Centuries of Massachusetts Furniture." Antiques and Fine Art 12, no. 3 (winter/spring 2013): 182–89. 10 color illus.

Johnson, Alex. Bookshelf. New York: Thames and Hudson, 2012. 272 pp.; 305 color illus., bibliography.

Judy Kensley McKie. Boston: Gallery NAGA, 2013. 35 pp.; color illus., chronology. (Includes short statements on McKie's work by Emily Zilber, Jonathan Fairbanks, Edward S. Cooke Jr., and others.)

Karasová, Daniela. The History of Modern Furniture Design. Prague: Museum of Decorative Arts and Arbor Vitae, 2012. 320 pp.; numerous color and bw illus., biographies, bibliography, index.

Kirk, John T. "The John T. Kirk Collection: I Bought It 'Ratty' and Left It Alone." In August Americana & Americana-Online. Boston: Skinner, August 10, 2013, 54. (See also lots 200–248).

Kirtley, Alexandra Alevizatos. "Front Parlor from the Powel House, Philadelphia, 1769–70." Winterthur Portfolio 46, nos. 2–3 (summer/autumn 2012): E12–E23. (Available as e-Book Edition from University of Chicago Press.)

———. "Museum Accessions." Antiques 180, no. 1 (January–February 2013): 82. 2 color illus. (Re Philadelphia dressing table, 1765–1775, acquired by the Philadelphia Museum of Art.)

Koenig, Gloria. Charles and Ray Eames, 1907–78, 1912–88: Pioneers of Modernism. 2005. Reprint. Cologne: Taschen, 2013. 96 pp.; numerous color and bw illus., chronology, bibliography.

Koeppe, Wolfram, Reinier Baarsen, et al. Extravagant Inventions: The Princely Furniture of the Roentgens. New York: Metropolitan Museum of Art, 2012. xi + 291 pp.; numerous color and bw illus., appendixes, bibliography, index. Distributed by Yale University Press.

Kolk, Heidi Aronson. "The Many-Layered Cultural Lives of Things: Experiments in Multidisciplinary Object Study at a Local House Museum in St. Louis." Winterthur Portfolio 47, nos. 2–3 (summer/autumn 2013): 161–95. 19 color and bw illus., 1 fig., 5 appendixes.

Kotula, Nickolas. "The Nathan Margolis Cabinet Shop's Last Apprentice: Memories, Impressions, and Lessons Learned." American Period Furniture: Journal of the Society of American Period Furniture Makers 11 (2011): 2–7. 3 bw illus.

Krawczynski, Keith. Daily Life in the Colonial City. Santa Barbara, Calif.: Greenwood, 2013. xxxv + 554 pp.; numerous bw illus., chronology, index.

Kyle, Robert. Review of Harmony in Wood: Furniture of the Harmony Society by Philip D. Zimmerman. In Pennsylvania History: A Journal of Mid-Atlantic Studies 80, no. 3 (summer 2013): 458–60.

Kylloe, Ralph. Ralph Kylloe's Rustic Living. Layton, Utah: Gibbs Smith, 2012. 368 pp.; numerous color illus., resource list. (Large-format picture book that depicts some furniture.)

Lacroix, Laurier, et al. Les arts en Nouvelle-France. Québec: Musée National des Beaux-Arts du Québec, 2012. 296 pp.; numerous color illus., maps, index.

Lahikainen, Dean Thomas. "The Derby Room from the Ezekiel Hersey Derby

House, Salem, Massachusetts, 1798–1799." *Winterthur Portfolio* 46, nos. 2–3 (summer/autumn 2012): E24–E36. (Available as e-Book Edition from University of Chicago Press.)

Lang, Brian J. "The Art of Seating: 200 Years of American Design." *Antiques and Fine Art* 11, no. 6 (spring 2012): 204–11. 8 color illus.

Leithauser, Mark, with contributions by Jon Frederick. "Masterpieces of American Furniture from the Kaufman Collection, 1700–1830." *Antiques and Fine Art* 12, no. 3 (winter/spring 2013): 220–25. 6 color illus.

[Loeser, Tom]. "Masters: The 2012 American Craft Council Award Winners." *American Craft* 72, no. 5 (October–November 2012): 70–71. Color illus. (Brief profile of furniture maker elected as Fellow of the ACC.)

[Lombard, Nathan]. "The Furniture and Life of Nathan Lombard to Open at Old Sturbridge Village Oct. 19." *Antiques and the Arts Weekly* (October 11, 2013): 3. 2 bw illus.

Long, Christopher. "Furniture." In *Norman Bel Geddes Designs America*, ed. Donald Albrecht, 214–27. New York: Abrams for the Harry Ransom Center, University of Texas at Austin, and Museum of the City of New York, 2013. 16 color and bw illus.

Lovelace, Joyce. "Structurally Sound." *American Craft* 73, no. 1 (February–March 2013): 50–55. Color illus. (Re furniture by Asher Dunn.)

Lovell, Margaretta M. Review of *Mahogany: The Costs of Luxury in Early America* by Jennifer L. Anderson. In *William and Mary Quarterly* 70, no. 3 (July 2013): 614–17.

[Lyndhurst]. "Current and Coming: Victoriana at Lyndhurst." *Antiques* 180, no. 5 (September–October 2013): 28. 2 color illus.

———. "Lyndhurst's 'Three Parlors' to Trace American Identity." *Antiques and the Arts Weekly* (June 7, 2013): 47. 2 bw illus.

Magnet, Myron. *The Founders at Home: The Building of America, 1735–1817.* New York: W. W. Norton, 2014. 472 pp.; numerous color and bw illus., index.

Maris-Wolf, Ted. Review of *Thomas Day: Master Craftsman and Free Man of Color* by Patricia Phillips Marshall and Jo Leimenstoll. In *Winterthur Portfolio* 47, no. 1 (spring 2013): 106–7.

"'Mark Hopkins: A New Look at Old Work' Opening June 14 at New Hampshire Furniture Masters Gallery." *Antiques and the Arts Weekly* (June 13, 2013): 13.

Marshall. Jennifer Jane. *Machine Art, 1934.* Chicago: University of Chicago Press, 2013. 204 pp.; 61 bw illus.

Martin, Ann Smart. Review of *Thomas Day: Master Craftsman and Free Man of Color* by Patricia Phillips Marshall and Jo Ramsay Leimenstoll. In *Journal of Modern Craft* 6, no. 2 (July 2013): 235–37.

Mascelli, Michael. "Upholstery for Period Furniture Makers." *American Period Furniture: Journal of the Society of American Period Furniture Makers* 12 (2012): 12–18. 12 color illus.

Mascolo, Frances McQueeney-Jones. "Frank Lloyd Wright Furnishings Acquired by the Huntington Museum." *Antiques and the Arts Weekly* (March 8, 2013): 1, 30–31. bw illus.

May, Stephen. "Masterpieces of American Furniture from the Kaufman Collection." *Antiques and the Arts Weekly* (May 10, 2013): 1, 30–31. 15 bw illus.

———. "Thomas Day: Master Craftsman and Free Man of Color." *Antiques and the Arts Weekly* (April 26, 2013): 1, 30–31. 15 bw illus. (Re exhibition at Renwick Gallery.)

McBrien, Johanna. "A Bit of Pennsylvania in Texas." *Antiques and Fine Art* 11, no. 6 (spring 2012): 144–57. Color illus.

———. "Kindred Spirits." *Antiques and Fine Art* 12, no. 4 (spring 2013): 16–31. Color illus.

———. "Serenity." *Antiques and Fine Art* 12, no. 6 (autumn/winter 2013): 128–43. Numerous color illus.

[McCallister collection]. *Important Americana: Property from the Collection of Dr. Larry McCallister.* New York: Sotheby's, January 26, 2013. 116 pp.; numerous color illus.

McCrosson, Alexis. *Marking Modern Times: A History of Clocks, Watches, and Other Timekeepers in American Life.* Chicago: University of Chicago Press, 2013. xvi + 255 pp.; illus.

[McCue collection]. *The McCue Shaker Collection II.* Marshfield, Mass.: Willis Henry Auctions, September 7, 2013. Unpaged; numerous color and bw illus., bibliography. (With some biographical material.)

McNamara, Martha J., and Georgia B. Barnhill, eds. *New Views of New England: Studies in Material and Visual Culture, 1680–1830.* Publications of the Colonial Society of Massachusetts, vol. 82. Boston: Colonial Society of Massachusetts, 2012. Distributed by University of Virginia Press. xxxv + 277 pp.; color and bw illus., index. (An anthology including several articles tangentially related to furniture.)

Meehan, William E., Jr. "What Modern Was." *Watch & Clock Bulletin* 55, no. 2 (March–April 2013): 138–44. 17 color illus.

Metropolitan Museum of Art. *MetPublications.* www.metmuseum.org/metpublications. (Online access to the museum's post-1964 books, catalogues, bulletins, journals, and online publications.)

Miller, Judith. *Mid-Century Modern: Living with Mid-Century Modern Design.* London: Miller's, 2012. 253 pp.; numerous color illus., index.

Mitchell, Rich. "Banjo Clocks, the Colonial Revival, and Wallace Nutting." *Watch & Clock Bulletin* 54, no. 5 (September–October 2012): 455–59. 13 color illus., table.

[Molesworth, Thomas]. "The Annenberg Commission by Thomas Molesworth: Property from Ranch A," 170–91. In *Important American Furniture, Folk Art, Silver, Paintings, and Prints.* New York: Christie's, September 25, 2013. Color and bw illus.

Moore, William D. "'You'd Swear They Were Modern': Ruth Reeves, the Index of American Design, and the Canonization of Shaker Material Culture." *Winterthur Portfolio* 47, no. 1 (spring 2013): 1–34. 22 color and bw illus.

"Museum of Arts & Design Presenting 'Against the Grain,' Works in Wood." *Antiques and the Arts Weekly* (April 26, 2013): 16. 1 bw illus.

[Museum of Early Southern Decorative Arts]. "Old Kentucky Chest Has New Home." *Maine Antique Digest* 41, no. 1 (January 2013): 9A. 1 bw illus. (Re late eighteenth-century cherry chest of drawers, made by Calvert-Tuttle-Foxworthy family of Mason County, Kentucky, acquired by MESDA.)

[Museum of Fine Arts, Boston]. "MFA Boston Buys Desk at Skinner Americana Sale." *Antiques and the Arts Weekly* (August 16, 2013): 41. 1 bw illus. (Re lot 38 in sale of August 10, 2013).

Mussey, Robert D., Jr. "Dowries for Two Daughters." *Historic New England* 13, no. 3 (winter/spring 2013): 34. 1 color illus.

———. "In Search of Classical Style." *Historic New England* 14, no. 2 (fall 2013): 10–12. 5 color illus.

Mussey, Robert D., Jr., and Rebecca J. Bertrand. "One Family's Treasure: Newly Discovered Collection of Seymour Furniture." *Antiques and Fine Art* 11, no. 6 (spring 2012): 190–97. 13 color and bw illus.

Muzio, David de. "Wharton Esherick's Music Room from the Curtis Bok House, Gulph Mills, Pennsylvania, 1935–1938." *Winterthur Portfolio* 46, nos. 2–3 (summer/autumn 2012): E58–E74. (Available as e-Book Edition from University of Chicago Press.)

"'Nakashima Woodworkers' at Moderne Gallery Sept. 20." *Antiques and the Arts Weekly* (September 6, 2013): 43. 1 bw illus.

New Hampshire Furniture Masters Association. *Celebrating Our 15th Year*. N.p.: New Hampshire Furniture Masters, 2010. 34 pp.; color illus.

New Hampshire Furniture Masters Association. *Furniture Masterworks 2013: A Celebration*. N.p.: New Hampshire Furniture Masters Association, 2013. 34 pp.; color illus.

New Hampshire Furniture Masters Association. *Inspired Design, Extraordinary Craftsmanship*. N.p.: New Hamp-shire Furniture Masters Association, 2011. 30 pp.; color illus.

New Hampshire Furniture Masters Association. *Unique Furniture with Style*. N.p.: New Hampshire Furniture Masters Association, 2012. 30 pp.; color illus.

[New Hampshire Furniture Masters Association]. "Fresh Look at Common Object at NH Furniture Masters Exhibition." *Antiques and the Arts Weekly* (April 12, 2013): 18. 1 bw illus.

[New Hampshire Furniture Masters Association]. "NH Furniture Masters and NH Art Association Unite for Collaborative Portsmouth Exhibit." *Antiques and the Arts Weekly* (April 19, 2013): 52. 1 bw illus.

[New Hampshire Furniture Masters Association]. "NH Furniture Masters Exhibit New Work." *Antiques and the Arts Weekly* (June 7, 2013): 20. 2 bw illus.

[New Hampshire Furniture Masters Association]. "NH Furniture Masters Gallery to Showcase Emerging Artists." *Antiques and the Arts Weekly* (September 6, 2013): 4. 1 bw illus.

[New Hampshire Furniture Masters Association]. "NH Furniture Masters to Exhibit at Boston's Society of Arts and Crafts." *Antiques and the Arts Weekly* (July 26, 2013): 3. 2 bw illus.

[New Hampshire Furniture Masters Association.] "3 Women Furniture Masters' Work at NHFMA Gallery February 15." *Antiques and the Arts Weekly* (February 8, 2013): 26. 1 bw illus.

Newell, Aimee E., Hilary Anderson Stelling, and Catherine Compton Swanson. *Curiosities of the Craft: Treasures from the Grand Lodge of Massachusetts Collection*. Boston: Grand Lodge of Masons in Massachusetts; Lexington, Mass.: Scottish Rite Masonic Museum & Library, 2013. 287 pp.; numerous color illus., index.

[Newport Historical Society]. "Newport Historical Society Desks in 'A Writer's Dozen' Exhibition." *Antiques and the Arts Weekly* (August 16, 2013): 9. 1 bw illus.

"Newport Restoration Foundation Presents Trio of Newport Highboys." *Antiques and the Arts Weekly* (May 17, 2013): 41. 1 bw illus.

[Newtown Historical Society]. "Newtown Clock Comes Home." *Antiques and the Arts Weekly* (September 13, 2013): 8. 3 bw illus. (Re tall-case clock by Ebenezer Smith [1745–1830] acquired by the society.)

Nicoletta, Julie. "Sisters' Retiring Room from the North Family Dwelling, Mount Lebanon, New York, ca. 1845." *Winterthur Portfolio* 46, nos. 2–3 (summer/autumn 2012): E37–E43. (Available as e-Book Edition from University of Chicago Press.)

Nylander, Richard. *Old Town by the Sea: Portsmouth, New Hampshire*. Boston: Historic New England, 2012. 24 pp.; color illus.

———. *A Tale of Two Houses, South Berwick, Maine*. Boston: Historic New England, 2012. 24 pp.; color illus.

Ostroff, Daniel. *Collecting Eames: The J. F. Chen Collection*. Los Angeles: J. F. Chen, 2011. 136 pp.; color illus.

Patoski, Christina. "Product Placement: High-Plains Classic." *American Craft* 73, no. 4 (August–September 2013): 16–17. 7 color illus. (Re Garza Furniture of Marfa, Texas.)

Pearce, Clark, Merri Lou Schaumann, and Catherine Ebert. "Robert McGuffin: Journeyman Extraordinaire, Part 1." *Antiques and Fine Art* 11, no. 6 (spring 2012): 168–73. 8 color illus.

Pepall, Rosalind, and Diane Charbonneau, eds. *Decorative Arts and Design: The Montreal Museum of Fine Arts' Collection, Vol. 2*. New York: Harry N. Abrams, 2012. 407 pp.; numerous color illus., index.

Porter, Susan, Jennifer Pustz, and Nancy Curtis. *Roseland Cottage, Woodstock, Connecticut*. Boston: Historic New England, 2011. 24 pp.; color illus.

Preservation Society of Newport County. *Newport: The Glamour of Ornament: Celebrating the Preservation Society of Newport County*. Newport, R.I.: by the society, 2013. 60 pp.;

color illus. (Contains articles by Charles J. Burns and others with some discussion of furniture and a checklist of the loan exhibition held in conjunction with the 59th annual Winter Antiques Show in New York City.)

Priddy, Sumpter, III, Adam T. Erby, and Jenna Huffman. "'The one Mrs. Trist would chuse': Thomas Jefferson, the Trist Family, and the Monticello Campeachy Chair." *American Furniture 2012*, 24–56. 27 color and bw illus.

Quartino, Daniela Santos. *The Bible of Classic Furniture: New Furniture Inspired by Classical Style*. Barcelona: Loft, 2012. 419 pp.; numerous color illus., glossary of woods, glossary.

Rago, David. "Paul Evans: Maker of Undeniably Weird Furniture." *New England Antiques Journal* 32, no. 3 (September 2013): 38–41. Color illus.

Raizman, David. "Giuseppe Ferrari's Carved Cabinet for the 1876 Centennial Exhibition: Presentation Furniture in the Cultural Context of World's Fairs." *West 86th: A Journal of Decorative Arts, Design History, and Material Culture* 20, no. 1 (spring/summer 2013): 62–91. 21 color illus.

Rauschenberg, Bradford L. "Documentary Evidence for Furniture Forms and Terminology in Charleston, South Carolina, 1670–1820." *Journal of Early Southern Decorative Arts* 34 (2013). Numerous color illus., bibliography. Online at www.mesdajournal.org/2013/documentary-evidence-furniture-forms-terminology-charleston-south-carolina-ii/#sthash.LjzJlQ4i.dpuf. (Not a traditional journal article but, rather, an incredibly detailed database of great utility for eighteenth-century furniture as a whole.)

Richmond, Daniel. "A Frontier Jack of All Trades: Joshua Shipman and the Business of Making Furniture in the Ohio Country." *American Period Furniture: Journal of the Society of American Period Furniture Makers* 12 (2012): 24–29. 8 color illus., table.

Ridner, Judith. Review of *Paint, Pattern, and People: Furniture of Southeastern Pennsylvania, 1725–1850* by Wendy A. Cooper and Lisa Minardi. In

Winterthur Portfolio 47, nos. 2–3 (summer/autumn 2013): 200–201.

Roubo, A.-J. *To Make as Perfectly as Possible: Roubo on Marquetry*. Fort Mitchell, Ken.: Lost Arts Press, 2013. 256 pp.; illus. (First English translation of Roubo's eighteenth-century text on woodworking; commentary by Donald C. Williams.)

Ruhling, Nancy A. "Life Style: Aesthetic Era Anew." *Antiques and Fine Art* 12, no. 3 (winter/spring 2013): 162–75. Color illus.

Russ, Kurt C., and Jeffrey S. Evans. "The Kahle-Henson School of Punched-Tin Paneled Furniture." *American Furniture 2012*, 57–83. 36 color and bw illus.

Scherer, Barrymore Laurence. "Eminent Victorians: John Whitenight and Frederick LaValley in Their Philadelphia Town House." *Antiques* 180, no. 5 (September–October 2013): 90–101. 19 color illus.

Schinto, Jeanne. Review of *Mahogany: The Costs of Luxury in Early America* by Jennifer L. Anderson. In *Maine Antique Digest* 41, no. 3 (March 2013): 10D. 1 bw illus.

Sherman, Sarah Way. *Sacramental Shopping: Louisa May Alcott, Edith Wharton, and the Spirit of Modern Consumerism*. Durham: University Press of New Hampshire, 2013. xiii + 316 pp.; index.

Sienkewicz, Julia A. "Critical Perception: An Exploration of the Cognitive Gains of Material Culture Pedagogy." *Winterthur Portfolio* 47, nos. 2–3 (summer/autumn 2013): 117–37. 5 figs.

Sims, Lowery Stokes, and Elizabeth Edwards Kirrane. *Against the Grain: Wood in Contemporary Art, Craft, and Design*. New York: Museum of Arts and Design and Monacelli Press, 2012. 160 pp.; numerous color illus.

Smit, Peter. "The Art of Thomas Nisbet." *Maine Antique Digest* 40, no. 10 (October 2012): 28C–29C. bw illus.

Society of American Period Furniture Makers. *A Tradition of Craft: Current Works by the Society of American Period Furniture Makers*. N.p.: by the society, [2012]. 49 pp.; numerous color illus.

Solensky, Jeanne. "The Furniture Designs of Gillow and Company." *Antiques and Fine Art* 11, no. 6 (spring 2012): 220–21. Color illus.

Solis-Cohen, Lita. "Forty M.A.D. Years." *Maine Antique Digest* 41, no. 11 (November 2013): 6B–10B. bw illus.

———. "Four Centuries of Massachusetts Furniture." *Maine Antique Digest* 41, no. 5 (May 2013): 16D–18D. 7 bw illus.

———. "The Kaufman Collection on Permanent View at the National Gallery of Art." *Maine Antique Digest* 40, no. 12 (December 2012): 24CS. 6 color illus.

———. Review of *American Furniture 2012* by Luke Beckerdite et al. In *Maine Antique Digest* 41, no. 8 (August 2013): 31C–33C. 1 bw illus.

———. Review of *Dream House: The White House as an American Home* by Ulysses Grant Dietz and Sam Watters. In *Maine Antique Digest* 40, no. 12 (December 2012): 30B–31B. 1 bw illus.

Sperling, David A. "The Clockmakers of Flemington, New Jersey, 1788–1850: Part 1, The Early Years: Thomas Williams, George Rea, and Richard Hooley." *Watch & Clock Bulletin* 55, no. 1 (January–February 2013): 35–41. Color and bw illus.

———. "The Hunterdon County Clock Case and the Enigmatic John Guild." *Maine Antique Digest* 41, no. 10 (October 2013): 11+ bw illus.

Spittler, Tom. "A Clock Mystery Unraveled." *Watch & Clock Bulletin* 55, no. 3 (May–June 2013): 289–95. 8+ bw illus.

Stewart, David Wood. "The Grandfather Clock: An 'Autobiography.'" *Watch & Clock Bulletin* 55, no. 5 (September–October 2013): 475–77. 5 color illus.

Stratton-Pruitt, Suzanne L., ed., et al. *Journeys to New Worlds: Spanish and Portuguese Colonial Art in the Roberta and Richard Huber Collection*. Philadelphia: Philadelphia Museum of Art, 2013. xviii + 204 pp.; numerous color illus., bibliography. (Contains a few entries on furniture by Jorge F. Rivas P. and Mark A. Castro.)

Sullivan, Gary R., and Kate Van Winkle Keller. "Eighteenth-Century Hit

Parade: Early American Musical Clocks." *Antiques* 180, no. 5 (September–October 2013): 132–39. 10 color illus.

Sweet, Fay. *Retro Furniture Classics*. London: Carlton Books, 2012. 223 pp.; numerous color illus., directory, index. (Published in 2007 as *Vintage Furniture*.)

Tarule, Rob. "The Tools Tell the Story: Authenticating the Bowles Cupboard." *New England Antiques Journal* 32, no. 2 (August 2013): 36–41. Color and bw illus.

Taube, Isabel L. *Impressions of Interiors: Gilded Age Paintings by Walter Gay*. London: Giles in association with Frick Art and Historical Center, Pittsburgh, 2012. 224 pp.; 105 color and bw illus.

Taylor, Lonn, and David B. Warren. *Texas Furniture: The Cabinetmakers and Their Work, 1840–1880*. 1975. Vol. 1. Rev. ed. Austin: University of Texas Press, 2012. xi + 378 pp.; numerous bw and color illus., checklist of Texas cabinetmakers, appendix, glossary, bibliography, index. (Published as vol. 1 of a two-volume set; see next listing.)

Taylor, Lonn, and David B. Warren, with a foreword by Don Carleton. *Texas Furniture: The Cabinetmakers and Their Work, 1840–1880*. Vol. 2. Austin: University of Texas Press, 2012. xi + 336 pp.; numerous color and bw illus., checklist of Texas cabinetmakers, glossary, bibliography, index.

Taylor, Mark, ed. *Interior Design and Architecture: Critical and Primary Sources*. 4 vols. London: Bloomsbury, 2013. 1,600 pp.; index. (A compilation of more than one hundred essays.)

Theobald, Mary Miley, with the Colonial Williamsburg Foundation. *Death by Petticoat: American History Myths Debunked*. Kansas City, Mo.: Andrews McMeel Publishing, 2012. x + 131 pp.; color illus. (Includes a few references to "myths" re furniture.)

Thompson, Rob. *Product and Furniture Design: The Manufacturing Guides*. New York: Thames and Hudson, 2011. 192 pp.; numerous color illus.,

line drawings, glossary, bibliography, index.

Trent, Robert F. "Boston Baroque Easy Chairs, 1705–1740." *American Furniture 2012*, 86–115. 41 color and bw illus.

Viera, Diane, Nancy Carlisle, and Emily Morris. "Four Centuries of Massachusetts Furniture: A Celebration of Craft and Industry, Tradition and Innovation." *Historic New England* 14, no. 2 (fall 2013): 2–6. Color illus.

Walczak, Leah. *Otis House, Boston*. Boston: Historic New England, 2011. 24 pp.; color illus.

Watts, Deward. "Cabinetmakers and Cabinetmaking in Fairfield County, Ohio, Prior to 1850." *American Period Furniture: Journal of the Society of American Period Furniture Makers* 11 (2011): 8–15. 8 color and bw illus., map.

Ward, Gerald W. R. *The Cabinetmaker and the Carver: Boston Furniture from Private Collections*. Boston: Massachusetts Historical Society, 2013. 64 pp.; color illus., note on sources. Distributed by University Press of Virginia

———. "The Cabinetmaker and the Carver: Boston Furniture from Private Collections." *Antiques and Fine Art* 12, no. 6 (autumn/winter 2013): 168–75. 14 color illus.

———. "Period Rooms and the New Art of the Americas Wing, Museum of Fine Arts, Boston." *Winterthur Portfolio* 46, nos. 2–3 (summer/autumn 2012): 195–212. 13 color illus.

———. Review of *Furnishing Louisiana: Creole and Acadian Furniture, 1735–1835* by Jack D. Holden et al. In *Winterthur Portfolio* 47, no. 1 (spring 2013): 107–9.

———. Review of *Woods in British Furniture-Making, 1400–1900* by Adam Bowett. In *Maine Antique Digest* 41, no. 7 (July 2013): 33A. 1 bw illus.

———, comp. "Recent Writing on American Furniture: A Bibliography." *American Furniture 2012*, 175–83.

Westman, Annabel. Review of *Capricious Fancy: Draping and Curtaining the Historic Interior, 1800–1930* by Gail Caskey Winkler. In *Furniture History Society Newsletter*, no. 190 (May 2013): 17–18.

White, Lisa. Review of *Woods in British Furniture-Making, 1400–1900* by Adam

Bowett. In *Furniture History Society Newsletter*, no. 190 (May 2013): 18–19.

Wilkinson, Philip. *Great Design*. New York: DK Publishing, 2013. 256 pp.; numerous color illus., index. (Published for the Smithsonian Institution.)

"Willard House and Clock Museum Hosts Exhibit of Rare Musical Tall Clocks." *Maine Antique Digest* 41, no. 11 (November 2013): 11A. 2 bw illus.

[Willard House and Clock Museum]. "Highlights: Keeping Time." *Antiques and Fine Art* 12, no. 6 (autumn/winter 2013): 82. 1 color illus.

———. "Willard Clock Museum to Host Rare Musical Grandfather Clocks." *Antiques and the Arts Weekly* (September 20, 2013): 43.

Winkler, Gail Caskey. *Capricious Fancy: Draping and Curtaining the Historic Interior, 1800–1930*. Philadelphia: University of Pennsylvania Press, 2013. xli + 292 pp.; 325 color illus., glossary, bibliography, index.

Winterthur Museum, Library, and Garden. Online museum collections database at http://museumcollection .winterthur.org. (This digital database with images, launched early in 2013, includes the majority of Winterthur's approximately 90,000 museum objects, including ceramics, furniture, glass, metalwork, paintings, prints, and textiles.)

———. *Uncorked! Wine, Objects, and Tradition*. Winterthur, Del.: Winterthur Museum, Library, and Garden, 2012. 40 pp.; color illus. (Includes some furniture and many period genre scenes; see also uncorked.winterthur.org).

[Wunsch, Eric Martin, collection]. *Important American Furniture, Folk Art, Silver, Paintings, and Prints*. New York: Christie's, September 25, 2013. 206 pp.; numerous color and bw illus., index.

Zwilling, Jennifer A. "Interior Woodwork from 1921 Arch Street, Philadelphia, Built 1871, Renovated Pre-1885." *Winterthur Portfolio* 46, nos. 2–3 (summer/autumn 2012): E44–E57. (Available as an e-Book Edition from University of Chicago Press.)

Index

Aaron Lopez & Co., 8

Abolitionism: Quakers and, 115–16(&fig.); Thomas Day and, 101–3, 136–37, 140, 144–45; Wesleyan Academy and, 137–38. *See also* Fifth Annual Convention for the Improvement of the Free People of Color in the United States

Albrecht, Charles, square piano, 256(fig. 92)

Acanthus carving, 57–58(&fig. 11), 59(fig. 13)

Acer pensylvanicum, 308

Acer pseudoplatanus, 284n19

Acer saccharinum, 308

Ache, Samuel, 252

Ackermann, Rudolph, 164, 166, 185(fig. 53), 195n39

Actions, piano, 264(&fig.), 265(fig. 106)

Adams, Robert, 158

Addison, Joseph, 8, 45n9

Adobe Photoshop, enhancing images in, 80, 93–94, 99

Aesculus, 305

Aesculus glabra, 308

Aesculus hippocastanutum, 305

Affleck, Thomas, 238, 239, 286n28

African Methodist Episcopal Church, 129, 142

African Repository (journal), 114, 121, 149n30

Agency in Behalf of the Free People of Color, 137

"Age of Mahogany" (Macquoid), 307

Agnus Dei, 213, 283n13

The AIC Guide to Digital Photography and Conservation Documentation (Warda), 96

Aiken, Joseph, 160, 161, 168–69

Alberti, Johann Philip, 209, 243(&fig. 70)

Albin, Eleazar, 222(&fig. 45), 283n16

Albrecht, C. F. L., 291n60

Albrecht, Carl, 254

Albrecht, Charles, 288–89n47, 288n46, 290n53, 290n55; clients, 270; competitors, 270–71; death and estate of, 267–68; documenting, 266–68; immigration to Philadelphia, 254; marriage of, 254–55; oldest known dated American-made piano and, 250, 253, 254(figs.); as piano importer, 267; pianos, 250, 253, 254(figs.), 255–66 (&figs. 91–104), 278, 289n48

Albrecht, Christian Frederick Lewis, 272

Albrecht, Daniel, 289n47

Albrecht, Elizabeth, 288n47, 289n47, 290n55

Albrecht, George, 252, 255, 257, 259, 266–67, 288n47; square piano, 258(fig.)

Albrecht, Henry, 255, 288–89n47

Albrecht, Jacob, 288n47, 289n47

Albrecht, Julias Augustus, 288n46

Albrecht, Margaret, 255, 288n47, 289n47

Albrecht, Maria Elizabeth, 288n46

Albrecht, Mary, 288n46, 290n53

Albrecht, Philip, 255, 268, 288–89n47

Albrecht/Albright, Philip, 268

Albright, George, 288n41

Alden, Harry, 304

Alder, 305

Allbrink, Henry Vinsalous (Wenceslaus), 288n46

Allen, Richard, 129

Alnus, 305

Amenzetter, Michael, 227, 229, 284n20

American Anti-Slavery Society, 112(fig. 13), 118, 132(fig.), 140, 144; Seventh Annual Meeting, 136–37

American ash, 308

American beech, 308

American Colonization Society, 114, 121

American Daily Advertiser (newspaper), 181

American Missionary Association, 143, 144

American Moral Reform Society, 127(fig. 24), 128, 129, 145n1

American Seating Furniture, 1630–1730 (Forman), 308

American silver maple, 308

American Slavery As It Is (Weld), 118(&fig.)

American Society for the Colonizing the Free People of Color in the United States, 149n29

American Society of Free Persons of Colour, 129

Amish, 206

Anderson, Jennifer L., 293–95

Andrews, Celia Tyler, 95n6

Andrews, John, 96n11

Andrews, Peggy, 95n6, 96n11

Andrews, Stephen, 95n6

Anglo-American Texas furniture, 302

Anisodactyl foot, 45n10

Antes, Henry, 273

Anthemion, 179, 180(fig.), 195n37

Anthony Wayne House (Paoli, Pennsylvania), 165(fig. 11)

Muhlenberg, Mary, 242(fig. 66), 267
Muhlenberg, Peter, 242, 267, 270, 277, 287n36, 290n54
Multispectral imaging, 96
Museum of Fine Arts, Boston, 302
Music, Pennsylvania Germans and, 250
Musical instrument making, in Philadelphia, 250
Music stool, 253(fig. 87), 288n44
Myers, Minor, Jr., 10

Nameboards, piano, 254(fig. 89), 255–57(&figs. 90, 91, 93, 94), 259(&figs.), 260(figs. 99&100), 263(&fig.), 266(fig.), 272(fig. 110), 273(fig. 113), 275(fig. 117), 289n49
Naph Hart & Co., 8
Nasby, David, 298–300
Nasby, Judith, 298
National Negro War (newspaper), 144
A Natural History of Birds (Albin), 222(&fig. 45)
Natural History of Carolina, Florida and the Bahama Islands (Catesby), 217(fig. 34), 222
A Natural History of Uncommon Birds (Edwards), 222
The Negro History Bulletin (journal), 103
The Negro in Our History (Woodson), 130(fig.)
Neisser, Augustin, 227, 284n20; tall-case clocks, 223(&figs.), 225–26
Nevill, Dinah, 115(fig.)
Newbern, Thomas R. J., 72, 80, 84–85, 86–87, 89–90, 91, 93, 94
New Brunswick, Thomas Nisbet and, 298–300
Newel posts, Thomas Day, 100(fig.), 108(figs.)
New Lutheran Church, in Fourth Street, Philadelphia (Birch & Birch), 198(fig. 4)
Newport (Rhode Island): bureau tables, 30(fig. 67), 41(fig. 92); card tables, 40(fig. 90), 42(fig. 94); chest of drawers, 37(fig. 83); desk-and-bookcase, 16(fig.); dining tables, 24(fig. 53), 26(fig. 57); document cabinet, 36(fig. 80); dressing table, 33(fig. 73); high chests of drawers, 12(fig. 16), 23(fig. 48), 27(fig. 61), 28(fig. 63), 29(fig. 65), 34(fig.), 39(fig. 89); mahogany high chests of drawers, 2(fig.), 4(fig.); pier table, 10(fig.); slant-front desks, 19(fig.), 21(fig. 44), 22(fig. 47), 38(fig.

86); tea tables, 26(fig. 58), 27(fig. 60), 31(fig. 69), 32(fig. 71)
Newsom, Margaret, 291n57
New York, piano production in, 272
New York Central College, 137, 153n62
New York City Vigilance Committee, 130
New York Society for the Promotion of Education among Colored Children, 144
Nicholls, Frederick, Jr., 285n24
Nicholson, Michael Angelo, 164, 187(fig. 57)
Nicholson, Peter, 164, 187(fig. 57)
Nicolls, Frederick W., 287n36
Niger, Alfred, 145n1
Nikon D70 camera, 98
Niles' Weekly Register, 157, 159
Nisbet, Thomas, 298–300
Nisbet, Thomas, Jr., 299
Noblitz, Stephen, 191n10
Nolt, Steven, 204
Nomini Hall (Virginia), 269
North Carolina: desk, 73(fig.); law barring free blacks from entering, 121–22; newel posts, 100(fig.), 108(figs.); repressive laws against free blacks, 107; restriction of education for free blacks, 107, 134–35, 153n58; restriction on movement of free blacks, 150n32; revocation of franchise from free blacks, 130; secretary presses, 74(fig.), 81(fig.); sideboard, 90(fig.); tympanum board, 92(fig.). *See also* Milton (North Carolina)
North Carolina Central, 141(fig. 34)
North Carolina Museum of History, 103, 104, 146n8
Northern white cedar, 305, 311
Nossitter, Thomas, 191n9
Nyssa, 305

Oak: *Brettstuhl*, 277(fig. 119); categorization of, 308; desk-and-bookcase, 18(fig. 37); dining table, 172(fig.); for pianos, 263; schrank, 214(fig.); secretary press, 74(fig.); sideboard, 163(fig. 7); *Tabernakelschrank*, 226(fig.). *See also* Red oak
Obadiah Brown & Co., 8
Oberlin College, 137, 153n62
Oblong Press, 306
Occupational taxes, 238–39
Octagon Library of Early American Architecture, 169

Oculus/oculi, 14, 15(fig. 25), 35, 223, 225(fig. 50)
Ogee heads, 8, 14
Ohio buckeye, 308
Old Lutheran Church, in Fifth Street, Philadelphia (Birch & Birch), 198(fig. 3)
Oneida Institute, 137
"Open Letter to the Public" (Garrison), 112(fig. 12)
Organs: Dieffenbach and, 270; Feyring and, 251; Klemm and, 251; Tannenberg and, 197, 199–200(&figs. 5&6), 200, 252; Taws and, 170, 171; Trinity Lutheran Church, 199–200(&figs. 5&6); Zion Lutheran Church, 197, 199, 200, 276, 280n1, 281n2
Ornament, classical, 272–73
"Ornament for a Frieze or Tablet," 272(&fig. 111)
The Orphan (Otway), 8, 45n9
Otto, Henrich, 217(fig. 35)
Otway, Thomas, 8
Ovolo-molded edges, bosses with, 176, 179(fig.), 182(fig. 46), 185(figs.), 187(fig. 57)
Ovolo moldings, 26, 176, 184(fig. 50), 185(fig. 53)
Owen, John, 131, 138

P. E. Brenan, 154n66
Pad feet, 35
Paleography, 72
Palmer, Fanny, 136(fig.)
Pannell and Son, 154n66
Paoli (Pennsylvania), Anthony Wayne House, 165(fig. 11)
Papageieinschrank, 221
Paquette, Michael A., 104
Parkin, Anna, 158
Parkin, Clara, 158, 190n3
Parkin, Hannah (Padley), 157
Parkin, Henry, 158
Parkin, Henry S., 190n3
Parkin, John, 157
Parkin, Richard, 157, 192n10, 192n15; armchairs, 181(fig. 45), 186(fig. 55); birth of, 190n2; bookcase, 177(fig.); Bullock and, 181; business after partnership with Cook, 159; Committee of Employers and, 161; death of, 190n2, 190n3; dressing table, 178(fig.); early life and family of, 157–58; Egyptian Hall and, 161–62; footstool, 185(fig. 53); furniture by, 178–90(&figs.);

41&42), 21–22(&figs. 43, 46), 23(fig. 49), 26(&fig. 59), 27(fig. 62), 28(&fig. 64), 47n23, 47n24; slant-front desks, 18–22(&figs.); tall-case clock and, 49n34; tea tables, 26(fig. 58), 31–32(&figs.); wealth of, 44n3

Townsend, Christopher, Jr., 44n3

Townsend, Job, 2, 49n34

Townsend, John, 7; apprenticeship with father, 4; baroque design and, 37; bureau table, 30(&figs.); card tables, 40(fig. 90), 42(&figs.), 43(fig.); chest of drawers, 37(figs.); construction techniques, 11, 13–14; dining table, 24(fig. 53), 25, 43n1; document cabinet, 35–37(&figs. 80–82); dressing table, 32, 33(figs.); fleur-de-lis style shell, 34(&fig.), 36(fig. 82), 37(fig. 84); high chests of drawers, 2(fig.), 4–9(&figs.), 12–17(&figs. 16–29), 22–25(&figs. 48–52), 34–35(&figs.), 39(&fig. 89), 40(fig. 91), 41, 44–45n5; inheritance from father, 44n3; inscriptions/marks, 5–6(&figs.), 8(&fig. 10), 15(&figs. 26–29), 22, 23(fig. 49), 25(figs. 54, 56), 34, 35(fig. 77), 36(fig. 81), 37(fig. 85), 38(fig. 87), 39(fig. 88), 42(fig. 95), 45n6, 48n29, 49n31; slant-front desk, 38(&fig. 86); tea tables, 26, 27(fig. 60), 32(fig. 71)

Townsend, Jonathan, 3, 44n3; bureau table, 41–42(&figs. 92&93), 48–49n32

Townsend, Mary, 8, 44n3

Townsend, Solomon, 3

"Tracing from Thomas Wilkinson from Designs of the laste Mr. George Bullock," 179, 180(fig. 43), 181

Trappe (Pennsylvania), 241; Augustus Lutheran Church, 243(fig. 69); Frederick Muhlenberg house, 243(fig. 68); Henry Muhlenberg house, 242(fig. 66)

Tray tops, 26

Trinity Church (Newport, Rhode Island), 3

Trinity Church (New York), 251

Trinity Lutheran Church (Lancaster, Pennsylvania), 251, 281n3, 283n13; organ, 199–200(&figs. 5&6)

Trist, Nicholas, 151n41

Tropical Timbers of the World (Chudnoff), 306

Trotter, Daniel, 238, 239, 240, 286n28

Trumble, Francis, 238, 239

Trute, Charles, 271

Tucker, Giles, 284n18

Tucker, Grace, 284n18

Tulip poplar: bedstead, 142(fig. 35); bureau table, 30(fig. 67); chest, 201(fig. 8); chest-on-chest, 231(fig.); étagère, 124(fig.); high chest of drawers, 12(fig. 16); keyboard instruments and, 251; lady's open pillar bureau, 125(fig.); music stool, 253(fig. 87); ornamental scroll, 109(fig.); passage rack, 142(fig. 36); pews, 105(fig. 3); for pianos, 263; pier tables, 165(fig. 12), 167(fig.); schrank, 214(fig.); sideboards, 163(fig. 7), 188(fig. 59); side chairs, 156(fig.), 183(fig.); slant-front desks, 19(fig.), 21(fig. 44), 218(figs.); sofa, 110(fig. 9); sofa table, 189(fig. 61); tall-case clocks, 213(fig. 27), 223(figs.), 229(fig.), 310(fig.); wardrobe, 176(fig. 38)

Tunebook, 269(fig.)

Tupelo, 305

Turlington, Robert, 149n26

Turnbull, Daniel, 189

Turnbull, Martha, 189

Turner, Nat, 144

Tyler, Celia, 95n6

Tyler, Elizabeth Rutland, 78, 95n6

Tyler, John, 78, 95n6

Tympanum, 14

Tympanum board, 92–95(&figs. 29–32)

Uhl, Reinhardt, 230, 241

Ulmus, 308

Ummensetter, Michael, 284n20

Uncle Tom's Cabin (Stowe), 117, 118

Underground Railroad, 133, 138, 140, 150n39, 151n44, 153n60

Underground schools, for African American children, 143, 144, 155n73

Union Seminary, 135, 141

Union Tavern (Milton, North Carolina), 106(&fig.), 133, 134, 142

The Universal Penman (Bickham), 255

University of Texas Press, 301

Upholstery evidence: backstools, 61–62(&figs. 19&20); governor's chair, 55–56, 62–63(&figs. 21–23)

Valuables cabinet, walnut, 220–21(&figs. 41–43)

Vance, Zebulon, 155n72

Van Deursen, William, 27

Van Rensselaer, Catherine, 30

Vashon, George, 153n62

Vashon, J. B., 140, 153n62

Veneers, 305. *See also* Mahogany veneer; Maple veneer; Rosewood veneer, Satinwood veneer; Walnut veneer

A View of the House of Peers (Cole), 64(&fig.)

View of Walnut Street between Third and Fourth Streets (Philadelphia), 159(fig.)

"View of Wilmington…Feb. 27, 1865" (Leslie), 143(fig.)

Vinhatico, 304

Virginals, 252

Virginia, free blacks in, 115–16

Virginia Gazette (newspaper), 118

Virginia Museum of Fine Arts, 96; desk, 72, 73(fig.), 83–89(&figs.)

Virginia royal governor's chair, 50(fig.), 51(fig.), 52(figs.), 55–56(figs.), 62–69(&figs.); acquisition of, 51; attached armorial, 65–67; backstools, 57–62(&figs.); history and historiography, 51–54; upholstery evidence, 55–56(&figs.), 62–63(&figs. 21–23); webbing, 68

Vleck, Jacob van, 268(fig.)

Volutes, 235

Vorbach, Andreas, 281n2

Vorbach/Forepaugh, George, 199, 281n2

Voting rights, free blacks and, 130

W. H. Sloane, 51, 52(fig. 3)

W. N. Seymour & Co., 136(&fig.), 153n60, 154n66

Wadkins, John, 149n28

Wady, James, 49n34

Wahl, Johann Georg, 225, 226(fig.)

Wainscot, 307

Wainscot chairs, 211

Walker, David, 107, 144, 146n11

Walker, Juliet E. K., 123–24

Walker's Appeal in Four Articles, 146n11

Walnut, 307; armchair, 186(fig. 55); chest-on-chest, 231(fig.); chest-over-drawers, 202(fig. 11); desk, 73(fig.); desk-and-bookcase, 221(fig.); étagère, 124(fig.); high chest of drawers, 27(fig. 61); looking glass, 206(fig. 16); lounge, 110(fig. 8); ornamental scroll, 109(fig.); pews, 105(fig. 3); schrank, 214(fig.); secretary presses, 74(fig.), 81(fig.); sideboard, 90(fig.); side chairs, 156(fig.), 183, 184(fig. 50), 210–11(figs.), 244(fig. 72), 249(fig. 81); slant-front desk, 218(figs.); spice box,